ALSO BY RANDY ROBERTS AND JAMES S. OLSON

★

John Wayne: American

A LINE IN THE SAND

The Alamo in Blood and Memory

RANDY ROBERTS

JAMES S. OLSON

A TOUCHSTONE BOOK
PUBLISHED BY SIMON & SCHUSTER
New York London Toronto Sydney Singapore

TOUCHSTONE
Rockefeller Center
1230 Avenue of the Americas
New York, NY 10020

FIRST TOUCHSTONE EDITION 2002
For information about special discounts for bulk purchases,
please contact Simon & Schuster Special Sales:
1-800-456-6798 or business@simonandschuster.com

Designed by Katy Riegel
Picture credits for the photo insert are as follows. Insert pages 1–10: The Daughters
of the Republic of Texas Library; 11: The University of Texas Institute of Texan Cultures at
San Antonio; 12–13: Paul Hutton Collection, Western Historical Association; 14: *Viva Max*:
The University of Texas Institute of Texan Cultures at San Antonio; *The Man from the Alamo*
and *Man of Conquest*: Paul Hutton Collection, Western Historical Association; 15: The
University of Texas Institute of Texan Cultures at San Antonio; 16: Paul Hutton
Collection, Western Historical Association.
Manufactured in the United States of America
1   3   5   7   9   10   8   6   4   2

The Library of Congress has cataloged the Free Press edition as follows:

Roberts, Randy
A line in the sand : the Alamo in blood and memory / Randy Roberts, James S. Olson.
p.   cm.
Includes bibliographical references and index.
1. Alamo (San Antonio, Tex.)—Siege, 1836. 2. Alamo (San Antonio, Tex.)—Siege,
1836—Influence. 3. Memory—Social aspects—United States. I. Olson, James Stuart,
1946– II. Title.

F390 .R67 2001   00-048421
976.4′03—dc21

ISBN 0-684-83544-4
0-7432-1233-9 (Pbk)

Contents

———— ✦ ————

Preface   vii

Map   xii

Prologue   1

1. In the Footsteps of History   5

2. "The Free Born Sons of America"   28

3. "The Bones of Warriors"   61

4. "Those Proud Tow'rs"   86

5. "VICTORY or DEATH"   121

Interlude   154

6. In Search of Davy's Grave   169

7. Retrieving the Bones of History   197

8. King of the Wild Frontier   230

CONTENTS

9. Only Heroes, Only Men   254

10. De la Peña's Revenge   277

11. The Third Battle of the Alamo   294

Epilogue   315

Notes   321

Bibliographic Essay   345

Index   349

PREFACE

———— ✦ ————

IN THE PREDAWN DARKNESS on the cold morning of March 6, 1836, the defenders of the Alamo died, but in their last stand they achieved a certain immortality. Today, millions of people visit the place where Travis, Bowie, Crockett, and the others perished. Most of the visitors stand silent, or shuffle about slowly and quietly, as if for once in their lives they are on ground commensurate to their reverence. Other visitors wander about with looks of scorn, sure that there is nothing sacred or even noble about the Alamo shrine. For all the visitors, the Alamo is both history and memory, as alive today as it was in the nineteenth century. Many historians have considered what happened at the Alamo, but few have explored the changing meaning of the battle. As a result, the story of what happened, why it happened, what it has meant, and what it still means has been left to an assortment of guides, politicians, television executives, and movie producers. More than 150 years after the storming of the Alamo, the two most important interpreters of the event are Walt Disney and John Wayne.

Perhaps this is not as strange as it seems. The history of the Alamo fits neatly into William Faulkner's notion of the past. "The past is never dead," the novelist wrote. "It's not even the past." He understood that history is contested territory. At the Alamo, the siege and battle served as a prelude to other fights and other battles, fought by preservers of our national culture and interpreters of our shared past. They continue to wrestle with the meaning of the Alamo and the objectives of its defenders. Were Travis, Bowie, Crockett, and the men who died with them patriots making a last stand for freedom and liberty? Or were the "heroes" of the Alamo merely a collection of greedy capitalists, men on the make, backwoods bullies, would-be statesmen, and washed-up politicians? Did they fight to win freedom or to preserve slavery?

In order to present the Alamo in the fullness and richness it deserves, we have opted for a broad canvas. The first half of *A Line in the Sand* sets the siege and battle of the Alamo in the context of a clash between two cultures and two political forces. Although in reality it was never as simple as Anglo-American versus Hispanic-American, many Texans of the time believed it was, and though their rhetoric appears extreme to us today, they believed what they said. It was a confusing time, and the defenders of the Alamo were in a more baffling position than most. Behind the walls of the Alamo, they knew very little about the events taking place on the outside. They were uncertain about the debate over independence and completely in the dark concerning the plans of Sam Houston and other military leaders. Nor did they have a much better understanding of the personality of General Antonio López de Santa Anna and the objectives of the government in Mexico City. They were, in a deadly sense, alone. They sent out contradictory messages; they received equally contradictory communications; they moved blindly and planned in the dark. And in the dark, a physical and metaphorical darkness, they died.

The second half of *A Line in the Sand* examines how Americans gave and continue to give meaning to the event. The battle cry of Texans during the battle of San Jacinto, and later the Mexican-American War, "Remember the Alamo," raises crucial cultural questions: How do we remember? What do we remember? Who governs our memory of historical events? The battle over memory has been as vibrant in its own way as the real battle, with a cast of characters equally committed to a cause. Presidents, filmmakers, preservationists, cultural critics, and a wild search for just how Davy Crockett died animate the second half of the book. In the end, the quest for the meaning of the Alamo has merged with the struggle to ascribe a meaning for America itself.

In the process of writing *A Line in the Sand,* we accumulated a number of debts, not the least of which are owed to such distinguished historians as Stephen L. Hardin, James Crisp, Alwyn Barr, Gregg Cantrell, Paul Lack, Paul Andrew Hutton, and William C. (Jack) Davis, and such Alamo specialists as Bill Groneman and Thomas Ricks Lindley, whose collective work on the revolution has given Texas and Texans a historiography as rich as any state in the country. We are especially thankful for the generosity of Jack Davis, who freely shared with us the research notes he collected in writing *Three Roads to the Alamo,* and Paul Hutton, who gave us access to his personal collection of Alamo memorabilia. To those scholars who read all or portions of the manuscript—Stephen L. Hardin, Gregg Cantrell, Kevin Young, John Payne, Ty Cashion, and Carolina Castillo-Crimm—we express our sincere gratitude. We should also acknowledge the financial support of the Center for Humanistic Studies at Purdue University, and Sam Houston State University.

On the personal side, our editor Bruce Nichols was a partner in this project from the beginning. He went beyond his duties as an editor, and sometimes even beyond his duties as a friend, and we will always appreciate his suggestions, intellectual generosity, and patience. Randy Roberts especially thanks his daughters, Kelly and Alison Roberts, and his wife Marjorie, for keeping the Alamo in perspective. Jim Olson extends the same appreciation to his wife and best friend Judy, who enjoyed the trips to San Antonio, tolerated the re-enactments in Brackettsville, and endured hearing more about the Alamo than she ever wanted to know.

Archivists and librarians at the University of Texas at Austin, the Institute for Texan Cultures in San Antonio, the Daughters of the Republic of Texas Library in San Antonio, and the Newton Gresham Library at Sam Houston State University helped us at every stage of the project. We are particularly grateful for the assistance of Paul Culp at Sam Houston State University, and Martha Utterback, Jeannette Phinney, Linda Edwards, Charles Gámez, Dora Guerra, Sally Koch, and Nancy Skokan of the DRT Library. Mark Jaeger and Cory Toole—our research assistants—saved us immense amounts of time in collecting and assembling our research materials.

Randy Roberts

James S. Olson

From amidst them forth he pass'd,
Long way through hostile scorn, which he sustain'd
Superior, nor violence fear'd aught;
And with retorted scorn his back he turn'd
On those proud Tow'rs to swift destruction doom'd.

JOHN MILTON

The past is never dead. It's not even the past.

WILLIAM FAULKNER

History is an unstable pattern of remembered things.

CARL BECKER

It is important to avoid partiality if one wants to be believed.
Be very careful because it is very difficult to be a historian.

JOSÉ ENRIQUE DE LA PEÑA

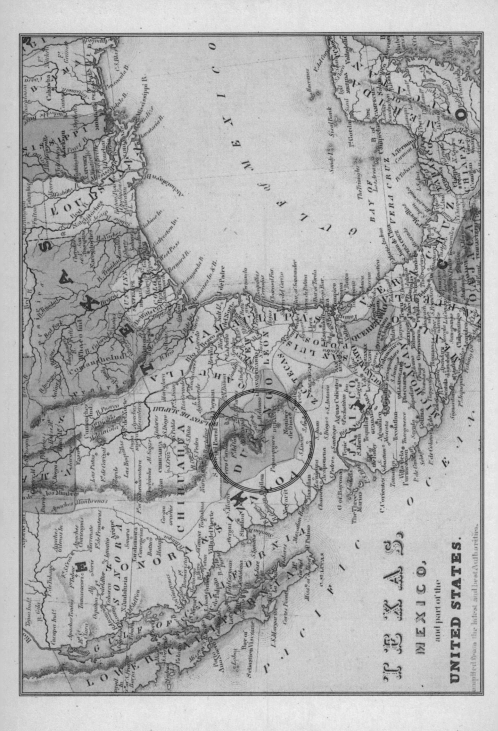

TEXAS, MEXICO, and part of the UNITED STATES.

Compiled from the latest and best Authorities.

PROLOGUE

The morning of March 3, 1836, dawned cold and clear, a cloudless sky frigid in the aftermath of a Texas blue norther. James Butler Bonham stirred up and got under way early, racing west as fast as he could go. Time was precious. Several hours later, he reined in his sweat-lathered white horse and pulled up short, probably cresting on Powder House Hill, with San Antonio de Béxar stretching out before him. Horse and rider were exhausted after several days of travel, often at breakneck speed, from Goliad, where Bonham had tried to hustle troops and supplies for the Alamo. Heavy brush and mesquite trees offered some cover as he surveyed the landscape below. Mexican soldiers by the thousands, dressed in white fatigue suits, busied themselves with breakfast and morning duty. The defenders were still holding out, but in the days since Bonham had left Béxar, the Mexicans had tightened the noose; their lines, trenches, and earthworks now crowded much closer to the Alamo, just out of range of the Kentucky long rifles. It must have been a chilling sight, one that suited the day—so many Mexicans and so few defenders.

On his way to Béxar, Bonham may very well have encountered Texans heading the other direction. Ever since February 23, when General Antonio López de Santa Anna and the Mexican army had pulled into town, Anglos and Tejanos had fled Béxar like prairie dogs escaping rising water.

They would almost certainly have updated Bonham, warning him that the Alamo was doomed, that the defenders stood no chance, that the red flag of "no quarter" still fluttered above the enemy encampment, that Santa Anna seemed determined to deliver on his dark promise. Perhaps they urged Bonham to turn his mount around and join them in a run for the Anglo-friendly coast.

In the days since Bonham had left Béxar, the situation inside the Alamo had changed dramatically. Jim Bowie lay sick in his room, dying; most of the Tejanos and a few Anglos had left the fortress, but dozens more Anglo Texans had arrived, carrying little more than guns and a few rounds of ammunition. Some had come to fight for freedom, others for land, and still others for the grand adventure of it all. Commanding this disparate force was Colonel William Barret Travis, aloof, a bit cold, but passionately committed to his cause. Few Texas politicians fully comprehended the plight of the Alamo's defenders. They didn't know that the men were running short of food and good water, that their ranks were wracked with dysentery and disease, that they had spent sleepless nights listening to the sound of Mexican artillery. Nor did Texas politicians realize how committed they were to the doomed defense of the ramshackle mission. Bonham probably sensed the hopelessness involved when he saw the ring of Mexican troops surrounding the Alamo. But if he did, it didn't alter his resolve.

Bonham was not about to turn back. He was a bearer of good tidings that Thursday morning and owned a monopoly on hope, the Alamo's shortest commodity. In his pocket, Bonham carried a letter from "Three-Legged Willie" Williamson, written on March 1, promising the defenders that help was on the way. Sixty Gonzales Volunteers would arrive soon, he promised, and "Colonel Fannin with 300 men and four pieces of artillery has been on the march toward Béxar three days now." Another three hundred volunteers were about to assemble in San Felipe. "For God's sake," Williamson told Travis, "hold out until we can assist you."[1]

Even empty-handed, Bonham would not have shunned a fight. The twenty-nine-year-old was a long way from home, light-years, it must have seemed, from the river bottoms of South Carolina's Edgefield district. Locked between the Blue Ridge Mountains and the Atlantic, Edgefield produced cotton, tobacco, and men with attitudes. In the late eighteenth century, the region had witnessed terrible massacres involving settlers and

Cherokee Indians; it had seen outlaw gangs run wild in an orgy of rape, murder, torture, and theft; it had watched vigilante Regulators restore order with the cruel hand of an Old Testament God. In the decades following the American Revolution, Edgefield became a physical and emotional wasteland. A returning minister commented that "all was desolation" and society itself "seems to be at an end. . . . Robberies and murders are often committed on the public roads. The people that remain have been peeled, pillaged, and plundered. . . . A dark melancholy gloom appears everywhere, and the morals of the people are almost entirely extirpated."[2]

Violence was not something that Edgefield's leading citizens boasted about, but a prickly sense of honor was a source of pride. Poorer white Edgefielders were quick to settle disputes with rough-and-tumble gouging matches, while their social betters used pistols and swords. Blood and kinship ran deep. They lived by a strict code that placed a premium on respect. It was quite simple, really: respect my wife, respect my family, respect my word, or else. South Carolina was one of the most violent states in the United States, and Edgefield was the most violent section of South Carolina. Santa Anna's menu of terror contained little that Jim Bonham had not already tasted. Growing up in Edgefield had inoculated him against fear. And anyway, his distant cousin William B. Travis, another Edgefield man, happened to be in command of the Alamo. Dying at a brother's side was infinitely preferable to living with the memory of abandoned kinfolk.

But Jim Bonham was no reckless fool either. Well educated and well read, he must have listened to the travelers, rehearsed the contents of Three-Legged Willie's letter, and calculated the risks. The Mexican army, several thousand strong, had swarmed over Béxar, and even with a few hundred reinforcements, the odds for survival—once Mexicans came over the Alamo's walls—were perilously short. Surrounded and outnumbered ten to one, the defenders would not prevail. But if Willie was right, if six hundred or so volunteers were on the way, and if Santa Anna procrastinated the final assault, the odds might improve quickly. Terrible "if's," to be sure, but like a true Edgefield man, Bonham was never faint of heart. His world harbored no lost causes. Back in 1827 the trustees of South Carolina College had expelled him after he led a protest march over poor food at the college boardinghouse. The whole senior class went out with him. A few years later, while practicing law in Pendleton, South

Carolina, he caned a lawyer who insulted one of his clients. When a local judge ordered an apology, Bonham threatened him too, earning a jail sentence for contempt. And in 1832, with South Carolina bordering on secession during the nullification crisis, Bonham showed up in Charleston brandishing sword and side arm, damning Andrew Jackson and his Yankee cohorts in Washington, D.C. At Texas's beckoning, Bonham acted on impulse, as Edgefielders so often did, arriving in November 1835 and offering his services to Sam Houston "without conditions. I shall receive nothing, either in the form of service pay, or lands, or rations."[3]

Bonham might have been less worried about getting into the Alamo than getting out once the battle commenced. In some ways, what Santa Anna had erected was more sieve than siege; couriers came and went, it seemed, at will, and thirty-two volunteers from Gonzales had breached the Mexican lines and entered the Alamo on March 1. On almost any night up to the early morning hours of March 6, 1836, the defenders could have made a run for it, and some would probably have succeeded. The Texans inside the walls were there because they chose to be, not because they had to be. They were not demigods, just men, products of their times. Like many others, they had troubled marriages, financial problems, and legal difficulties. Like George Washington, Thomas Jefferson, and Andrew Jackson, they promoted equality and individual rights in the same breath that they defended slavery, without feeling a twinge of hypocrisy. And like most Americans, they were willing, sometimes even anxious, to make money at the expense of others.

But now and again, common men rise to uncommon heights, getting caught up in the sweep of events, sometimes involuntarily, usually not, and discover a cause worth dying for. Bonham had found his; so had Davy Crockett, Travis, and Bowie, and such Tejano defenders of the Alamo as Juan Abamillo, Juan Antonio Badillo, and José Esparza: TEXAS. Sometime before 11 A.M., Bonham tied a white handkerchief to his hat so that it would blow in the wind, a sign to the defenders that he was one of them. Spurring the horse to a gallop, he leaned his body over the side of the mount and raced through the Mexican lines and past the sentries, dodging bullets to resounding cheers from inside the walls. The gates of the Alamo opened for Bonham, and seconds later, the doors of destiny closed behind him, trapping inside a band of brave men whose sacrifice and secrets would shape the destiny of Texas.[4]

1

IN THE FOOTSTEPS
OF HISTORY

ALWAYS GAMES. Life itself was a game of winners and losers, life and death. A game of glory or disgrace that only the most compulsive gamblers, the ones with still hands and icy nerves, played. And during the lulls between the biggest games, there were always the cocks. At least that was how Antonio López de Santa Anna approached life.

All his life, Santa Anna was drawn to the games. He loved to gamble on cockfights, though he generally preferred when the matches were fixed in his favor. And he was devoted to political gambles, though militarily he preferred fixed fights there as well. Soon he would face a bettor's odds at the Alamo.

By 1835, at the age of forty-one, the gambling had begun to exact its toll. Not the heaviest—he still had both legs. But his handsomeness, his almost aquiline beauty, was fading. Though he was still tall and muscular, tropical diseases had yellowed his skin and he was adding weight. Small imperfections, really. His eyes, piercing and dark, could still strike terror if he chose, and his ability to dominate men, women, and even a nation seemed intact. He remained a hero for a romantic age. With his hair swept forward à la Napoleon and his air of reckless-ness, he was Byronic, a man destined to conquer worlds or perish in some act of self-destruction. As one historian commented, "He did not have a messiah complex. He skipped that level. He thought he was God."[1]

But a peculiar type of "God"; in fact, not so much the biblical God as a classical god, in whom heroism and audacity mixed naturally with laziness, licentiousness, and vanity. He wanted to conquer worlds but had no real interest in ruling them. He wanted to "save" Mexico but not administer his country. He saw his duty as sweeping out of the green paradise of Jalapa, performing some life-threatening, heroic act, then retiring back to his less than humble hacienda—a nineteenth-century Cincinnatus stripped of all notions of simplicity, a Mexican George Washington shorn of the need to be virtuous or to spend eight years as president. The sort of life Byron might have invented for himself.

But in retirement—or between conquests—he could never really relax. Farming or writing or any sort of contemplative pursuit held no attraction for him. Where was the excitement in watching something grow? Where was the thrill in putting sterile words on paper? So he gambled, especially at the famous cockfighting pit in San Agustín de las Cuevas, a village just south of Mexico City. At the Plaza de Gallos, Santa Anna was in his glory, placing bets, shouting encouragement, and watching the birds flash together in a blur of color. The ritual was unchanging. Every day during the festivals, seven sets of cocks, razors strapped to their legs, fought to the death while sharp-eyed brokers trolled the arena taking bets. Trainers tried to influence their cocks—pulling feathers to infuriate them, splashing water on their heads to refresh them, blowing breath into their beaks to revive them. After two or three rounds a fight would be over.[2]

Unlike the contest in the pit, Santa Anna's game was rigged. A man named Guillermo Prieto left a description of Santa Anna at the cockfighting pit: "He was something to see at the fights, surrounded by the leading loan sharks of the city, taking the money of others, mingling with employees and even with junior officers. He borrowed money but did not repay it, was praised for contemptible tricks as if they were charming manners, and when it seemed that he was growing tired of the matches, the fair sex would grant him their smiles and join him in his antics."[3]

Santa Anna possessed voracious appetites—for sex, power, and money, but most of all for adulation—and he dominated his country. He lusted for absolute power. A contemporary later said of him, "He lives in perpetual agitation, he gets carried away by an irresistible desire to acquire glory. . . . Defeat . . . maddens him." Late in his life, recalling the ambitions of his youth, Santa Anna wrote, "How impatient I was to climb the stair of life! With the typical eagerness of youth, I wished to vault its steps two by two, four by four." And in the end, his destiny became Mexico's. "Providence willed my history to be the history of Mexico since 1821," he later wrote.[4]

In the 1820s, when Santa Anna surfaced into political prominence, the United States and Mexico were, for all intents and purposes, equals on the world stage, possessing comparable landmasses, populations, natural resources, and seemingly, futures. Both countries had thrown off colonial powers. After the Mexican Constitution of 1824 was adopted, both had federalist, democratic systems. Mexico had even banned slavery, and despite a hierarchical society with built-in prejudices similar to those of the United States, Mexico might have had a better claim to living up to its ideals of freedom. Except that its political leaders were prone to conspiracies. Santa Anna became a small-time Napoleon. By the mid-1840s, Mexico would be eclipsed, severed in two, and relegated by its northern neighbor to the backwaters of world history. Santa Anna would bear much of the responsibility.

It was the season of blood in the early spring of 1835, and Santa Anna was heading for Zacatecas to draw even more. He awakened in the upstairs bedroom of a white-stuccoed mansion at El Encero, his hacienda twelve miles from Jalapa. Nestled high in the Sierra Madre Oriental, Jalapa's cool, crisp air had for centuries lured the wealthy rulers of Mexico out from Vera Cruz's disease-ridden, mosquito-infested lowlands. At 4,700 feet in elevation, balanced between the ocean and the high tablelands, Jalapa was, according to a Spanish traveler, "a piece of heaven let down to earth." Its clean streets were lined with one- and two-story stone homes, each whitewashed, trimmed in red, blue, yellow, pink, or green, and topped with a slanted roof of red tiles. Local Indians insisted that "Jalapa is paradise."[5]

Perhaps Santa Anna sat for a few moments on the second-story veranda, surveying through open arches an estate, including the El Encero and Manga de Clavo haciendas, that stretched beyond the horizon, nearly to the Gulf of Mexico, and included thousands of acres and tens of thousands of cattle and sheep. Orchards of bananas, oranges, figs, mangoes, olives, and coffee filled the eastern and northern horizons as far as the eye could see. To the south and west, snow-covered peaks seemed to go on forever, with 18,855-foot Citlaltépetl, or Mount Orizaba, presiding over them all. Santa Anna's spectacular fortune was already a national scandal. Mexicans joked sarcastically that "God must open heaven every so often and shower Santa Anna with pesos. How else did he become so rich?" In front of El Encero, a cavalry troop hovered around the president's carriage, the horses poised and ready to start. Another carriage housed his beloved fighting cocks. Santa Anna exited his hacienda, said his good-byes, then stepped aboard the carriage and ordered the driver to head west.[6]

Few men have spent so much of their lives fomenting or crushing rebellions. Santa Anna was a criollo (a Spaniard native to Mexico), born in Jalapa on February 21, 1794, to parents only recently immigrated from Spain. His pale complexion, high forehead, nose, and full head of dark hair testified to European origins—a mother's ancestry in southern France, a father's roots in northern Spain. Years later Frances Calderón de la Barca, the wife of a Spanish diplomat, described him as a "gentlemanly, good-looking, quietly-dressed, rather melancholy-looking person . . . [with] fine dark eyes, soft and penetrating, and an interesting expression on his face." As a sixteen-year-old, Santa Anna joined the Spanish army, hoping with military exploits to earn a place for himself in a world dominated by *gachupínes* (natives of Spain).[7]

The young cadet soon found himself under the command of Colonel José Joaquín de Arredondo, a Spaniard who served first as governor of New Santander and from 1813 to 1821 as commandant general of the Eastern Interior Provinces of New Spain, which consisted of Texas, Nuevo León, Coahuila, and Santander (Tamaulipas). Arredondo was at first charged with putting down Chichimeca uprisings. Spaniards employed the term "Chichimecas" loosely, attaching it to various nomadic, warlike indigenous peoples in central and northern Mexico. Adept at bow-and-arrow warfare, the Chichimecas had battled Spaniards for centuries. During a fight near San Luis Potosí in 1811, a warrior drew first blood, shooting an arrow into Santa Anna's left arm. The young soldier shrugged off the wound and kept on fighting, leading Arredondo to praise him as one "who had enough constancy to suffer the inconveniences of continuous marches, giving an example in his way to the troops, and demonstrating the most vivid desires to give credit to their great valor." In February 1812, Santa Anna was promoted to second lieutenant, and six months later to first lieutenant.[8]

At some point he began to ache with ambition, a lust unburdened by ideology or philosophy. He lived for power and the personal pleasures it afforded. He exploited, used, abused, and killed those who stood between him and his desires, exhibiting little interest in the needs of others unless they could somehow be turned to his advantage. Years later, a contemporary described him as "a man who has within him some force always driving him to take action but since he has no fixed principles nor any organized code of public behavior, through his lack of understanding he always moves to extremes and comes to contradict himself." Contradictions, about-faces, inconsistencies, and mood swings were as common in Santa Anna's life as humidity in a Vera Cruz summer. On August 29, 1821, his duplicity first revealed itself when he accepted a promotion in the Spanish army to lieutenant colonel. Later in the day, when offered the rank of colonel in the rebel forces, he abruptly switched sides, declaring himself a Mexican, pledging eternal loyalty to rebel leader Agustín de Iturbide, and later telling his troops, "Let us hasten to proclaim the immortal Iturbide as emperor and offer ourselves as his most faithful defenders."[9]

Santa Anna's instincts eventually flowered into an uncanny gift for political intrigue. Calderón de la Barca once likened Mexican politics to "a game of chess, in which the kings, castles, knights, and bishops are making all the moves, while the pawns look on without taking part in the game." Nobody played better than Santa Anna. Within eighteen months, he had turned on Iturbide, leading a rebellion that forced the emperor's abdication. He later conspired with Vicente Guerrero to depose President Manuel Gómez Pedraza, and then intrigued yet again, helping incite a new rebellion that eventually put Guerrero in front of a firing squad. One year later, Santa Anna became a national hero when Spain tried to reconquer Mexico. In the blazing sun and sweltering heat of August 1829, the Spanish navy landed twenty-six hundred soldiers about forty miles south of Tampico. Actually, Spanish incompetence and Tampico's legendary yellow-fever-bearing mosquitoes inflicted most of the damage, and the Spanish armada had immediately returned to Cuba, leaving the army trapped along the coast, with Santa Anna blocking the route to higher ground. He waited a month to attack, giving the deadly mosquitoes time to feast. Then he went on the offensive and eliminated what was left of the army. Spain surrendered, and within a matter of weeks, millions of Mexicans knew Santa Anna as the "Hero of Tampico," the "Fearless Son of Mars," the "Support of the People."[10]

He finally reached the summit of power in 1833, becoming president after again negotiating the dark catacombs of Mexican politics. Anastasio Bustamante, whose government Santa Anna brought down in 1832, told Congress, "There is hardly a Mexican . . . who is ignorant of the dissembling and perfidious character of the chief of the insurgents [Santa Anna]." Beginning with his first inauguration, in 1833, Santa Anna would serve *eleven* times as president of Mexico, entering and exiting the political stage more often than a character in an Italian opera. Each time he sported a different ideological costume, masquerading as conservative or liberal, centralist or federalist, royalist or rebel, whatever political circumstances demanded. He was a complete enigma, and those who knew him best recalled his contradictions—a heart where kindness and viciousness, and forgiveness and revenge, coexisted peacefully, even comfortably, and a mind as capable of brilliance as it was of stupidity.[11]

Santa Anna seized power in a country whose early modern traditions were even more violent than colonial America's. In March 1835, as he departed El Encero, he assumed as his own Mexico's legacy of conquest. In the capital, he would assemble an army and then march north, rescue his country from traitors, and enshrine himself forever in the pantheon of Mexican heroes. The nearly four-hundred-mile journey from Jalapa to Mexico City, which traversed three mountain ranges and a desert, roughly followed the route taken 316 years before by Hernán Cortés. Drawn by rumors of fabulous Aztec riches, the Spanish conquistadors had marched eighty-three days getting to Tenochtitlán, in the Valley of Mexico. (Santa Anna did it in less than three weeks—but he did not have thousands of people to kill along the way; not yet at least.) The conquistadors attacked their foes to the traditional strains of the *degüello*—a medieval ballad played through centuries of wars with the Moors—whose haunting rhythms announced "no quarter" to the vanquished, only imminent "beheadings," "throat slittings," and "ruin." It was an appropriate military anthem for Mexico.

As Cortés made his way to the interior, he encountered the Aztec taste for human sacrifice. In the past seven centuries, North America has witnessed three major episodes of military and cultural imperialism, the last of which assumed the title Manifest Destiny. The Aztecs brought about the first. In the thirteenth century, they began leaving mountain redoubts in northern Mexico for points south and soon overwhelmed indigenous peoples, creating a bloody empire of their own, taking land that was not theirs to take, plundering towns that were not theirs to plunder, and killing millions who did not deserve to be killed. An eighteenth-century Jesuit historian wrote that Aztec civilization "when the Spaniards discovered them greatly surpasse[d] that of the Spaniards themselves when they came to be known by the Greeks, the Romans, the Gauls, the Germans and the Bretons. . . . [Their] religion was very bloody and . . . their sacrifices cruel . . . but there is no nation in the world that has not sometimes sacrificed victims to the god they adored." Convinced of their own superiority and invoking the names of their gods in justification, the Aztecs took what other peoples in Mexico were incapable of defending.[12]

Sometime in the mid–fifteenth century, Aztecs had accepted the efficacy of human sacrifice to appease the gods, secure military victories, and guarantee good harvests. Repeatedly in 1519, as Cortés and his followers made their way toward Tenochtitlán, they explored Indian temples reeking with the smell of death, walls dripping blood and floors slippery with body fluids and human entrails. In temple plazas, the Aztecs stacked victims' skulls into macabre sculptures. Bernal Díaz del Castillo, who accompanied Cortés, remembered one plaza with the skulls "so neatly arranged that we could count them, and I reckoned them at more than a hundred thousand. I repeat that there were more than a hundred thousand."[13]

Several points along Santa Anna's fateful 1835 journey recalled the sanguinary fields of the past. Two weeks into his trip, he passed through Tlaxcala, eyes raised toward La Malinche, a 14,636-foot snow-covered peak named after Cortés's Indian mistress and interpreter. There, in August 1519, Cortés had encountered a Tlaxcalan army of forty thousand troops. When his expedition of four hundred Spanish soldiers and several hundred Indian allies approached, the Tlaxcalans massed into groups and—armed with slings, bows, javelins, and two-handed obsidian-bladed clubs—hurtled themselves at the foreigners. The battle raged for a week, bloodying the Spaniards but taking a heavy toll on the Tlaxcalans. Díaz remembered that poor infantry tactics doomed the Tlaxcalans. "One thing saved our lives," he later wrote, "and this was that they were many and massed such that the shots wrought havoc among them." A fiercely independent people constantly at war with the Aztecs, the Tlaxcalans battled Cortés to a draw. When the Tlaxcalan chief proposed a Spanish-Tlaxcalan military alliance, Cortés readily agreed. As Díaz wrote, the Spaniards were worrying about "what would happen to us when we had to fight Moctezuma [and the Aztecs] if we were reduced to such straits by the Tlaxcalans."[14]

Backed by thousands of Tlaxcalan warriors, Cortés had headed south for Cholula, a major religious center, home to four hundred temples and a hundred thousand people. A huge, 177-foot-high pyramid dedicated to the god Quetzalcóatl dominated the Cholulan skyline. When Santa Anna passed through Cholula in mid-April 1835, the pyramid looked more like an overgrown hill, topped by a Catholic church that Spaniards had erected to diminish Aztec glory, since Aztec theology held that someday the god Quetzalcóatl would return from the east in power and glory. More than a few Indians had wondered if Cortés might represent his reincarnation. But perhaps the Indians had not expected a god so bloodthirsty. On October 18, 1519, at the base of the pyramid, Cortés assembled Cholula's elite, massacred three thousand people in two hours, and then turned Tlaxcalan warriors loose to plunder and kill for several days more. Eventually Cholula was littered with ten thousand corpses. A victorious Cortés then turned west for Tenochtitlán.

Cortés traversed the 12,000-foot-high pass that now bears his name, flanked by the legendary Popocatépetl and Iztaccíhuatl volcanoes, and then descended into the Valley of Mexico. Just as he passed over the shoulders of Popocatépetl, the volcano came alive after years of dormancy, sending plumes of smoke heavenward and convincing even more people that Cortés might indeed be Quetzalcóatl. But Cortés was no god; he brought power to the valley but no glory, only death and misery, commodities that Santa Anna trafficked in as well.

Like Cortés before him, Santa Anna descended into the Valley of Mexico, passing through pine forests to Amecameca, crossing the great lava flows to Tlalmanalco, and riding by Ayotzingo, Mixquic, Cuitlahuac, and Iztapalapa. When he reached Mexico City on April 18, 1835, throngs greeted him similar to those that had greeted Cortés. He enjoyed grand entrances—magnificent Arabian stallions, ornate carriages, honor guards, armed dragoons, formally dressed civil and military dignitaries, blaring bands, fireworks, cannonades, and cheering crowds. Just one year before, he had staged another grand entrance. On April 19, 1834, after hiding out at Manga de Clavo and testing the political winds, he had descended on the capital to dismantle the liberal, federalist constitution. Mexico was in trouble, suffering the aftershocks of its independence movement. Political instability had prompted a flight of capital. Gold and silver had flown the country, and without hard currency, the economy reverted to barter. Congress made a bad situation worse by minting worthless copper coins and triggering a hyperinflation that sent the economy into a steeper decline. Wages lagged woefully behind prices, food shortages appeared, crime skyrocketed, and the social fabric unraveled. One foreign visitor described the streets of Mexico City as "no longer worthy of the name; they are chasms, precipices and disgusting sewers. Its suburbs are heaps of ruin, horrific dung heaps, centers of corruption and disease. . . . Its most public thoroughfares are sites of scandal and indecency and there is a tavern, vice and prostitution on almost every street. Nowhere is safe from crime."[15]

Chaos mocked revolutionary hope. For three centuries, the Catholic church and the Spanish monarchy had anchored Mexican society, producing a relatively fixed social order where most people understood their place. At the top were white Europeans, divided into Spanish-born *gachupínes* and Mexican-born criollos. By virtue of birth and the backing they received from Madrid and Rome, *gachupínes* controlled the colonial establishment. Criollos' power, on the other hand, was rooted in land and commerce, and they resented the stranglehold *gachupínes* exercised over the government, the army, and the clergy. Beneath criollos seethed a large working class of mestizos, the offspring of Spanish and Indian parents. They resented the smug Spaniards who controlled political, social, and economic power. Finally, poverty-stricken Indians occupied the bottom rung of the social ladder. Criollos, mestizos, and Indians had little affection for one another, but together they loathed *gachupín* arrogance and in the 1810s had transformed resentment into revolution.

The rebel victory sent Spanish-born public officials, army officers, and priests scurrying back to Spain, leaving Mexico to the feuding revolutionaries. The criollos, with property and status to protect, desired a mere coup d'état, maintaining the old order, only with themselves at the top. Many mestizos, on the other hand, hoped to convert the rebellion against Spain into a genuine reform movement that would lead to universal male suffrage, individual civil liberties, and separation of church and state. A few even lobbied for breaking up large estates and giving the land to peasants and Indians.

Ethnic rivalries destabilized the periphery. To the north, across the borderlands frontier, Anglo-American settlers penetrated Texas, New Mexico, and California. Their political and economic compass pointed east, not south, and their patience with interference from Mexico City would soon prove startlingly shallow. And across Mexico's southern tier, from Chiapas to the Yucatán, Mayan Indians kept a vigil of their own. Like a jigsaw puzzle being shaken by a child, Mexico was coming part. Revolts and revolutionaries were everywhere—in California and Texas in the north, in the Yucatán in the east, in Chiapas in the south, and everywhere in between.

Conservative elements of Mexican society—primarily criollo merchants, businessmen, army officers, clerics, and professionals—looked nostalgically to a past when, they believed, law and order prevailed, the moral code stood unchallenged, and the upper classes ruled without rivals. Unless change came soon, they predicted violence, anarchy, and national disintegration. Concerned criollos, or *hombres de bien* ("men of goodwill") as they came to be known, blamed the Constitution of 1824. By extending near sovereignty to each state government, it had encouraged local autonomy, emasculated the central government, and sown the seeds of anarchy. Federalism, they concluded, could no longer hold Mexico together.[16]

Sensitive to shifts in the political wind, Santa Anna traded his liberal costume for a conservative uniform. Within weeks of his arrival in the capital on April 19, 1834, he had deposed Acting President Valentín Gómez Farías, dissolved Congress, launched a systematic purge of liberals, and denounced the 1824 Constitution. Specially arranged elections in the summer of 1834 produced a new legislature dominated by *hombres de bien*—Catholic priests, army officers, lawyers, large hacienda owners, and well-to-do businessmen, all of whom demanded the stability that Santa Anna somberly promised. Liberals knew exactly what was coming. "Caesar has crossed the Rubicon," wrote a liberal editor in June 1834, "and has already proclaimed himself a tyrant."[17]

Within a matter of months, Santa Anna had created centralized, dictatorial authority. All state governors henceforth would hold office only at the whim of the central government; all state legislatures would be replaced by five-man councils that advised the governor; and a uniform tax, civil, and criminal code would be imposed throughout the country. Congress then set its sights on the state militias, which regular army officers resented and conservatives viewed as symbols of state autonomy. Santa Anna's followers accused the state militias of representing a "cruel servitude for the people, a focus of corruption and immorality and a harmful distraction for industrious people . . . [militias were] the worst plague of society." A centralist newspaper likened state militias to "hirelings of the sansculottes . . . [who] install and remove governments at their whim, to take revenge on anybody they choose." At the end of March 1835, Congress placed a ceiling on the size of state militias, limiting them to a maximum of one recruit for every five hundred citizens.[18]

The demise of the constitution and reduction of the militias aroused instant, bitter resentment throughout Mexico. Several states—including San Luis Potosí, Querétaro, Durango, Guanajuato, Michoacán, Yucatán, and Jalisco—expressed discontent, and outright rebellion erupted in Zacatecas and Texas. The local newspaper in Zacatecas accused Santa Anna of "conspiring to crush freedom in an immoral assault on federalism." The Zacatecas legislature labeled the measure "an affront to Zacatecan sovereignty and an assault on our liberty" and on March 30, 1835, passed a resolution authorizing the governor to "use all of the State Militia to repel any aggression."[19]

The Zacatecan militia was the largest in Mexico, with twenty thousand men on its muster rolls and four thousand armed, uniformed, and ready to serve. Santa Anna suspected that centralists would soon prevail politically in most states, but he decided to move quickly on Zacatecas, where he could not afford to lose control of valuable silver mines, and Texas, where Anglo settlers threatened to detach the region and hand it over to the United States. He vowed to crush the rebellion "with the most inflexible severity."[20]

Command of the local militia fell on Francisco García, the governor of Zacatecas, who, unfortunately, had no military experience. Even with Santa Anna on the move, García made few preparations, except for placing some artillery along the ravines leading to Zacatecas, in case *el presi-*

dente decided to invade the city. He also decided to establish a defensive perimeter on the east side of the town of Guadalupe, about four miles southeast of Zacatecas. García naively believed that the advantages of his position—a field of battle nearly one thousand meters in length, flanked by mountains on his left and a ravine to his right—would give the militia an advantage against Santa Anna's regulars.[21]

Hundreds of miles to the north, Anglo Texans occupied common philosophical ground with the Zacatecans. Thousands of Anglos had crossed the Texas border; most were from Southern states. They identified as U.S. citizens, and to them Santa Anna's orders evoked visceral passions dating back to the American Revolution, when British soldiers had occupied their cities and their homes. The "shot heard round the world" on April 19, 1775, which launched the war for independence, occurred after British regulars marched on Lexington and Concord to seize the weapons of the Massachusetts militia. Texans, like most U.S. Southerners and Westerners, took their firearms and their militias seriously. When Mexico's Congress announced the demise of the state militias, one Texas rebel termed it "the last final blow at their liberties . . . [that lit] the flame of civil war; the civic militia had all times previously proven the sure and safe bulwark of the liberties of the People . . . to deliver up their arms, was to deliver themselves over to an aristocracy, whose object was plainly Monarchy." The legislature of Coahuila y Texas similarly proclaimed that when "the Civic Militia are reduced . . . the only bulwark of liberty, and the right of the community are destroyed."[22]

Santa Anna aimed to punish Zacatecas first and then to move to Texas. In 1546 Juan Tolosa and a small contingent of Spanish soldiers, Indian auxiliaries, and Franciscan friars had explored what would later become the city of Zacatecas, reaching a hump-shaped mountain decorated with green-streaked crests and sharp craggy outcroppings. He dubbed the mountain La Bufa—or Hog's Bladder. At the sight of the Spaniards and their horses, the local Indians fled into La Bufa's canyons and caves. But neighboring Chichimecas, some of whom had escaped slave labor in the Taxco silver mines, knew how to pacify the white men. In return for freedom, they showed Tolosa vast seams of silver coursing like frozen rivers through the Zacatecan mountains. The town of Zacatecas sprang up almost overnight as silver prospectors by the thousands threw up shanties in the twisting gullies and ravines. Whitewashed stone monuments, identifying mining claims, soon dotted the mountainsides. For the next three centuries, a river of silver flowed from Zacatecas. Santa Anna was not about to lose his grip on the mother lode.[23]

The expedition began on April 18, 1835, when Santa Anna left Mexico City for the northern frontier with three armies totaling more than four thousand *soldados*. Behind them trailed hundreds, perhaps even thousands, of *soldaderas,* or camp followers—prostitutes, cooks, and infantry wives and children too poor to survive at home while their husbands and fathers went to war—and government officials, teamsters, and supply contractors. The highway out of Mexico City to Querétaro retraced the route of the Calzada de Tepeyac, an Aztec highway that once crossed Lake Texcoco from Tenochtitlán to the mainland.

The Mexican population in 1835 had yet to recover to its pre-Cortés level. On Good Friday 1519, the day Cortés stepped ashore near what is today Vera Cruz, Mexico's indigenous peoples had numbered in the tens of millions; by 1600, less than a million survived. Their brothers and sisters, fathers and mothers, grandfathers and grandmothers, uncles, aunts, and cousins had all succumbed to a Spanish arsenal of lances, harquebus muskets, cannons, crossbows, pikes, swords, horses, bacteria, and viruses. From the heart of New Spain in the Valley of Mexico, the Spaniards then radiated steadily outward, in increasingly wide concentric circles, killing and subduing the indigenous peoples in the jungles of Chiapas and Yucatán, the deserts of Sonora and Chihuahua, and the Sierra Madre Oriental and Sierra Madre Occidental. What Spain wrought in the sixteenth, seventeenth, and eighteenth centuries would be a forerunner of the Manifest Destiny Americans imposed in the nineteenth.[24]

In April 1835, as Santa Anna's Army of Operations marched along the highway from Mexico City, urban sprawl gave way to the peaceful Bajío—vast fertile valleys punctuated by burnt brown mountains stretching toward the cities of Querétaro, Guanajuato, Morelia, and León. Although the word *bajío* means "lowland" in Spanish, the Bajío is actually a vast highland plain between 5,500 and 7,000 feet in altitude. Fertile soil rooted in volcanic ash had transformed the Bajío into Mexico's breadbasket, and Spanish soldiers and settlers had driven the Chichimecas off the land. They then enslaved them to extract silver from the Bajío's vast subterranean lodes. The rich land became the cradle of Mexican liberty. Towns and villages bear the names of revolutionary heroes—Miguel Hidalgo, Ignacio de Allende, Juan de Aldama, Mariano Jiménez, Agustín de Iturbide, and José María Morelos y Pavón. During the 1810s, Santa Anna had been involved directly or indirectly with all of them, serving with them or chasing them throughout the Bajío.[25]

On April 25, his army reached Guanajuato, down the road a few miles from Dolores, the birthplace of the Mexican Revolution. There, on September 15, 1810, four months after Santa Anna had joined the Spanish army, Miguel Hidalgo, a criollo priest turned revolutionary, set out to secure "restitution of the holy rights granted by God to the Mexicans, usurped by cruel, bastard, and unjust conquerors." That morning, he sounded the church bell in Dolores, and before a crowd of Indians and mestizos announced—in what is remembered as the *grito de Dolores*—"Death to the Spaniards! Long live the Virgin of Guadalupe!" He hoisted a painted canvas of the Virgin of Guadalupe on a pole and marched around the town square, encouraging his followers, "Take! My children! Because everything is yours!" Poverty-stricken Indians and peasants, who had spent their lives suffering while Spaniards became rich, rallied by the tens of thousands, and within a matter of weeks Hidalgo's revolution had engulfed central Mexico.

The revolt soon flamed out of control. In Guanajuato, as Hidalgo's army massed on the outskirts, Spanish families fled to the protection of the Alhóndiga de Granaditas, a walled grain-storage compound. Hidalgo's followers attacked and slaughtered every Spanish man. Those who surrendered were beaten and tortured before being executed. Spaniards died in the Alhóndiga as if (according to a contemporary Mexican historian) "history were taking an atrocious revenge for the massacres of the Indians by the conquistadores at Cholula and the great temple of Tenochtitlan." The revolutionaries then spread out, hunting down Spaniards like animals, slitting their throats in tribal rituals to liberty, ransacking homes and businesses, raping women, stealing everything they could carry. Hidalgo opposed "any settlement which did not provide for the liberty of the nation and the rights which the God of nature granted to all men, rights that are truly inalienable, and they would be protected with rivers of blood if it becomes necessary."[26]

Blood did flow, Hidalgo's included. Full of vision but devoid of strategy, he self-destructed. With Spanish soldiers pursuing him, he fled the Bajío for safety in the northern deserts. But a contingent of Spanish soldiers captured him in Baján, just north of Monclova, where his revolutionary dreams turned quickly into a personal nightmare. Along with four coconspirators, Hidalgo spent three weeks in Monclova's jail before Spanish officials transported him to Chihuahua for trial. In short order he was convicted and sentenced to death. On July 30, 1811, the defrocked priest, clutching a silk-embroidered image of the Virgin of Guadalupe, faced execution. No member of the firing squad wanted to be responsible for killing him, and after three lines of soldiers had fired, Hidalgo was still alive, though wounded in the legs, arms, feet, spine, shoulders, and abdomen. The commander then took two soldiers and ordered them to shoot point-blank into Hidalgo's heart. As he gave the order to fire, Pedro Armendáriz remembered, "Hidalgo just stared straight at us with those beautiful eyes." His coconspirators were executed as well. A headman then decapitated the corpses of Miguel Hidalgo, Ignacio de Allende, Juan de Aldama, and Mariano Jiménez, and the heads were transported to Guanajuato, impaled on spikes inside iron cages, and hung on the four corners of the Alhóndiga de Granaditas, site of Hidalgo's bloodiest depredations. The cages remained in place for ten years, stark reminders of the perils of rebellion.[27]

For Santa Anna, the Bajío conjured violent memories. He had crisscrossed the region as a young cadet and learned, under the tutelage of José Arredondo, how to treat a defeated enemy. To teach others a lesson, prisoners of war needed to be tortured and sympathetic noncombatants punished. In the afterglow of victory, Arredondo often ordered his troops back through Chichimeca villages, where they "swept off all they found, confusing the peaceful inhabitants with fighting men." They leveled villages, burned homes and granaries, assaulted women, horsewhipped boys, cut men's throats, and shot livestock.[28]

Several years later, Santa Anna had returned to the Bajío to put down insurgent rebellions and Indian uprisings. He was now under the command of Agustín de Iturbide. There Santa Anna learned new lessons in the art of the *degüello*. According to one contemporary, Iturbide had few peers when it came to viciousness. "He left a trail of blood in his wake . . . [and was] harsh beyond measure with the Insurgents. . . . [He] sullied his victories with a thousand acts of cruelty." Iturbide had a penchant for summarily executing prisoners of war and sympathetic civilians, usually denying them the last rites of the church so that their final moments would be especially torturous. To punish platoons and companies accused of dereliction or cowardice, he forced soldiers to draw lots to determine who would be executed. On one occasion, to send a message to potential insurgents, Iturbide targeted their wives, ordering that "one woman in every . . . three arrested at any distance from their disloyal fathers, husbands, or brothers, etc., should be beheaded without possibility of reprieve whenever the traitors committed specific outrages."[29]

As Santa Anna passed through the Bajío, he was prepared to inflict similar punishments on Zacatecas and Texas. As with El Cid, Cortés, Montezuma, Arredondo, and Hidalgo, his sense of mission knew few limitations. He arrived in Aguascalientes on May 1, setting up his general headquarters in the Palacio de Gobierno, an elegant, two-story edifice built of dark red volcanic stone with a column-lined courtyard and stone staircases. The palace rested on the south side of the Plaza de la Patria, where Santa Anna paraded his army, giving local citizens a glimpse of his power. On another, more leisurely occasion, he might have spent a few weeks in Aguascalientes. At more than 6,000 feet in altitude, the city enjoyed near perfect weather, especially in the spring and summer; some of the best vineyards and wine cellars in Mexico; and hot springs known widely for their medicinal powers. But there was no time. On May 5, the Army of Operations moved on.[30]

Zacatecans had a reputation as an arrogant people—fiercely independent, resentful of authority, quick to anger, and slow to forgive. An old Mexican adage described them as "as proud as a stallion, as stubborn as a mule, and as ill-tempered as a rattlesnake." They came by such traits honestly. Before Aztec warriors commenced their thirteenth-century migration to the Valley of Mexico, they sharpened spears in the mountains of Zacatecas, erecting small pyramids, sacrificing humans to invisible gods, carving telltale plumed serpents, and driving lesser tribes into the parched northern deserts. When the Aztecs departed, Chichimecas filled the vacuum, waging violent guerrilla campaigns against neighboring peoples and establishing their own reputation for stubborn ferocity.

A vibrant middle class contributed to Zacatecan independence. The silver mines had lured merchants, muleteers, miners, textile workers, lawyers, small landowners, doctors, and skilled craftsmen to Zacatecas, and with prosperity came the desire to control their own affairs. Liberalism had long thrived because property there had been more evenly divided and large haciendas were few and far between. In 1833 the

Zacatecas governor had purchased large haciendas with public funds and then distributed the land to smaller property owners. Zacatecans became notoriously jealous of their privileges and resentful of outsiders—Spanish or Mexican—bent on limiting their opportunities.[31]

On May 9, Zacatecan scouts informed the governor that the Army of Operations had nearly reached Guadalupe, about four miles southeast of Zacatecas, and bivouacked in Tolosa. The news surprised nobody. In addition to thousands of soldiers and camp followers, Santa Anna's army included oxen, cattle, horses, wagons, carts, and artillery pieces. The army kicked up clouds of dust that could be seen for miles.[32]

The Zacatecan troops not already at the front arose early on the morning of May 10, donning militia uniforms—rough sailcloth trousers and dark blue, red-collared tailcoats once used by regular army troops. Their bellies full of tortillas stuffed with beans and an extra portion of shredded beef, the part-time soldiers marched down Avenida Hidalgo and Avenida de la Independencia, smiling and joking, waving to crowds, acting as if they were heading for a fiesta. They collected downtown in front of the main church of Zacatecas, erected to honor Nuestra Señora de la Asunción, ready to pray for victory and to receive a priest's blessing.

Morning shadows dappled the church's ornate, three-story facade, giving life to the angels, saints, cherubs, and gargoyles sculptured into pink sandstone. A huge rose-colored window sparkled. Tangles of elaborately carved vines, grapes, fruit, shells, and feathers twisted their way around the stone pillars, and dominating the display was a figure representing God, attended by horn-playing angels. When the troops were properly blessed, the Zacatecans formed into columns, cast last looks at La Bufa, and set out for battle, while friends and neighbors tossed flowers and urged them on to victory for federalism and freedom.

The six-kilometer march took a few hours. Upon their arrival, García, the militia commander, rested his troops for an hour, letting them eat lunches that wives had prepared the night before. Knapsacks disgorged more beans, tortillas, beef, cheese, rice, and slivers of a Zacatecan delicacy—*tuna en crepa,* a semihard candy known as *el dulce de Dios,* "the candy of God." But the wives knew to ration God's candy. *Queso de tuna* is also a potent laxative, and men going into battle ate it sparingly. During lunch, the citizen soldiers relaxed and joked with one another. It looked more like a picnic than a war. García also installed snipers in the

Guadalupe chapel, the local convent, and on the rooftops of dozens of houses.[33]

At 5 P.M., Santa Anna reconnoitered the Zacatecan position, observed García's preparations, and decided quickly that he faced an amateur. Couriers from Santa Anna delivered a curt message to García, informing him that the Army of Operations intended to occupy the city of Zacatecas and giving the militia eight hours to surrender its weapons and disband. García stood firm, citing the Constitution of 1824 and the sovereignty it awarded the states of Mexico. His defiance irritated Santa Anna, who blamed the local politicians for the terror about to befall.

The Zacatecans were better armed than most militias; local taxes on silver had generated a steady revenue, and García had purchased a good supply of .753 caliber British India Pattern muskets, known as the Brown Bess, and British Baker .61 caliber rifles, the same weapons wielded by Santa Anna's infantry and cavalry. Most of the militiamen actually carried more than one weapon into battle. They also had twelve pieces of artillery. On paper, the Zacatecans appeared to be a match for the Army of Operations. But war games, not wars, are fought on paper, and in the field the Zacatecans did not stand a chance. In the heat of battle, infantry troops must fire their weapons, cycle back to the rear to reload, and then return to the front line to fire again, all in coordinated lines. Reloading the Brown Bess took no less than nineteen separate maneuvers by soldiers moving back and forth in rank, often under fire. Managing such an intricate combat task required elaborate training, which Santa Anna knew how to administer, putting his men through round after round of repetitive, disciplined practice, boring them, frustrating them, and enraging them, but also preparing them for battle.[34]

Zacatecans, on the other hand, were a motley crew of businessmen, peasants, artisans, and farmers, men who worked every day and had little time for drill. They talked war, dreamed about war, and played war, but their lives had little to do with real war. And they were under the command of a man with only the foggiest notions of infantry tactics.

The field of battle radiated waves of brilliant colors, glistening hues of red, blue, yellow, and orange shimmering off fields of green. The rainy season had arrived early in 1835, and drizzles had germinated wildflower seeds. García positioned his militia in the open space, clustering his troops like bees on hives, buzzing with courage, patriotism, and dreams of glory, but possessing little sting. Moreover, the Zacatecans let down their guard, failed to send out scouts, and posted few sentries.

In a matter of hours, Santa Anna developed an operational strategy. He had no intention of taking heavy casualties; next year's campaign against Texas would require full strength. He needed the tactical advantage of choosing when and where to fight, and he counted on militia inexperience to hand him an easy victory. After dark on May 10, Santa Anna set his trap. Scavengers collected cartloads of brush and scrap wood, and when the sun set, they ignited dozens of huge bonfires. Santa Anna left behind several hundred troops, ordering them to make noise— laughter, jokes, yelling, singing, dancing, and fighting—to convince Zacatecans, if any were listening, that the battle was likely to be postponed. Once the Zacatecan sentries fell asleep, the Mexican army moved out. To muffle the sound of wooden wheels scraping on wooden axles, teamsters applied extra portions of lard to the artillery mountings and wrapped wheels in blankets and animal skins. Quietly and slowly, teams of men towed the artillery pieces to the front. The Mexicans positioned cannon and cartloads of ammunition less than 150 yards from the slumbering Zacatecans.

Santa Anna's attack plan was disarmingly simple. Several companies of regular infantry, armed with Brown Bess muskets and backed by fourteen artillery pieces, took up positions several hundred yards east and west of the Zacatecan encampment, with instructions, once artillery detonations sounded, to form into firing lines and attack the enemy's left flank. Once enemy troops were within seventy yards—the range of their weapons—the foot soldiers would open fire. The general also assembled a special company of *cazadores*—infantry sharpshooters—armed with British Baker .61 caliber rifles and ordered them to operate independently, picking off Zacatecan soldiers from as far away as 250 yards. They were also to shoot down enemy horses and oxen, so that wounded troops could not be evacuated from the field, and to target Zacatecan artillery crews. Most militias, Santa Anna knew from experience, were notoriously undertrained, which made it unlikely that competent backup crews would replace fallen comrades. Well to the rear so that fidgety horses could not be heard, Santa Anna readied his cavalry, each man bearing a lance, a saber, and a short-barreled British Paget carbine. Once the battle commenced, with the infantry advancing in overlapping segments, General Juan José Andrade would race his cavalry up the Zacate-can right flank and attack from the rear. A reserve division under Santa Anna's command would feint a frontal attack on the Zacatecan line.[35]

Tested on a dozen battlefields, Santa Anna's men, though poorly equipped and grossly underpaid, understood the confusion of battle and knew that discipline won wars. At 7 A.M., the bugles sounded and the sleepy-eyed militia stumbled out from blankets and bedrolls, hastily donned uniforms, pulled on shoes, boots, or sandals, and grabbed their weapons. They fumbled with the muskets, trying to load and cursing the drizzling rain that had moistened their powder. Santa Anna bided his time. Canister and cannonballs plow through standing men much better than sleeping men. Once the militia firing lines shaped up, Santa Anna unleashed the artillery.

The first salvos struck panic into the Zacatecans. A round shot at close range can turn dozens of men into chunks of shattered flesh, while canister and grapeshot slice off arms, legs, fingers, hands, feet, and faces. Exploding bones become organic shrapnel to kill and maim on their own. The Mexican artillery cut the Zacatecans down, shredding their lines, turning courage into panic, and sprinkling the wildflowers with blood and body parts. Fallen men screamed and moaned in vain. Others walked about in a daze, already in shock, sporting bloody stumps or cradling their own intestines, waiting to bleed to death. The Zacatecan artillery crews got off a salvo or two of their own, but the *cazadores* cut them down one by one, silencing the enemy cannoneers. The *cazadores* also dropped Zacatecan horses and oxen, littering the battlefield with carcasses.

Then, to the sounds of the "Degüello," Santa Anna ordered his infantry to advance. Dressed in blue coattee uniforms with red collars and red cuffs and loose-fitting blue or gray trousers, the foot soldiers marched forward in linear formation. The carefully orchestrated front lines fired and then methodically withdrew to the rear to prime and reload, while a new line of musketeers moved to the front. The Zacatecans returned fire, but in all the confusion, with so little training and so much wet powder, their best efforts proved hopelessly ineffectual; they downed a Mexican soldier here and there more by luck than by design. Concealed Zacatecan snipers brought down a few more. All the while, General Andrade maintained his ruse and kept the Zacatecan cavalry at bay.

Like a battering ram, Santa Anna's foot soldiers pushed into the Zacatecan left flank, forcing the militiamen steadily toward the center. So much destruction, so fast. In ten minutes the Mexican column split the Zacatecans in two, driving the enemy far to the right, where more Mexican infantry, their muskets primed and loaded, awaited their turn. The doomed Zacatecans eventually broke ranks, dropped their weapons, and fled toward the Mexican blocking parties—exactly as Santa Anna had anticipated. Primed and waiting soldiers mowed down the terrified militia and sent survivors into a wholesale retreat back up the highway toward Zacatecas. By that time, the Mexican cavalry had turned the right flank and was descending down the Zacatecan road toward the fleeing militia. With the escape route sealed, the cavalry finished the job. Some troopers swept down on the battlefield, killing the wounded with well-aimed thrusts of the lance. The wildflowers had been trampled into a killing field.

Capricious as always, Santa Anna decided not to slaughter all the Zacatecans. Two hours into combat, he ordered a cease-fire. As the dust settled and the smoke cleared, the extent of his victory became clear. The Army of Operations counted only about one hundred dead, but the Zacatecan militia had been destroyed. Francisco García sent four thousand men into battle, and Santa Anna took 2,723 prisoners of war. Estimates of the Zacatecan casualties ranged as high as twelve hundred men. The panic-stricken militia had abandoned more than six thousand muskets on the field of battle, along with all twelve artillery pieces.[36]

But Santa Anna was not finished. He ordered the Army of Operations to advance on the city of Zacatecas, leaving behind the prisoners of war under armed guard. He was being cautious. The mountains, ravines, and canyons of Zacatecas were a paramilitary's dream, and Santa Anna worried that García might be luring his troops into an ambush. He also feared hand-to-hand combat inside the city, which had been built along a series of gullies and ravines, with narrow streets and crowded buildings. But the Army of Operations encountered little resistance. News of the militia's horrendous defeat reached Zacatecas well ahead of Santa Anna, and thousands of citizens fled for the countryside. His troops entered an eerily quiet city, which looked almost as if Zacatecans were busy begging God for mercy.

If God gave them mercy, Santa Anna did not. While the general made his way out to the silver mines of Fresnillo to augment his personal fortune, he left his troops behind, giving them forty-eight hours to plunder Zacatecas. For two full days, they ransacked homes and businesses, emptying jewelry and cash boxes, cleaning shelves of inventory, pilfering clothes from racks and closets, carting away shoes and furniture, stealing horses, and slaughtering pigs and cattle. The exercise turned into an orgy of destruction, with soldiers raping women, bludgeoning men, poisoning wells, and setting fires. They stuffed bags and suitcases and hauled the loot out of town to camp-following wives, children, and prostitutes, who were more than ready to enjoy the fruits of victory. Cavalry troops rode out to local farms and haciendas. Infantry regiments invaded the neighboring settlements of Parrés, Fresnillo, and Sombrerete. When Santa Anna finally called off his men in the evening of May 13, Zacatecas was a ghost town, its commercial infrastructure destroyed. The offices and printing presses of *La Imprenta,* the local newspaper, had been leveled, and the paper went out of print and would remain so for two years. Schools and the local market remained closed for months.[37]

The Zacatecas defeat and rampage that followed sent a clear message north to Texas. Not that it was needed; Santa Anna loathed Anglos, perhaps because to him their greed and arrogance matched his own, perhaps because they seemed so intent on raping Mexico. During the battle of Zacatecas and the subsequent sacking of the city, he ordered the summary execution of all North Americans. Anglo engineers had provided technical assistance to Zacatecan mine owners, Anglo accountants had offices in La Casa de Moneda—the city's bank—and Anglo filibusterers had worked as military advisers to the Zacatecan militia. Santa Anna considered them all "pirates," "brigands," and "freebooters," subject to draconian retribution. Mexican infantry went house to house and room to room, rousting out cowering gringos and killing them on the spot.[38]

Santa Anna lingered in Zacatecas for two weeks, establishing a military government under the command of General Joaquín Ramírez y Sesma. On June 13, in recognition of the new order of things, Ramírez y Sesma organized citywide festivities to celebrate his own birthday. By that time Santa Anna was touring Mexico in triumph. At the end of May, the city fathers of Aguascalientes hosted him with a parade and a series of parties. He then proceeded to Guadalajara, where special masses, parties, toasts, and huge fireworks displays greeted him. There he learned that at Anahuac, Texas, on June 20, insurgents upset about government attempts to collect customs duties had attacked and overrun a Mexican garrison. While the leading ladies of Guadalajara installed a fine silk mattress in a carriage so that he could travel comfortably, Santa Anna fumed and plotted revenge. The governor of Jalisco sponsored three days of celebrations, and in Morelia, honor guards welcomed Santa Anna with cannon salutes and the bishop opened the cathedral doors, sprinkled him with holy water, and blessed him. The general arrived back in Mexico City on July 21, 1835, where Congress had proclaimed him "Benemérito de la Patria," or "Hero of the Fatherland." Everywhere, he labored to create an elaborate cult of personality. Handbills and broadsides by the thousands proclaimed his virtues; streets, plazas, and parks were rededicated in his name; statues were erected in his honor; and his portrait was displayed ubiquitously. Only after nine days of parades, festivals, and receptions did he depart for Manga de Clavo to recuperate before dealing with Texas. What Santa Anna did not anticipate north of the Rio Grande, however, was an enemy as violent and determined as himself.[39]

2

---★---

"The Free Born Sons of America"

Like the heroes of the Sir Walter Scott novels he read so voraciously, William Barret Travis longed for fame and fortune, but mostly for fame. "He hungered and thirsted for fame," remembered a friend, "not the kind of fame which satisfies the ambition of the duelist and desperado, but the exalted fame which crowns the doer of great deeds in a good cause." Travis thought he had made the right moves. Well read and well educated, he had settled in Claiborne, Alabama, in 1828 and studied law under James Dellet, the county's most successful attorney. He attended a Baptist church, supported the Claiborne Temperance Society, and joined a Masonic lodge. He accepted a commission in the local militia, opened a law office, and edited the *Claiborne Herald*. When he turned twenty-one, on August 1, 1830, he seemed destined to become a leading citizen.

But real success eluded him. The newspaper never turned a profit and drained what little income the law office generated. Debts piled up, and he found himself borrowing money to make partial payments, each time adding new obligations, alienating friends, and spoiling his reputation. Creditors hounded him and retained local attorneys, including James Dellet, to collect the delinquent notes. In March 1830, Travis found himself heading the county's docket of deadbeats. And while legal difficulties emptied his pocketbook, marital troubles drained his emotional reserves. A marriage to Rosanna Cato had produced one son but little happiness, and the likelihood of a stint in debtors' prison left him looking for a way out. "Never have I seen a more impressive instance of depression from debts," a fellow attorney recalled. Desperate to find a new route to fame and fortune, Travis decided, like millions of other Americans, to migrate west. In April 1831, leaving a pregnant wife with empty promises, he rode out of Claiborne and crossed the Alabama River into Mississippi.[1]

★

Travis fled for Texas just two years after Andrew Jackson had been sworn in as president. The so-called Jacksonian age, however, predated its namesake. America crackled with talk of individual rights, praising "equality" though defining it narrowly. Few American leaders would have included women, blacks, and Indians under democracy's blanket, but their discussion of equality and rights nevertheless transcended the Revolutionary generation's vision. During the 1770s and 1780s, when Americans spoke of rights, they had focused on such government abuses as the seizure of private property, double jeopardy, unreasonable searches and seizures, and cruel and unusual punishments. The framers of the Constitution did not consider voting rights a civil liberty. In 1800 less than half of white men owned enough property to vote.

By the early 1800s, however, Americans expanded their notion of individual rights to include the franchise. "We are the free born sons of America," Andrew Jackson told his troops in 1812, "the only people on earth who possess rights, liberties, and property which they dare call their own." White men of all classes demanded the right to vote, and their logic was compelling. Kentucky entered the Union in 1792. When a large landowner at the state constitutional convention suggested "limiting the vote to those with substantial interests to protect," delegates shouted him down. Tennessee entered the Union in 1796 and Ohio in 1803, both with low property requirements. Between 1816 and 1821, Indiana, Maine, Illinois, Mississippi, Alabama, and Missouri entered the Union with no limits on white male suffrage.[2]

The civil rights movement then spread east. In 1807 New Jersey abolished property requirements for voting, and Maryland followed suit three years later. Connecticut amended the state constitution in 1818, as did Massachusetts and New York in 1821. By 1828 only three states—Virginia, Louisiana, and Rhode Island—still denied some white men the right to vote. Just over 250,000 men cast ballots in the election of 1824; four years later, the number jumped to more than 1.25 million. The trend continued. In the election of 1840, more than 78 percent of white men cast ballots. Never again would such a high percentage of eligible Americans take politics so seriously.

Political deference, in which the poor acquiesced to the wisdom of the well-to-do, died along with the aristocratic dress codes of the eighteenth century. Alexis de Tocqueville, the French traveler and writer, observed in 1830, "Equality, which makes men independent of one another, naturally gives them the habit and taste to follow nobody's will but their own. This . . . independence makes them suspicious of all authority." The absence of deference startled wealthy Europeans and Latin Americans. They complained about the lack of first-class accommodations in steamboats and railroads, about sharing rooms with "uncouth scoundrels" in roadside inns and eating family style with poor farmers and laborers in boardinghouses. They could not find servants to take care of them. Americans acknowledged free labor and slavery but nothing in between. The word "servant" fell into disuse. Those who cooked someone else's food, washed someone else's clothes, or tilled someone else's land called themselves "hired help" but never "servants."[3]

The conjunction of republicanism, equality, and reverence for majority rule produced a boundless confidence that seduced de Tocqueville, who predicted that "the time will therefore come, when one hundred and fifty millions of men will be living in [the United States]. . . . The rest is uncertain, but this is certain; and it is a fact new to the world,— a fact which the imagination strives in vain to grasp." Mexico would become one more victim. "The province of Texas is still part of the Mexican dominions," de Tocqueville wrote, "but it will soon contain no Mexicans; the same thing has occurred wherever the Anglo-Americans have come in contact with a people of a different origin." William Barret Travis was part of that Anglo-American vanguard. Early in May 1831, he arrived at San Felipe de Austin in the Mexican state of

Coahuila y Texas. Feeling debt free and family free, at least for all practical purposes, Travis resurrected his dream.[4]

✱

In 1821 the advance elements of two great civilizations collided at the
Sabine River dividing Louisiana and Texas. The Spanish had marched
first, and had intermarried with Indians since the time of Cortés. Texas
mestizos traced their roots back 150 years, when their ancestors had left
central Mexico and settled north of the Rio Grande. There they wiped
out more than sixty tribes of indigenous peoples. The mestizo priests and
soldiers who manned the missions and presidios carried the bacterial bag-
gage of European civilization, and the natives fell to a variety of infectious
diseases. Immunologically vulnerable and technologically deficient, the
Indians, wrote one historian, "just seem to have faded away"—though it
was not exactly a peaceful process. The empty land was steadily settled
by Spanish-speaking immigrants, known later as "Tejanos." Their Texas
empire stretched northeast to the Sabine River, anchored by the Nuestra
Señora de Guadalupe mission near Nacogdoches.[5]

After the American Revolution, Anglo settlers in the American South
had pushed their frontier west, similarly disposing of indigenous peoples
and behaving, as had Spaniards and mestizos, as if they enjoyed a divine
right to the land. Kentucky came into the Union in 1792, Tennessee in
1796. By that time more than three hundred thousand Anglo-Americans
had settled west of the Mississippi, and Spanish officials pondered how
they could defend North America against such aggressive settlers. Illegal
American settlers had penetrated the Spanish colonies of East Florida and
West Florida, and in 1819 Spain had given up, surrendering the Floridas
to the United States in return for American recognition of Spain's sovereignty over Texas and the federal government's assumption of $5 million
of Spanish debts to American citizens. A deputy to the Spanish legislature
saw history repeating itself and urged caution in letting foreigners into
Texas because of the "great risk of dismemberment of that part of America in which Texas" was located. For Spain it was all soon a moot issue.
Texas was lost anyway in 1821, when Mexico secured its independence.[6]

The collision at the Sabine was a gross mismatch. Although the United
States and Mexico appeared equal on paper—two young nations, born in

revolution, with bright futures—they could hardly have been more different. While the United States had enjoyed four decades of independence, Mexico was an infant republic. The American population was booming with new immigrants and a high birth rate; Mexico's was shrinking after ten years of warfare. The U.S. economy was growing by leaps and bounds, while Mexico's was in ruin.

Spain had tried, at the last moment of its Mexican empire, to develop Texas. Government officials hatched an ambitious scheme, naming the Connecticut-born Moses Austin an *empresario,* with the right to settle, or "colonize," three hundred families along the Brazos River, in return for which he would receive handsome land grants and cash. Austin died in June 1821, soon after closing the deal, and his son, Stephen F. Austin, inherited the contract. The final expulsion of Spain from Mexico, in 1821, threw the scheme into turmoil, but when the Constitution of 1824 left states in charge of colonization, the *empresario* system became the official policy of the state of Coahuila y Texas. The immigrants had to be or become Roman Catholic and live on the land. Each family would receive 4,428 acres and would be exempt from taxes for ten years. Mexican citizenship came with settlement. In 1823 the colonists received a seven-year exemption from customs duties. During the next several years, the state legislature negotiated thirty *empresario* contracts.[7]

On paper, the *empresario* system appeared orderly and effective, but the term "orderly" would never characterize Texas. American settlers in a rush for land ignored the niceties of international boundaries, and for every Anglo family that settled legally in an *empresario* colony, many squatted illegally. Even the legal Anglo colonists posed a problem for Mexico, because almost all of them came from the United States. Practically speaking, Mexico was giving Texas away. The Sabine was as porous for illegal immigrants in the 1820s as the Rio Grande would be in the 1990s. In December 1821, the Mexican population of Texas amounted to roughly twenty-five hundred people. Within a decade, Anglos outnumbered Tejanos ten to one, a ratio that only continued to swell. "If, then, the condition of Texas is so prosperous," complained Mexican official Juan Almonte, "what precludes Mexicans from enjoying its prosperity? Are they not the owners of those precious lands?"[8]

Several nagging differences quickly soured Anglo-Mexican relations. The United States had already earned Mexico's distrust. During Mexico's late colonial period, Spain endured no less than eight threatening incursions by American filibusterers bent on detaching Texas from the empire. Between 1791 and 1801, Philip Nolan staged four military expeditions. He was actually more interested in stealing horses from Indians and bringing them back across the Sabine for sale, but Spain nevertheless regarded him with considerable suspicion. On the fourth expedition, Nolan's group included twenty-seven armed men. When Mexican troops caught up with him on March 21, 1801, they stopped him with a bullet to the head.[9]

General James Wilkinson, a former U.S. Army officer whom President Thomas Jefferson appointed governor of Louisiana, became involved in 1804 and 1805 with Aaron Burr's schemes to invade Mexico, peel off a slice of Spanish territory, and establish a new nation west of the Mississippi. Actually, he was more than "involved"; he was a clear-cut traitor, far more dedicated to treason than was Burr. Spain lodged vigorous diplomatic protests, and Jefferson removed Wilkinson as governor. But the controversy did not change Wilkinson's obsession. He negotiated with Mexican authorities in the early 1820s but died before securing an *empresario* contract.[10]

In 1811 José Bernardo Gutiérrez de Lara visited Washington, D.C, hoping to rally support for Mexico's rebellion against Spain. Gutiérrez secured nothing formal, but in Natchtitoches, Louisiana, he enlisted the backing of Augustus Magee and several hundred Anglo adventurers, and they invaded Texas in August 1812. During the course of the next year, the Magee-Gutiérrez expedition battled Spanish forces from Nacogdoches to La Bahía to San Antonio de Béxar. Magee died near La Bahía, and Spanish troops under General Joaquín de Arredondo drove Gutiérrez and his supporters back across the Sabine.[11]

In November 1816, Francisco Xavier Mina, a Spanish liberal dedicated to striking a blow against King Ferdinand XII by invading Mexico, secured financing from New York and New Orleans businessmen, and assembled an invasion force in Galveston. On April 7, 1816, he sailed into the Gulf of Mexico with eight ships and 235 men, en route for Soto la Marina in Tamaulipas. Mina's troops landed on April 15 and headed inland, fighting several minor skirmishes with Spanish troops before being captured on October 27, 1816. Taken to Mexico City for trial, Mina was convicted of treason and executed, along with twenty-eight of his men.[12]

Finally, James Long, a merchant in Natchez, Mississippi, organized in 1819 a military expedition against Texas. Angry that the Adams-Onís Treaty of 1819 between Spain and the United States had recognized the Sabine as the international frontier and left Texas to Spain, Long raised enough money to launch an invasion of the disputed territory. In Nacogdoches in June 1819, he proclaimed Texas independence. Governor Antonio Martínez deployed five hundred troops to crush the rebellion, and they captured Long at La Bahía. He was sent under armed guard to Mexico City and conveniently murdered before trial.[13]

Although the United States denied backing the filibusterers, official policy grew steadily more menacing. Soon after arriving in Washington, D.C., in 1822 as Mexican minister to the United States, José Zozaya complained about the "haughtiness of these Republicans who see us not as equals but inferiors, and who think that Washington will become the capital of all the Americas. . . . They love dearly our money, not us, nor are they capable of entering into an alliance agreement except for their own profit." The Americans, he went on, "ha[ve] no other object than that of fulfilling their ambitious designs on the province of Texas. . . . They will be our enemies." As if to prove Zozaya correct, in 1826 President John Quincy Adams offered $1 million for Texas, and when the Mexicans refused, he pursued a series of heavy-handed diplomatic initiatives to change their minds. Four years later, President Andrew Jackson upped the ante to $5 million, never hiding his intentions to see the Stars and Stripes waving over Texas. Mexico had too much territory, far more than it could ever develop. Detaching Texas through purchase or bribery, he said, would not be too difficult, since "I scarcely ever knew a Spaniard who was not the slave of avarice."[14]

With Mexican-American relations deteriorating, Anglo Texans grew increasingly restless. The independent government in Mexico City already considered them an impetuous and recalcitrant people. The Fredonian Rebellion of 1826 would prove the correctness of their view. In April 1825, Haden Edwards received an *empresario* grant allowing him to settle eight hundred families near Nacogdoches. He immediately offended earlier settlers by challenging their land titles, prompting Mexico to cancel his grant and send in troops from Béxar. On December 21, 1826, Edwards entered into open revolt, drafted a declaration of independence for the Republic of Fredonia, and appealed for U.S. military assistance. The revolt was stillborn and Edwards fled to Louisiana before the troops arrived, but the rebellion raised suspicions in Mexico City about the loyalty of other Anglo-Americans.[15]

Other controversies transformed suspicion into certainty. Nothing loomed larger than slavery. Two thousand slaves accompanied the first twenty thousand settlers to Texas, and like most white Southerners, these white immigrants considered slavery central to their way of life. Yet anti-slavery sentiments ran strong in postrevolutionary Mexico, the federalist Constitution of 1824 vaguely condemning it and leaving details to the states. Texans often found themselves lobbying in Saltillo, the capital of the state of Coahuila y Texas, and in Mexico City to protect the "peculiar institution." In January 1827 the state constitution recognized slavery but prohibited importing new slaves after November and declared that children of slaves would be free at birth. A few months later, the state legislature outlawed the slave trade and freed the slaves of owners who had died without heirs. Texans protested every step, and Stephen F. Austin maneuvered a subterfuge through the legislature guaranteeing "contracts made by emigrants to this state or Inhabitants of it with the servants or hirelings they introduce." Texans cynically freed their slaves and then forced them to sign contracts as lifetime indentured servants. But what the state legislature gave, the central government took away. On September 15, 1829, Mexican president Vicente Guerrero freed all slaves. Only with great difficulty did Texans secure an exemption, and in 1832, when the state legislature limited labor contracts to ten years, some Texans raised the issue of separate statehood as a solution. The American heroes who would die at the Alamo were fighting for many causes—including slavery.[16]

Immigration laws aggravated tensions. In 1828, Manuel de Mier y Terán, a Mexican patriot and head of the country's boundary commission, conducted an extensive tour of the northern frontier, hoping to help establish a firm boundary between Mexico and Texas, assess the threat posed by Native Americans in the region, and determine whether the swarms of Anglo-Americans settling in Texas threatened Mexican sovereignty. Just a few weeks into his journey, as soon as he arrived in Béxar, Mier y Terán had already reached some ominous conclusions. The Anglos had been given "the best land that exists anywhere in Texas" and had done the most possible with it. "Industry in the colony is outstanding, not only in the cultivation of the land for the harvesting of cotton and other cereals, but also in artisanry." Local Tejanos, Mier y Terán went on, would not be able to "resist the feared uprising of the colonies and of the foreigners . . . [who] cross the country in different directions without [the authorities] knowing . . . [and] if it happens that all the ingredients that have accumulated begin to ferment, this lovely portion of Mexican territory will be hopelessly lost."[17]

Mier y Terán's continuing tour of Texas only reinforced his early opinion. Mexico needed to study history. "The department of Texas," he insisted, "is contiguous to the most avid nation in the world. The North Americans have conquered whatever territory adjoins them. In less than half a century, they have become masters of extensive colonies which formerly belonged to Spain and France." Unless immediate steps were taken, Mexico would face the same fate. "If the colonization contracts in Texas by North Americans are not suspended," Mier y Terán wrote in November 1829, "and if the conditions of the establishments are not watched, it is necessary to say that the province is already definitely delivered to the foreigners." Mier y Terán then proposed several remedies. To guarantee Mexican sovereignty, he urged Congress to prohibit future Anglo immigration, flood Texas with Mexican and European settlers, encourage commercial relations between Texas and Mexico and discourage those with the United States, and strengthen the Mexican military presence in Texas. In February 1830, Congress debated his recommendations. When the final bill passed on April 6, 1830, it adopted many of them and also prohibited future Anglo immigration and the introduction of new slaves.[18]

Stephen F. Austin immediately went to work lobbying to amend the law, which he considered a disaster, telling President Anastasio Bustamante that it was certain to "destroy in one blow the happiness and prosperity of this colony which Your Excellency has always protected." For Austin and like-minded Texans, the Law of April 6, 1830, clouded the future. Blocking further immigration would eventually reduce them to a minority, and without slaves, they would be unable to work the land. Austin secured an exemption for his own colony and that of Green DeWitt, but Mexico City canceled the contracts of those *empresarios* who had not completed their colonies. In 1834 Mexico repealed the ban on Anglo immigration.[19]

Anglos complained incessantly about the Mexican political system, which seemed cumbersome and inefficient. When they crossed the Sabine, they carried with them a distinct set of assumptions about law, politics, and individual rights that were, they believed, inalienable and God-given, regardless of where a person had been born. Devoted to republicanism, they believed that the best government was local government because it was highly accountable. Having the state legislature and appellate courts in Saltillo, more than four hundred miles from Béxar and six hundred miles from Nacogdoches, produced isolation and alienation. Judicial proceedings taking place in Spanish, not English, frustrated them as well, as did the absence of trial by jury. Conditions seemed to improve in the spring of 1834 when the state legislature passed a law allowing Anglos to buy land at reasonable rates, granted Texas three seats in the legislature, declared English an official language, established new local municipalities—at Matagorda, San Augustine, Bastrop, and San Patricio—and provided for trial by jury. An ecstatic Stephen F. Austin declared, "In short, every evil complained of has been remedied."[20]

But there was another issue, the tariff, that constantly chafed Texans. To encourage settlement, Congress in 1823 had granted Anglo settlers a seven-year exemption from Mexican tariff laws, and as 1830 approached, Texans clamored for an extension. In 1831–32 Mexico deployed customs agents and soldiers to Nacogdoches, Velasco, and Anahuac, on Galveston Bay. For William Barret Travis, this new conflict was an opportunity. After securing a nice piece of land in San Felipe de Austin, he had relocated to Anahuac. Customs collections would produce work for an attorney. He taught himself Spanish and studied Mexican law.

But Travis would find fame not as a lawyer but as a revolutionary. In Anahuac, Anglo-Americans resented the Mexican soldiers, many of whom were conscripted convicts. "The common soldiers at this post," wrote a visitor, "were men of a most depraved character, while they were believed to be as cowardly as they were wicked and ignorant." Smoldering resentments grew hotter as ship captains tried to negotiate Mexico's byzantine customs bureaucracy, merchants handed over good money to customs officials, and prospective settlers were locked in detention. Angry protesters harassed customs agents. In June 1832 in Anahuac, the local political chief arrested Travis, who was already despised by local authorities for his antigovernment rhetoric and his part in organizing an illegal militia. Back in Claiborne, Alabama, Travis had frequently used the pages of the *Herald* to editorialize about the evils of high tariffs and the virtues of limited government, and now in Anahuac he found Mexico City guilty on both counts. He let pass no opportunity to criticize local officials, whom he considered venal and capricious. When he tried to recover an escaped slave for a client, Travis was arrested, charged with sedition, and held in a brick kiln. On more than one occasion during his incarceration, he was tied up and had the barrel of a rifle aimed at his head; such threats of summary execution only aggravated his opposition to the local government. At one point, when more than two hundred armed Texans arrived on the scene to rescue him, a Mexican official ordered Travis shot if an attack was launched. When Travis heard the threat, he shouted out, "Blaze away upon the fort." One Texan was moved by his bravery, remembering that he "never shrunk but called on his friends to witness that he would die like a man." Negotiations eventually prevailed, and Travis was released. A few days later he gloated, "Mexicans have learned a lesson. Americans know their rights and will assert and protect them."[21]

As part of the Anahuac disturbance, another battle erupted in nearby Velasco. On June 26, 1832, Colonel Domingo Ugartechea, commander of Mexican forces at Fort Velasco, learned that a band of Texans was trying to ferry a cannon from Brazoria to the rebels in Anahuac. When Ugartechea tried to board the vessel for an inspection, a rebel force of 100 to 150 armed men attacked, and in the ensuing melee, ten Texans died and eleven were wounded (against Mexican losses of five dead and sixteen wounded). But the Mexicans ran out of ammunition on June 29 and surrendered. The Texans treated Ugartechea well, awarding him favorable terms and allowing him to sail back to Mexico. He reported to his superiors that Americans intended nothing less than "to separate the territory from the Govt of the state and the federation." Mexican troops were then withdrawn from Anahuac, Nacogdoches, Fort Tenoxtitlán, and Velasco, but Stephen F. Austin knew that the troubles would continue. "My own and general wish," he told Ramón Músquiz, political chief of the department of Texas, "is to see Texas forming by itself as a State of the Federation, and as long as it is not so, we can expect no peace, progress, nor government, in fact nothing."[22]

For a time between 1832 and 1835, statehood became the panacea for Texans. Although laws coming out of Mexico City and Saltillo had repeatedly threatened their interests, the Constitution of 1824 had protected them. By giving so much authority to state governments, the constitution provided Texans an opportunity to lobby for exceptions. But workable exceptions were hard to come by. In the legislature of Coahuila y Texas, where representation was based on population, Texans constituted a tiny minority; Coahuilans vastly outnumbered them. If Texas separated from Coahuila and secured separate statehood, Texans would enjoy a free hand to govern themselves, or so men and women steeped in Jacksonian values expected.

During the first week of October 1832, fifty-five delegates gathered for an extralegal state convention at San Felipe de Austin. Béxar and Victoria did not send delegations. For president, the delegates elected Stephen F. Austin. Among other things, the delegates passed resolutions calling for an armed militia, a three-year extension in their exemption from customs duties, repeal of the prohibition on Anglo immigration, the sale of public lands to fund public schools, and most important, separate statehood. They also established committees of safety and correspondence in each municipality and a seven-man central committee with authority to call future conventions. The resolutions never reached Saltillo or Mexico City. Austin believed the timing was not right, since he knew that Ramón Músquiz considered the convention illegal. Only state legislatures could petition Congress, not rump meetings of malcontents. As expected, Músquiz annulled the resolutions.

At the time of the Convention of 1832, Travis had been in San Felipe for little more than a month, having relocated his law practice from Anahuac. In San Felipe he finally found the fortune that had eluded him. His law practice thrived, he acquired more land, and he became secretary to the local council, a position that carried an annual salary of $400 and required him to translate documents and file reports. His politics steadily evolved as well, one Texan remembering him as someone who was "not backward in revolutionary movements."[23]

Many Texans were bent on self-government, although most of Stephen F. Austin's colonists, for fear of losing their large land grants, opposed it. It seemed increasingly likely that a revolution was the only means to that end. The central committee called another convention for April 1833.

Again Músquiz denounced the proceedings, and again fifty-odd delegates appeared and promoted statehood. This time the delegates, considering Stephen F. Austin a bit too conciliatory, elected the more radical William H. Wharton as president. A native of Virginia who had graduated from the University of Nashville, Wharton had settled in Texas in 1827 and quickly became a Texas patriot. The delegates to the Convention of 1833 revived the earlier convention's demands and presumptuously drafted a new state constitution. Acknowledging Austin's gift for diplomacy, the delegates appointed him to deliver the resolutions to Mexico City. Before leaving, Austin optimistically wrote his cousin, "The course taken by the convention is the true one I think. . . . I can see no just reason why any offence should be taken [to] it by the Government . . . nor why it should be refused."[24]

In Mexico City, amid a deadly cholera epidemic and renewed political chaos, Austin's optimism died. On October 2, 1833, he sounded like a revolutionary in a letter to a friend: "I hope that you will not lose one moment in sending a communication to all the Ayuntamientos of Texas, urging them to unite in a measure to organize a government independent of Coahuila, even though the general government withholds its consent." Soon thereafter, however, Austin's diplomacy helped secure a congressional repeal of the law prohibiting Anglo immigration, and Santa Anna even paid lip service to Texas statehood, at least when the province's population should reach the minimum eighty thousand.[25]

Ironically, however, as Austin returned northward, Mexican authorities intercepted his October 2 letter, and on January 2, 1834, he was arrested in Saltillo. He languished in jail for more than a year. The jailing of Austin, the best diplomat and by no means the most radical among the Texans, shook Texas, and radicals favoring independence became known as the "War Party." The "Peace Party" of Austin and others was losing strength. Finally, in April, when Santa Anna deposed Acting President Gómez Farías, dissolved Congress, purged liberals, and denounced the federalist Constitution of 1824, statehood was a dead issue. Austin saw the implications immediately. So did William Barret Travis. "Texas is forever ruined unless the citizens make a manly, energetic effort to save themselves from anarchy and confusion," he wrote. Several weeks later he added, "I am, however, for Texas, right or wrong, and never will oppose anything for her benefit."[26]

In January 1835, Santa Anna had deployed Mexican troops and cus-toms agents to Anahuac to resume tariff collections. Several months later local citizens resolved that since the "Custom House officers at this place have neither been reasonable, just or regularly legal . . . no duties should be collected in this port." When Travis learned that Captain Antonio Tenorio, the new local military chief, had arrested two merchants on smuggling charges, he decided that "we have come to the cool determi-nation to submit to no more imposition of the kind that will prove ru-inous to the country by destroying the commerce and stopping the emigration." Travis assembled a volunteer militia and sailed to Galveston Bay, where Tenorio surrendered on June 29. The victory elevated Travis's status in the War Party. When he returned to San Felipe de Austin at the end of August, crowds hailed him, and he responded by screaming, "Huzza for Texas! Huzza for Liberty, and the rights of man." News that Mexico was sending troops to crush the rebellion only emboldened Travis, who insisted, "Let the towns be once garrisoned, and we are slaves. . . . We shall give them hell if they come here. . . . Let us be men and Texas will triumph." His sense of individual rights deepened. "If we are encroached upon, let us resist until our bodies & our property lie in one common ruin, ere we submit to tyranny. . . . We have sworn to sup-port a federal republican govt. not a military usurpation."[27]

Santa Anna knew that the insurgency had to be crushed. He had just finished with the Zacatecan rebels. He flirted briefly with the notion of leading the Army of Operations north, but they and he needed to recu-perate. The national treasury was drained, the quartermaster's supplies depleted, and the troops exhausted. Instead, Santa Anna's brother-in-law General Martín Perfecto de Cos, only recently appointed commander of military forces in Texas, was ordered to disarm the rebels in the north of his own region, crush the rebellion, and deport anybody remotely con-nected with the insurgency.

Cos especially wanted Travis. On August 1, 1835, he ordered Ugartechea to arrest the "ungrateful and bad citizen W. B. Travis who headed the revolutionary party. He ought to have been punished long since." Cos ordered Mexican military authorities in La Bahía to arrest Travis and try him for sedition. But Travis went into hiding, fleeing San Fe-lipe de Austin. A $1,000 bounty was placed on his head, and one Mexican official promised to "swing said Travis at his yard arm in less than half an hour after his delivery." But Mexican authorities could never find him. In the environs of San Felipe, he enjoyed too much political support, with few Anglo Texans wanting to see him in a Mexican jail.[28]

✷

Even Stephen F. Austin had changed his mind by the time of his release from prison. He had scuttled any pretense of compromise. "A gentle breeze shakes off a ripe peach," he wrote. "Can it be supposed that the violent political convulsions of Mexico will not shake off Texas so soon as it is ripe to fall[?] . . . The fact is, we must, and ought to become a part of the United States. . . . I wish a great immigration this fall from Kentucky, Tennessee, *every where,* passports, or no passports, *any how.* . . . [N]othing will daunt my courage or abate my exertions to complete the main object of my labors—*to Americanize Texas.*" He reached Brazoria on September 8, 1835, where he made his position immediately clear, calling for a representative assembly to determine whether Texans were going to "relinquish all or a part of their constitutional and vested rights under the Constitution of 1824."[29]

Cos arrived in Texas on September 21. A native of Vera Cruz whose father was a prominent attorney, Cos became a cadet in the Mexican army in 1820 and guaranteed his rise through the ranks by marrying Santa Anna's sister. More sycophant than tactician, his personal loyalty to Santa Anna was absolute. His promotion to brigadier general in 1833 had its roots in kinship, not in battlefield skill. Cos brought his troops by sea from Vera Cruz to Copano Bay, and when he landed in Texas, he was determined, as he told one Texan, "to repress with a strong arm all those who, forgetting their duties to the nation which has adopted them as her children, are pushing forward with a desire to live at their own option without subjection to the laws." Austin's position hardened. "Conciliatory measures with Gen[eral] Cos and the military at Béxar," Austin wrote, "are hopeless. WAR is our only recourse." Cos wasted little time moving inland. On September 28 he reached the Mexican outpost at Lipantitlán on the Nueces River, and on October 1 he moved into Goliad.[30]

A political confrontation of momentous proportions loomed. Cos was the product of an authoritarian regime in which opportunist politicians shedded political philosophies like snakes molting in the spring. He expected blind obedience. "The plans of the revolutionists in Texas," he announced, "are well known . . . it is quite useless and vain to cover them with a hypocritical adherence to the federal constitution. The constitution by which all Mexicans may be governed is the constitution which the colonists of Texas *must* obey, no matter on whāt *principles* it may be formed." Cos may have considered political principles expendable, but Texans did not. He was ignorant of how closely they held to their political values and how tightly they gripped their long rifles. If anything, they felt more strongly than the Zacatecans. Their reverence for democracy, federalism, and individual freedom transformed political culture into theology. At a July 5, 1835, protest meeting in San Felipe de Austin, rebel leader R. M. Williamson warned, "They are coming to compel you into obedience . . . to compel you to give up your arms; to compel you to have your country garrisoned; to compel you to liberate your slaves; to compel you to swear to support and sustain . . . the Dictator; to compel you to submit to the imperial rule of the aristocracy, to pay tithes and adoration to the clergy."[31]

Early in October 1835 Domingo Ugartechea, now military commandant of Coahuila y Texas, asked the Texans in Gonzales to hand over an artillery piece they had acquired four years earlier. Although Ugartechea was diplomatic, Texans were not so inclined. When a Mexican platoon showed up on October 2, 1835, to seize the cannon, the Texans draped it in a banner proclaiming, COME AND TAKE IT. Two Mexicans died in the ensuing firefight and the others withdrew without the artillery piece. A frustrated Ugartechea wrote Stephen F. Austin, requesting his efforts to secure the cannon and warning that without it, "I will act militarily and the consequence will be a war declared by the Colonists, which shall be maintained by the Government of the Nation with corresponding dignity." Austin was not intimidated. News of the "battle of Gonzales" spread throughout Texas, and volunteers signed up in droves. Travis exulted. "Let us go at it heart & hand. Stand up like men & we have nothing to fear."[32]

Cos underestimated his adversaries. He had wasted little time in Goliad, preferring to move inland to Béxar, where he would stage the reconquest. But he soon found himself cut off and on the run. News of his landing brought more rebel volunteers, including Tejanos, from all over southeast Texas, as did rumors that he carried a war chest stuffed with

$50,000. On October 9, 1835, volunteers in Victoria captured the mood and pledged their eternal support for "the Republican institutions of the constitution of 1824. . . . For . . . [its] redemption . . . we pledge our lives, our property, and our sacred honor." They began redeeming the pledge in a matter of hours. On October 10, 1835, in a surprise attack that lasted only thirty minutes, Texan volunteers overwhelmed the Mexican presidio at La Bahía, taking fifty prisoners and capturing several hundred muskets, carbines, lances, and bayonets, and a cache of desperately needed food and supplies.[33]

What appeared to be a minor setback was actually a strategic disaster for Cos. The Texans had severed his supply lines to the sea. Mexican ships could still land at Copano Bay, but muleteers and teamsters, without army escorts, could never penetrate the Texan lines. Cos now had to look south across four hundred miles of desert for supplies. In relatively short order, the Texans drove the Mexican army out of Goliad, San Patricio, and Copano. Cos and his troops were forced to dig in at Béxar, reinforce its barricades, deploy twenty artillery pieces, and prepare for a siege.[34]

The rebels tightened the noose. On October 11, 1835, the insurgents in Gonzales held elections for a commanding officer. Several men vied for the post, but early in the afternoon Stephen F. Austin, still enfeebled from his incarceration, rode into camp to the cheers of the men. A Texan immediately nominated Austin for command, arguing that he could "come nearer uniting the people than any other man, and, furthermore, it will give us better standing abroad." By acclamation, Austin was chosen to head up the "Army of the People."[35]

As they moved out of Gonzales for Béxar on October 12, the Texans seemed no match for Cos and could hardly have stood the scrutiny of a professional commander. A motley crew, they marched in street clothes, buckskins, or a collage of secondhand uniforms from unnamed militias and armies, their heads covered by an assortment of sombreros, coonskin caps, and hats. Shoes and moccasins, not boots, covered their feet. "Our only arms," remembered veteran Noah Smithwick, "were Bowie knives and long single-barreled, muzzle-loading flintlock rifles." A few carried shotguns. They lugged gourds instead of canteens. They faced combat short of everything except faith in the virtue of their cause and individual courage. "[We must have appeared] a fantastic military array to a casual observer, but the one great purpose animating every heart clothed us in a uniform more perfect in our eyes than was ever donned by regulars in dress parade," Smithwick recalled.[36]

Determined to drive Cos's forces out of Texas, Austin went on the offensive. He sent a ninety-two-man reconnaissance patrol, led by James Bowie and James Fannin, to push to the outskirts of Béxar and establish a base of operations. A native of Kentucky reputed to be America's best knife fighter, Jim Bowie had made a living in land speculation, slave trading, and sugar production, and in 1830 had he settled in Texas, eventually marrying Ursula de Veramendi, daughter of one of Béxar's most illustrious Tejano families. James Fannin, born in Georgia in 1804, dropped out of West Point after two years and came to Texas in 1834. He settled in Velasco and became a slave trader. Both men believed fervently in the cause of Texas independence. Bowie, eight years Fannin's senior, assumed tactical command and established a defensive position several miles south of Béxar at a bend in the San Antonio River, near the mission Purísima Concepción. It was precarious ground—their backs were to the river and there was no escape route. But the river cut its way six feet below the grassy flatlands, and the men tethered their horses and dug in below the bank, hoping to angle for Mexican soldiers and lure them into a trap. Cos should have known better, but he took the bait. At dawn on October 28, 1835, with heavy fog blanketing the river, he deployed four hundred troops into the cul-de-sac, preparing the way with two field cannons throwing canister and grapeshot at the rebels. The riverbank provided the Texans a perfect cover. Noah Smithwick remembered—perhaps with some exaggeration—how artillery fire "thrashed through the pecan trees overhead, raining a shower of ripe nuts down on us, and I saw men picking them up and eating them with as little concern as if they were being shaken down by a norther."[37]

The long rifles shredded enemy lines, mowing down the Mexicans, according to Smithwick, "at a rate that well might have made braver hearts than those encased in their shriveled little bodies recoil." Texan sharpshooters, with rifles accurate up to two hundred yards, picked off the artillerymen, silencing the cannon. Mexicans charged into the cross fire, but their Brown Bess muskets, accurate up to only seventy yards, were ineffective, and even rounds reaching their target had little effect. The Mexican powder could not propel the lead with any velocity. "We wondered," remembered one Texan veteran, "to see that their balls often fell short of us. . . . [Some] were struck by balls which were far too spent to break the skin, and only caused an unpleasant bruise." The Mexicans finally broke ranks and fled, and Bowie charged, turning their own artillery on them. When the smoke of battle and the morning fog cleared, one Texan was dying, compared to upwards of sixty dead and wounded Mexicans. The victory had been deceptively easy, convincing Texans of their own superiority. According to veteran William T. Austin, the battle "proved the fact that Texians with their rifles and pistols were formidable. . . . sufficient to cope with Mexican troops even with greatly superior numbers."[38]

Stephen F. Austin arrived at Concepción with the Mexicans in full retreat. With Cos's troops in disarray, he wanted to press the advantage, but advisers urged caution. A frontal assault on Béxar, with its carefully constructed fortifications and entrenched defenders, might prove suicidal. Once he had seen Béxar's perimeter, Austin agreed. "The fortifications are much stronger than has been supposed and the difficulty of storming of course greater," he told Bowie and Fannin. Instead, the rebels opted for a siege, hoping to seal Béxar from the outside world and starve Cos into submission.[39]

On the day before the battle of Concepción, Austin had ordered Travis to raise a cavalry company. Travis's troops arrived at Concepción just as the Mexican rout commenced, and he chased some of Cos's men all the way to the outskirts of Béxar. He then took his troops south of Béxar, trying to avoid detection by camping at night without fires, eating cold food, and sleeping without tents, all to locate and capture a rumored encampment of Mexican soldiers and livestock. On November 10, he succeeded, surprising the Mexicans and capturing more than three hundred horses and mules. On November 13, he crossed the San Antonio River with those horses to the acclaim of Austin, who officially commended "Citizen Wm. B. Travis for his personal worth and distinguished service." The citizens of San Felipe de Austin welcomed Travis home as a hero.[40]

Soon after Concepción, the Texans returned to politicking. News of Anahuac had spread through eastern and central Texas, and radicals and moderates suggested another general meeting, although they hesitated to label it a convention, since Mexico City considered grassroots aggregations illegal. Instead, they came up with "consultation." War Party loyalists hoped to use the consultation to establish Texas sovereignty; Peace

Party voices wanted only to debate and recommend. The consultation was scheduled for October 15, 1835, but the rush of events—Cos's arrival, the skirmish at Gonzales, and the battle of Concepción—forced postponement. The delegates did not pull together a quorum until November 3. This time, independence was declared in all but name. The delegates proclaimed their "right" to make such a declaration, established a provisional government, elected War Party leader Henry Smith as governor, assured soldiers in the field of generous rewards of public land for their service, authorized a regular army, and awarded its command, with the rank of major general, to Sam Houston.[41]

✳

A recent generation of historians has viewed the Texas Revolution in social and ideological terms, divining the source of the insurgency in racism and ethnocentrism, not in genuine, conflicting views of politics and individual rights. Many express contempt for the Alamo. According to Jeff Long, the Texans "wallowed in freedom like hogs in mud." They were "pirates," "mercenaries," and "adventurers" in whose lives and deaths freebooting masqueraded "as heroism, wrong as right, aggression as defense"—men who aspired only to "greater heights of folly, racism, and violence," nothing but "white trash and outlaws whose roots in Texas were no deeper than their boots." For Rodolfo Acuña, they were "smugglers" and "filibusterers," and any history that praises them is a "mixture of selected fact and generalized myth." Most contemporary Mexican historians, such as Josefina Vásquez, agree with such characterizations of the Texas Revolution.[42]

But viewing the Alamo through an ideological lens distorts history, kidnapping flesh-and-blood people from their own time and holding them hostage to a contemporary standard. To be sure, most Anglo Texans were racists, products of a Southern culture that put whites on a pedestal, held people of color in disdain, and saw no contradiction in owning slaves and hailing liberty. Creed Taylor, a veteran of the Texas Revolution, later recalled, "I thought I could shoot Mexicans as well as I could shoot Indians, or deer, or turkey; and so I rode away to a war." Another Texan in 1835 described Mexicans as "degraded and vile; the unfortunate race of Spaniard, Indian and African, is so blended that the

47

worst qualities of each predominate." And David G. Burnet attributed the revolution to the "utter dissimilarity of character between the two people, the Texians and the Mexicans. The first are principally Anglo-Americans; the others a mongrel race of degenerate Spaniards and Indians more depraved than they."[43]

Anglo Texans were certainly ethnocentric, convinced that their own culture enjoyed a friendship with destiny. In 1822 Stephen F. Austin commented that most residents of Mexico City were "miserably poor and wretched, beggars are more numerous than I ever saw in any place in my life—robberies and assassinations are frequent in the Streets—the people are biggoted and superstitious to an extreem, and indolence appears to be the general order of the day." More than a decade later, his opinion had not changed, and he held the Catholic church responsible. "Rome! Rome!" he wrote, "until the Mexican people shake off thy superstitions & wicked sects, they can neither be a republican, nor a moral people." Few Anglos doubted the outline of the future. War Party leader William H. Wharton predicted that Anglo-Americans were "destined to be for ever the proprietors of this land of *promise* and *fulfillment. Their* laws will govern it, *their* learning will enlighten it, *their* enterprise will improve it. . . . [T]*heir* latest posterity will here enjoy legacies of 'price unspeakable,' in the possession of homes fortified by the genius of liberty, and sanctified by the spirit of a beneficient and tolerant religion."[44]

Certainly many Texans were uncouth and unruly, especially when lubricated with enough corn liquor, often more interested in drinking than working or fighting. South and west of Pennsylvania, America had been settled by the Scots-Irish. They tended to be reckless and argumentative, militaristic and short tempered, quick to take offense, sensitive about personal honor, and highly politicized about individual rights. They were super-Celts and hyper-Jacksonians, strained through the pores of Southern culture in a uniquely American process of natural selection. Immigrants—whether those leaving Europe for America or those abandoning Eastern communities for frontier settlements—have always been risk takers, willing to take a chance on the New World. Cautious, timid, conservative people—bound to home by family, occupation, or tradition—stayed put. Texas in the 1820s and early 1830s represented the final extension of several immigrant Scots-Irish generations, each more assertive than its predecessor, each more willing to take chances, each more prone to violence, each more certain of its place in the world.[45]

For such people, picking a fight was easy, but making a success of revolution was less so. Launcelot Smither, a farmer and physician, wrote to Stephen F. Austin complaining that one group of rebel volunteers "treated the wimon of this place worse than all the comanshee nation could have done and dragged me out of the house and nearly beat me to death. . . . The conduct of wild savages would be preferable to the insults of such Canebols." Austin could not have agreed more. The rebel volunteers drank too much, bickered too much, womanized too much, and as soldiers, were too often insolent and disobedient. When the alcohol flowed, soldiers fired their weapons, wasted precious ammunition, and drove Austin to distraction. He begged his officers to "preserve order and regularity and to prevent shooting without leave." But the troops ignored his pleas. The soldiers under his command, Austin said, "went where they pleased and came when they chose. . . . In the name of Almighty God, send no more ardent spirits to this camp—if any is on the road turn it back." And many Texans loved fighting for its own sake, for the fun of it. One veteran of the Gonzales skirmish remembered how anxious the men were for combat. The more they waited, the more frustrated they became. "Some were for independence," he recalled, and "some were for the Constitution of 1824; and some were for anything, just as long it was a row." Similar frustrations during the siege of Béxar would prompt one rebel to complain that they "had come to whip the Mexicans, and if they could not fight, they would go home, as they did not propose to remain in an army that ran away every time it saw a Mexican."[46]

Violence was theirs by birthright. Most Texas rebels were Southerners raised in a culture that revered the redemptive shedding of blood—for family, for country, and for individual honor. At the slightest provocation, they resorted to battle, sometimes in no-holds-barred fisticuffs characterized by gouging, biting, scratching, pulling hair, and "groining." In early-nineteenth-century Southern culture, one historian has written, when men began to "drink together, tongues loosen, a simmering of old rivalry begins to boil; insult is given, offense taken, ritual boasts commence; the fight begins, mettle is tested, blood redeems honor, and equilibrium is restored." A Kentuckian bragged with evident exaggeration about one of his recent performances: "I socked my thumb in his eye, and with my fingers took a twist on his *snot box,* and wit the other hand, I grabbed him by the back of the head; I then caught his ear in my mouth, gin his head a flit, and out come his ear by the roots! I then flopped his head over, and caught his other ear in my mouth, and jerked that out in the same way, and it made a hole in his head that I could have rammed my fist through." Throughout the early-nineteenth-century South, and in Texas too, it was common to encounter maimed men who had lost noses and eyes and ears in near-mortal combat, and they wore the scars like battle ribbons.[47]

These Southern transplants in Texas were advance agents of the greatest land rush in history. The country's potential took their breath away. Texas "is immense in extent," wrote settler Daniel Cloud in December 1835, "and fertile in its soil, and will amply reward all our toil." Davy Crockett found Texas "the garden spot of the world." Speculating on the future, Alexis de Tocqueville concluded that Americans would take Texas as their own. In spite of treaties delineating the Sabine as the border, the Americans would "shortly infringe it. Vast provinces, extending beyond the frontiers of the Union towards Mexico, are still destitute of inhabitants. The natives of the United States will people these solitary regions before their rightful occupants. They will take possession of the soil, and establish social institutions, so that, when the legal owner at length arrives, he will find the wilderness under cultivation, and strangers quietly settled in the midst of his inheritance."[48]

But the racist, rowdy, and land-hungry Texans did not exactly confront in Mexico City a repository of political virtue. The Mexican ruling class was steeped in an ethnocentrism and racism of its own. In 1825 Joel Poinsett, the United States minister to Mexico, noted that "the most important distinction, civil and political, was founded in the colour of the skin. Here, to be white was to be noble; and the rank of different casts [*sic*] is determined by their nearer or more distant relation to the whites." Perched at the top of the social pyramid was a small minority of lighter-skinned criollos who dominated commerce, clergy, and government, even though mestizos and Indians outnumbered them five to one. They considered people of color to be inferior. At least in the United States in 1820, the racial pyramid had been stood on its head, with a racist white majority dominating a much smaller minority. It was the opposite in Mexico, where a racial minority oppressed millions of darker-skinned people.[49]

As for religious loyalties, the Mexicans were just as certain of Catholicism's truth as Anglo Texans were of Protestantism's virtues. At the end of the Revolution in 1821, Catholicism was proclaimed the accepted religion. In his Plan of Iguala in 1821, Agustín de Iturbide identified purity of religion as one of the "Three Guarantees," and in 1824 the Mexican Congress passed legislation outlawing freedom of religion. Mexico denied burial rights to Jews, Protestants, and Muslims, and foreign nations had to negotiate treaties to provide funerals for deceased nationals in Mexico. Non-Catholics could not be interred in regular cemeteries, and the segregated sites eventually set aside for them were regularly vandalized. G. F. Lyon, an American who traveled widely throughout Mexico in the 1820s, remembered being nearly stoned to death in Zacatecas by anti-Semitic mobs convinced that he was Jewish and that he had tucked a tail under his trousers. When people were invited to settle in Texas, they were expected to convert to the state religion. And many Mexicans looked down on Anglo Texans as a repulsive people. After winning independence, several Mexican officials warned about the dangers of Anglo settlement. The government should "take measures to prevent the planting of a population [Anglo-Americans] composed of abominable people of bad conduct." If anything, the Texas Revolution constituted a struggle for power between two groups of equally prejudiced people.[50]

Those who see the Texas Revolution simply as an uprising of racist Anglos ignore similar rebellions throughout Mexico, many of them rooted in identical political principles. The Zacatecas uprising of 1835 is one example, but there were many more. In April 1837, Lieutenant Colonel Ramón García Ugarte, proclaiming "Federation or Death," launched a rebellion in San Luis Potosí that had to be put down by the army. Several months later, José Urrea assembled a convention in Sonora and reorganized the state government along federalist lines, reassuring the Sonoran legislature that his actions had restored state autonomy. Gordiano Guzmán incited a federalist insurgency in Michoacán, and Mariano Olarte in Vera Cruz. In the spring and summer of 1838, federalist rebellions erupted in Morelia, Tuxtla, Aguascalientes, and Tampico. Federalists in Yucatán declared independence in 1840, and for the next three years warfare raged; Yucatán did not return to Mexico until 1843, when federalists received guarantees of virtual autonomy. During the 1830s and 1840s, Mexico was full of people—Anglo Texans as well as criollos, mestizos, and Indians—who considered the centralist regime of

Mexico City a morally bankrupt government that had surrendered its own legitimacy.

Many Tejanos were among them. The advent of Santa Anna's centralized dictatorship divided Tejanos into rival camps, just as it divided political opinion and made civil war endemic. Liberal federalists rallied behind the Constitution of 1824 and accused Santa Anna of tyranny, while conservative centralists yearned for order, even if it was oppressive. To be sure, as the civil war in Texas progressed and demands for statehood yielded to demands for independence, many Tejanos lost enthusiasm for the fight, but in its initial stages, many were just as supportive of the Constitution of 1824 as any Anglo and just as contemptuous of Santa Anna. As one historian wrote, after Mexico gained its independence, "Members of the educated elite in Mexico soon were divided into liberal and conservative camps. For the next half-century, control of the government changed back and forth between representatives of these factions. Upon taking power, the next group not only changed the government personnel, it also rewrote the laws and even the constitution to reflect its philosophy."[51]

Like federalist compatriots throughout Mexico, many Tejanos rallied to the cause. On October 7, 1835, when the Texas militia marched on La Bahía, José Padilla, Silvestre de León, Plácido Benavides, Mariano Carbajal, and thirty others signed on, anxious to give General Martín Perfecto de Cos a taste of Tejano will. During the assault on La Bahía, local Tejanos supplied the rebels with the axes needed to break down doors and barriers. Later in October, Juan Seguín and his Tejano cavalry acted as advance scouts for the rebels at Concepción. A week later, profederalist Tejano ranchers in Victoria and Goliad provided dozens of horses and thirty head of cattle to the rebel army. And many Tejano volunteers would be wounded fighting side by side with Anglo rebels in the hand-to-hand combat about to take place in Béxar. To view the Texas Revolution simply as an illegitimate crusade of white racists ignores the attitudes of federalist Tejanos anxious to restore the Constitution of 1824.[52]

Anglo Texans had become accustomed in the United States to peaceful transitions every four years. By 1835 the United States had seen seven democratically elected presidents, but between 1821 and 1835, Mexico had witnessed Agustín de Iturbide crown himself emperor and then die before a firing squad; Guadalupe Victoria establish the liberal Constitution of 1824, only to see his government rendered impotent by military conspiracy, rigged elections, and widespread corruption; Manuel Gómez Pedraza deposed by Vicente Guerrero, who assumed the presidency but soon died before a firing squad; Anastasio Bustamante deposed by Antonio López de Santa Anna; Santa Anna elected president in 1833 but failing to attend his own inauguration and leaving the presidency in the hands of Valentín Gómez Farías; and Santa Anna returning in 1834 and deposing Gómez Farías. Mexican politics had become little more than would-be caudillos clawing their way up the heap and announcing themselves king of the hill. Simón Bolívar, the great liberator of South America, had only contempt for how quickly Mexico mortgaged its destiny. "The casual right to usurpation and pillage has been enthroned as King in the capital of Mexico," he wrote in 1829. "There is no good faith. . . . The treaties are papers; the constitutions are books; the elections are combats; freedom is anarchy; and life a torment." William Travis agreed. "I wish to know," he wrote, "for whom I labor—whether for myself or a *plundering*, robbing, autocratic, aristocratical jumbled up govt. which is in fact no govt. at all—one day a republic—one day a fanatical heptarchy, the next a military despotism—then a mixture of the evil qualities of all."[53]

Many Texas rebels regarded their American Founding Fathers as demigods, read the Declaration of Independence like scripture, and believed that the only legitimate government was one that obeyed the principles of the U.S. Constitution. Many Mexicans resented the unwillingness of Anglo immigrants to leave their political philosophies on the east bank of the Sabine. Manuel de Mier y Terán complained in 1828 that the Texans "all go about with their constitution in their pocket, demanding their rights and the authorities and functionaries that [their constitution] provides." But telling an Anglo immigrant to forget the Declaration of Independence and renounce the U.S. Constitution was tantamount to demanding that he renounce the King James Version of the Bible. A rebel sympathizer in Columbia, Texas, in August 1835 put the issue quite clearly: "Texas . . . [is] . . . the only portion of the civilized part of the globe which has no government at all. True there are some officers, who still hold on to the authority acquired under the State constitution, but they are mere tenants at will, and liable to be removed at any moment. The source from which they derived their power has failed and hence, their functions have expired." At a town meeting on August 15, 1835, the residents of Nacogdoches resolved that "governments are designed for the rational control of human actions, and for the preservation of human rights. When these objects are disregarded or abused, the . . . compact is virtually dissolved." For many Texans, the government in Mexico City was no longer legitimate. Travis had certainly arrived at that conclusion. "We are virtually and *ipso facto* without any legal government in the state or nation," he wrote in October 1834. "We are subject legally and constitutionally to no power on earth, save our *sovereign selves*. We are actually in a situation of revolution and discord, when it becomes the duty of every individual to protect himself."[54]

At a time when the spirit of Jacksonian democracy was sweeping away political barriers based on privilege and property, Mexico seemed headed in the opposite direction. Sentiment was mounting there to denounce democracy and limit the franchise. Already, the Congress in Mexico City was drafting a new constitution that, when enacted in 1836, would limit citizenship and the right to vote to men with an income of at least 100 pesos a year, restrict service in the chamber of deputies to men with incomes of at least 1,500 pesos a year, and confine the office of senator to men with incomes of at least 2,500 pesos a year.[55]

In contrast, Texans remembered that their fathers and grandfathers had resisted the autocratic excesses of King George III and the tyranny of a distant central government. Although the American Revolution and the Texas Revolution were hardly analogous, many Anglo-Texans considered them so, and they viewed themselves as a later generation of freedom fighters. James Allen, who would be the last courier to leave the Alamo, had grown up listening to his father's tales of Indian wars in the Ohio Valley. John Sutherland, another courier, remembered his father's service in the Continental Army. John Baylor, who in 1835–36 would fight in Béxar, Goliad, and San Jacinto, bragged of his grandfather's exploits as a member of General George Washington's personal guard. Bowie's father had fought with Francis Marion, the "Swamp Fox," and his guerrillas during the American Revolution. Samuel Evans and Joseph Kerr, who would not survive the Alamo, each had a father who had served as generals in the U.S. Army. Alamo courier and scout Ben Highsmith's father was a veteran of the War of 1812. Christopher Parker, who would die at the Alamo, boasted of his father's service with General Andrew Jackson at the battle of New Orleans in 1815. Others were veterans themselves. Micajah Autry did not get out of the Alamo alive, but he had survived three years of military service during the War of 1812. Bowie and Crockett had fought in the Indian wars, as had Alamo defenders John Davis and Robert Musselman. Almaron Dickinson, whose wife and infant daughter would survive Santa Anna's assault, had most likely completed a U.S. Army tour of duty as an artilleryman.[56]

The Texas rebels could not escape history. When Mexico deployed a standing army to Nacogdoches, Velasco, and Anahuac, the Texans saw parallels with the 1760s and 1770s, when British troops occupied Boston and New York City. Mexican assurances that the troops were there only to protect colonists from Indians raised Texans' suspicions, just as their ancestors' suspicions had been raised by similarly hollow assurances from British politicians. When Travis heard rumors in April 1835 of Santa Anna's plans to invade Texas, he wrote, "Such a measure would kindle a flame in Texas that would burn in twain the slender cords that connect us to the ill fated Mexican confederation." Texans despised the Law of April 6, 1830, seeing in its provisions frightening reflections of British behavior during the American Revolution. The imposition of tariffs and duties, the outlawing of trade with the United States, and the stationing of customs officials at Texas ports called to mind the Navigation Acts, the vice-admiralty courts, and the Coercive Acts; the prohibition on new immigrants resembled the Proclamation of 1763, when Parliament forbade American settlement west of the Appalachians; and banning the importation of slaves sounded like the British confiscation of Southern slaves during the Revolution. The legislature of Coahuila y Texas proclaimed that when "the Civic Militia . . . are reduced . . . the only bulwark of liberty, and the rights of the community are destroyed."[57]

At every turn, to justify the insurgency and bolster their courage, the Texans resorted to the rhetoric of the American Revolution. On the eve of the battle of Gonzales on October 1, 1835, the Reverend W. P. Smith, a local Methodist minister and veteran of the battle of New Orleans, reminded his congregation that "the same blood that animated the hearts of our ancestors in '76 still flows in our veins." In November 1835, from Nacogdoches, Texas, Charlie Parker announced his decision to set out for San Antonio because "the Texians, as you will see, have made a Declaration of Independence—[at least] it amounts to a Declaration, although not worded in the same manner as old Tom Jefferson's." Amos Pollard, a physician in the rebel army, saw the 1835 triumph of Mexican centralists through the lens of the American Revolution. "The [T]ory party," he wrote, "have . . . usurped the government to themselves,—but the people will not stand this. . . . God grant that we may create an independent government."[58]

The Texans also insisted that Mexico had reneged on a deal, breaking a promise made in good faith by trying to take back individual rights already granted. Like the Americans of the Revolutionary era, who claimed that George III and Parliament had violated their God-given rights as English subjects, the rebels felt Santa Anna had done the same. Richard Ballentine, a native of Scotland who would fall at the Alamo, said he made his decision to fight in Texas because he wanted to "relieve our oppressed brethren who have emigrated thither by inducements held forth to them by the Mexican government, and rights guaranteed to settlers of that province, which that government now denies them." The situation of Texans, Ballentine went on, "is assimilated to that of our forefathers, who labored under tyrannical oppression."[59]

✯

Throughout November 1835, the Army of the People waited, swilling corn liquor, bickering with one another, growing short of food and fodder, waiting in vain for General Cos to play his hand. But Cos had decided to exact a heavy price for Béxar. The Texans would have to storm the barricades. Few Texans relished that assignment, except Stephen F. Austin, but on November 12, 1835, the consultation named him commissioner to the United States. The troops elected Edward Burleson to replace him as commander in chief. Natives of North Carolina, Burleson's family had moved to Alabama, and during the War of 1812 he fought the British as a member of Perkins's Regiment. He then relocated to Missouri Territory and on to Tennessee, participating actively in local militia units. Burleson was a commanding officer Jacksonians could truly love, a rough, plain man whose shock of unruly hair topped a rugged face reddened by years in the sun, except for a shiny white forehead hidden under a hat. He had arrived in Texas in 1830, served as a member of the *ayuntamiento* that governed San Felipe de Austin, Béxar, Goliad, and Guadalupe, and led militia units against marauding Indian bands.[60]

Like Austin before him, Burleson soon found himself outside Béxar trying to command a rabble, and he all but lost heart. What Texans fondly remember as the Grass Fight—a skirmish just outside Béxar on November 26 in which Burleson's troops routed a detachment of Mexican cavalry and infantry—buoyed morale for a while, but cold weather and the prospects of an assault against Cos's formidable position soon discouraged the rebels. On December 4, 1835, just when Burleson was about to end the siege and order the army to winter quarters in Gonzales, Ben Milam showed up, enraged at such lack of will. A native of Kentucky, Milam knew a little about combat, more about Mexican soldiers, and a great deal about Mexican politics. He was a veteran of the War of 1812, had served as a colonel in the Mexican army, and had received an *empresario* grant. In 1835, while in Monclova lobbying the state legislature to provide Texas settlers with legal land titles, Milam got lost in the wilds of Mexican politics. When Santa Anna scrapped the Constitution of 1824 and imposed a military dictatorship on Mexico, he had Milam arrested. After serving some time in jail, Milam escaped and made his way back to Texas, convinced that independence was the only course of action.[61]

Milam burst into Burleson's tent and convinced the commanding officer to let him lead an attack on Béxar. He exited the tent with Burleson to the rear and assembled the rebel soldiers. He appealed to their patriotism and asked for the ultimate sacrifice. Everybody knew what they were up against. Cos enjoyed greater numbers and artillery superiority, and held an entrenched defensive position. The Texas Revolution hung in the balance. "Who'll go with old Ben Milam into Béxar?" Milam shouted out to them. A deafening roar of "I will" and "We will" echoed back. Deftly turning his rifle on end, according to historian Jeff Long, Milam scratched out a line in the sand. "Well," he said, "if you are going with me, get on this side." Roughly three hundred men crowded across.[62]

That afternoon, Milam developed a plan, hoping to distract the Mexicans with a feigned attack on the Alamo while sending two columns into Béxar. (The Alamo, founded in 1718 as the San Antonio de Valero mission, had become by 1835 a dilapidated walled compound across the San Antonio River from the town of San Antonio de Béxar. The town had risen up to serve the needs of local friars, soldiers, and Indians.) The assault would begin the next morning. Actually, Cos's position appeared stronger than it really was. The powder his troops used in their firing pans had the texture of charcoal dust, not at all like the rebels' hard-grain DuPont powder, and the Mexicans would be unable to use their Paget carbines and Brown Bess muskets to full effect. The siege had also done its damage, leaving Mexican cavalry mounts starving for fodder and the troops subsisting on restricted rations. Discontent riddled the ranks, and within a matter of days Cos would lose four cavalry troops—more than two hundred men—to desertion. Some reinforcements arrived with Colonel Domingo Ugartechea, but most were convicts dragooned into service. Once in Béxar and out of their chains, they refused to obey orders, assaulted officers, stole food, and tried every avenue of escape. Instead of standing resolute and dying for their country, they bickered, fought, and malingered.

Early the next morning, a norther blew in, reducing temperatures to near freezing and Milam's rebel force to only 210 men. The others had scattered. Milam managed to get an artillery piece across the San Antonio River, within range of the Alamo. With the wind roaring and the men shivering, he ordered two columns of troops to close in on Béxar and wait for the sound of artillery. At around 3 A.M., James C. Neill maneuvered a cannon to the east bank of the San Antonio River, just above the Alamo. Neill fired the cannon at 5 A.M., and its sound, along with the crash of the ball into the Alamo wall, awakened the Mexican troops, who scrambled for position. "The hollow roar of our cannon," remembered one veteran of the siege, "was followed by the brisk rattling of drums and the shrill blasts of the bugles. Summons, cries, the sudden trampling of feet, the metallic click of weapons mingled in the distance with the . . . heavy rumblings of the artillery. Our friends had done the trick." Both troop columns moved unopposed into Béxar.[63]

Entering the city proved to be the easy part. The Mexican soldiers recovered quickly, and the Texans soon found themselves fighting their way down narrow, winding streets, dodging artillery canister and musket fire, and trying to locate Mexican snipers. The battle quickly degenerated into hand-to-hand combat, fought from street to street and from house to house. On the second day of the assault, Milam died instantly when a Mexican sniper armed with a Baker rifle shot him in the forehead. But after four days of fighting, Cos's situation became untenable. He faced surrender or annihilation, and on the morning of December 9, 1835, he told Colonel José Juan Sánchez Navarro to meet with the Texans and negotiate terms. Cos raised a flag of truce and Sánchez Navarro approached the Texans. He could hardly believe his eyes. Before him stood no army. He was surrendering to a contemptuous, catcalling mob proudly wearing silver spurs, bloodied uniforms, blankets, hats, and helmets pilfered from Mexican corpses. "We were surrounded with crude bumpkins, proud and overbearing. Whoever understands the character of the North Americans will appreciate the position in which we found ourselves," Sánchez Navarro said later. How could that mob, Sánchez Navarro no doubt wondered, have achieved such a lopsided victory? The Texans had sustained thirty or so casualties, with five or six dead, to Cos's 150 casualties. Béxar was a mess. One veteran observed, "Every thing looked miserable . . . heaps of dirt and Stone ashes from the burning of some wood breast works . . . with dead animals lieing about cannon balls & shot of every description thick on the ground with the plastering shot of[f] the outside of the walls of the houses."[64]

The Texans behaved well in victory, acknowledging Cos as a worthy adversary and treating him with respect and equanimity. In fact, the rebels acted the part of professional soldiers, exacting gentlemanly promises from a vanquished foe. In return for Cos's pledge to pull back south of the Rio Grande and "in no way [to] oppose the re-establishment of the [Texas] Federal Constitution of 1824," the Texans offered his force enough food for the withdrawal, six days for recuperation, and ten rounds of ammunition each to go along with their rifles and muskets. Some Texans would have preferred a slaughter, or at least sterner terms. "We should have made a Treaty," argued veteran William Carey, "and not a child's bargain." On December 15, 1835, the Mexicans departed Béxar and headed south. Texans hoped their victory would give Santa Anna pause. "Some say that Santa Anna is in the field with an immense army," Micajah Autry wrote, "and near the confines of Texas, others say that since the conquest of St. Antonio by the Texans and the imprisonment of Genl. Cos and 1100 men . . . that Santa Anna has become intimidated for fear that the Texians will drive the war into his dominions and is now holding himself in readiness to fly to Europe." Santa Anna had other intentions. "As soon as the war in the south is over," he had already promised, "I shall send four to six thousand men to Texas with the purpose of punishing those turbulent, insolent North Americans. . . . [I]f they resist in the least, all their property will be confiscated; and I shall convert Texas into a desert."[65]

3

───────── ✦ ─────────

"THE BONES OF WARRIORS"

ON FEBRUARY 21, 1836, his forty-second birthday, Santa Anna's past and his future met on the banks of a river. He spurred his mount ahead, leaving behind the forward elements of his army. Repeatedly in the previous two months, he had charged ahead, getting way out in front of the main column, sometimes irritating other general officers. At 1:45 P.M., full of anticipation and anxious to revisit a defining moment in his life, Santa Anna reined in his horse at the top of a crest overlooking the Medina River, fourteen miles south of San Antonio de Béxar. More than two decades before, on that very spot, he had won medals and promotion for bravery in combat. The grove of oak, hickory, pecan, and mesquite trees before him had not changed much. Except that it had become a shrine of sorts.[1]

In 1828, French scientist Jean-Louis Berlandier had crossed the Medina River and noticed that very grove of trees, soft in the late afternoon sun, offering a perfect site for a camp or bivouac. When Berlandier reached the grove he was greeted by human bones—bleached and smoothed by blistering summers and rainy springs—littering the sandy soil: a femur here and a humerus there, clumps of knuckles and carpals and tarsals, knots of vertebrae, skulls scattered like pumpkins in a field, vacant eye sockets bearing witness to an earlier generation's carnage.

"When we passed over the place where the battle was unleashed," he wrote in his notebook, "the bones of warriors were still to be found everywhere." As if the bones were not enough, a large cross carved at eye level into the bark of a majestic oak marked the battlefield. Soldiers from the presidio at Béxar, like religious pilgrims, frequently stopped to refresh the engraving.[2]

Santa Anna never recorded how long he stayed on his mount, savoring the moment and a time before his hair had thinned and his waist had thickened. In 1813 he had helped slaughter an American army of anti-Spanish rebels there. From the hill rising above the Medina, Santa Anna could almost see Béxar on the horizon. Another rabble of arrogant Americans was out to steal a slice of Mexico—his country—and Santa Anna again was ready to punish them. Once again he would experience the acrid smell of spent powder, the ear-splitting boom of cannon, the eye-stinging smoke, the shouts of the victors, and the moans of the vanquished. The time was near.

★

Santa Anna was a world younger in 1810, when Father Miguel Hidalgo launched the Mexican Revolution and Tejano sympathizers in Texas followed, throwing in their lot with land-hungry Americans anxious to stake out claims west of the Sabine River. That was when José Bernardo Gutiérrez, a rebel merchant and Texas insurgent, with the tacit support of the United States, traveled through Kentucky, Louisiana, and Tennessee, finding sympathy for the Mexican cause. He concluded that the Americans "would make up a considerable army of volunteers, with which, under my command, we would invade the provinces of Mexico and sweep before us the oppressors of our liberty." Mexican rebels committed to freedom and independence signed on; so did Anglo-Americans in Louisiana.

Gutiérrez assembled on the eastern bank of the Sabine a motley army of hunters, trappers, Indians, and Tejano rebels. He pegged them the "Republican Army of the North," and on August 8, 1812, crossed the Sabine and invaded Spanish territory. Some volunteers hoped to liberate Mexico from Spanish oppression; others yearned for nothing more than land and loot. They occupied Nacogdoches several days later, and victory swelled the ranks when Gutiérrez guaranteed them free land, Mexican citizenship, and the right to "work and dispose of any mines of gold, silver or whatever." By November 1812, the Republican Army of the North included nearly one thousand troops, mostly Americans. They fought their way across Texas, defeating royalist forces at every turn, and on April 1, 1813, Manuel de Salcedo, governor general of Texas, surrendered San Antonio de Béxar without a fight. The invaders proclaimed Texan independence and announced their liberation from "the chains which bound us under the domination of European Spain."[3]

Feigning courtesy to a defeated foe, Gutiérrez offered a military escort to Governor Salcedo and thirteen other royal officials, promising them evacuation to La Bahía, where they could secure passage back to Spain. Two hours into the journey, however, the troops butchered the royalists, hacking them to death and leaving their bodies to the vultures. When news of the murders reached Béxar, residents filled the streets in joyous celebration. Many Anglo residents were aghast at what had happened. Although Gutiérrez denied complicity, he took more than a little comfort in Salcedo's demise since the governor had regularly committed atrocities against the Tejano people.[4]

Béxar was more sleepy village than bustling town in 1813, but it was still the last outpost of Spanish civilization on the southern plains. Spain was not about to give it up so easily. Spanish authorities ordered the reconquest of Béxar and gave the job to Colonel José Joaquín de Arredondo, former military governor of New Santander. Early in August, Arredondo's expedition crossed the Rio Grande and approached Béxar from the southwest, up the dusty Laredo Road. In one of the cavalry regiments rode Antonio López de Santa Anna, a nineteen-year-old lieutenant.

Arredondo set an ambush. More than fourteen hundred troops of the Republican Army of the North, now under the command of José Alvarez de Toledo, who had deposed Guitiérrez on August 4, marched out of Béxar and assumed a position about three miles east of the Medina River, hoping to surprise the invaders. But after reconnoitering the site on August 16, Arredondo had already identified a perfect trap about fourteen miles from Béxar on the west side of the river. There he waited patiently. Thick trees provided perfect cover, and heavy sand between the river and the trees made for bad footing. The rebels would emerge wet from the river and find themselves tiring in foot-sucking sand, marching up a gradual incline. Arredondo positioned 1,830 troops and several artillery pieces on both sides of a V-shaped ambush formation. On August 18 he ordered Colonel Ignacio Elizondo and a company of cavalry to cross the Medina, engage the enemy, quickly break off the battle, and then, feigning panic, implement a wholesale retreat, luring the enemy into the trap.

Elizondo carried out the charade exquisitely, and the insurgents, against the orders of their suspicious commanding officer, surged west, riding and running into a withering cross fire. The rebels proved brave but impetuous, victims of zealous arrogance. "Believing that they were already glorious victors and masters of the field, and had only to take the spoils . . . ," Arredondo later reported, "they advanced bravely and blindly" to their deaths. Musket and artillery fire raged into the afternoon, and the rebels sustained huge casualties. After four hours, the dehydrated, wasted insurgents, leaving behind hundreds of dead and wounded comrades, broke and fled east.

Arredondo offered no quarter. He ordered several infantry platoons, armed with lances and sabers, to finish off the wounded. Distinguishing the living from the dead required little effort. Under the Texas sun, corpses bloated quickly. Bodies swelled, splitting cloth uniforms and popping buttons. Spanish dragoons walked casually through the sand, systematically slaughtering the living while covering their noses to ward off the stench. "The field was covered with many wounded," Arredondo reported to his superiors, and "they have been executed as just punishment for their crimes."[5]

Arredondo then ordered his cavalry to hunt down the fleeing rebels. In a brutal scorched-earth policy, the cavalrymen, Santa Anna among them, laid waste to everything between Béxar and the Sabine. The royalists burned barns and farmhouses, torched crops in the fields, murdered suspected rebels, and seized horses and cattle. As an example to be remembered, Elizondo executed rebels in front of their wives and children, then denied the corpses a decent burial and forced families to remain on the scene until vultures picked at the dead. They captured more than one hundred prisoners and then led them on what amounted to a death march to Béxar. The badly supplied Spanish troops pillaged and plundered, stealing everything they could carry. They stuffed sacks and suitcases with booty, loaded down their horses like pack animals, and drove the prisoners of war before them. Many rebels died of dehydration, others of exhaustion. Arredondo's cavalry then returned triumphantly toward Béxar. Rebel women and children were incarcerated in a jail that locals sarcastically referred to as "La Quinta" ("Country Retreat"). In the sweltering August heat, La Quinta was more oven than jail.

On August 19, fresh from the slaughter of the rebel army, Arredondo entered Béxar. Crowds that only a few months before had toasted the rebels now lined the streets and cheered the crown. Unmoved, Arredondo ordered a house-to-house search, imprisoning rebels one day and executing them the next. Inside the walls of La Quinta, their wives and children worked eighteen-hour days grinding corn and making tortillas for his troops, their chores interrupted every hour by another execution, which they anxiously witnessed through small openings in the cell walls, hoping that their fathers and husbands were not the victims. Within two weeks, a total of 327 rebel prisoners lost their lives, most by firing squads but some from dehydration or by being hacked to death.

The rebellion was over and the Texas republic only a memory. The Tejano and Anglo-American rebels who survived did so only by escaping east of the Sabine into Louisiana. Huge sections of the land lay fallow, without people or crops. Between 1810 and 1820 the non-Indian population of Texas fell from forty-five hundred to less than two thousand. The region between San Antonio and the Sabine became a no-man's-land of empty fields, abandoned ranches, evacuated towns and villages, and burned-out buildings. As Stephen F. Austin later remarked, Texas had become little more than "a howling wilderness."[6]

★

In mid-November 1835, Texas was an incipient free republic and Spain no longer ruled Mexico. But to Santa Anna, the Anglo rebels were all the same. He vowed another offensive. Like the carved figurines in Aztec temples, Santa Anna's general officers and staff sat in stunned silence, unable to absorb his words or fathom his logic. Perhaps the cult of personality—with its portraits, statues, banners, and street names littering public places all over Mexico—had gone to the general's head. On a shoestring budget he had proposed an invasion of Texas, expecting his troops to cross hundreds of miles of unforgiving desert before engaging an intemperate army of Americans, whom he fully expected to walk into any trap he set. Santa Anna's staff shared his El Cid–like passion for the *reconquista*, but his strategic vision bordered on lunacy. "Nothing could influence Santa Anna to change his plan to march on Béjar," wrote Colonel José Enrique de la Peña, a member of Santa Anna's staff. Or maybe he was sipping too much laudanum, an elixir of alcohol and opium that soothed troubled souls. Worse yet, perhaps the generalissimo had slipped into madness, convinced of his own infallibility.[7]

Often he thought and talked about Napoleon. The ghost of Bonaparte haunted the Army of Operations. Santa Anna fancied himself Napoleon's latter-day reincarnation. As a young man, he had devoured biographies of the French emperor, and in the early 1820s he had served under Agustín de Iturbide, a general with his own Napoleonic fantasies. Santa Anna revered Bonaparte, adopting Napoleonic poses and collecting Napoleonic memorabilia. Sycophants of every stripe, with gifts of French collectibles, could garner a moment of the general's time, attract an imperious nod, extract a small favor, or gain a tiny political advantage over an enemy. Beautiful young women in the latest French fashions always turned his head. In 1835, especially after Zacatecas, when he flirted with the notion of becoming emperor of Mexico, Santa Anna had a bust of Napoleon placed in the halls of Congress, prompting a flurry of newspaper speculations about his intentions. At Manga de Clavo and El Encero, he lived in the splendor of a European court and adorned the walls with portraits of Napoleon. An American visitor once wondered about all the "ordinary oil pictures of the history of Napoleon." Santa Anna shamelessly promoted himself as the "Napoleon of the West." Detractors joked; Santa Anna did not.[8]

His Napoleonic tastes extended to fashion. Although his army was a patchwork of different uniforms, most infantry sported dark blue coats adorned with red scarlet collars, cuffs, and lapels, along with white piping and brass buttons. They wore barracks hats with bands and tassels. Some had tall black shakos. Cavalrymen wore bright red tailcoats with green collars, lapels, and cuffs, dotted with white buttons, and blue riding pants with antelope skin inserts and red seam stripes. Across their torsos rested white-leather carbine and cartridge-box straps. Tin-plated iron cavalry spurs, instead of being strapped on, were screwed into wooden heels.[9]

Even the weapons had Napoleonic roots. Many regular infantry carried the smoothbore .753 caliber musket known as an *escopeta*. Nicknamed the "Brown Bess," the musket had been manufactured in Great Britain by the Tower Arms Works and had played a key role in the Napoleonic wars, especially at Waterloo in 1815 when Wellington overwhelmed Napoleon. British generals had scrapped the Brown Bess, a cumbersome and outdated musket, and sold the surplus to Mexico.[10]

General Joaquín Ramírez y Sesma let no opportunity pass to hail Santa Anna as Bonaparte's reincarnation, and he publically fancied himself as "His Excellency's Murat," playing on the memory of Joachim Murat, Napoleon's flamboyant cavalry commander. Others were critical of Santa Anna's ego. General Vicente Filisola complained that the general "would listen to nothing which was not in accord with [Napoleon's] ideas." De la Peña sarcastically wrote that Santa Anna's "flatterers have had the audacity . . . to compare him with the man of the century [Napoleon], although he is as distant from him as our planet is from the sun. . . . General Santa Anna would have needed a century of indoctrination to resemble [him]."[11]

In terms of military tactics, Santa Anna was a slave to his alter ego, insisting that his troops march exactly as Napoleon's had. According to Napoleon's tacticians, infantry were to march into battle in ranks separated by "one pace, two feet," and each man in rank "two paces" from the other. Individual battalions were separated by twenty yards. They strutted into combat at a constant tempo—seventy-six steps, or sixty yards, per minute. Double time required one hundred steps, or eighty yards, per minute, and running required double that again. Drill instructors put troops through the synchronized steps, measuring paces in inches and insisting on perfectly timed cadences. Cavalry units underwent tactical training requiring similarly rote movements and precision timing, almost as if horses in the smoke of combat could count.[12]

Finally, and most disastrously for the Army of Operations, Santa Anna now decided that he could pull off a Napoleonic *offensive*, marching across northern Mexico much as Napoleon had once swept over central and eastern Europe, moving over vast stretches of territory and living off the land. The differences between 1812 and 1836, however, were enormous. Napoleon had traversed the grain belts of Europe, plump with prosperous villages, towns, and cities and irrigated with abundant lakes, rivers, and streams, whereas Santa Anna's army confronted hundreds of miles of desert with precious little water; scattered, poverty-stricken villages; and isolated ranchos and haciendas. Napoleon's quartermasters pulled wagons with strongboxes full of hard currency and negotiable bonds; Santa Anna requisitioned supplies at fire sale prices and paid with worthless chits. And where once Napoleon led columns of battle-hardened professional troops, Santa Anna led an army riddled with conscripts, convicts, and corruptibles. The plan, de la Peña wrote in his diary, "was a great mistake, an error that brought serious consequences."[13]

★

Back in March 1835, when he had first contemplated the assault on Zacatecas, Santa Anna had learned that although the Army of Operations's muster rolls listed 38,715 troops available for duty, only 18,219 were *permanentes,* and of those only 3,500 could actually be put into service. Federalist unrest in other regions of Mexico required troop deployments throughout the country. Santa Anna's decision to go on the offensive had been made quickly, and he found himself hastily assembling the available soldiers. On October 23, 1835, while resting at Manga de Clavo after the Zacatecas campaign, he had received news of the outbreak of hostilities in Texas. He soon forwarded instructions to Minister of War José María Tornel, arranged for a cavalry troop, and in a caravan that included a luxurious carriage for his fighting cocks, set out for the capital. Santa Anna also ordered Brigade General Joaquín Ramírez y Sesma to move from Zacatecas to Laredo, assume command there of the Morelos Battalion, and prepare for an offensive against the rebels in Texas. Ramírez y Sesma's brigade eventually came to include 1,541 men and eight cannon. Santa Anna was stern in his orders to Ramírez y Sesma: "The foreigners who wage war against the Mexican nation," he wrote, "have violated all laws and do not deserve any consideration, and for that reason, no quarter will be given them. . . . They have audaciously declared a war of extermination . . . and should be treated in the same manner." On October 29, Tornel appeared before Congress, acknowledging a state of war and requesting military appropriations.[14]

On November 14, 1835, the general's entourage arrived in the capital and proceeded to the country town of Tacubaya, a former Aztec ceremonial center located just beyond the outskirts of Mexico City. He took up residence in the luxurious archbishop's palace, constructed a century before as a summer residence for prelates of the church but more recently expropriated by Congress. Sheltered by the cliffs of Chapultepec, Tacubaya was an autumnal paradise, warm in the afternoons and cool in the evenings, its air pungent with the aromas of fresh fruit wafting up from thousands of apple, peach, orange, cherry, and olive trees. Its haciendas, mills, granaries, and ranches sustained a steady flow of beef, pork, wheat, and maize to the capital. The Mexican elite gathered there on weekends and in summers for rest and recuperation. The palace was also close to the cockfighting pits at San Agustín de las Cuevas. Santa Anna was drawn to the *gallera*, or cockpit.[15]

Now that they knew of his plans, aides questioned the wisdom of the invasion. Santa Anna regularly received politicians and foreign diplomats, to whom he waxed expansive and bragged about the upcoming offensive, assuring death for the rebels. Around closer associates, however, he was more ill-tempered than arrogant. Heated arguments disturbed his mood. His aides argued that Béxar had little strategic or political significance; the winds of revolution in Texas blew much stronger to the east and southeast, where Americans had crossed the Sabine and spread over the landscape like army ants. At best, Béxar sat at the edge of civilization, a border outpost that could afford to be ignored. Left to their own devices, the American rebels, stuck there with little to do except drink, gamble, argue, and become bored, were more likely to scatter than become the vanguard of revolution. Even if they remained sober in the stone fortress, they would have little military impact. "We should have attacked the enemy at the heart instead of weakening ourselves by going to Béjar, a garrison without any political or military importance," de la Peña later remembered.[16]

Even an amateur strategist armed with a decent map would have picked La Bahía (Goliad), on the north bank of the San Antonio River, as a better point of attack. For more than a century, supply caravans had plied the river and roads between the Gulf Coast, La Bahía, and Béxar. Aides wanted Santa Anna to assemble an army in Vera Cruz, transport the troops by sea to San Antonio Bay, and then march up the San Antonio River to Goliad. With well-rested troops and secure supply lines to

Vera Cruz, they could lay waste Anglo settlements on the San Antonio, Guadalupe, Colorado, and Brazos Rivers.

Such a strategy, however, entailed major risks. If Mexico's army was weak, its navy was moribund. United States naval forces patrolled the Gulf Coast, and President Andrew Jackson was sympathetic to Texas independence. A close friend of Sam Houston, Jackson had tried more than once to purchase Texas from Mexico. If Santa Anna put to sea and Jackson ordered the United States Navy to destroy the flotilla, Mexico would disintegrate. Financial reality also mitigated against a maritime invasion. A naval expedition equipped to move thousands of troops over hundreds of miles of open sea required a huge initial investment; few Mexican merchants or shipowners loved their country enough to lease expensive vessels to Santa Anna. And timing mattered. Outfitting a maritime expedition would take months, a delay that Santa Anna felt he could not afford.[17]

The general was in a hurry. The war needed to be over before April. Santa Anna remembered the nasty summer of 1813, when he crossed the Rio Grande Valley chasing Comanches, Anglo filibusterers, and Mexican insurgents. Intense heat, day and night, sapped energy, and water shortages threatened troops with dehydration. Even worse were the insects. Along riverbanks and streambeds, especially in the evenings, mosquitoes were so thick that men could grab them from the air. Nasty horseflies raised stinging welts, and chiggers—tiny bloodsucking insects that burrowed into the skin—drove troops into itching frenzies. To ward off the pests, locals greased themselves thoroughly with alligator, cattle, and buffalo fat and at night huddled close to buffalo and cow chip fires, making sure that the malodorous smoke penetrated every pore. "If the only four favorable months of the year were not taken advantage of," Santa Anna remembered, "the army . . . would perish of hunger and the effects of the climate, upon those who composed the army under my command, who were accustomed to a more temperate climate."[18]

New Anglo depredations aggravated Santa Anna's itch for revenge. Within hours of reaching Tacubaya, he learned of an insurgent attack on Tampico. José Antonio Mexía, an ardent federalist and former associate of Santa Anna, had fled Mexico when the *hombres de bien* assumed power. In New Orleans he conspired with North American filibusterers to invade Mexico. Mexía felt certain that most Mexicans despised Santa

Anna and that an invasion would inspire a spontaneous uprising. Advertising as a broker offering land to settlers, he signed on several dozen Americans, who had no clue about his real intentions. The expedition aboard the schooner *Mary Jane* set sail on November 6, 1835, and once on the high seas, Mexía briefed the settlers on his real intentions. When they learned of the expedition's military nature, most of the recruits balked, but it was too late. On November 8, the *Mary Jane* ran aground off Tampico, and Mexican troops captured thirty-one prisoners.[19]

The Tampico expedition sent Santa Anna into a predictable rage. He ordered the execution of the prisoners, in spite of clear evidence that most were guilty only of stupidity, not rebellion. Three died in captivity and the others were shot. "These unfortunate men," wrote the American chargé d'affairs in Mexico City, in a myopic analysis that ignored Mexía's role, "were victims of the offended vanity and uncontrollable passions of General Santa Anna, merely because the people of Texas have dared to oppose his will. . . . This horrible crime is the work of General Santa Anna alone." Santa Anna then asked and received from the Congress confirmation of his extermination orders to Ramírez y Sesma. The Texan rebels would receive no quarter.[20]

Mexía escaped Tampico aboard an American schooner and returned to Texas. Santa Anna took it personally and vowed to get even, which made a quick invasion of Texas even more urgent. Their paths would not intersect again until 1839, when Santa Anna crushed another Mexía-led rebellion. Mexía would be captured in the fighting, and Santa Anna would grant him three hours to write letters before meeting God. Mexía wrote the general, "If the captor and captive had been reversed in position I would have allowed [you] only that number of minutes, not hours." On that same day—May 3, 1839—Mexía was executed by a firing squad.[21]

On November 27, 1835, Santa Anna ordered General Vicente Filisola's brigade to San Luis Potosí, where the Army of Operations would take final shape. Accompanied by a fifty-troop cavalry escort, Santa Anna left Tacubaya the next morning. He soon overtook Filisola's main force, and the two generals jointly entered Potosí on December 5. With Ramírez y Sesma on his way to Béxar, *el presidente* worried about possible command and control problems, since Ramírez y Sesma and Cos enjoyed similar ranks. To avoid any confusion, he named Division General Vicente

Filisola as second commander in chief and dispatched him to Béxar as well.[22]

Potosinos did not exactly welcome the Army of Operations with open arms. They had memories of Santa Anna's youthful excesses. In 1821, as a new general, he had swept into San Luis Potosí like a conquering hero, commandeering homes and apartments, pilfering cattle and sheep to feed his troops, and raiding the city treasury. Like Iturbide, whom one contemporary accused of "being driven to enrich himself by any manner or means," Santa Anna had coveted Potosí's silver mines, sequestering enough bullion to add a few thousand acres at Manga de Clavo. Nor had he controlled his troops, who indulged their own lusts. And on more than one occasion, his soldiers fell to quarreling among themselves; the rivalry between infantry and cavalry units was intense enough to produce firefights. At the Alameda de Bracamonte, a large, downtown city park, infantry and cavalry had opened fire on each other, and before officers could intervene, dozens were killed and wounded, including innocent bystanders.[23]

This time the troops were more circumspect. Santa Anna established a headquarters, assembled his army, and made further preparations for the Texas campaign. Ramírez y Sesma's brigade of 1,541 troops included 1,110 foot soldiers, 369 cavalry, and 62 artillerymen. To General Antonio Gaona, an arrogant Cuban, Santa Anna assigned a brigade of 1,600 troops, and to General Eugenio Tolsa, 1,839 infantry and six cannon. General Juan José Andrade led a cavalry brigade that consisted of 437 mounted soldiers, and General José Urrea had 601 foot soldiers and mounted troops. Presiding over it all was Santa Anna, with Italian-born Vicente Filisola second in command. The original plan was for Urrea to move on Goliad via Laredo, and for the other brigades to cross the Rio Grande at what is today Guerrero and advance on Béxar from the southwest. Santa Anna busied himself "issuing . . . orders for the divisions, assembling . . . army equipment, and arranging everything . . . necessary for the beginning of the campaign." To inspire the *soldados*, Secretary of War José María Tornel established the Legion of Honor, Mexico's highest military honor, to be awarded only to veterans of the Texas campaign.[24]

During the month in San Luis Potosí, Santa Anna trained the troops, reorganized the Army of Operations, and renamed its various units, hoping to exploit the memory of the Revolution to build esprit de corps. Instead of bearing the older numerical designations, infantry battalions were renamed after revolutionary heroes—Hidalgo, Allende, Morelos, Guerrero, Aldama, Ximénes, Landero, Matamoros, Abasolo, and Galeana. Cavalry units replaced numerical designations with the sites of the revolution's great military triumphs—Dolores, Iguala, Palomar, Cuautla, Vera Cruz, and Tampico.[25]

In reality, Santa Anna was engaged in the makings of a national catastrophe that would not reveal itself for another ten weeks, on the muddy banks of the San Jacinto River. His low regard for Americans kept him from thinking strategically, planning carefully, or acting prudently. He should have been worrying, wrote de la Peña, about weather, climate, maps, and topography; supplying wagons, ambulatory hospitals, and draft animals; keeping powder dry and soldiers fed; and crossing rivers and negotiating mountain passes. Instead, he fixated on teaching Americans another lesson. "What was lacking," wrote de la Peña, "was prudence, planning, order, foresight, clear and precise judgment. . . . The operation was done in a fashion so offensive to humanity as to appear incredible, were it not for the numerous testimonies attesting to it."[26]

Of the approximately six thousand troops under command, nearly half were raw recruits shanghaied into service. As the army trekked north out of Mexico City, platoons of troops and press gangs scattered throughout the cities, towns, and villages of Querétaro and San Luis Potosí, rounding up beggars and the homeless, dragooning drunks in cantinas, and emptying jails and prisons. Conscripts were chained together and forcibly marched to San Luis Potosí. Hundreds of Indians taken captive were pressed into military service as well. "Scarcely a day [goes by] that droves of these miserable and more than half naked wretches are not seen thus chained together and marching through the streets to the barracks, where they are scoured and then dressed in a uniform," wrote an American observer. Santa Anna called it a *sorteo,* meaning "draft" or "conscription," but the process really amounted to kidnapping. Most conscripts had never handled a musket, let alone engaged in drill or combat. Mayan Indian troops did not even speak Spanish or have shoes. Most of the so-called ghost soldiers were hungry, poverty stricken, and in poor physical condition, hardly prepared for a forced march over hundreds of miles of desert and combat in a strange land. De la Peña condemned "the thoughtless violence with which forced recruiting was carried out. . . . There were many too young, some too old, some of these succumbing under the weight of their weapons and knapsacks. . . . How could these men withstand the long and tedious marches and rapid maneuvers they had to execute?"[27]

Financial exigency exacerbated the situation. Congress charged Santa Anna with the job of crushing the rebellion but gave him precious little money to do so. To provision the troops, he turned to the *agiotistas,* or loan sharks, who refused to come up with 400,000 pesos until the bidding reached a crushing 48 percent interest rate. To secure the loan, Santa Anna put up custom house receipts and allowed the greedy bankers to import military supplies duty-free through Vera Cruz and Matamoros. Several thousand additional pesos came from well-to-do *hacendados* and the chapter of the Monterey cathedral. The governors of Nuevo León and Coahuila contributed some money as well.

Of course, Santa Anna brokered the bond sales himself, siphoning off a handsome fee, and then established a special agency to manage the account, with Ricardo Dromundo, his brother-in-law, supervising the operation. Ramón Martínez Caro, Santa Anna's secretary during the Texas campaign, later described the general's behavior as "slanderous. . . . Though the terms of the contract proved very disadvantageous to the nation, the transaction yielded His excellency negotiable bonds of considerable value. . . . The Comissary can testify whether this amount was ever turned in to the general treasury of the army of operations . . . If not, where did it go?"[28]

Precarious logistics revived the debate. Subordinates tried to dissuade Santa Anna from the overland invasion, but he was a poor listener. "His irascible temperament did not lend itself to discussion," remembered de la Peña. The general "became especially annoyed when [discussion] tended to touch on the topic of taxes, at which time he would do nothing but make speeches, regret the shortage, and quarrel with everyone." Traversing mountains and deserts on rationed resources posed huge risks, but the general discarded caution, assuring everyone that patriotic *hacendados* and church officials along the way would keep the troops fed and clothed. He told General Joaquín Ramírez y Sesma to rely on "the enthusiasm of the citizenry of the towns along your route." This too, he said, had worked for Napoleon. The governors of Nuevo León and Coahuila y Texas tried to talk him out of it, as did close aides. They "counseled wisely and gave the best advice," de la Peña observed, but Santa Anna

"had become quite obsessed . . . and he refused to listen to reason, trusting only in his good fortune, which in war does not play the major part."
Insisting that the overland invasion would catch the rebels off guard and
allow for a surprise attack in a minimum amount of time, Santa Anna declared the case closed.[29]

In the middle of the debate at San Luis Potosí, Santa Anna learned that
his brother-in-law General Martín Perfecto de Cos had surrendered Béxar
to the rebels. Hoping to keep news of Cos's surrender from reaching
Mexico City, Santa Anna buried the dispatch by ordering that it not be
sent south by courier. He had no intention of supplying ammunition to
his political enemies. He talked incessantly of accelerating the campaign,
of shedding blood for *la patria,* of sacrifice in the name of national honor,
of revenge, vendettas, and retribution. At the end of December 1835, he
ordered Generals Eugenio Tolsa and Antonio Gaona and their brigades,
to march to Saltillo. General Pedro de Ampudia's artillery units headed
out the same day. On January 1, 1836, General Juan José Andrade's cavalry also set out for Saltillo. Cos's surrender at Béxar forced Santa Anna
to alter his original plan. When Ramírez y Sesma learned of Cos's defeat,
he diverted his forces from the road to Béxar and headed for Laredo,
where he joined up with Cos's army. Instead of marching to Goliad, Urrea's forces were redirected to Guerrero, where Urrea was to place his
men under General Filisola's command. Unaware of the orders, Filisola
had already relocated to Laredo and joined forces with Cos and Ramírez
y Sesma. Santa Anna, protected by a fifty-man cavalry detachment, departed Potosí on January 2.[30]

On the afternoon of January 6, 1836, after several days navigating
Mexico's vast interior plateau, Santa Anna's carriage crested the mountains surrounding Saltillo, passed a large reservoir, and descended into a
valley of pastel-colored stone and adobe buildings, scattered farms thick
with mesquite, chaparral, and cactus, and haciendas supplying beef,
pork, wheat, and corn to as many as fifteen thousand Saltilleros. Until
March 1833, Saltillo had served as the capital of Coahuila y Texas. The
encircling, gently sloping Sierra Madre Oriental, composed largely of
slate and limestone, sprouted little vegetation, and the range's earth tones
at sunrise and sunset melted imperceptibly into the orange hues of the
horizon. Winters there were said to be mild. "For the past five years,"
wrote a French traveler in the early 1830s, "the winters have not been

very rigorous . . . no snow has been seen in recent years. During our stay in that town the temperature was quite moderate and its variations scarcely noteworthy." Such reports might have convinced Santa Anna that a winter invasion of Texas would not really be too hazardous.[31]

At Saltillo, the invasion army took shape. But the strategic argument revived on January 20 when Cos reached Saltillo. His men had just crossed the desert and understood its dangers. Cos agreed with General Filisola's suggestion that instead of attacking Béxar by way of Monclova and Guerrero, which meant a desert campaign, the army should head east out of Saltillo, skirt Monterey, cross the Rio Grande at Mier, and then march on Goliad. From Goliad, with supply lines secure, the Army of Operations could wipe out the insurgents in southeast Texas and march on Béxar. But Cos did not press his point of view. The mere fact that his brother-in-law had accepted him with open arms all but rendered him mute. Santa Anna was bent on revenge, and the desert campaign would proceed. He then ordered Cos and his troops to Monclova for rest, recuperation, and refitting.[32]

On January 15, couriers had arrived in Saltillo bearing rumors of an upcoming rebel attack on Matamoros; Santa Anna ordered General José Urrea to Matamoros to intercept any rebel offensive. After crushing the invasion force, Urrea was to secure Goliad and then advance on Béxar. But during his maneuvers, Urrea had noticed throughout "the towns of the north, from Matamoros to Guerrero, great adherence to the constitution of 1824, and the people, believing that the colonists were upholding it, kept in touch with them, being disposed to take up arms and join their cause." His reports convinced everyone except Santa Anna that the Army of Operations would find little support among civilians, which would make the overland invasion less tenable. Governor Pedro Lemus of Nuevo León traveled to Saltillo with a plea that the desert invasion be reconsidered. If there were no other reason, attacking Texas from the vicinity of Monterey rather than Monclova would at least assure the army relatively abundant supplies. Santa Anna remained unmoved and unconvinced. Nothing, according to de la Peña, "could influence Santa Anna to change his plan to march on Béjar." When funds came in from wealthy *hacendado* Don Melchor Sánchez, Santa Anna's confidence was boosted even more.[33]

On January 24, he assembled the army for a full dress parade. Thousands of troops stood for review and marched through the streets of Saltillo. From a distance, they appeared impressive, but on closer inspection many uniforms were threadbare and patched, with brass buttons tarnished and white buttons stained. Many infantry were barefooted or wearing sandals. Some cavalrymen wore leather helmets with brass shields and goat's pelt crests, topped with plumes of black horsehair. Others had the same barracks caps as the infantry. Most dragooned Indians and their Mayan brothers from the south did not have a clue about close order and were ill at ease in their uniforms. But to the citizens of Saltillo cheering along the parade route, the infantry, cavalry, horses, oxcarts, wagons, and cannon were an impressive sight. At the head of the column was the generalissimo, looking Napoleonic in a uniform of gray trousers and a blue pigeon-tailed jacket with bright red front pieces and cuffs, and a high collar embroidered with golden palm, olive, and laurel leaves. Golden epaulets graced his shoulders and a blue sash covered his waist. Jet black riding boots stretched from toe to knee, and a black, gold-laced hat, complete with plumes of green, white, and red ostrich feathers, rested on his head. Such a resplendent leader, the gawkers no doubt concluded, could conquer the world.[34]

Between January 26 and 28, several brigades departed Saltillo for Monclova. At the end of the month Santa Anna and his general staff left Saltillo in the company of Andrade's cavalry brigade. They covered the 120 miles to Monclova in less than a week. The town had little to offer the Army of Operations except a few head of cattle and some bushels of local walnuts. And memories, of course, for the general. In March 1811, at the nearby village Nuestra Señora de Guadalupe de Baján, Spanish authorities had trapped and arrested Miguel Hidalgo, hero of the Mexican Revolution. They then incarcerated him in Monclova, along with Ignacio de Allende, Juan de Aldama, and Mariano Jiménez, his coconspirators. Contemporary Mexican travel guides still cite Hidalgo's confinement as the city's only real claim to fame.[35]

Monclova had also witnessed the beheading of a Tejano rebel in 1811. When Miguel Hidalgo launched the Revolution in 1810, Juan Bautista de las Casas, a former militia captain living in Béxar, had shouted Hidalgo's name and taken up arms against the royal government, attracting to the cause hundreds of poor soldiers and lower-class citizens. He pulled off a coup d'état on January 11, 1811, occupied government offices, took the governor general prisoner, and then dispatched him under armed escort to Monclova. But Las Casas proved a better rebel than administrator. During the course of the next six weeks, he alienated everybody in Béxar. Too much property was confiscated and too many people were arrested, leading to too much crime and instability. On March 2, a coalition of regular army officers, priests, and well-to-do citizens staged a counterrevolution, arrested las Casas, and despatched him to Monclova for trial, where he was convicted of treason and sentenced to death.

On August 2, 1811, the evening before his execution, Las Casas met with priests and government officials. When asked if he had any last words, the condemned rebel dictated a will, making sure that provisions were made for payment of his debts. The next morning, he was escorted from his cell, officially demoted from the officer corps, forced to kneel with his back to the firing squad, and then shot. Ignacio Yngloria, the acting headman, wasted no time sawing off Las Casas's head and placing it in a wooden box. Two soldiers were given the assignment of carrying the souvenir to Béxar, an onerous journey of three hundred miles. In Béxar, the decaying head was impaled on a small spike, placed in an iron cage, and dangled from a post in the center of town, a grim reminder of the perils of revolution. It remained there for two years, perhaps long enough for a young Antonio López de Santa Anna to catch a glimpse of it.[36]

Santa Anna did not tarry long in Monclova. His sense of urgency baffled several aides, who could not understand his willingness to put himself at risk by moving far in advance of the main body of troops. Colonel José Sánchez Navarro, who was part of General Cos's staff, sarcastically wondered if Santa Anna had decided that "his name alone would conquer the rebels."[37]

On February 9, Santa Anna headed into the 150 miles of desert between Monclova and the Rio Grande, where he planned to rendezvous with Ramírez y Sesma's brigade. On the eve of their departure, he promised his officers, who in turn reassured worried soldiers, that food, blankets, and water would be waiting at the Rio Grande, where he had established a headquarters. It was an empty promise delivered by a general unconcerned with his troops. Santa Anna was prepared to get to Béxar at all costs. Nothing awaited at the Rio Grande except another two hundred miles of desert. On the evening before their departure from Monclova, according to Ramón Martínez Caro, the general "ordered that the troops should be placed on half rations of hard-tack and that each man be allowed one *real* a day. The officers were to provide themselves with their necessary supplies out of their regular pay, without receiving an extra campaign allowance." Many of the troops became quite cynical about the shortages in supplies. One officer observed, "It is pitiful and despairing to go looking for provisions and beasts of burden, money in hand, when there is plenty of everything in the commissaries and to have everyone from the quartermaster general . . . to the humblest clerk . . . reply, 'We cannot sell that, we cannot let you have it . . .' Consequently, we are perishing from hunger and misery in the midst of plenty." Greed and graft explained much of the lack of supplies. "I have been unable to find out the reason for this unjust and mysterious order," Caro complained. "In San Luis Potosí the Commissary General of the Army, Colonel Ricardo Dromundo, brother-in-law of His Excellency, had been given the necessary funds for two months' provisions and supplies for 6,000 men. What became of these provisions and supplies? When we arrived in Monclova the said Commissary was already there. If he had secured the supplies that he was supposed to get, why, then, was the soldier put on half rations?" Caro knew. Manga de Clavo and El Encero, as well as lenders and relatives, had swallowed the money.[38]

On its way out of Monclova, the Army of Operations was distinguished more by what it lacked than by what it possessed. One column of troops was without a hospital, other columns' hospitals were without surgeons, surgeons were without medicines, horses were without fodder, and infantry were without boots. There were muskets without decent powder, wagons without mules, mules without muleteers, and cavalry without saddles. Soldiers marched into the desert without water barrels and with near-starvation rations of eight ounces of hardtack or corn cake a day. A disgusted de la Peña wrote, "To deprive an officer during a campaign of allowances . . . would have been praiseworthy, had communities not been burdened with heavy demands and had the funds not been used to let a few rascals live in luxury. But one cannot recall how the soldier was deprived of his due when he in turn was offering his life and was receiving only the bare necessities to sustain him, without feeling the most profound indignation and wanting to curse the perpetrators of such suffering." Ramón Caro remembered having to "put in the wagons (though already filled to capacity) some of the dying wretches we found on the road. I remember particularly, the General must remember him too, a poor wretch whom we found, at the point of death, unable to move, loaded down with his gun and pack. . . . [H]e expired before the day's journey was over."[39]

They were also burdened with thousands of *soldaderas*—primarily the wives, girlfriends, and children of enlisted men and conscripts. The *soldaderas* had long been part of the Mexican army, since most troops could not afford to enlist and leave families behind. *Soldaderas* worked as nurses, cooks, and scavengers, but they also slowed the pace of a march and consumed the already pitifully meager rations. Soldiers found themselves worrying more about wives, sweethearts, and children than about the upcoming campaign.[40]

Roving bands of Indians only complicated matters. Santa Anna had let his own hatred of the Texans cloud his judgment about Indian loyalties, assuming that the Comanches and Apaches would side with Mexicans against the Anglos. But Comanches and Apaches viewed Mexicans and Texans with equal disdain; both represented aggressive European societies bent on conquest. The fact that Mexican invaders happened to be expanding from the south and Anglos from the east mattered little to the Indians, who hated to see cattle displace buffalo and cabins replace tipis. Conversely, an army officer captured Mexican contempt, and Mexican intentions, for the Comanches: "The Comanches are composed of more than ten thousand souls . . . but they never move in great numbers because they do not have a leader to direct them and do not recognize anyone as such. . . . A Mexican is equal to five of them. . . . With a force of six hundred men the whole country could be overrun in any direction, and by engaging them in detail, I believe that in the course of two or three years they could be totally eliminated." The Comanches sensed that Mexicans, no less than Anglos, were bent on genocide.[41]

At every opportunity, marauding Comanches and Apaches attacked the Army of Operations, picking off and scalping stragglers, scouring ranchos clean of materiel, raiding supply depots, and fouling water. More than once Santa Anna dispatched dragoons and presidial troops, who were experts at guerrilla warfare, to track down and punish the Indians. The generalissimo even had to loan precious muskets and ammunition to local politicians and hacienda and rancho owners for their defense, a decision that deprived his own troops of weapons. All along the way, especially south of the Rio Grande, wary officers kept extra sentries on night duty, just in case Comanche and Apache warriors came scalp hunting. "The savages . . . were in the habit of roaming the camps where we had spent the previous night to see what could be found there, sometimes venting their cruelty on those left behind or deserters. These fierce people customarily scalp their victims, sometimes before sacrificing them, sometimes after, and then have a celebration during which many hours are spent dancing around the scalp."[42]

In addition to serious logistical deficiencies and hostile Indians, the Mexicans had to deal with unpredictable weather. The desert took its toll in many ways. Good water was scarce. Troops and the accompanying *soldaderas* engaged in forced marches from water hole to puddle to stream. "It broke one's heart to see all this," Filisola later wrote, "especially many women with children in their arms, almost dying of thirst, crying for water. The tears they were shedding were all that they could give them to drink." The poorly trained, poorly conditioned conscripts were particularly bad off. "They were so weak and so little accustomed to the fatigue of the marches that they had fallen far behind," Filisola recalled. "Although water was sent to them, several of them never managed to drink because they were already dying; others died as they drank." And sometimes drinking the water was as dangerous as going without. Desert water holes, at best putrid and stagnant, and sometimes littered with animal carcasses, left soldiers with dysentery and high fevers from a disease known as *tele*. Without feed grains or even forage, the horses, mules, and oxen lost weight and strength, and they too suffered from lack of water, many of them dying in their tracks.[43]

What the desert failed to exact, a brutal winter storm, or "blue norther," did. Such storms were not uncommon. In February 1828, a French traveler near Laredo wrote that "on the ninth of February, with a southeast wind, the thermometer rose to 25 degrees centigrade, whereas on the eleventh of the same month at ten o'clock in the morning, a norther caused the temperature to drop to 4.4 degrees centigrade." Almost to the day, eight years later, the Army of Operations, scattered across hundreds of miles of desert, encountered a numbing arctic storm. By February 13, 1836, Santa Anna and his general staff had reached Guerrero, near the Rio Grande. Ramírez y Sesma's first infantry had already crossed the river and was headed northeast toward the Nueces

River. The second and third infantry brigades were several days' march out of Monclova, and Andrade's cavalry had barely departed Monclova.[44]

The forward elements of the Army of Operations felt the weather change late in the afternoon of February 13. At first, almost imperceptibly, the heavy, humid air that had been blowing steadily from the southeast surrendered to cool intermittent gusts out of the north. After slogging their way for days through wet air that had clung to them like Spanish moss, the troops no doubt welcomed the pleasant breezes that dried sweaty brows, cleared bronchial passages, and lifted spirits. They may not even have noticed, an hour later, when a dark, ominous cloud approached over the northern horizon. Hungry, thirsty soldiers on forced march rarely acknowledge environmental subtlety, even when lives depend on it. Burdened with heavy packs and weapons, the *soldados* stoically pushed ahead, short step by short step, heads down, eyes staring at the ground in front of them.

After another hour, the refreshing gusts turned to cold gales sweeping across the desert's open vistas. At dangerous moments, nature's cacophony harmonizes, and the Mexican soldiers would soon be hard pressed to distinguish howling winds from howling coyotes. Their uniforms—dank, damp, and stale from weeks of marching against an enemy no more formidable than the dew point—trapped cold air and conveyed it to warm skin. Troops and *soldaderas* scrounged for coats, blankets, and scarves, anything fresh and dry, and bundled up. Fingers numbed, and they blew warm breath into their hands.

The day before, a huge crater of low pressure had settled on northeastern Mexico and southern Texas, setting off a whirligig of counterclockwise winds, sucking wet air off the surface of the Caribbean and the Gulf of Mexico and then dumping it on the southern plains, generating unusually humid temperatures that bedeviled the soldiers, aggravating their allergies, reddening their rashes, and dehydrating their tissues.

Now, dry, frigid arctic air, cooled by months of dormancy over frozen tundra, raced south and collided with moist Gulf air. On the northern horizon, as the sun set, the thin dark cloud line stacked up layer after layer, reaching as much as 50,000 feet, its dense, dark mass blackening the sky and inking out moon, stars, planets, nebulae, and Milky Way, everything that emanated light, making it difficult for soldiers to see their hands in front of their faces. Troop columns lost track of one another and the trail, breaking companies into platoons, platoons into squads, and squads into long lines of stragglers. Within a few hours of sunset, the Army of Operations was scattered across the landscape, disoriented and unable to navigate, men and animals wandering in every direction.

The wind grew steadily colder. Then, after a detour through the stratosphere, the humid Gulf air showed up again as freezing rain and ice crystals. Santa Anna's army found itself marching head-on into cutting frozen winds, with gusts up to forty miles per hour, being pelted with high-velocity ice crystals that hurt on impact and even raised welts. "The night was very raw and excessively cold," wrote General José Urrea. "The rain continued and the dragoons, who were barely able to dismount, were so numbed by the cold that they could hardly speak." As the men marched forward, the wind drove condensed, exhaled breath back into their faces, crusting mustaches, eyebrows, sideburns, and eyelashes with ice, turning soldiers into ice men. General Urrea later recalled how "a violent norther accompanied by rain" brought his own maneuvers to a halt. Ramón Caro complained that the troops had "set out on their long march over deserts, in the middle of winter, which is very severe in those regions, without sufficient clothes, particularly among the wretched recruits who in the main were conscripts and were practically naked."[45]

There was nowhere to hide. In winter, much of Mexico's northern desert resembled a lunar landscape, devoid of plants, shrubs, and trees, except for an occasional cactus and clumps of mesquite and chaparral. Natural shelter was as scarce as water. So were tents. When they despaired of marching anymore, the *soldados* clung together like frozen fingers, hoping to keep one another warm enough to survive the night. Fingers and toes ached at first and then turned numb as frostbite set in. Horses, mules, and oxen collapsed and died, and the men burrowed under the south side of the carcasses, a few of them probably butchering the animals and squeezing into their empty bellies for protection. "The snowfall increased and kept falling in great abundance," wrote de la Peña. "At dawn it was knee-deep. It seemed as though it wished to subdue us beneath its weight. Indeed, one could not remain standing or sitting, much less lying down." When morning came, "as far as one could see, all was snow. The trees, totally covered, formed an amazing variety of cones and pyramids, which seemed to be made of alabaster." Dotting the landscape were mogul humps of snow covering dead horses, oxen, mules, and humans, and splotches of blood where men and animals had collapsed and died. De la Peña wrote, "Many mules . . . as well as some horses, died, for those that fell and tried to get up inevitably slipped from being so numb, and the weight of their loads would make them crack their heads. The snow was covered with the blood of these beasts." Snowfall eased the next day and temperatures began to rise, but the troops, driven ahead by Santa Anna's anger, faced a new torture—desert sands turned into a cold, slushy mud that penetrated socks and boots. Desertions increased, muleteers quit, and teamsters abandoned the campaign for warmer climes south. Napoleon's ghost returned. With animal carcasses, abandoned ox-carts, empty boxes, cast-off barrels, fresh graves, and shivering, frostbitten soldiers stretching from Monclova to the Rio Grande, "We could not help recalling on this date," wrote de la Peña, "the illustrious conquerors of many nations who in 1812 had succumbed beneath the snows of Russia."[46]

If Santa Anna knew the full extent of the suffering behind him, he did not mention it. As always, he was focused on the glory ahead. He crossed the Rio Grande, near Guerrero on February 16, and then drove north-northeast at a quickened pace, overtaking Ramírez y Sesma's brigade two days later at the Frio River. Then he pushed ahead to the Medina, arriving at 1:45 P.M. on February 21, 1836. Stretched out behind, for a distance of nearly three hundred miles, was the rest of his army. That evening, at the site of his boyhood triumph, Santa Anna celebrated his birthday. When de la Peña reached the Medina, he dutifully noted that "this was the place where General Arredondo [and Santa Anna] had fought against the colonists who had rebelled during the Spanish regime."[47]

During the next several days, as the rest of the Army of Operations caught up with its general, anticipation and excitement about the looming battle mounted. Santa Anna and his general staff did not take the Anglo rebels seriously. In 1834 Colonel Juan Nepomuceno Almonte had conducted an inspection tour of Texas and reported back that the Anglo settlers, "being from the southern states of the [United States] . . . are considered there as the least advanced in civilization, [and] introduced customs that were somewhat crude . . . these customs are not compatible with the manners practiced by persons of good breeding." Others took at face value the assurances of Secretary of War José María Tornel that the "superiority of the Mexican soldier over the mountaineers of Kentucky and the hunters of Missouri is well known. Veterans seasoned by twenty years of wars can't be intimidated by the presence of an army ignorant of the art of war, incapable of discipline, and renowned for insubordination." These thoughts were reinforced by the cross on the giant oak tree, recalling how the stupid Americans in 1813 had charged headlong like sheep to a slaughter. General Manuel Fernández Castrillón proved even more contemptuous. On January 31, 1836, Colonel Carlos Sánchez Navarro had overheard Castrillón and several officers ridiculing the fighting abilities of the Texans. Castrillón predicted that the battle would be nothing more than a military parade and that the Texans would not get off a single volley. Sánchez Navarro, who had been with General Cos at Béxar a few months before, replied that the Texans were a formidable enemy, not to be taken lightly, and that they would probably get off thousands of shots. He feared that his comrades were badly underestimating the Texans.[48]

Santa Anna, on the other hand, may still have entertained dreams of sweeping across North America just as Napoleon had cut a swathe through Europe, defeating every army put in his path, crushing all opposition, and redrawing the political boundaries of the continent. At a November 1835 meeting in Tacubaya with diplomats from France and Great Britain, he had boasted about the upcoming military expedition: he would sweep through Texas and "continue the march of his army to Washington and place upon its *Capitol* the Mexican *flag*."[49]

But first the rebels outside Béxar, and the Alamo.

4

---✦---

"THOSE PROUD TOW'RS"

NO ONE KNOWS exactly when he got the idea, but it might have been that December night in 1833 at the Washington Theater. Congressmen David Crockett of Tennessee had recently returned to the capital, exultant after his narrow reelection victory. Unlike in 1831, the forces aligned with President Andrew Jackson had failed to engineer Crockett's defeat, and his people were again his people, at least by a margin of 173 votes. But if it had been only by a single vote, what would it have mattered? He would still have been Congressman David Crockett, a man of importance, even though he struggled with debts, felt the limits of his meager education, and laid claim to few political or economic accomplishments. For Crockett, the position was significant. He yearned to be a respectable gentleman, trying to dress the part and associating with prominent Whigs. A seat in Congress put him in the same room, if not quite the same social circle, as Daniel Webster, Henry Clay, and John Quincy Adams. For a man born and raised in the hardscrabble poverty of the West, who married young only to discover that he was "better at increasing [his] family than [his] fortune," and whose primary talent was making other people like him, sitting close to Webster, Clay, and Adams would have to do—at least for the moment.[1]

But something was changing in the United States. There was profound movement in the social and political landscape, some subtle shift that signaled the arrival of Crockett's moment—and not only Crockett's but that of a whole nation of Crocketts, white men from nowhere important who dreamed to be going somewhere and doing something. The change was acknowledged that cold December night at the theater. Crockett had gone to see actor James Hackett play the part of Colonel Nimrod Wildfire in James Kirke Paulding's play *The Lion of the West*. The part, as almost everyone knew, had been modeled on Crockett. Frontiersman Wildfire dressed in buckskin, wore a wildcat-skin hat, and spoke the patois of the West—or at least what Easterners assumed was the patois of the West. Like the popular image of Crockett, Wildfire was known for his exaggerated boasts. In the play he claimed that he had "the fastest horse, prettiest sister, the quickest rifle, and the ugliest dog in the states," and that he could "jump higher, squat lower, dive deeper, and come up drier than any other fellow in the world." The play had opened in late 1831, had been performed across the country and in Great Britain, and had filled the house everywhere.[2]

Crockett took his seat for the performance. No doubt pleased with himself, he looked at Hackett, who was ready to start his imitation of David Crockett. Hackett, dressed in his stage buckskin, saw Crockett, the real Crockett, then nodded to David and bowed. Crockett, dressed like a gentleman, nodded back, rose to his feet, and turned to acknowledge the other spectators, who by this time were clapping for Hackett, Crockett, and the sheer, pure theater of that moment. Crockett bowed, Hackett bowed, and an odd fusion took place. Legend and man, myth and reality, backwoodsman Davy Crockett and Congressman David Crockett—they had become one and interchangeable. If the word had existed in its modern meaning—which it did not until about 1850—Crockett would have realized that he had become a celebrity, famous not for anything he had actually accomplished but simply for being famous. He had become not so much a man of deeds as a figment of the American imagination, the sum total of the country's desires.[3]

Maybe it was then that the glimmer of a thought became a fully formed idea. Why shouldn't he, David/Davy Crockett, get cut in for a piece of himself? Hackett and Paulding were making a small fortune from incantations of his life. So was Matthew St. Clair Clarke, who in January 1833 had published *Life and Adventures of Colonel David Crockett of*

West Tennessee, an exaggerated portrait of Crockett, "that same David Crockett, fresh from the backwoods. . . . Half-horse, half-alligator, a little touched with snapping turtle." If Crockett did not understand that Paulding and Clarke had helped to make him a celebrity, he did sense that he might become rich by selling an image of himself that Americans were hungry for. He went right to work writing his own account of himself, *A Narrative of the Life of David Crockett, of the State of Tennessee,* to which he appended, "by Himself." The autobiography appeared in March 1834 and was a great success, moving into its sixth printing within a few months and easing Crockett's debt. In the language of an American he told the story of an American, the great tale of democracy. Using phonetical spelling and frontier grammar, he told his story with great humor, demonstrating that while he was better than no other man, he was no worse either.

Unlike any autobiography before it, it was the story of a Jacksonian man, yearning for success in Jacksonian America. Unlike Benjamin Franklin, whose accomplishments merited an autobiography, Crockett wrote one simply because he could and because he gleaned a market for it. In a sense, it was not so much a record of his accomplishments as an accomplishment in itself, an announcement that he had arrived because he had written that he had arrived. And the beauty of his life, as he told it, was that it was so common, so down-home-Western common. He was born and raised honest, hunted bears and fought Indians, went to Congress, and became a toady for no man. That was about it—poverty, hunting, fighting, electioneering—representing the common man by being a common man. And he said it all in the language of the common man.

The language, the language was everything—words that followed no standards for spelling or usage. Words that were scattered in odd combinations and took on new meanings. Words that were as fresh and powerful and malleable as America itself, ever changing and mutating and transforming, always moving west on a vast mythical and physical landscape. Only a few years before the appearance of Crockett's autobiography, Frenchman Alexis de Tocqueville had toured America, studying the nature of Jacksonian democracy. He was shocked at the impact of democracy on language, suggesting that Americans believed that one person's use of a word was as good as the next's. "An author begins by a slight deflection of a known expression from its primitive meaning, and he adapts it . . . A second writer twists the sense of the expression in another way; a third takes possession of it for another purpose." The end result is that words and expressions, like Jacksonian men, are self-made. Tocqueville analyzed and understood the process; David Crockett lived and was the process.[4]

The autobiography had its desired effect, making Crockett even more famous, encouraging his Whig supporters to think of him as a potential presidential candidate. He just might be the Whig answer to Andrew Jackson. He just might be able to out-Jackson any politician the Democrats could throw at him. They had plans, important plans, for him; at least that was what Whig Party men indicated. Plans for a trip along the East Coast to broaden his political base, plans for speeches to show Americans the quality of him, plans for the White House, a symbolic place for a symbolic man. Congress was in session, but Crockett had bigger worlds to conquer. Texas, part of another country, was the furthermost thing from his mind.

In the spring of 1834, with dreams of the White House pushing him ahead, Crockett hit the road and traveled widely throughout the Northeast, drawing crowds and newspaper coverage at every stop, giving prospective voters a close look at a legend. But on May 13, 1834, he returned to Washington, D.C., tired and moody. David Crockett had grown tired of politics probably even before politics had grown tired of him.

The trip had gone passably well. Crockett had said all the right things, making people laugh when he wanted to and criticizing the administration of Andrew Jackson whenever the chance appeared. If he wanted to become the Whigs' presidential nominee in 1836, he had to become as familiar in Boston as he was in Nashville, as loved in Pennsylvania as in Tennessee, and the tour was designed for that purpose—that and to embarrass Jackson. But still, being all things to all people, even if the nomination hung in the balance, wearied an honest man in body and soul, and David Crockett, whatever people thought, was an honest man.

Congress now bored him. Too many speeches, too much hot air that was expended on blowing up grand balloons that always seemed to burst. Increasingly, he had stopped listening and left his seat, drifting out of the Capitol back to his boardinghouse or to a Washington watering hole. Although Congress was scheduled to adjourn on June 30, Crockett adjourned himself earlier, traveling to Philadelphia to pick up the finished rifle that had been promised to him during his spring tour. It was a beautifully crafted weapon with an alligator, a possum, and a deer etched in the silver plate on the stock. Along the barrel, in an inlaid gilded arrow, was Crockett's motto, *Go Ahead*. "Pretty Betsey," Crockett dubbed the fine rifle, and he promised to use it in defense of America. As he said on the Fourth of July 1834, "I love my country." And he meant it. He may have developed a passionate dislike of Jackson and an itchy feeling sitting in Congress, but he had not lost his love of his country.

Back home in Tennessee, Democrats grumbled about Crockett's jaunts from Congress when he was paid $8 a day to be there looking after the interests of the people. But David knew that the $8 a day was not nearly enough to pay off the mountain of debt that he had accumulated. His only hope was to return to writing, following up the success of his *Narrative of the Life of David Crockett, of the State of Tennessee* with another account. During the fall and winter he labored on a narrative of his Northeastern trip, which was published in 1835 as *Col. Crockett's Tour to the North and Down East* and was not nearly as popular as his earlier work. But it helped to relieve some of the debt and encouraged him to believe that writing and politics might be his economic salvation.

That was the order—writing and politics. When Congress reconvened he spent more time preparing his book than he did tending to his congressional duties. And when he did attend a session and take the floor it was usually to attack Jackson or Martin Van Buren, the politician Democrats believed would be the next president of the United States. The thought of "Mr. *martin vanburen*," all pink and clean, maneuvering his way into the White House infuriated Crockett. If that happened, he thought, he would pack up and leave the United States. "I will go to the wildes of Texas" and live under Mexican rule, Crockett wrote a friend.

In truth, the Crockett phenomenon was on the wane. In three terms in Congress he had failed to push through a single piece of legislation. As a political wag, his act was becoming repetitive and weary. The same stories, the same attacks on Jackson and Van Buren—it was wearing thin with both his Whig patrons and his Democratic friends. In the August 1835 congressional election against pro-Jackson Adam "Blackhawk" Huntsman, Crockett tried to explain away his failures and excuse his slightly amiss expense accounts. He could still speak the language of his backcountry constituents and he remembered how to make them laugh, but the combination of his turning on Jackson and Jackson turning on Crockett's home district was a distinct liability. Still, he fought a good fight, again proclaiming that a loss would not be the worst thing in the world. Texas was still west of Louisiana and south of Arkansas, and if by chance his people voted him out of office, by damn he would go to Texas.

By a thin margin Crockett lost his bid for a fourth term. He took it badly. In his own mind he had become some sort of heroic figure standing for truth and honesty against the most base tyranny; he had become a nineteenth-century version of Milton's Abdiel, the one true man in a crowd of false gods, transforming Jackson into Satan. He knew in his heart that he was right, but the mob had followed Jackson, or more precisely, followed Jackson's money. Now, like Abdiel, he would turn his back on them, turn his back on "those proud Tow'rs to swift destruction doom'd." Shortly after the election, he announced in the press that "I never expect to offer my name again to the public for any office."[5]

When Crockett made the statement, he probably meant it, for defeat had never come easy to him. When he had tasted it previously, he had gone on a long hunt, forcing public affairs out of his mind and surrounding himself with friends whose loyalty was absolute. Now, more than ever, he needed nature, not society—friends, not political allies. For a decade his life had centered on politics and celebrity. He had drifted away from his family, his home in Tennessee, and perhaps even from himself. He had drunk too much, talked too much, and occupied too much of his time with things that didn't really matter. Over the years his Davy persona had hogtied and swallowed his David self.

The more he thought about Texas, the more the idea grew on him. Texas had wild game, good men like Sam Houston, and the promise of emotional, perhaps even political, regeneration. In Texas there were land and adventures and maybe even a future. It was certainly worth a look. In October he held a barbecue in his honor and spent the day drinking, eating, and talking, complaining about the past and speculating about the future. He was determined to go west and south.

On the first day of November 1835, the forty-nine-year-old Crockett, accompanied by his nephew William Patton and friends Lindsay Tinkle and Abner Burgin, set out for Texas. The news spread fast, and what started as a modest expedition began to swell and contract as men joined up with him for a day or a week or more and then left for home or to some other destination. At times as many as thirty men rode along, sharing stories and a jug with one another. They swept through Bolivar and

Jackson, Tennessee, then turned southwest toward Memphis and the Mississippi River. All along his route people came out to gape and gawk and shake his hand. They wanted to meet Davy Crockett, wanted to hear him speak. "He was like a passing comet," noted an acquaintance, a perfect description for the year that Halley's comet tracked across the sky.

In Memphis he drank with friends—always with friends—at the Union Hotel and Neil McCool's saloon. Crockett's friends carried him on their shoulders and he made a speech standing on McCool's bar—the "Go to hell, I am going to Texas" speech. The next morning he crossed the Mississippi and set off overland to Little Rock. Along the way he shot game, which he toted with him. In Little Rock once again there were speeches to deliver, liquor to drink, and people to meet. Why was he going to Texas? In a letter to his brother-in-law penned before his departure from Tennessee, Crockett had written, "I want to explore Texas well before I return." In Little Rock he hinted that he had an interest in the revolutionary activities taking place there, and one reporter recalled that Davy said he would "have *Santa Anna's* head and wear it as a watch seal."[6]

From Little Rock Crockett veered southwest toward the Red River and into Texas. As he moved west, a fresh, virgin land opened before him, a flat prairie landscape filled with herds of bison and wild horses, as well as an occasional bear. It was a land to stir a man's imagination. In his first letter from Texas to his daughter, he wrote that Texas "is a garden spot of the world, the best land & best prospects of health I ever saw is here, and I do believe it is a fortune to any man to come here." He said that he planned to settle on the Bois D'Arc or Choctaw Bayou or Red River, where the soil was the richest, the springs the finest, and the streams the clearest, where buffalo herds pass by twice a year and there are "bees and honey a plenty." What Crockett described was a paradise straight out of the mind of Daniel Boone.[7]

The dream of Texas gripped him tightly. There was simply so much of everything that a man could not help but be content there. He planned on becoming a land agent and attracting his friends to follow him. Texas, then, would be his financial salvation. Texas would get him out of debt and back on his feet. "I am rejoiced at my fate," he wrote. "I had rather be in my present situation than to be elected to a seat in Congress for life. I am in great hopes of making a fortune for myself and my family bad as has been my prospects."

Texas seemed as enthralled with Crockett as he was with it. He may have crossed over from the United States, but he had not passed beyond the border of his fame. He wrote his family that he had been "received by everyone with open arms of friendship, I am hailed with a hearty welcome to this country, a dinner and a party of Ladys [sic] have honored me with an invitation." Texans feted Crockett, and Davy told them what they wanted to hear in the language they wanted to hear it. Now he hardly needed to give a reason for his move. "To satisfy your curiosity at once as to myself, I will tell you all about it. I was, for some years, a member of Congress. In my last canvass, I told the people of my District, that, if they saw fit to re-elect me, I would serve them faithfull as I had done; but, if not, *They might go to hell, and I would go to Texas.* I was beaten, gentlemen, and here I am." It was still a story that never failed to bring whoops and hollers.[8]

✫

Crockett was only one of hundreds of ambitious, patriotic men making their way to Texas. Raised by their fathers and grandfathers on a steady diet of Revolutionary and military rhetoric—the war for American independence, the War of 1812, and the Indian wars—they treated combat as a refiner's fire that made men of boys. They looked to the Texas Revolution as *their* turn, their opportunity to make history. The subtleties of federalism versus centralism, independence versus statehood, and the Constitution of 1824 versus the Law of April 6, 1830 all blurred into an epic battle of democracy versus dictatorship, freedom versus oppression, and America versus Mexico. And they knew they were not alone in the world; men were bleeding and dying in similar wars over similar issues on distant battlefields. Many of the men arriving in Texas considered themselves liberals fighting to rid the world of absolutism, aristocracy, and privilege.

In some ways they were right. Mexico and Texas were not the only scenes of liberal uprisings and civil wars. Europe was awash in revolutions that captured the romantic imagination. Nineteenth-century European liberalism rested on several assumptions—individual rights, the efficacy of people governing themselves through elected legislatures, government protection of private property and promotion of economic development, an expanding franchise, and free trade. Uprisings against conservative, centralist regimes occurred in Spain and Naples in the early 1820s, in Poland and France in 1830, and would occur again in France and throughout the Hapsburg empire in 1848. In Europe and the United States, liberals followed the rebellions closely, hoping to see democracy and freedom unfold.

The Greek war for independence, in particular, stirred the imagination. Proclaiming vaguely liberal principles, Alexandros Ypsilantis in 1821 had precipitated a rebellion against the Ottoman empire that quickly evolved into a war for independence. The revolution had all the ingredients of high political drama—Greek versus Turk, Christian versus Muslim, democracy versus absolutism, freedom versus oppression. A generation of American and European liberals, educated in the classics and soon to be labeled "Philhellenes," saw the war as a struggle between good and evil. In 1821 the British Poet Percy Shelley wrote, "We are all Greeks, our laws, our literature, our religion, our art have their roots in Greece. But for Greece . . . we might still have been savages and idolators." Warming to the memory of Homer, Plato, and Aristotle, the Philhellenes insisted, as Shelley wrote, that the modern Greek "is the descendent of those glorious beings."[9]

Philhellenes from France, England, Scotland, the Netherlands, and German-speaking principalities scrambled to Greece, hoping to lend a hand in a glorious cause. They quickly learned, of course, that the Greek patriots of the 1820s were hardly the demigods of Mount Olympus, but their cause still seemed righteous. Shelley's friend the poet Lord Byron raised the Byron Brigade to fight alongside the Greeks. Once in Greece, he urged his friends to get in on the glory, to do something useful with their lives. In a letter to Edward Trelawny, Byron had written, "My dear T.,—You must have heard that I am going to Greece. Why do you not come with me? I want your aid . . . I am serious . . . they all say I can be of use in Greece. I do not know how, nor do they; but at all events let us go." Byron, at the age of thirty-six, died there in April 1824 during the siege of Missolonghi, becoming in death a cult figure among romantic revolutionaries. Leaving one's own country to fight for freedom abroad was now Byronic.[10]

Many Americans felt much the same way. Greek independence attracted considerable attention in the United States. In October 1823 former president Thomas Jefferson assured a Greek patriot, "No people sympathise more feelingly than ours with the sufferings of your country-men, none offer more sincere and ardent prayers to heaven, for their suc-cess. . . . Possessing ourselves the combined blessings of liberty and order, we wish the same to other countries and to none more than yours, which, the first of civilised nations, presented examples of what men should be." On January 22, 1824, freshman congressman Sam Houston of Tennessee took the podium in the House of Representatives and urged his col-leagues to come to the aid of Greece. "The Greeks are struggling for their liberty, and the Turk is determined to exert all his power to prevent it. . . . [The Greeks] have determined to stand manfully, and perish before they submit. . . . Let us encourage them. . . . Principles remain unchanged and eternal. The distance of the people from us does not alter the principle." Soon, when a similar struggle began across the Sabine, he would feel a similar urgent need to do his duty there.[11]

In 1830s Mexico, people enjoyed neither liberty nor order, and in Texas, when the rhetoric of individual rights escalated into rebellion and revolution, many Americans enlisted in the cause. Like Lord Byron, they trudged to Texas to fight the noble battles, to take a stand for freedom and liberty. "I am a volunteer from Kentucky," wrote John M. Thurston, "and have come to Texas to aid in her struggle. . . . I wish to remain in the cause of Texas until the termination of her struggle." Writing home from Natchitoches, Louisiana, late in December 1835, Daniel Cloud said, "We go [to Texas] with arms in our hands, determined to conquer or die; re-solved to bury our all in the same ditch which ingulphs [sic] the liberties of Texas." John C. Goodrich, another new Texan, wrote family members from Washington-on-the-Brazos on November 8, 1835: "I feel a great de-sire to render some service to this country of my adoption in her struggle for freedom."[12]

And like Lord Byron, they recruited others. Advocates of Texas inde-pendence held rallies to sign up volunteers in Boston, New York City, Philadelphia, New Orleans, Mobile, Nashville, Lexington, Cleveland, and Baltimore, and Texas residents wrote home urging friends to join the crusade before it was too late. "Mississippi must send forth her gallant sons to aid us," Charles Parker wrote from Nacogdoches in November 1835. "Many have come—God bless them—like brave descendants of worthy sires." Come they did. Between October 1835 and April 1836, more than fifteen hundred Americans enlisted in the Texas army. Some of the volunteers had lived in Texas for years, others for only weeks, but they came to fight for freedom, as individuals and in such groups as the Mobile Greys, the Tennessee Mounted Volunteers, the Tampico Blues, the Georgia Battalion of Permanent Volunteers, or the Gonzales Ranging Company.[13]

No volunteer company was more enthusiastic than the New Orleans Greys. On October 13, 1835, Thomas Banks, a Texas patriot, convened a meeting in the coffee room of Bank's Arcade in New Orleans. Herman Ehrenberg, a young German immigrant, remembered the meeting. "Everyone was eager to hear the message of the colonists, whose delegates and friends now came forward to explain the cause of the rebellion and to ask for support and sympathy. . . . These short, spontaneous speeches roused the enthusiasm of their hearers to the highest pitch, for on that night there was no need of eloquence to secure loud applause. Everyone in the audience already admired the Texans for their pluck." Before the night was over, nearly 120 men signed on to fight for Texas, and they were each outfitted with weapons—a rifle, a pistol, and a Bowie knife—and uniforms of gray pants and jackets and sealskin hats. Organized into two companies, they entered Texas that same month.[14]

When one company arrived in San Augustine, Texas, on its way to Béxar, local patriots treated them to a dinner of beefsteaks and roasts. Herman Ehrenberg recalled, "As we sat down to eat, the simply laconic 'Help yourselves' of our hosts was the only ceremony used." Another feast greeted the Greys in Nacogdoches, Texas. A 150-foot-long table displayed a recently killed and only partially dressed black bear, complete with "hide and bones, meat and claws." The locals referred to the bear as "Mr. Petz" and stuck between its teeth a Mexican flag. Raccoons, turkeys, squirrels, and slabs of beef covered much of the rest of the table. Ehrenberg remembered that the Greys gorged themselves and gulped corn liquor, toasting the virtues of Texas and the evils of Mexico. "Political speeches were [then] made. The causes of the war were discussed; inflammatory appeals resounded . . . and it was already very late when the feast was over." The next day, the Greys pushed on for Béxar.[15]

Some of the Americans fighting for Texas explicitly viewed the crusade as part of a global confrontation between the forces of liberty and of absolutism. Frank Johnson, a firebrand and early member of the War Party, called Texans to join a worldwide movement: "To arms! then, Americans, to aid in sustaining the principles of 1776, in this western hemisphere. To arms! native Mexicans, in driving tyranny from your homes, intolerance from your altars, and the tyrant from your country. In this very hour the crowned despots of Europe have met in unholy conclave, to devise the means of crushing liberal principles. Louis Philippe of France, faithless to his oath, now sits side by side with the monarchs of Russia, and Austria, and Prussia, and Spain, and the minister of Santa Anna is among them. . . . [T]he genius of liberty demands that every man do his duty to his country." A later generation might scoff at such passion, treating these Texans as naive, racist mercenaries, but they were sincere. They came to Texas to fight for freedom.[16]

★

While Davy and his companions dreamed of what lay ahead, the Army of Operations ground its way north. From the Mexican interior, two highways led to the rebels. The Atascosito Road wound north from Goliad at the San Antonio River, Victoria on the Guadalupe River, and San Felipe de Austin on the Brazos River, to the Trinity River near present-day Liberty, Texas. As one traveled north on the Atascosito Road, Tejano rhythms gave way to Anglo music. The second artery into Texas was the Old San Antonio Road, or Camino Real, which crossed the Rio Grande at Paso de Francia and inched up northeasterly, through Tejano Texas, to Béxar, Bastrop, Nacogdoches, and San Augustine before reaching the Sabine. In the late winter of 1836, Santa Anna's troops crowded both highways, *el presidente* himself leading a column toward the Old San Antonio Road and General José Urrea advancing along the Atascosito Road. Along those routes, long ago, Spain had constructed the Alamo at Béxar and La Bahía near Goliad. As 1835 turned to 1836, Texans realized that both places needed defending against Spain's inheritors.

But that was all they could agree on. Petty bickering and personal squabbles threatened to achieve what Martín Perfecto de Cos had failed to do: crush the rebellion. When the consultation had adjourned back in mid-November 1835, Texas had a provisional government consisting of a governor and a Council, but the division of powers between the two was vague and poorly defined, guaranteed to produce infighting, backbiting, and recrimination. Henry Smith had been named provisional governor, and he felt the urgency of the hour. With a Mexican army occupying Béxar, he pleaded with legislators to "call system from chaos; to start the wheels of government, clogged and impeded as they are by conflicting interests." Cos's surrender in December placed an even greater premium on political stability. After all, nobody knew for certain whether Santa Anna would let the rebels go or would avenge his brother-in-law and lay waste to Texas. Smith remained concerned, warning the Council that "it is now time for the Government to bring every thing under its own proper control, and pursue the organic system in place of confusion, or desultory warfare."[17]

His pleas had about as much effect as a whispering voice in a Texas storm. Rather than exchange chaos for stability, he was about to watch chaos turn to anarchy. Smith and the Council quarreled like rancorous children, calling one another names and sending unsubstantiated accusations ricocheting throughout the territory. In children's quarrels, however, the stakes are never so high. Smith backed the radicals, abandoning any hope of reconciliation with Mexico, advocating immediate independence, and calling for the establishment of a regular army. He also agreed with Sam Houston that Texans were unlikely to secure support from sympathetic federalists in Mexico. Houston had no faith in them. "Our proclamations to the other states of the Mexican Confederation," he told his troops, "asking them to support us in our struggle for the restoration of our former rights, and for the protection of the Constitution of 1824, have . . . been without results." Nor could most Tejanos be trusted. "Even many of the Mexicans who live between the Sabine and the Rio Grande," he went on, "have disdainfully forsaken the cause of freedom. . . . [H]e who is not with us is against us."[18]

An influential faction of the Council, however, proved more deliberate, worrying about Tejano sensibilities and the wisdom of a standing army. For support they looked to Stephen F. Austin, who for a brief period in December 1835 and early January 1836 had grown somewhat cautious and expressed concern about an immediate declaration of independence, which would "expose the old settlers and men of property in this country to much risk." Busily working, still unsuccessfully, to secure formal United States support for the Revolution, Austin wanted to buy time, urging the Council to defer independence for a proclamation of statehood and to provide troops to Mexican federalists battling Santa Anna's regime, all in hope of confining the military struggle far to the south. He feared that Texas was ill prepared for the Army of Operations. Although Austin soon returned to the cause of independence, many Council members quoted him in their power struggle with Governor Smith and the War Party. Opposing the Peace Party, on the same day that Stephen F. Austin appealed for moderation, rebels in Goliad wrapped independence in the blanket of Jacksonian democracy. As long as Texans remained shackled by the chains of Mexican oppression, they would never realize the full meaning of natural rights. The Goliad rebels proclaimed that only independence would bring Jacksonian democracy to Texas, "a new; invigorating; & cherishing policy . . . a policy extending equal; impartial; and indiscriminate protection to all—to the low, as well as the high, the humbly bred, & the well-born;—the poor, & the rich; the ignorant, and the educated; the simple, & the shrewd." In independence, they insisted, Texans would discover a "work of political, or of moral renovation."[19]

By early February 1836 the provisional government had become fully dysfunctional; so many Council members left for home that a quorum could not be assembled. Most hoped that the upcoming convention, scheduled for Washington-on-the-Brazos at the end of the month, would fix what they had broken. In a concerned letter to Sam Houston, a former consultation member wrote, "I sincerely hope that the Convention will remedy the existing evils and calm the Public mind. If not Texas must be lost." But time favored the radicals. Every day, more Anglo-Americans arrived in Texas, bringing attitudes that were decidedly anti-Mexico, anti-Mexican, and anti-Tejano.[20]

Early in January 1836, Texas faced a moment of decision on the Atascosito Road, where warmongers had hatched the idea of invading Matamoros. Philip Dimmitt, a well-known radical who had become rebel commander of Goliad after its capture in October 1835, first proposed the incursion. Capturing Matamoros, he argued, would guarantee Texas independence. Rather than wait at La Bahía for a Mexican army to march up the Atascosito Road, Texans should assume the offensive, march down the road themselves, and invade across the Rio Grande. Customs duties from the port would finance the Army of the People; federalist supporters of the Constitution of 1824 would rally to the rebellion and overthrow *santanistas* in Tamaulipas State; and Santa Anna would have no choice but to cancel his assault on Texas. He could not afford to lose Matamoros, which would rob him of valuable revenues and sever his supply lines to the sea. By attacking Matamoros, Dimmitt promised, Texans could "hurl the thunder back in the very atmosphere of the enemy, drag him, and with him the war out of Texas. The liberal of all classes would immediately join us, the neutrals would gather confidence, both in themselves and us, and the parasites of centralism, in that section, would be eventually panic-struck and paralyzed."[21]

On the surface, his logic seemed compelling, and the Council approved the invasion over the objections of Governor Smith, who declared the scheme complete folly and certain to "destroy the very institutions which you are pledged and sworn to support." During the next several weeks, political relations deteriorated rapidly, and late in January 1836, Smith dissolved the Council just as it impeached him. Seeing General Sam Houston as a Smith ally, the Council then relieved him, too, as commander in chief. Their reasoning was as murky as their rhetoric was hysterical. Council members accused Smith of plotting to overthrow the government, arrest and imprison his enemies, and impose a military dictatorship. Smith was no less shrill, labeling the Council members "corrupt as hell. . . . They have taken grampers hold on the dry tits of the Treasury and hunch on like long tailed pigs hoping the milk will come after a while. Nothing short of an unqualified declaration of Independence can save the country."[22]

As government officials engaged in political fratricide, Houston ignored the Council and at Smith's request headed for Goliad to assume command of the Matamoros expedition. He might be able, Smith hoped, to sound a voice of reason among the rabble assembling on the Atascosito Road. At the same time, however, the Council awarded command of the invasion to two firebrands—Frank Johnson *and* James W. Fannin—and then designated Lieutenant Governor James W. Robinson acting governor. Sam Houston was now a military commander without portfolio, a soldier fighting for a country that had no government.[23]

A native of Tennessee, Frank Johnson was widely known for his hair-trigger temper and contempt for Mexico. During the siege of Béxar, he had enthusiastically rallied to Ben Milam's call for volunteers, led a militia column into the town, and fought the Mexicans. When Cos surrendered, Johnson received command of the Texas army, and he was determined to make good use of it. James Fannin, a native of Georgia who had settled in Velasco, Texas, in 1834 to raise cotton and traffic in slaves, was at least Johnson's equal with the hot adjectives of rebellion. In 1835 he fought in the battles of Gonzales and Concepción and early in 1836 was recruiting volunteers when he learned of the Council's decision to give him cocommand of the Matamoros expedition. Cluttering the command issue even more, Frank Johnson had cast his lot with James Grant, a native of Scotland and a land speculator who had become secretary to the legislature of Coahuila y Texas. Grant and Johnson had been partners in several land schemes that went belly-up with the overthrow of the Constitution of 1824. Anxious to win Texas independence and resurrect their real estate empire, the two men promoted the Matamoros campaign. "We can calculate with certainty on our liberals," Johnson assured Lieutenant Governor Robinson. "The moment is appropriate and should not be lost and you may rely on my embracing it with every soldier that can be spared...[I]f we are not interfered with by the officers of the regular army . . . you may rely on all going well." When Johnson was not around, Grant frequently referred to himself as "acting commander" of the Matamoros assault force. The expedition, a disaster waiting to happen, now had four commanders in chief: Sam Houston, James Fannin, James Grant, and Frank Johnson.[24]

On January 3, 1836, with the blessing of the Council, Johnson ordered his men out of Béxar for Goliad, and James Grant accompanied them. When Houston arrived in Goliad on January 14, 1836, to assume command, he was too late. Johnson, Grant, and Fannin were all jockeying for position and seemed to enjoy the confidence of the troops. Houston had only contempt for Grant. "[H]as [he not] resided in Mexico for the last ten years?" he later wrote Governor Smith. "[D]oes he not own large possessions in the interior? . . . [Is] he not deeply interested in the . . . claims of land which hang like a murky cloud over the people of Texas? . . . [I]s he not the man who took from Bexar . . . cannon and other munitions of war, together with supplies necessary for the troops of that station, leaving wounded and the sick destitute of needful comforts?"[25]

Houston kept his own counsel and made no effort to pull rank on Fannin, Johnson, and Grant, joining the expedition as it marched south down the Atascosito Road, hoping for an opportunity to reassert his authority. It never came. He eventually abandoned all thoughts of command, but not before subtly sowing seeds of doubt in the troops.

Houston cautioned them about invading Matamoros, where the odds against success were short. The invasion army of several hundred men, short of supplies and ammunition, was to attack a city of twelve thousand people. If federalists did not rally to the rebels, Houston warned, the Texans were destined for hand-to-hand combat with enraged urban mobs. He also left a few tidbits intimating that land speculator James Grant might just be trying to recover his properties in Mexico, and he asked his men if they were willing to shed good red blood to green his pockets. And they could expect no forgiveness from Mexicans. Texas would die fighting far from home, he suggested, either in combat or at the end of a rope. If captured, Houston warned, the men would be treated as pirates, not as soldiers. "In war," he confided, "when spoil is the object, friends and enemies share one common destiny." Many men listened to "Old Sam." Within days, the Matamoros expedition fell apart, its warriors dispersing to fight other battles. Fannin replaced Sam Houston as commander in chief of the Army of the People, about-faced the Matamoros expedition, and marched his troops back up the Atascosito Road to Goliad. For the time being, the Revolution's center stage shifted to Béxar and the Alamo, on the Old San Antonio Road.[26]

*

While the the Matamoros expedition was self-destructing, Davy Crockett crossed the Sabine into Texas. Texans turned out for him in Nacogdoches and San Augustine, listening to his stories and telling him their own grand tale, the narratives of Texas and Mexico and the dream of independence. They told how they defeated General Cos in Béxar and how they had won other skirmishes. In Nacogdoches in mid-January he took the "oath of the government"—insisting that the word "republican" be inserted into his oath as the type of future government he would support—and thought it likely that he would get elected as a member of the convention to form "the Constitution of the Provence [sic]." Others in San Augustine felt the same way. One citizen wrote Lieutenant Governor James Robinson that Crockett "is To Represent them in the Convention."[27]

Without knowing exactly what he was getting into, he had been swept along. But into what? Land speculation? Politics? War? Revolution? Treason? In Crockett's mind they were probably all tied together. To get into politics, he had to take the oath. To get land, he had to volunteer to fight. And the sum total of the politics and fighting was revolution and perhaps even treason.

Of course, there was also a very good chance that Crockett would not have to fight at all. It was only a little more than a month since General Cos had surrendered, and though there were rumors that a bigger fight was brewing, no one knew that for certain. If Crockett was lucky, he might have missed the fighting but arrived in time to stand for election. In Nacogdoches he promised, if necessary, "to grin all the Mexicans out of Texas." That said, he set his sights on San Antonio de Béxar, some 280 miles southwest of Nacogdoches. Supported by other men who had taken the oath and called themselves the Tennessee Mounted Volunteers in Crockett's honor, the famed frontiersman and former congressman, who still probably nursed dreams of becoming president of the United States, rode west toward his destiny. It was the middle of January 1836. "Do not be uneasy about me," he had written his daughter. "I am among friends."[28]

Davy and his friends took a leisurely course south, roughly following the Old San Antonio Road, diverting along the way to track down big game and scout out good river bottomland. Accompanying Davy was Micajah Autry, a veteran of the War of 1812 who had become, successively, a farmer, schoolteacher, and lawyer in Tennessee. Autry also happened to be a talented musician and artist. Chasing land and opportunity, he had reached Nacogdoches, Texas, early in January 1836, and teamed up with Crockett. On the way to Béxar, Autry frequently wrote home, filling his wife, Martha, with high hopes. "I feel more energy than I ever did in anything I have undertaken. I am determined to provide you a home or perish." Autry knew what he was getting into, telling her a week later that the "war is still going on favourably to the Texans, but it is thought that Santa Anna will make a descent with his whole force in the Spring." Whatever the risk, for Autry, it was worth it. "I go to the whole Hog in the cause of Texas . . . for it is worth risking many lives for. . . . Be of good cheer Martha I will provide you a sweet home. I shall be entitled to 640 acres of land for my services in the army and 4444 acres upon condition of settling my family here."[29]

On the evening of January 11, 1836, Autry drew a shift of nighttime guard duty, and the two hours standing alone in the dark inspired hope

and nostalgia. The moon rose above the eastern horizon, and he wondered what the future might bring for his family. Two days later, he
penned a note to Martha: "We stand guard of nights and night before last
was mine to stand two hours during which the moon rose in all her . . .
majesty. . . . I imagined that you might be looking at her at the same time.
Farewell Dear Martha."[30]

Daniel Cloud, a Kentucky lawyer who rode for a time with Autry and
Crockett, shared those sentiments. Just before crossing the Sabine, he told
family members, "Next week, heaven willing, we shall breathe the air of
Texas. . . . If we succeed, a fertile region and a grateful people will be for
us our home and secure to us our reward. If we fail, death in defense of
so just and so good a cause need not excite a shudder or a tear."[31]

Farther down the Old San Antonio Road, the defenders of the Alamo
busied themselves preparing for a siege. When Frank Johnson and James
Grant had abandoned Béxar on January 3, 1836, they left behind a skele-
ton force of only 104 men under the command of Captain J. C. Neill. Before departing, Johnson stripped Béxar cleaner than a picked-over prairie
carcass, removing everything that the Matamoros expedition might need,
and could carry, for a strong offensive. For the men remaining, Neill was
a natural choice for command. A native of North Carolina, he had settled for a time in Alabama before moving his family to Texas in 1831. He
was forty-five years old in 1835, a veteran of the Creek war who had been
wounded at the battle of Horseshoe Bend. During his military service under General Andrew Jackson, he had acquired some expertise in artillery.
One Texan military veteran remembered him as "the first in our camp
whose experience was sufficient to mount and point a cannon at the enemies of Texas."[32]

Neill knew by experience that defending Béxar would be difficult, especially if the invaders enjoyed numerical superiority. General Cos had
been unable to hold Béxar even with numbers in his favor. Armed only
with a few brave men and high hopes, Neill decided that the best defense
required a retreat across the San Antonio River into the Alamo. Cos and
his men had left behind a stock of artillery pieces, and if the Texans could
install the batteries and strengthen the fortifications, they might be able
to hold off the Army of Operations—at least for a while. Perhaps the old
walls of the Alamo would protect them from destruction.

In 1718 Fray Antonio de Olivares, a Franciscan friar, had arrived to establish the San Antonio de Valero mission, and in 1724 he selected the Alamo site for the chapel and mission compound. Construction proceeded over the course of several decades, with the cornerstone of the chapel laid in 1744. Although the mission's purpose was to educate and convert local Indians, the work proved slow; by culture, economics, and inclination, the local tribes were loath to settle down, except for some Payaya, Jarame, and Pamaya peoples, who joined the new mission. After 1765 missionary activities declined, and they were abandoned altogether in 1793, when the mission was handed over to secular clergy. The Franciscan friars withdrew, secular priests replaced them, and the small community surrounding the former mission became a recognized, self-governing town.

In 1803 the abandoned mission became a military barracks when the Second Flying Company of San José y Santiago del Alamo de Parras, an element of Spain's colonial army, relocated there from Coahuila, Mexico. Some historians believe the site became known as the Alamo at that time; others insist that the term "Alamo" derives from *álamo*, the Spanish word for the cottonwood trees that grew abundantly on the banks of creeks and streambeds. The Alamo remained a military post of the Spanish and then the Mexican army until December 9, 1835, when General Martín Perfecto de Cos surrendered it to the rebels.[33]

Aware that he had to defend Béxar against a rumored Mexican advance up the Old San Antonio Road, Neill immediately put his men to work. Green Jameson, a native of either Kentucky or Tennessee with some engineering experience, supervised the project. It was a daunting task. Although Spanish and Mexican occupants had improved the Alamo's defenses over the course of a century, it was never intended to serve as a state-of-the-art military post, but merely to defend presidial troops against Indian attack. Its walls, for example, were rambling and irregular in height and width, bastion enough to repel Comanche and Apache arrows but not thick enough to defy modern, artillery-backed infantry. The Alamo could not survive a siege and assault without major engineering improvements. In a letter to Sam Houston, Jameson admitted as much: "You can plainly see by the plot that the Alamo never was built by a military people for a fortress." Still, he had plans for the old mission. "It is a strong place and better that it should remain as it is after completing the half moon batteries than to rebuild it."[34]

Jameson, Neill, and the garrison put in long days, seven days a week, strengthening the fortifications. The Alamo's longest continual wall faced west, toward Béxar, and had numerous windows and doors that had to be closed and barred. The Texans mounted the eighteen-pounder cannon on the southwestern corner and two other artillery pieces at the north-western corner. In order to create an opportunity for enfilade and cross fire against enemy troops, Neill also dug a deep semicircular trench on the outside center of the west wall, and with the excavated dirt erected a pal-isade. At an opening in the wall behind the earthen redoubt, the Texans mounted another cannon. The presence of the semicircular redoubt per-mitted riflemen, backed by artillery, to cut down invading infantry at a variety of firing angles. Outside the southwestern corner of the wall, just below the eighteen-pounder, the Texans began construction on another semicircular trench backed by a wooden stockade wall. Of course, the two semicircular redoubts outside the west wall also increased the Alamo's perimeter and, therefore, the need for troops.

The north wall, just a third of the length of the west wall, was in an ad-vanced state of deterioration and would have been an easy mark for ar-tillery bombardment. To reinforce it, an elaborate wood outerwork cribbing had been erected, with the open space between the wood and the wall filled with tons of dirt. Just outside, at the center of the north wall, the Texans dug another trench and erected another palisade, providing more opportunities for cross fire but also increasing the perimeter and the need for reinforcements. Atop the north wall, just above the earthen re-doubt, the Texans mounted three eight-pounder cannons.

The south wall, roughly equal in length to the north wall, consisted primarily of old buildings and the main gate to the Alamo compound. Housed in the buildings that formed the south wall were a room for the water well, a barracks for troops, and a jail cell. At the center of the south wall stood the Alamo's main gate, and to protect it, a trench had been dug and a lunette erected. The lunette, a semicircular fortified structure, was armed with three artillery pieces, one facing south, one east, and one west. Inside the main gate facing out, at point-blank range, was another mounted battery consisting of two artillery pieces.

To the east, the compound's perimeter consisted of two walls. The in-ner wall was actually less a wall than a series of one and two-story build-ings. At the southernmost point of the inner east wall stood the old mission convent building. Its second floor was used as a hospital and its ground floor as an armory. Next door to the old convent was a dilapidated building known as the long barracks, and from there, moving north, were a building to house infantry and then a series of small rooms providing a barracks for artillerymen. Behind the inner east wall buildings were a cattle pen and a horse corral, each separated by an interior wall and both enclosed by a low, outer six-to-ten-foot adobe wall. Inside the cattle pen was the compound's latrine. Mounted at the northeast corner of the horse corral was an artillery piece. Another was positioned at the same corner of the cattle pen. Outside the cattle pen's northeast corner, the Texans erected another semicircular palisade. The back of the Alamo chapel formed the southeast corner of the compound. The chapel was roofless and its interior was filled with debris. During the siege of the Alamo in November and December 1835, Cos's engineers had constructed a high, two-story platform and mounted a battery of three artillery pieces.

The compound's greatest weakness was a sixty-foot gap between the chapel and the south wall. Neill knew that a flood of Mexican infantry could pour through the breach. The Texans dug a trench across the opening and erected an earthen palisade fronted by an eight-foot-high wall of vertical timbers. Outside the palisades, they placed an abatis, or barrier, of fallen cottonwood trees, their outward-pointed limbs sharpened to cut up invaders. At the center of the palisade rested a single artillery piece.[35]

Jameson put everything he had into strengthening the Alamo, trying to turn what had once been a mission into a real fort, and after investing enormous amounts of personal energy in the project, he admired his work. The walls, trenches, palisades, abatis, redoubts, and artillery batteries inspired confidence, even hubris, and Jameson waxed eloquent about the Alamo's virtues, promising anyone who would listen that, if assaulted, the Texans would be able to "whip 10 to 1 with our artillery." He verged on the cardinal sin of military planners—not taking his enemy seriously. "The mexicans have shown imbecility and want of skill in this Fortress as they have done in all things else."[36]

Green Jameson may have been an engineer, but he was no military tactician; courage and confidence would not be enough to compensate for mathematical deficiencies. Santa Anna was bringing more than a ten-to-one numerical superiority, and the calculus of Alamo architecture spelled defeat. When General Cos surrendered back in December 1835, he had left behind nineteen artillery pieces, including a huge eighteen-pounder, all of which Neill and his men had hauled into the Alamo compound. The cannons, they presumed, would supply enough firepower to hold out against a besieging enemy. But with only 104 troops at his disposal, Neill was in trouble. Operating an artillery piece at maximum efficiency required a six-man crew; Neill needed 114 men just to keep cannonballs, grapeshot, and canister flying. He also had tactical problems defending the adobe- and stone-walled perimeter of the Alamo compound, which stretched more than a quarter of a mile in circumference. Positioning men at four-foot intervals around the perimeter would require at least another 350 troops. Neill and his garrison, almost as soon as Cos withdrew, recognized a critical need for reinforcements if the Alamo was to survive.

J. C. Neill was not nearly as sanguine as Green Jameson. He had seen combat in his day and remembered the damage that Andrew Jackson's troops had inflicted in 1814 on inadequate Cherokee defenses. Again and again, he tried to make a case for reinforcements. He faced an impossible situation, trying to motivate hungry men, many of them without adequate clothing or boots, who had not been paid in months. On January 14, 1836, he wrote Sam Houston pleading for help: "The men all under my command have been in the field for the last four months. They are almost naked. . . . There are at Laredo now 3,000 men under the command of General Ramírez . . . and . . . 1,000 of them are destined for this place. . . . We are in a torpid, defenseless condition. . . . I hope we will be reinforced in eight days, or we will be over-run by the enemy." Neill also wrote to the governor and the Council, begging them for food and supplies and complaining that he did not even have enough horses to send out reconnaissance patrols. "Unless we are reinforced and victualled, we must become an easy prey to the enemy."[37]

By mid-January, invasion rumors saturated Texas. A Mexican army was on the march. In retaliation for the defeat of his brother-in-law, to mete out revenge for the Anahuac disturbances, and to teach uppity, self-righteous Texans a lesson, Santa Anna was driving north in force, leading thousands of Mexican regulars in an overland invasion. Both a smaller army, under General José Urrea, advancing up the Atascosito Road, and a larger one, under *el presidente* himself, most likely coming up the Old San Antonio Road, were bound for Texas. "We have had loose discipline untill [sic] lately," Green Jameson wrote to Sam Houston from Béxar on January 18, 1836. "Since we heard of 1000 to 1500 men of the enemy being on their march to this place duty is being done well and punctually." Two days later, David Cummings learned in Gonzales that "letters have been intercepted to the Mexican citizens of Bexar informing them of the arrival of 2,000 troops on the Rio Grande, and now coming to retake that place in consequence of which, many of the Mexicans have secretly left the place."[38]

Alarmed at J. C. Neill's plight and the imminent invasion by Santa Anna, Acting Governor James Robinson rallied Texans to the fight, trying to encourage more militia and regular army enlistments and appealing to love of country, home, and family. "Rally then my brave countrymen," he proclaimed on January 19, "to the standard of constitutional liberty. . . . Your homes, your families, your country call, and who can refuse to obey. . . . March then . . . to the western frontier . . . where victory awaits you, and the genius of freedom spreads her banner. . . . [M]ake the tyrant feel the fiery sun of blazing, burning, consuming war. . . . [G]ive him 'war to the knife and knife to the hilt.'"[39]

In mid-January, while sorting out the Matamoros mess, Sam Houston reached a decision about Béxar. Worried that the resources of the Army of the People had been stretched too thin, and that defending both the Atascosito Road and the Old San Antonio Road might be impossible, he considered abandoning the Alamo and Béxar. "I have ordered the fortifications in the town of Bexar," he wrote Governor Henry Smith, "to be demolished, and, if you will think well of it, I will remove all the cannon and other munitions of war to Gonzales and Copano, blow up the Alamo and abandon the place, as it will be impossible to keep up the Station with volunteers." In other words, he was prepared to scuttle defense of the Old San Antonio Road and to concentrate his resources on the Atascosito Road, where he could protect the heart of Anglo Texas.[40]

To assess the situation in Béxar, Sam Houston turned to one of the few men he could trust—Jim Bowie. Although Bowie's reputation did not equal Crockett's, he was well known throughout the South. A native of Kentucky, Bowie had been raised in southeastern Louisiana, where his father cultivated sugarcane, cotton, and cattle, and traded in slaves. Like Crockett, the younger Bowie was an avid hunter and had a knack for wrestling alligators. Bowie grew up to be, in the words of his brother, "a stout, rather raw-boned man, of six feet height, weighed 180 pounds." He possessed a full head of sandy blond hair and steely gray eyes, "rather deep set in his head." After service in the War of 1812, Bowie spent a decade speculating in Louisiana real estate and playing fast and loose with the law, repeatedly resorting to forgery and counterfeiting to close deals. He also went into partnership with Jean Laffite, the Galveston-based pirate, who captured slave shipments in the Caribbean and sold them to Bowie, who then marketed them in Louisiana. Bowie spent money faster than he made it. "His style of living," remembered an associate, "was like a man who had plenty of money," but he was constantly fending off creditors.[41]

He also possessed a fierce temper, an exaggerated sense of personal honor, and an overpowering need for revenge. "He was a clever, polite gentleman," insisted a former friend and neighbor. "He was a true, constant, and generous friend, an open, bitter enemy, who scorned concealment, and any unfair advantage. He was a foe no one dared to undervalue, and many feared. . . . When fired by anger his face bore the semblance of an enraged tiger." Another friend warned that "it was his habit to settle all difficulties without regard to time or place, and it was the same whether he met one or many."

And there was that knife, the Bowie knife, that made Jim Bowie a household name throughout the Deep South. In 1826, after Bowie got into a violent argument with Sheriff Norris Wright of Rapides Parish, he acquired and wore a huge hunting knife capable of butchering man or beast. One year later, on a sandbar in the Mississippi River near Natchez, Bowie was acting as a second at a duel between Samuel Wells and Thomas Maddox. Neither man was hit in the first exchange of fire, but observers then got into a quarrel and more shots were fired. In the ensuing melee, Sheriff Wright decided to finish off Bowie. He put a bullet through Bowie's chest. The wounded Bowie went after Wright on foot, and two of Wright's friends shot Bowie in the leg and stabbed him several times. Known to his friends as a man of "great will power, unbending firmness of purpose, and unflinching courage," Bowie would not give up the chase and finally caught up with Wright. Weakened by bullets through his lung and thigh, a savage blow to the head, and seven deep stab wounds, he still managed to grab hold of Wright and thrust the long knife into the man's chest. Bowie later boasted that he had "twisted it to cut the heart strings."

News of the "Sandbar Fight" got into the regional newspapers and turned the Bowie knife into a Southern icon, elevating Bowie to heroic status as a man beyond intimidation, ready to defend his honor with the blade and feeling no remorse about drawing another's blood. The story soon billowed into mythology, transfiguring Bowie into the country's greatest knife fighter, which endeared him to frontiersmen and Southern brawlers everywhere. Throughout Louisiana, Mississippi, Kentucky, and Louisiana, blacksmiths received orders for the Bowie knife, and Bowie enjoyed free drinks in any bar, tavern, or saloon in the country. Sam Houston picked him to relieve Béxar partly because Bowie would already enjoy respect among the recent Anglo settlers of Texas.

But he also knew that Bowie had good Tejano contacts. In 1830, Bowie had filed for Mexican citizenship and large Mexican land grants, and he purchased a textile mill in Coahuila. Early in 1831, he married Ursula de Veramendi, daughter of one of Béxar's more prominent families, and they settled in San Antonio. Bowie spent much of his time searching for lost gold mines and killing Indians, but the marriage to a Veramendi still brought him into the Tejano community. Juan Seguín remembered that Bowie "was known among the Mexicans from Saltillo to Béxar." Many Tejanos loved Bowie, and just as many loathed him as *"fanfarrón Santiago Bowie"* ("James Bowie the braggart"). But like him or not, Seguín remembered, Tejanos "knew that he was absolutely brave, and that they could depend upon his being fair to foe and loyal to friends."

In 1833, however, Bowie's fortunes turned. A bout with malaria or yellow fever almost killed him, and a case of cholera took his wife and her father, the influential Juan Martín de Veramendi. With their demise, Bowie lost much of his political capital in Tejano Texas, and whatever money he had accumulated had long since disappeared into a bottomless pit of bad debts and expensive lawsuits. Bowie continued to dabble in land speculation, but in 1835 he had to flee Monclova when Santa Anna ordered the arrest of all Texas businessmen operating there. Bowie returned to Texas in a belligerent mood, traveling back and forth between Nacogdoches and San Felipe de Austin as a spokesman for the War Party, urging independence from Mexico. He led Texan troops at the battles of Concepción and Béxar late in 1835. A veteran acknowledged that "Bowie was a born leader . . . never needlessly spending a bullet or imperiling a life. His voice is still ringing in my old deaf ears as he repeatedly admonished us, 'Keep under cover boys and reserve your fire; we haven't a man to spare.'"[42]

Bowie and his thirty or so volunteers wasted no time, riding into town on January 19, 1836, prepared to follow up on Houston's orders, if necessary, to blow up the Alamo and withdraw to the east. Bowie conveyed those orders to Neill, who agreed, if "trams could be obtained here by any means to remove the Cannon and Public Property I would immediately destroy the fortification and abandon the place." But Governor Smith never ordered the demolition, and when Bowie saw the Alamo, he took note of the improvements. He was quite familiar with the compound, having lived in Béxar for years and having battled Cos and the Mexicans during the siege of 1835. He immediately joined in the effort to strengthen the fortifications, assuring Governor Smith that "we are still labouring night and day, laying up provisions for a siege, encouraging our men, and calling on the government for relief." Bowie heaped praise on J. C. Neill. "I cannot eulogise the conduct & character of Col Neill too highly. [N]o other man in the army could have kept men at this post, under the neglect they have experienced." Perhaps Bowie believed Green Jameson's predictions and decided that the Alamo could repel Santa Anna. Perhaps he was just happy to be home again. In any event, he made a final decision. "Col. Neill & Myself have come to the solemn resolution that we will rather die in these ditches than give it up to the enemy."[43]

The Texans faced two enemies—Santa Anna and a government unwilling or unable to assist its own soldiers. Although Neill had a difficult time distinguishing between rumor and fact, he nevertheless knew that the Army of Operations was steadily marching north. On January 23, 1836, he wrote the governor and Council, "Santa Anna has arrived at Saltillo with Three thousand troops, also . . . there are at the town of Rio Grande Sixteen hundred more. . . . [H]e says that he will reduce [Texas] to the State it originally was in 1820." The Council's neglect raised an even darker cloud. Endemic feuding rendered the provisional government impotent and discouraged the rebel army. Neill wrote to the governor and the Council that he had received their "despatches . . . and [am] truly astonished to find your body in such a disorganised situation—Such interruptions in The General Council of Texas have bad tendancies—they create distrust & alarm. . . . Our Govt.

appears to be without a legitimate head." Sam Houston echoed Neill's frustration. In a letter to Governor Smith, he wrote, "I trust sincerely, that the first day of March may establish a government on some permanent foundation. If this state of things cannot be achieved, the country must be lost." William Travis agreed. "Our affairs are gloomy indeed," he wrote on January 28. "The people are cold and indifferent. They are worn down and exhausted with the war, and, in consequence of dissensions between contending and rival chieftans, they have lost all confidence in their own government."[44]

When he was not lamenting the provisional government's demise, Neill was begging anybody and everybody for help—money, ammunition, livestock, grain, and troops. Couriers bearing requests left Béxar with alarming regularity. On January 28, Neill asked that the "efforts of the government be all concentrated and directed to the support and preservation of this town, that supplies of Beef, pork, hogs, salt etc be forthwith forwarded . . . men, money, rifles and cannon powder are also necessary." His requests produced nothing of use. Five days later Jim Bowie tried his hand with the governor: "*Relief* at this post, in men, money, & provisions is of *vital* importance & is wanted instantly. . . . The salvation of Texas depends in great measure in keeping Bejar out of the hands of the enemy." Men of fainter heart would have left long before the Army of Operations forded the Rio Grande.[45]

Two days after Bowie arrived in Béxar, William Barret Travis received his marching orders. Responding to J. C. Neill's inability to send out cavalry reconnaissance patrols, Governor Smith directed Travis to raise up a company of one hundred volunteers and reinforce Béxar. The government issued him a measly $100 for supplies. During the next six days, Travis found it easier to secure provisions than volunteers. On January 24, when he threw saddlebags, with *Wm. Travis* hand-carved into the flaps, over his horse, Travis counted only twenty-six men with him. They were short of food, equipment, ammunition, clothing, and confidence. "I have done every thing in my power to get ready to march to the relief of Bexar," he wrote Smith. "I shall however, go on & do my duty." Riding with a couple of dozen men into an army of thousands of Mexicans gave him more than a little pause for thought. Travis soon wrote Smith again, requesting that he "recall the order for me to go on to Bexar in command of so few men. I am unwilling to risk my reputation (which is ever dear to a soldier) by going off into the enemie's country with such little means, so few men, & them too badly equipped." Smith was either not listening or just unable to help, and Travis pushed on, arriving in Béxar on February 3.[46]

Crockett and his companions lingered for two days at Washington-on-the-Brazos, from January 22 to 24, where they learned that Santa Anna and the Army of Operations might already be approaching the Texas end of the Old San Antonio Road. He knew that a small band of Texans stood at Béxar, and he headed for the fray to the southwest. At each stop along the Old San Antonio Road, Texans hailed the folk hero. "Few could eclipse him in conversation," remembered John Swisher, with whom Crockett spent a few days. "He was fond of talking, and had an ease and grace about him which, added to his strong natural sense and the fund of anecdotes that he had gathered, rendered him irresistible." Like most other Anglo immigrants arriving in Texas during the last act of the revolutionary drama, Crockett had only the most muddled sense of the politics involved. He and his traveling companions passed through Gonzales, briefly considered proceeding on to Goliad, but finally veered southwest for Béxar. Crockett arrived around February 5, welcomed like a conquering hero.[47]

While hoping for a flood of reinforcements, J. C. Neill got only a trickle. He worried about the future. His men were ill clothed, ill fed, ill paid, and ill prepared; an army of thousands had its sight on the Alamo; and the provisional government was in complete disarray. If Santa Anna arrived before the government got its act together, the Alamo—and perhaps Texas—was doomed.[48]

On February 11, 1836, Neill learned that sickness had befallen his family, and he left Béxar to care for them. His departure underlined the garrison's sense of foreboding. Neill had been indefatigable in attending to the Alamo and rallying his men, and they missed him. In a letter to Governor Henry Smith, a dejected Green Jameson wrote, "Col Neill left today for home on account of an express from his family informing him of their ill health. There was great regret at his departure by all of the men though he promised to be with us in 20 days at furtherest." Actually, the defenders still had twenty-three days of life left, but Neill got delayed. He attended to his family's needs and hustled up $90 of his own money to buy provisions for his brothers in arms, but Santa Anna reached Béxar before he could return.[49]

Neill awarded command of the Alamo to William Travis, who held a regular commission in the Army of the People, but the volunteers in the garrison refused to accept him. He was no doubt too formal for them, a man who preferred uniforms to buckskins and felt hats to coonskins, a man of books and learning, a lawyer whom they found a bit self-absorbed. True, he *was* a Southern boy from Edgefield, South Carolina, but he was also a regular officer and thus not to be trusted, someone appointed by a distant, invisible elite. They had become accustomed to choosing their own officers. And most of them had never seen Travis in battle. The volunteers were willing to stand, fight, and die, but only under the command of one of their own. They knew Jim Bowie and rallied to him.[50]

Suddenly Travis found himself balancing on a political tightrope, enjoying the command but not the confidence of his troops. "My situation is truly awkward & delicate," he wrote Governor Smith. The Army of the People, a largely voluntary organization, had all the permanence of clouds, coming and going to rhythms of their own. With no pay and little enough food, the soldiers complained constantly and departed frequently. In mid-January, when he first appealed for help, Neill had warned Sam Houston that among his poverty-stricken troops, "almost every one of them speaks of going home, and not less than twenty will leave tomorrow." One month later, nothing had improved. Travis and Bowie warned Governor Smith that "it is useless to talk of keeping up the garrison any longer without money as we believe that unless we receive some shortly the men will leave." To keep the garrison intact, Travis agreed to a formal election. The results left him in command of regular troops and cavalry and Bowie in charge of the volunteer companies.[51]

A little authority went quickly to Bowie's head, as did too much corn liquor. Travis complained that since Bowie's "election he has been roaring drunk all the time; has assumed all command—& is proceeding in a most disorderly and irregular manner." Frustrated with the exodus of Béxareño families, who knew of Santa Anna's advance and his vengeful reputation, Bowie on February 12 ordered them to halt and seized the property of those who refused to do so. He also forced local authorities to release his friends from jail—Tejanos and Anglos. "Things passd on this way yesterday & to-day until at length they have become intolerable," J. J. Baugh wrote to Governor Smith. At one point, when Judge Erasmo Seguín refused to obey Bowie's order to release a prisoner, Bowie "sent to the Alamo for troops and they immediately paraded in the Square, *under Arms,* in a tumultuously and disorderly manner, Bowie, himself, and many of his men, being drunk which has been the case ever since he has been in command." Feelings between Travis's contingent and Bowie's chafed into raw resentment. "There was a bitter feeling between the partisans of Travis and Bowie, the latter being the choice of the rougher party in the garrison," remembered a veteran. To make sure that he was not implicated in Bowie's antics, and to keep a civil war from erupting within the Alamo, Travis took his own troops on patrol out of Béxar and south to the Medina River.[52]

Into such chaos came news of the invasion. Juan Seguín's Tejano patrols reported that elements of the Army of Operations had reached the Rio Grande River and would soon be moving on Béxar. Travis anticipated Santa Anna's arrival around March 15 and knew he had to resolve the feuding within the Alamo garrison. When Bowie woke up on the morning of February 14, bleary eyed and hungover, he realized that he had gone too far the day before, acting more like the leader of a mob than of an army. He approached Travis contritely, or at least as contritely as Jim Bowie could ever act, and negotiated a rapprochement. Until Neill returned and resumed command, Travis would continue with the regulars and Bowie with the volunteers, but they would both countersign all orders and correspondence. To make sure that things remained under control, Travis's men quartered themselves in town and Bowie's stayed in the Alamo. Bowie also apologized to Judge Seguín.[53]

During the next week, Travis and Bowie picked up where Neill left off, continuing to work on the fortifications and appealing for help. They ordered wells dug, trenches excavated, scouts deployed, missives dispatched, recruiters assigned, and scroungers sent out to forage. On February 16 or 17, Travis sent out a series of letters with James Butler Bonham, hoping Bonham would be able to drum up support from Governor Smith, Acting Governor Robinson, the Council, Sam Houston, James Fannin, Frank Johnson, James Grant, or anybody else who might be helpful. Travis trusted Bonham, who was also from Edgefield, South Carolina, and also a lawyer. Bonham had spunk and determination. In

October 1835, he had led a pro-Texas rally in Montgomery, Alabama, trying to generate money and volunteers for Texas, and he quickly bought into his own words, organizing the Mobile Grays, a volunteer militia company, and leading them across the Sabine. He reached Texas in November 1835 and opened a law office in Brazoria. But with war afoot, he had little interest in deeds, debts, or dockets. By early January 1836, Bonham had joined the Matamoros expedition, and when Sam Houston ordered Bowie to the Alamo, Bonham went along, entering the compound on January 19.[54]

Perhaps more than anyone else inside the Alamo, Travis realized that no amount of courage or willpower could compensate for shortages of food, boots, clothing, and ammunition. Even before being ordered to the Alamo, he had written Sam Houston, pleading for five hundred troops, more money, and more provisions. "Enthusiasm may keep up an army for a few days," he told the general, "but *money,* and money alone, will support an army for regular warfare." The missive Bonham carried east to Governor Smith bore the same message: "I hope your Excelly. will send us a portion of the money, which has been received from the U.S. as it cannot be better applied, indeed we cannot get along any longer without Money: and with it we can do every thing." Travis ended his letter eloquently: "Should we receive no reinforcements, I am determined to defend it to the last, and, should Bejar fall, our friends will be buried beneath its ruins."[55]

After February 18, rumors concerning the Army of Operations darted around Béxar. Santa Anna was said to be here, and Ramírez y Sesma there. Tolsa was on the move and Gaona was closing in fast. Urrea, according to the reports, was advancing rapidly, and Filisola was on his way too. Travis and Bowie discounted many of the stories as Tejano hyperbole, but the steady exodus of Béxareños lent some credibility to them. Did they know something the Texans did not? On Saturday, February 20, Juan Seguín informed Travis that General Ramírez y Sesma's army had crossed the Rio Grande and was on its way. Travis and Bowie summoned a council of war, at which the garrison's officers discussed the credibility of the report. Still convinced that the Army of Operations was at least two weeks away, they adjourned the meeting without making any decision.[56]

Sunday, February 21, 1836, passed quietly, except that Seguín asked

Travis and Bowie to issue furloughs to Tejano troopers whose farms and ranches lay south along the Old San Antonio Road. The Tejano troopers worried about Santa Anna's capricious moods and whether he planned to take out his anger on women and children. Zacatecas still loomed large on the horizon of Texas. Travis did not want to spare the men. Yet neither could he deny them the right to protect their own families. "I think a distinction ought to be made between those who lost property while in our service and those who were against us or were neutral," he told a Tejano friend. Later in the day and early Monday morning, perhaps a dozen of Seguín's men left Béxar and headed home, each with Travis's blessing.[57]

Monday, February 22, dawned with wet, cloudy skies, and throughout the day thunderstorms drenched Béxar. Still, it was a perfect day to ponder the meaning of liberty. Throughout the United States, patriots celebrated George Washington's birthday, and as they hailed the father of their country, thoughts of nation building must have drifted across Texas. Of course, nobody in Texas came close to filling George Washington's shoes; the leading politicians picked at one another constantly, and the Army of the People suffered from endemic command and control problems. In Béxar, Jim Bowie and William Travis still jockeyed to lead a mixed regiment of regulars and volunteers; James Grant and Frank Johnson commanded small clusters of troops in and around San Patricio; James Fannin, with nearly four hundred troops, stuck close to Goliad; and Sam Houston, supposedly the commander in chief, was without an army. In fact, nobody was in charge politically, since the Council had dissolved and two men—Henry Smith and James W. Robinson—claimed to be governor.

But a holiday was a holiday. A cloudburst early in the afternoon gave the air a fresh, clean smell, and after dinner, unaware that Antonio López de Santa Anna and the forward elements of his army were already at the Medina River, the Texans gathered at Domingo Bustillo's place on Soledad Street for a fandango celebrating Washington's birthday. Not that they needed the excuse. At the drop of a hat, the Texans were ready for revelry—cards, craps, and corn liquor, singing and dancing, practical jokes and outlandish tales, and perhaps even a quiet interlude upstairs or even in a barn with some willing señoritas.

Tejanos in Béxar were no less ready to have fun. The fandango, a popular dance among Mexican peasants and urban workers, had roots reaching deep into medieval Spain, and by the 1830s "fandango" was often used synonymously with "fiesta." Although the exact nature of the celebration that night is unknown, it no doubt resembled a typical Mexican fandango. Word of its location spread throughout a community, and at the appointed time, a band of musicians—equipped with brass instruments, guitars, harps, and primitive accordions—struck up some tunes announcing the beginning of the festivities. Men and women then walked to the party. The dancing took place indoors and outdoors, depending upon the size of the crowd and the weather. Couples would face each other with hands elevated, and synchronizing with the rhythms of the music, would step lightly toward each other and just as lightly back, and then around and around, chemises twirling with the turns and revealing the colored petticoats.[58]

Béxareños and Anglos flocked to the party on Soledad Street, with charcoal braziers cooking. The Texans, with plenty of beef roasting and fiddles playing, danced Kentucky, Tennessee, and Virginia reels and tried their feet on guitar-driven Mexican dances. They shared cigarettes with Mexican women, ate barbecued steaks, beef ribs, enchiladas, and tamales, and downed enough corn liquor to blur their vision, puff their egos, and loosen their tongues. Jim Bowie probably declined on his invitation. Too many bullet holes, too many stab wounds, and too much corn mash had taken their toll on his constitution. He had fallen ill. A high fever was coming on, along with chills, aches, pains, and fatigue. But Crockett was there playing the fiddle and regaling everyone with his tall tales, double entendres, and political satire. Even Travis probably left some of his stiff demeanor behind at his quarters and enjoyed a good time.

They celebrated into the early morning hours. Rumors later insisted that on the evening of February 22, 1836, Santa Anna had entered Béxar incognito, made his way in disguise down Soledad Street, and even idled away some time at the fandango, taking the measure of his foe and concluding that there was little to fear. Men who danced with an enemy at the gates need not be taken seriously. The rumors were undoubtedly false, but Santa Anna was not far away. All day he had contemplated, from his redoubt on the Medina, a surprise attack on Béxar, where he hoped to capture or kill the rebels before they could get behind the Alamo's walls. But the day's cloudbursts had filled the river, and his army was delayed until the raging torrent subsided and fording was easier. Without the rain, there might never have been a siege of the Alamo. In the wee hours of February 23, 1836, Travis, Bowie, Crockett, and the boys collapsed into their beds. It would be the last good night's sleep they would ever get.[59]

5

"VICTORY OR DEATH"

PERHAPS TRAVIS AND A FEW OTHERS had some vague sense that something was different when they were awoken early on February 23 by the sound of horses and wagons and Spanish voices drifting down the streets of the town and heading toward the open country to the north and east. Tejano Béxar was on the move in much greater volume than before, and the creaking carts, lowing oxen, and neighing horses made it hard to miss. Those with carts had them packed full; those on foot carried supplies on their shoulders. Although Travis had other concerns to occupy his attention, he was troubled by the rapid and unexpected exodus. He had his soldiers detain a few peripatetic stragglers for questioning.[1]

He asked some where they were going, and they answered evasively, talking about the need to begin spring planting. Unsatisfied, Travis had a few arrested, but that tactic also failed to loosen their tongues. Finally, Nathaniel Lewis, a local merchant, told Travis what every Tejano seemed to know: a Mexican army had been sighted at León Creek, less than eight miles southwest of Béxar. They were coming, and the Tejanos had been warned. Exactly how and by whom was uncertain. José María Rodríguez, a child in 1836, long afterward recalled that early in the morning of February 23 a man named "Rivas called at our home and told us that he had seen Santa Anna in disguise the night before looking in on a *fandango* on Soledad Street." Rodríguez's father was away "with General Houston's army," but his mother made the decision to bury their money in the clay floor of their home, pack their goods into oxcarts, and go to the ranch of Doña Santos Ximénes.[2]

Rodríguez's memories, though seventy-five years after the event, probably faithfully captured the mood of Béxar that morning. Rumors of Santa Anna sighting, always inaccurate, mixed with reports of the size of the army, always exaggerated. Added together they equaled fear. Any unrecognized man in a poncho and a broad-brimmed hat might be Santa Anna, and an army of ten thousand, fifteen thousand, twenty thousand, or more was on the outskirts of town. Remember what happened in Zacatecas the year before, or after the 1813 insurrection in Béxar itself. If the army was coming, local wisdom dictated that every resident of Béxar should scurry out of harm's way.

At first Travis was unconvinced, but after a few more reports he took precautions. Accompanied by John Sutherland and a few other men, Travis climbed to the belfry of the San Fernando Church between the Main Plaza and the Military Plaza and squinted toward the southwest. Nothing. But to be on the safe side he posted a reliable man as a sentinel with orders to ring the bell if he spied the enemy. Hours passed. Travis looked after other affairs. Then in the early afternoon the bell clanged wildly. Once again Travis scaled to the top of the square tower, glared out into the sun, and saw nothing save a wide prairie broken by patches of mesquite and thickets of chaparral. But the sentinel insisted that he had seen Mexican soldiers out there in the direction of the sun. They had simply disappeared in the bushwood.[3]

Sutherland wanted to ride out and take a look, and Travis agreed that he should take John W. Smith, a local carpenter who knew the country, and reconnoiter the area along the Laredo Road. Sutherland told Travis if "he saw us returning in any other gait than a slow pace, he might be sure that we had seen the enemy."

If Sutherland and Smith took the Laredo Road, they rode directly south. At the same moment, the vanguard of Santa Anna's army was approaching Béxar from the southwest. The night before, the Vanguard Brigade under General Joaquín Ramírez y Sesma had camped along the Alazon Creek, above which a ridgeline afforded the view of the entire San

Antonio River Valley. There he could only watch the heavy rains foil hopes of taking the town unprepared. Santa Anna would later write that had the surprise attack taken place it "would have saved the time consumed and the blood shed later in taking of the Alamo."[4]

Crossing over the crest of the slope, Sutherland and Smith got a good look at what the sentinel had seen only at a distance. There must have been fifteen hundred soldiers, Sutherland later remembered, "their polished armor glistening in the rays of the sun, as they formed in a line between the *chaparral* and the mesquite bushes." In 1836 Mexican soldiers were not wearing breastplates, so no armor glistened in the sun, but Sutherland did not spend much time looking. He and Smith wheeled their horses and spurred north. In a moment, however, Sutherland was on the ground. His horse had slipped in the mud, thrown him, and rolled on top of his leg. Smith helped his dazed companion back onto the saddle and they rode hard into Béxar.

The confirmation that the Mexicans were coming in force sent another wave of panic through the town. Travis ordered his men to cross the San Antonio River and take cover in the Alamo. Herding cattle before them and raiding *jacales*—poor people's shacks—along the way for corn and supplies, they moved in an orderly fashion toward the old mission. Juan Seguín, one of the Tejano revolutionary leaders, recalled that as the Texans walked east on Potero Street toward the river, women stood by watching and exclaiming, "Poor fellows you will all be killed, what shall we do?"[5]

Travis was wondering the same thing. He had a force of about 150 men, a loose collection of volunteers and regular army, under the joint command of himself and Bowie. In his group were colonels, captains, lieutenants, and sergeants—designations that were hardly based on any sort of education or training. In truth, he had a body of men, a group of patriots and adventurers, among whom were some natural leaders like David Crockett, James Bowie, Juan Seguín, William C. M. Baker, and William Blazeby, but none were experienced officers.

Even more than officers, Travis needed men, and he needed them fast. Seeing that Sutherland was too injured from his fall to be of much use, at 3 P.M. Travis penned a hasty note to Andrew Ponton in Gonzales and sent him off with it. "The enemy in large force is in sight," he wrote. "We need men and provisions. Send them to us. We have 150 men and are determined to defend the Alamo to the last. Give us assistance." Later he wrote a similar note to James Fannin in Goliad, promising to "make such a resistance as is due to our honour, and that of the country, until we can get assistance from you, which we expect you to forward immediately." It was an urgent message, more an order than a request. Travis, determined *"never to retreat,"* deemed "it unnecessary to repeat to a brave officer, who knows his duty" that he needed help, but he wrote it nonetheless.[6]

While the Texans occupied the Alamo, Santa Anna's Vanguard Brigade marched into Béxar. "I will never forget how that army looked as it swept into town," Juan Díaz recalled. "At the head of the soldiers came the regimental band, playing the liveliest airs, and with the band came a squad of men bearing the flags and banners of Mexico and an immense image that looked like an alligator's head." Thousands of Mexican soldiers had moved into Béxar that afternoon, and what they saw confirmed the rebellious nature of the Texans. Above the Military Plaza, and then the Alamo, flapped a tricolor flag with two stars. The stars represented Coahuila and Texas, and the flag signified that the Texans were in rebellion against Santa Anna's violations of the Mexican constitution. Answering flag with flag, Santa Anna ordered a blood red flag raised on the bell tower of the San Fernando Church, a mere thousand yards from the Alamo. In the center of the flag were the skull and crossbones. The flag meant no quarter, no surrender, no mercy—death for every man who opposed the Mexican government. The Texas rebels, Santa Anna believed, were filibusterers, pirates, and traitors, not soldiers of an established nation, and would be treated accordingly.[7]

The Texans inside the Alamo responded to the flag with a blast from their eighteen-pounder. If Santa Anna wanted a battle without quarter, then so be it. The Texans were ready, just as they had been a few months before when Cos occupied the Alamo. The ball landed harmlessly in the town, raising dust and hurting no one, but the action was an eloquent note of defiance. Santa Anna answered fire with fire. Two Mexican howitzers rained four grenades toward the Alamo. Several shells exploded inside the fort but did no real damage. From inside the Alamo a new flag stretched above the west wall. A white flag. The Texans wanted to talk. Santa Anna responded by ordering a parley sounded.[8]

Talk, yes—but about what? Both Texans and Mexicans were confused about the exact order of the opening sequence of events. Did the Texans fire first, or did the Mexicans? Was the red flag misinterpreted? Had Santa Anna sounded a parley during engagements, or even before the first shot? Someone inside the Alamo told Bowie that he distinctly heard the notes of a parley, and Bowie ripped a page out of a child's copybook and scribbled a hurried message to Santa Anna asking for clarification. "I wish, Sir, to ascertain if it be true that a parlay was called, for which reason I send my second aid, [Green B.] Benito Jameson, under guarantee of a white flag which I believe will be respected by you and your forces." "Dios y Mexico," he ended his note, but after second thoughts he crossed it out and penned, "God and Texas!" Though ill and in a ticklish military situation, he still wanted Santa Anna to know that he was not a man to bend. "God and Texas" said it nicely.[9]

Santa Anna was above answering a rebel. He refused to meet—let alone negotiate with—Jameson. Instead, he instructed aide-de-camp Colonel José Batres to answer Bowie. "I reply to you, according to the order of his Excellency, that the Mexican army cannot come to terms under any conditions with rebellious foreigners to whom there is no other recourse left, if they wish to save their lives, than to place themselves immediately at the disposal of the Supreme Government from whom alone they may expect clemency after some considerations are taken up. God and Liberty!"[10]

The reply was pregnant with possibilities. Though its general tone was tough, it was by no means a blood-red flag. A phrase like "if they wish to save their lives" and a word like "clemency" sounded vaguely hopeful. But what about "after some considerations are taken up"? What did that mean? Perhaps that most of the Texans would be pardoned but their leaders—certainly hotheaded Travis and traitorous Bowie—would be put to the sword? Bowie undoubtedly read the reply under the lamp of history. The Texans had treated Cos decently, but Zacatecas suggested that the Mexicans would not do the same to them.

Bowie and Travis were following independent courses. Bowie signed his note "Commander of the volunteers of Bexar," distancing himself from the regular army, and acted without consulting his cocommander. Now Travis wanted a parley of his own, and he sent Albert Martin to speak for him. Since his arrival in Texas via Tennessee and New Orleans, Martin had been deeply involved in the independence movement, and Travis trusted him completely. He rode out to the parley site on the banks of the San Antonio, meeting with Colonel Juan N. Almonte and several other Mexican soldiers. Educated in America and fluent in English, Almonte, perhaps, might be sympathetic with the Texans. Martin brought a verbal message from Travis: if the Mexicans wanted to negotiate terms, Travis "would receive [him] with much pleasure." As one Mexican source later recalled, Travis wanted respect for himself and his army, asserting that he would surrender the fort if he and his men could march out and join their government, as they had allowed Cos to do. If those terms were not met, he would stay put and fight.[11]

Almonte may have been sympathetic, but he was not stupid enough to alienate his commander by promising generous terms he could not deliver. He answered that "it did not become the Mexican Government to make any propositions through me, and that I only had permission to hear such as might be made on part of the rebels." Nothing had changed. Santa Anna had stated his position in the Batres communication: surrender without terms. There was not much more to say. Martin took the message back to Travis, who sent word back to Almonte that he would consider it. If the unbending terms were acceptable, Travis would communicate this to Almonte. If they were unacceptable, he would fire a cannon.

Travis probably knew he had sent Martin on a fool's errand, that if Santa Anna would not budge on his terms for Bowie, the dictator would certainly not bend for him. Perhaps he simply wanted more propaganda ammunition to take to his men, to fire them with resolve and get their blood up for a fight. Juan Seguín later recalled that shortly after Martin returned, Travis gave an incendiary speech to the garrison, reminding them why they were fighting and what to expect if they were defeated. They were fighting for Texas and their families, for their God-given rights and their futures—and for their lives. The blood red flag told them as much. This said, he ordered a cannon shot.[12]

The next day in an open letter addressed to "the People of Texas & all Americans in the world," he explained the position of the men in the Alamo: "The enemy has demanded a surrender at discretion, otherwise, the garrison are to be put to the sword, if the fort is taken. I have answered the demand with a cannon shot, & our flag still waves proudly from the walls. *I shall never surrender or retreat.*" In language unambiguous and defiant, he challenged his countrymen in Texas and the

United States to support his cause. "I call on you in the name of Liberty, of patriotism & every thing dear to the American character, to come to our aid with all dispatch. . . . If this call is neglected, I am determined to sustain myself as long as possible & die like a soldier who never forgets what is due his own honor & that of his country." He ended the letter, "VICTORY or DEATH."[13]

Travis had crossed his own private Rubicon. He would not waver from the position he took on February 23. Now it was time to hunker down and wait. Several things he knew with certainty. First, the Alamo was not a particularly defensible fortress. As military historian Stephen L. Hardin observed, "By the standards of the day, the Alamo was certainly no fortress. It lacked mutually supporting strong points—demilunes, bastions, hornworks, ravelines, sally ports, and the like. There were simply no strong points from which its defenders could oppose an assault." In addition, the walls had no firing ports, which meant the defenders would have to expose their upper bodies when they manned the Alamo. Travis and Bowie knew the weaknesses of their haven and understood that the Mexicans had the cannons to destroy the Alamo. They chose to stand their ground nonetheless.

Second, even if the Alamo had been defensible against siege weapons, Travis did not have enough soldiers to defend it. Needing five hundred soldiers to man the perimeter, he had about 150 to 160. And not only did he have too few men to defend the walls, he had too few cannoneers to fire all the cannons.

Third, even if the Alamo had been a defensible structure and Travis had had enough men to defend it, the garrison lacked food, supplies, and gunpowder to hold out against a protracted siege. Never expecting Santa Anna to mount such an early offensive, the defenders had not stockpiled the necessary supplies. Instead, as they moved to the Alamo they requisitioned what they could find, an unfortunate way to begin a defense against a siege. Nonetheless, Travis chose to stay and fight.[14]

Santa Anna had problems of his own. If time was not on the Texans' side, it was not on his either. His forces were like a pearl necklace strung out over miles and days of south Texas territory. When he took his position in Béxar on February 23, his heavy siege guns were days behind. In theory General Vicente Filisola was right: "By merely placing twenty artillery pieces properly, that poor wall could not have withstood one hour of cannon fire without being reduced to rubble." But Santa Anna needed time for the heavy cannons to arrive and to dig the trenches to get them into proper position. And time could change everything. Time could mean reinforcements for the Alamo. The thought that Texans were on the march toward Béxar concerned Santa Anna more than his eventual confrontation with the men inside the walls, and he sent General Ventura Mora and a cavalry detachment to scout the land to the east and north. Santa Anna was under no illusions about where most Texans stood. He was an invader in enemy territory, far from the center of Mexico and closer to the border of the United States.[15]

Santa Anna in Béxar and Travis and Bowie inside the Alamo had begun the elaborate and deadly game of war. Santa Anna had the numbers and the experience; Travis and Bowie had the advantage of a defensive position. For the moment, it was a game of waiting. But like every important contest, smaller games took place within the larger one. The blood red flag, for instance, was more than just a message. It was a psychological weapon.

That night, and during the following nights of the siege, Santa Anna maintained the psychological pressure. Like other military leaders he knew that lack of sleep would drain resolve and make brave men question their commitment to any cause. On the first night he kept the Texans alert by periodic shelling of their position. Then when darkness fell on the second day, he ordered his band to serenade the defenders, and Mexican music filled the night air. Then without warning the music would stop and hollow iron balls filled with black powder would rain into the Alamo, exploding when they hit the ground and spraying fragments. Then more music. The next time it stopped, the Mexicans might cry out and fire their muskets as if they were attacking or destroying a band of reinforcements bound for the Alamo. All sound and fury signifying nothing, perhaps, but it was enough to keep any man with an imagination awake and wondering. Were the Mexicans attacking? Would they attack that night? When would they attack? Questions began to replace sleep.[16]

Those men inside the Alamo who had slept at all through the first night's activities awoke on Wednesday, February 24, to an overcast day and a south wind that promised rain. Bowie probably rested less than the others, and when the sun rose he could not even lift himself out of bed. Ill for weeks, he had still moved about and done his duties. Now a hard fever had set in and his condition was grave. Juana Navarro de Alsbury, wife of Texas doctor Horace Alsbury and a relative through marriage of Bowie, tended the colonel and said that he had typhoid. It might instead have been some form of consumption, or perhaps pneumonia or some bacterial infection. The garrison physician simply called it "a peculiar disease of a peculiar nature." Diagnosis was of less concern to Travis than the reality of Bowie's condition. Bowie was flat on this back, suffering from chills and the shakes. He was probably suffering through bouts of vomiting and bloody diarrhea as well. He was too sick to walk, too sick to think clearly, and certainly too sick to command.[17]

That left Travis in charge of the defense of the Alamo. Travis, as most observers recorded, was not a man to be trifled with. He struck some people as vain, others as ambitious, brusque, prideful, overly sensitive, self-important, and occasionally hotheaded. He may even have been a bit pompous. But no one considered him incompetent, cowardly, or dumb, and he accepted full command determined to perform his duty to the best of his abilities. Undoubtedly a sense of his new position seeped into his February 24 letter to "the People of Texas & all Americans." The masterful, emotional appeal became Texas's unofficial declaration of independence, and it bespoke a man who took himself and his cause—his duty and his country—seriously. The words "Liberty . . . patriotism & every thing dear to the American character" resounded across Texas and the United States, and the promise "*I shall never surrender or retreat*" fired imaginations. The sign-off, "VICTORY or DEATH," meant just that to Travis.

Brilliant with words, he was also a clear-thinking commander. During February 24 and 25, Travis labored to strengthen the Alamo and to clear a field of vision around it. Although the Mexican artillery did not seriously injure any of the defenders, it blasted away parts of the fortress, making repairs necessary. Inside the fort the men were kept busy digging trenches, fortifying walls, and generally moving dirt. But of even more concern to Travis were the actions of the enemy. Intent upon pounding the walls and weakening the structure of the Alamo, Santa Anna began to encircle the fortress. On the night of the twenty-third he erected a small battery just west of the Main Plaza near the San Antonio River. During the next two days and nights he established other batteries—one just across the San Antonio about 150 yards southwest of the Alamo, and another south of the fortress in an area known as La Villita. He also set up several entrenched camps to the south. Santa Anna's moves inched his guns and troops closer to Travis and his men.

On February 24 Santa Anna mounted his horse and reconnoitered the land around the mission, passing within musket shot of its walls. Exactly what Santa Anna was thinking is difficult to know, for he tended not to disclose his plans until the last moment, but by placing batteries to the south and southwest he undoubtedly planned to attack the Alamo at its main gate. Perhaps he hoped a quick attack would break through the Texans' defenses and result in painless victory. Or maybe his concern over reinforcements motivated him to attack before his full army had arrived in Béxar. Or he might simply have wanted to test the Texans' resolve. Were the men inside the Alamo truly willing to die defending four walls far away from their homes and families?[18]

On the morning of February 25 the Mexican batteries began to shell the Alamo, forcing the defenders to seek cover. While the bombardment was taking place, Santa Anna then ordered two infantry battalions—cazadores (riflemen) from the Matamoros Battalion and foot soldiers from the Jiménez Battalion—to ford the San Antonio River and move into the mud-and-thatch jacales of Pueblo de Valero, outside the Alamo's main gate. General Manuel Fernández Castrillón led the attack, but Santa Anna himself hovered close to the action. Travis, Crockett, and the other defenders watched the Mexicans coming closer, looking for cover while steadily moving forward. They all well knew the effective range of their weapons—seventy yards for a musket, two hundred or so for a long rifle. They waited. Waited on the piles of dirt looking over the Alamo's south walls. Waited in the artillery batteries at the southwest corner, main gate, and palisade. Waited in the trenches and ditches outside the Alamo. Then they opened fire. Travis wrote Sam Houston that the Mexicans "arrived within point blank shot, when we opened a discharge of grape and canister on them, together with a well directed fire from small arms which forced them to halt and take shelter in the houses 90 to 100 yards from our batteries."[19]

The Texas barrage drew blood. After regrouping, Santa Anna's forces began a slow advance, moving from one covered position to the next. The Texans killed several of the attackers and wounded a few others. Despite being bombarded by "balls, grape and canister," the Texans maintained their fire. Travis gloried in the performance of his officers and men, writing Houston that they "conducted themselves with firmness and bravery . . . with such undaunted heroism" that it was unfair to single out only a few. But Travis did comment that David Crockett "was seen at all points, animating the men to do their duty."

Though the Texans repelled the attack, the assault did underscore one of the major weaknesses in their position. The *jacales* of Pueblo de Valero and La Villita, to the south of the Alamo, offered too much protection for the enemy. The Texans needed a greater field of fire. Seeing this, Charles Despallier, a recent arrival in Béxar from Rapides Parish, Louisiana, and Robert Brown, who had been in Texas for more than a year, "gallantly sallied out" and torched several abandoned structures close to the Alamo.

The fighting continued in bursts while the low clouds spit light rain on the combatants. After two hours the Mexicans pulled back and the shooting stopped. The fight had certainly not elevated Mexican soldiers in Travis's eyes; his men had fought and won the day, sustaining only one injury and a few soldiers "slightly scratched by pieces of rock." But one day's skirmish would be meaningless in the final battle. The enemy was encircling him. Batteries were sprouting at night like mushrooms. His position was becoming increasingly tenuous. "I have every reason to apprehend an attack from his whole force very soon," Travis wrote Houston, "but I shall hold out to the last extremity, hoping to secure reinforcement in a day or two. Do hasten on aid to me as rapidly as possible, as from the superior number of the enemy, it will be impossible for us to keep them out much longer." At the end of the letter Travis shifted, as he often did, from a factual account of the day's events to a somber emotional appeal. "If they overpower us, we fall a sacrifice at the shrine of our country, and we hope posterity and our country will do our memory justice. Give me help, oh my country!"

That night both sides continued to prepare for a major confrontation. The Mexicans conducted a probing assault against the "rear of the fort" and received a volley of grape and musket fire for their efforts. The Texans concentrated their energy on burning more *jacales* and clearing the space between themselves and their enemy. The night was alive with musket and rifle fire, cannon blasts, and exploding shells, with cries of soldiers and whispers of raiders. Men shivered against the night air, suddenly colder as the first wisps of a norther swept off the plains.[20]

For how long could the Texans stand? That night a council of the Texans met to decide upon a course of action. They needed reinforcements, but so far Travis's urgent pleas had either disappeared on the prairies of Texas or been ignored. The council needed someone of standing, someone with deep roots in Texas who commanded respect, to ride to Goliad and convince James Fannin to come to their aid. Tejano Juan Seguín was only twenty-nine years old, but he was a man whose opinions carried weight throughout Spanish-speaking Texas. He had married into an important ranching family, served as a political chief in Béxar, and led a militia company against the centralist government, taking part in the storming of the Alamo the previous December. Moving easily between Spanish and Anglo Texas, Seguín was the ideal courier. His mission was clear: convince Fannin to act.[21]

*

Ninety-five miles down the San Antonio River, sitting in the presidio of La Bahía, overlooking the town of Goliad, James Walker Fannin prepared for his role as a savior with all the resolve of Prince Hamlet. At his disposal were some four hundred soldiers, passionate and ready to fight, waiting only for Fannin's order to march, lingering while Fannin thought through his options. On February 23, Travis and Bowie jointly signed a letter pleading for assistance, demanding that Fannin, like themselves, act honorably. "We hope you will send us all the men you can spare promptly," they wrote. Time was of the essence and Fannin's army was a five- or six-day march from the Alamo.[22]

Fannin received the letter on February 25, and he recognized his duty at once, though he was not the sort of man to fulfill it. A native of Georgia, he had been raised by his grandfather on a cotton plantation near Marion and entered the U.S. Military Academy at West Point in 1819. He left the academy before graduating, having acquired an apprentice's knowledge of strategy, tactics, logistics, and artillery but a journeyman's sense of rank, command, control, authority, and obedience. Settled in Velasco, Texas, in the fall of 1834, he raised a bit of cotton, traded slaves, and sided with the radicals on the question of Texas independence. Fannin became a member of the committee of safety and correspondence of Columbia in August 1835, wrote letters inviting West

Point officers to come to Texas and join the cause, fought in the battles of Gonzales and Concepción in October, and early in January 1836 began raising volunteer troops for the Matamoros expedition. When the expedition fizzled out, he fell back to Goliad, which he hoped to defend against José Urrea's army advancing up the coast. He was bivouacked there on February 25, 1836, when a courier delivered the plea for help from Travis and Bowie.[23]

Fannin faced difficult political, military, and personal choices. In the chaos of the Matamoros expedition and the disintegration of the provisional government, the Texas army suffered badly. The power struggle between Governor Henry Smith and the Council had clouded command issues in a political fog. At one time or another in January and early February, James Fannin, Sam Houston, Frank Johnson, and James Grant had either been designated or tried to assume the role of commander in chief. Fannin knew he occupied critical ground, but he had no idea what to do about it. "General Houston is absent on furlough," he wrote to Acting Governor James W. Robinson on February 22, "and neither myself nor the army have received any *orders* as to who should assume the command."[24]

Fannin's long letter to Robinson reveals the depth of his psychological torment. He begins by complaining that he is overworked, then details a lottery he conducted that renamed La Bahía "Fort Defiance." Next he emphasizes how "many men of influence view me with an envious eye, and either desire my station, or my disgrace. The *first,* they are welcome to—and many thanks for taking it off my hands." Unlike Travis, Fannin has no desire to lead and requests that Robinson and the Council relieve him of command. "I am a better judge of my military abilities than others, and if I am *qualified* to command an *Army, I have not found it out.*" After making this stark admission, Fannin starts rambling from one point to another, ranging from the best way to select a commander and ideas for the proposed Texas constitution to qualified officers he has known. Taken as a whole, the letter should have been enough to convince Robinson that La Bahía—Fannin's Fort Defiance—was rudderless.

Fannin also found himself in a strategic dilemma. While Travis begged him to march west and break the siege of the Alamo, he had orders from the provisional government to hold Goliad. Urrea was marching steadily north from Matamoros, up the coastal prairies, headed straight for Goliad and Copano Bay, the mouth of the San Antonio River and Béxar's logistical lifeline. If Fannin attempted a rescue of the Alamo, he risked leaving the southwest coast undefended and giving Urrea an opportunity to cut Béxar's links to the sea, sweep north into the heart of Anglo Texas, and conquer the settlements along the Guadalupe, Colorado, Brazos, and Trinity Rivers.

Even worse, Fannin knew that he was ill equipped to confront either Santa Anna or Urrea. West Point had given him enough tactical and logistical training to understand the inherent limits of his position. If he heeded Travis's pleas and deployed to Béxar, his troops would have to fight their way into the Alamo through thousands of regular Mexican troops and, once there, with limited provisions, defend it against concentrated artillery bombardment and infantry assault. The prospects of remaining in La Bahía seemed better. If he remained there, he would face Urrea's army of 641 men and eight cannon from a fine defensive position. If war was a gamble, the odds of staying put seemed better than playing against the house in Béxar. But—and Fannin lived in a world of buts—José Urrea was the best general in the Mexican army, a veteran of the Revolution, the failed Spanish reconquest, and the Apache wars. "General don José Urrea," a Mexican army officer would soon write, "was without doubt the General who most distinguished himself in the Texas campaign."[25]

Desperate for more men, more money, and more materiel, Fannin forwarded repeated requests to the provisional government. In a February 16 letter to Acting Governor James Robinson, he had pleaded, "Send from twelve to fifteen hundred men to Bexar immediately, and provisions plenty." He wrote to Robinson again the next day, even more urgently. "Let me implore you to lose no time and spare no expense in spreading these tidings throughout Texas, and ordering out the militia 'IN MASS.'" Without reinforcements and provisions, the Texans were doomed.[26]

In almost every way, Fannin was ill suited for command of the Army of the People. A beggar for help, he was also choosy. He wanted reinforcements but none like the troops he already had—Jacksonian individualists who elected their own officers, chose which orders to obey, and drifted in and out of service with the consistency of birds lighting in a tree. "Stir up the people," he told Governor Robinson, "but do not allow them to come into camp unless *organized*. I never wish to see an election in a camp where I am responsible in any manner." He felt somewhat better a week later: "I have been troubled to get my militia to work or do any kind of garrison duty: But I am now happy to say, that I have got them quite well-satisfied, and being well-*disciplined,* and doing *good work.*"[27]

Fannin's troops had little trouble sensing his misgivings and perhaps his lack of respect for them. La Bahía in the winter of 1836 was nothing like the hills of West Point in 1819 and 1820, where humble, obsequious plebes had instinctively, enthusiastically obeyed every word coming from the mouth of an upperclassman, let alone an army officer. They found Fannin distant and arrogant, a windbag filled with personal ambitions, scarcely hidden fears, and unusually high expectations. "I am sorry to say," wrote Private J. F. Ferguson, "that the majority of the soldiers don't like [Fannin]. For what cause I don't know whether it is because they think he has not the interest of the country at heart or that he wishes to become great without taking the proper steps to attain greatness."[28]

On February 26, before Seguín ever reached La Bahía, Fannin finally decided that he had to march to the Alamo to relieve the siege. Or perhaps his men decided the issue for him. In any case, he seemed, at least temporarily, full of resolve. The day before, in a letter devoted to financial matters, he had written Robinson, "I am aware that my present movement toward Bexar is any thing but a military one. The appeals of Cols. Travis and Bowie cannot however pass unnoticed—particularly by my troops now on the field—Sanguine, chivalrous Volunteers—Much must be risked to relieve the besieged." Leaving just one hundred men behind, he cautiously began to lead three hundred troops up the San Antonio River, heading for Béxar with all the enthusiasm of a condemned man approaching the executioner. From the first, nothing went as planned. A wagon broke down and they spent much of the first day trying to lug their artillery across the San Antonio River. Hungry after that effort, they discovered that they had not packed nearly enough rations—"Not a particle of bread stuff, with the exception of half a tierce of rice, with us,—no beef, with the exception of a small portion which had been dried—and, not a *head* of cattle, except those used to draw the artillery, the ammunition, etc." At the end of the day they had moved only two hundred yards closer to the Alamo. That night, while they camped along the river, several oxen wandered off. That was enough for Fannin. He was never keen on the mission, and the small problems gave him an excuse to reconsider the entire expedition. The next morning the man who had raged against democracy in the military held a war council, reporting that "it was by them unanimously determined, that, inasmuch as a proper supply of provisions and means of transportation could not be had; and, as it was impossible, with our present means, to carry the artillery with us, and as by leaving Fort Defiance without a proper garrison, it might fall into the hands of the enemy, . . . and as by report of our spies . . . we may expect an attack upon this place, it was deemed expedient to return to this post and complete the fortifications." In short, Fannin—now the democrats' democrat—scuttled the rescue attempt.[29]

Fannin had barely returned to La Bahía when he learned just how close Urrea was. Late in the evening of February 26, Urrea's division reached the Nueces River just one mile above Lipantitlán. When a reconnaissance patrol discovered seventy Texans at San Patricio, Urrea decided to surprise them. At 3:30 A.M. on February 27, Mexican troops attacked, routing the Texans in a matter of hours, killing a total of twenty rebels and taking thirty-two prisoners. For Fannin, the enemy had closed to within fifty miles. "The enemy have the town of Bejar, with a large force—and I fear will soon have our brave countrymen in the Alamo," he wrote on February 28. "Another force is near me—and crossed the river yesterday, and attacked a party by surprise . . . and routed them." Rescuing Béxar was now completely out of the question.[30]

Announcing his decision in a letter to Governor Robinson, Fannin lamented his dwindling supplies and the possibility that famine might compel his army "to cut our way through the enemy leaving the artillery & munitions of war in their hands." As for the men in the Alamo, he wished them well and then washed his hands of the matter.

> We hope, however, for the best—we hope that before this time the people have risen and are marching to the relief of Bexar & this post—but should the *worst* happen—on whose head should his burthen of censure fall—*not* on the *heads* of those brave men who have left their homes in the United States to aid us in our struggle for Lib-

erty—but on those whose all is in Texas & who notwithstanding the repeated calls have remained at home without raising a finger to keep the Enemy from their thresholds. . . . Will not *curses* be heaped on the heads of the sluggards who remain at home with a knowledge of our situation.[31]

★

Juan Seguín never made it to La Bahía. On the road he met one of Fannin's officers at the Ranch of San Bartolo and was told that Fannin and four hundred soldiers were on "his way to render assistance to the defenders of the Alamo." Deciding to wait at the ranch for Fannin, Seguín sent back a message that time was critical. Later that same day Seguín talked with another of the colonel's men and learned that Fannin had aborted the mission and returned to La Bahía to defend it against General Urrea. Fannin had his own orders and concerns, the messenger said, adding that Seguín should travel to Gonzales to confer with General Houston. Seguín did just that, arriving in Gonzales and setting to work organizing a Tejano force.[32]

The situation in the Alamo was critical. On February 26 a norther dropped the temperatures to just above freezing and sent a strong, numbing wind across south Texas. William Fairfax Gray, a Virginian on his way to the Texas convention at Washington-on-the-Brazos, noted in his journal that a norther "is sometimes so excessively cold that persons have been known to freeze to death in crossing the plains. Long observation has taught [Texans] to expect a norther between the 20th of February and 1st of March, and that generally closes winter." Whether this one spelled the end of winter or not, Gray could not answer. But he was so cold that he did not commence his journey until noon. Only the news from Béxar warmed Gray's blood. Travis was going to fight. Texas would respond, Gray was sure. "The people now begin to think the wolf has actually come at last, and are preparing for a march."[33]

A march away from Gray, the cold forced the defenders to huddle by their fires, where they used the dwindling supply of coffee to make a weak brew. It also made painfully clear what they lacked. The well they had dug inside the Alamo did not satisfy their needs, and the wood they burned to keep themselves warm was quickly vanishing into embers. Outside the walls was their answer—water from the acequia to the east and wood from the jacales of Pueblo de Valero and La Villita to the south. Between the Alamo's walls and the resources were Mexican *cazadores* armed with Baker rifles and soldiers carrying Brown Bess muskets. It made for dangerous work, but it was necessary. During the day Texans ventured out into enemy territory, gathering water and wood and torching a *jacal* here and there. Meanwhile, Mexican soldiers continued their reconnaissance efforts. Occasionally small, opposing groups clashed, fired shots, and ran for cover. A few Mexicans died during the day, and undoubtedly at least several Texans were hit.[34]

The bombardments and burning *jacales* lit Béxar and the Alamo that night. The next day, Saturday, February 27, the wind and the search for supplies continued. Now not only the Texans but the Mexicans scoured the landscape. Santa Anna sent parties to surrounding ranches with orders to requisition—or simply take—corn, cattle, and hogs. While his men foraged, Santa Anna planned. In a letter to another officer, he bragged, "From the moment of my arrival I have been busy hostilizing the enemy in his position, so much so that they are not even allowed to raise their heads over the walls, preparing everything for the assault which will take place when at least the first brigade arrives, which is now sixty leagues away. Up to now they still act stubborn, counting on the strong position which they hold, and hoping for much aid from the colonies and from the United States, but they will soon find out their mistake."[35]

On February 28 the weather improved and for a time it seemed as if the defenders' position would too. Fannin was on his way with several hundred—at least, that was a rumor that spread through the Mexican camp. Juan Almonte noted in his journal, "It is not true." But for a time it seemed real enough that Santa Anna sent a cavalry detachment southeast to intercept Fannin. Santa Anna could not have known that Fannin was too cautious to come. Perhaps the rumor penetrated inside the walls and allowed the imaginations of the defenders to soar with thoughts of victory. Yet an afternoon rain coupled with no sign or word from Fannin dampened spirits.[36]

There was no Fannin on the Goliad–Béxar Road, but throughout Texas and the United States the name William Barret Travis and the fight at the Alamo was on people's lips. The stand of the defenders and Travis's impassioned pleas had quickly assumed a romantic mantle. Travis intended that his letters be published, and they were, along with other equally emotional appeals. Governor Henry Smith called upon his fellow Texans "to fly to the aid of your besieged countrymen and not permit them to be massacred by a mercenary foe. I slight none. I call on ALL who are able to bear arms, to rally without a moment's delay." He challenged their manhood: "Do you possess honor? Suffer it not to be insulted or tarnished! Do you possess patriotism? Evince it by your bold, prompt and manly action!" Across Texas and in ports like New Orleans the message was the same. Save Travis. Save the Alamo. Save Texas. There was not a moment to spare. The barbarians were at the gate. In another statement, Smith pleaded: "Citizen of Texas, descendents of Washington, awake! arouse yourself! . . . The eyes of the world are upon us! let us fly at once to our arms, march to the battle field, meet the foe, and give renewed evidence to the world, that the arms of freemen, uplifted in defense of their rights and liberties, are irresistible."[37]

The appeals of Smith and the other politicians and journalists did not penetrate the Alamo, where they would have been appreciated almost as much as reinforcements. Leap Year's gift, February 29, came and passed like the previous day, without Fannin and without any hopeful news. But the day did begin a short lull in the fighting, which may even have been a brief armistice. Santa Anna may have entertained the idea of not attacking the Alamo. In his 1837 account of the campaign he claimed, "I still wanted to try a generous measure, characteristic of Mexican kindness, and I offered life to the defendants who would surrender their arms and retire under oath not to take them up again against Mexico." These were essentially the same terms that the Texans had given Cos in December. *El presidente* also wrote that Almonte delivered the message. In his own journal, however, Almonte detailed the weather and Mexican troop movements but no peace missions, so Santa Anna may have been sprucing up his image after the fact.[38]

Still, the fighting stopped and a number of Tejanos—perhaps the only people Santa Anna included in his armistice—reconsidered their place in the Alamo. Seguín, their leader, was gone, and several of them sought out Bowie for advice. Unlike Bowie, Travis, and the other Anglos, they had not enlisted or taken the oath, even if they disapproved of the government of Santa Anna. They trusted Bowie; he was as close to being one of them as an Anglo settler was likely to get. And Bowie, though sick and unable to get out of his cot, expressed concern for them. "All of you who desire to leave here may go in safety," he told them. It was their decision. A few stayed to fight. When Bowie asked Gregorio Esparza if he wanted to leave, Esparza answered, "No. I will stay and die fighting." Esparza's wife then told her husband, "I will stay by your side and with our children die too. They will soon kill us. We will not linger long in pain." But most left.[39]

★

The weather had turned nasty again. It was another norther, only this one was colder, louder, and stronger than the previous one. The winds were galelike, and the night was violent and alive with lightning, thunder, rain, and hail. José Enrique de la Peña, moving toward Béxar from the south to join Santa Anna, spent the night in a riverbed shielded from the wind but not the snow. He noted that it was impossible to write messages because the ink had frozen in the inkwells and bottles. William F. Gray had gone to sleep on a warm night in Washington-on-the-Brazos, throwing off some of his clothes to cool down, so the norther hit him especially hard. He was from Virginia and was unaccustomed to the shifting moods of the weather on the Texas plains.[40]

Something else was happening outside the Alamo's walls. Out in the darkness there were some sort of unusual activities: voices—English-speaking voices—and horses. The men guarding the Alamo had learned during the previous week to shoot first and ask questions later, assuming that anything moving toward them from the outside was the enemy. So when one of them saw a movement he shot. A man hit in the foot swore an oath in English, and someone else told the Texans to hold their fire. The men on the outside were Texans and Americans, thirty-two of them and mostly from Gonzales, come to the Alamo to aid their brothers. In a moment the postern swung open and the reinforcements were inside. It was 3 A.M., and as far as Travis was concerned, this proved that it was possible to get men into the Alamo.[41]

The origins of the Gonzales expedition went back to the first day of the siege, when Travis sent Dr. John Sutherland and John W. Smith to Gonzales for help. Though Sutherland had injured his knee when his horse had thrown him on February 23, his voice was still good and he told the men in Gonzales that the Alamo was facing stiff odds. A day or two later

Captain Albert Martin, a Gonzales man, had arrived back at home with Travis's "VICTORY or DEATH" letter, and he too said the situation at the Alamo was urgent. Texas needed help. The Gonzales Ranging Company of Mounted Volunteers, thirty-two men with horses and rifles, seemed duly constituted and honor bound to help.[42]

As a group, the men of Gonzales formed a cross section of frontier Texas—old and young, modestly successful and dirt poor, educated and illiterate. Isaac Millsaps was forty-one; William P. King was sixteen. Thomas R. Miller, a well-off resident, had just lost his young bride to Johnnie Kellogg, so he joined up. So did Kellogg. So did John W. Smith and Albert Martin, both eager to rejoin their comrades. Thirty-two men altogether made the decision to ride into hostile country, into the teeth of the Mexican army, to join a group of Texans who were badly outnumbered and facing the blood red flag of no quarter. They had a choice; many had wives and families. But they decided to follow Smith and Martin.[43]

That they got to the Alamo at all was probably pure, blind luck. The Mexican forces that had encircled the Alamo had been thinned by the departure of a cavalry unit in search of Fannin. And the night was so cold and ugly that the sentinels were probably more concerned with keeping warm and dry than looking for Texans sneaking across the plains. The Gonzales men could see the Mexican fires and sentries and adjusted their path accordingly, moving from bush to bush and ravine to ravine.

Their only scare came when a mysterious man speaking English appeared out of nowhere and told them to follow him. They followed for a while, but soon the scout in Smith became suspicious. Something was wrong—the man's voice, his posture, the distance he kept. "Boys," Smith called out, "it's time to be after shooting that fellow!"[44]

The stranger spurred his horse and disappeared into the same darkness from which he had appeared. The Gonzales men didn't need him anyway. Smith knew the country and could guide them about anywhere. Except for the man who was shot by an Alamo guard, they got inside the walls without further incident.

Young Enrique Esparza, in the Alamo with his mother and father and siblings, later recalled that March 1 was a day of general celebration. "The Texans beat on a drum and played on a flute." The fact that reinforcements had passed through the Mexican ring and entered the fort, even if only thirty-two of them, was a triumph. Outside the walls a more subdued but significant celebration took place. Joaquín Ramírez y Sesma, who had led the Fannin search party, returned from his voyage down the Béxar–Goliad Road and reported that there was no enemy in sight. Neither side knew exactly what the other knew, but the sum total of the information was this: thirty-two men had joined the defenders in the Alamo; two hundred or more had rejoined the attackers. Without that net loss, the Alamo might have been saved.[45]

✼

By the beginning of March the defense of the Alamo had become the visible incarnation of Texas, its present crisis and its future hopes. For many Texans and Americans it represented a people fighting against tyranny and arbitrary rule, and for personal liberty and the rule of law. For others it signified the fight for a prosperous future built on land, cotton, and slaves. Of course, there *was* no Texas, at least no constituted, independent, and free Texas. So while the Alamo stood strong as a symbol, politicians trudged to Washington-on-the-Brazos to embody its dream.

The delegates to the Convention of 1836 began riding into Washington-on-the-Brazos on February 28. They rode along muddy paths into rain and hail and freezing temperatures. The forty-one delegates who arrived by the first day crowded into a half-finished frame house at 1 P.M. Before starting the work of birthing a new nation, they tacked cotton cloth over the open windows. As a group, they contrasted sharply with those who attended the Conventions of 1832 and 1833 and the Consultation of 1835. They were younger and relative newcomers to Texas, and an unusually large number of them were military veterans of the battles of Gonzales, Concepción, and Béxar. Most were radical, War Party firebrands, men who loathed Antonio López de Santa Anna and believed that only in independence could Texans fulfill their destiny.[46]

They sensed that everything was at stake. For more than a month, the provisional government had ceased to exist, its officials fighting with one another to the point of effective abdication. Now a somber mood blanketed the sessions. Mexico's Army of Operations menaced like a Sonoran scorpion, its two pincers—Urrea to the southeast and Santa Anna to the southwest—ready to sting. Most Texan rebels realized that the future of their country hung in the balance, that the moment of truth was at hand.[47]

The delegates may have been somber about their military chances, but they were decidedly meaner than before about their opponents. With farms, families, homes, and lives threatened with destruction, an anti-Mexican streak, always lurking just below the surface, spewed forth from many. During the political battles of the previous fall, Anglo Texans had walked a racial tightrope, not wanting to alienate federalists in the Mexican interior or sympathetic Tejanos in their own backyard. But Santa Anna had crushed liberal forces at least temporarily, and once Anglo Texans realized they could expect no help from the south, their racial prejudices bubbled to the surface. At a meeting in Texana on January 20, 1836, citizens from the municipality of Jackson resolved that "the great mass of . . . [Mexicans are] incapable of appreciating or even comprehending the Blessings of free institutions." Another Texan justified independence because "we separate from a people one half of whom are the most depraved of the different races of Indians, different in color, pursuits and character." David G. Burnet, soon to be Texas's interim president, would later tell Senator Henry Clay of Kentucky that "Texas has pronounced a final separation from the miserable and revolutionary government of Mexico. . . . The causes . . . are too numerous to be detailed in a single letter; but one general fact may account for all; the utter dissimilarity of character between the two people, the Texians and the Mexicans. The first are principally Anglo-Americans; the others a mongrel race of degenerate Spaniards and Indians more depraved than they."[48]

Anglo attitudes toward Tejanos had deteriorated as well, particularly when so few rallied to the rebellion. Writing to Acting Governor James W. Robinson on February 21, 1836, James Fannin warned against trusting Tejanos. "Whilst I am in command, both private and public enemies will be attended to. There is more danger from these spies, who are so intimately acquainted with the country, than from twenty times the number of armed soldiers. I again tell you," Fannin summarized, "we must not rely on Mexicans."[49]

For many Anglo Texans, and perhaps on both sides, the rebellion was assuming the dimensions of a race war—American against Mexican, white against brown. In a February 12 letter to Governor Henry Smith, William Travis insisted that Santa Anna was "denouncing vengeance against the people of Texas—and threatening to exterminate every white man within its limits." James Fannin shared those sentiments, telling Acting Governor Robinson, "Not the least doubt should any longer be entertained, by any friend of Texas, of the design of Santa Anna to overrun the country and overrun or exterminate every white man within its borders."[50]

Like so many other Southerners, the Anglo Texans feared that a race war would culminate in a sexual apocalypse against white women. Leering, sexually depraved Mexican soldiers were marching north to deflower Texas women, they thought. "What can be expected for the *Fair daughters* of chaste *white women,*" James Fannin insisted, "when their own [Mexican] country-women are prostituted by a licensed soldiery, as an inducement to push forward into the Colonies, where they may find *fairer* game?" Other Texans raised the specter of rape and ruin. "Their [Mexican] war cry is, 'death and destruction to every Anglo-American, west of the Sabine'; their watchword, actually, 'beauty and booty.' . . . And will you *now* as Texian freeman . . . suffer the *colored* hirelings of a cruel and faithless despot, to feast and revel, in your dearly purchased and cherished homes? . . . Your beloved wives, your mothers, your daughters . . . given up to the dire pollution, and massacre of a band of barbarians." To be sure, mass rapes were not unheard of in wartime, then or later—but Santa Anna preferred execution and pillage to sexual brutalization.[51]

These racial fears undoubtedly helped fan the flame of independence, but to their credit, the Texans had much higher motives. To George Childress fell the task of drafting the Texas Declaration of Independence. A well-educated attorney and native of Tennessee, he had arrived late in Texas, settling in an *empresario* colony founded by his uncle Sterling Robertson. But he wasted no time clothing himself in the fabric of rebellion. Just three weeks after arriving in Texas, Childress won a seat in the Convention of 1836, representing Milam municipality. He called the convention to order on March 1 and chaired the five-man committee charged with drafting the declaration. He had probably carried a draft of the declaration in his saddlebags as he rode to Washington-on-the-Brazos, because the committee submitted it to the delegates less than twenty-four hours later. On March 2, with Santa Anna tightening his grip on Béxar and José Urrea racing toward Goliad, the delegates did not even bother to debate the document, approving it in a matter of minutes.[52]

★

The Texas Declaration of Independence crackled with the rhetoric of natural rights and popular sovereignty. The thinking and writings of John Locke and Thomas Jefferson echoed throughout the document. More than a century and a half earlier, the Englishman John Locke had planted a major seed of American political culture, arguing that human beings formed governments to protect the natural rights God had bestowed upon them, particularly the rights to liberty and property. Governments derived their authority, Locke maintained, from the consent of the governed, and citizens retained the right to withdraw consent when government failed to protect or abused their natural rights.

The Founding Fathers, of course, had adopted Locke's ideas. In the Declaration of Independence of 1776, Thomas Jefferson had written that when government failed to fulfill its obligation to protect individual rights, the people had the right and even the duty to dissolve it and erect in its place a new government, capable of achieving those ends. Philosophically, at least, revolution was as American as open spaces. Jefferson famously said (not in the declaration) that "the tree of liberty must be refreshed from time to time with the blood of tyrants," and the Texans were quick to agree. The rebels were certain that Santa Anna had wrought what Locke and Jefferson had feared, a despotic state committed not to protecting individual rights but to aggrandizing its own power. The Mexican government, so the declaration went, had "ceased to protect the lives, liberty, and property of the people, from whom its legitimate powers are derived . . . [and had become] an instrument in the hands of evil rulers for their suppression." Under such circumstances, Santa Anna had surrendered all political legitimacy. "When, in consequence of such acts of malfeasance and abduction on the part of the government," the declaration argued, "anarchy prevails, and civil society is dissolved into its original elements, in such a crisis, the first law of nature, the right of self-preservation," gives the people the right "to take their political affairs into their own hands . . . to abolish such government, and create another in its stead, calculated to rescue them from impending dangers, and to secure their welfare and happiness." The Texans had little regard for the fact that they had moved from the United States to Mexican sovereignty. Rights were rights, given by God to people everywhere. Their Declaration of Independence insisted that when Anglo-Americans had crossed the Sabine, Mexico had promised that they "should continue to enjoy that constitutional liberty and republican government to which they had been habituated in the land of their birth, the United States of America."

Heading the Texan list of grievances was the fact that the "federal republican government, which they have sworn to support, no longer has a substantial existence . . . and has been forcibly changed from a restricted federative republic, composed of sovereign states, to a consolidated military despotism." Among other things, Santa Anna had "suffered the military commandants, stationed among us, to exercise arbitrary acts of oppression and tyranny, thus trampling upon the most sacred rights of the citizens, and rendering the military superior to the civil power." Mexican customs collectors, said the declaration, had "made tyrannical attacks upon our commerce . . . commissioning desperadoes, and authorizing them to seize our vessels, and convey the property of our citizens to far distant parts for confiscation." Furthermore, Mexico City "denies us the right of worshipping the almighty according to the dictates of our own conscience, by the support of a national religion." The Mexican government "has demanded us to deliver up our arms, which are essential to our defense—the rightful property of freemen—and formidable only to tyrannical governments." And finally, the central government had been "during the whole time of our connection with it, the contemptible sport and victim of successive military revolutions, and hath continually exhibited every characteristic of a weak, corrupt, and tyrannical government." Worshiping God, owning guns, protecting property, and preventing anarchy were worth dying for.

No sooner had they inked their signatures on the Declaration of Independence than the Texans set about writing a constitution. It would not be ratified until March 17, 1836, but it also drew on ideas developed long before Santa Anna's final assault on the Alamo. All but quoting John Locke, the constitution argued that "all men, when they form a social compact, have equal rights. . . . All political power is inherent in the people, and all free governments are founded on their authority, and instituted for their benefit, and they have at all times the inalienable right to alter their government in such manner as they think proper." The constitution then outlined a Declaration of Rights based on the Bill of Rights of the U.S. Constitution, providing to all citizens the right "to worship God according to the dictates of our own conscience"; guaranteeing private property, due process, and freedom of speech and the press; protecting citizens from unreasonable searches and seizures; outlawing debtors' prison, excessive bail, and cruel and unusual punishments; requiring grand jury indictments and speedy and public trials in which guilt or innocence was decided by juries; and extending to every citizen "the right to bear arms in defense of himself and the republic." Blind to what later generations would consider obvious, the delegates tolerated and even endorsed slavery, seeing no discrepancy between praising the virtues of liberty and individual natural rights while condoning human bondage. The constitution denied citizenship to Africans, descendants of Africans, and Indians (though not to Mexicans), and prohibited the immigration to Texas of free blacks. "All persons of color who were slaves for life previous to their emigration to Texas," the constitution provided, "and who are now held in bondage shall remain in the like state of servitude." Pushing Southern slave codes to the limit, the constitution even made abolition—individual or otherwse—all but impossible: "Congress shall pass no laws to prohibit emigrants from bringing their slaves into the republic with them. . . . [N]or shall Congress have the power to emancipate slaves; nor shall any slave holder be able to emancipate his or her slaves without the consent of Congress."[53]

In this respect, the Texas constitution was worse than its model. Otherwise, it was quite similar, if less well thought out. But time was short.

★

As the delegates proclaimed independence, General José Urrea was showing James Grant that Mexico was bent on crushing Texas's rebellion. Unaware that Urrea had taken San Patricio a few days earlier, Grant and about fifty soldiers were returning from a horse-hunting expedition. Urrea's scouts found them driving hundreds of wild horses north toward San Patricio. The general set a trap for them at Agua Dulce Creek, twenty-six miles south of the settlement, concealing forty riflemen and eighty dragoons in the tree line. Several hours after sunrise, the Texans rode into the ambush. Grant and an associate, Reuben Brown, made a run for it, but Urrea's cavalry caught up with them after a seven-mile chase. Once surrounded, Grant and Brown reined in their mounts to make a last stand. Grant fell quickly to cavalry lances and Brown was captured. He remembered watching Mexican troops hack at Grant's body with their sabers. Several other Texans who surrendered were similarly butchered. Forty-one comrades died with Grant that morning.[54]

Travis was completely in the dark, of course, about both the new constitution in the making and the destruction of Grant's army. He was unaware that his "VICTORY or DEATH" letter had been published in the *Brazoria Texas Republican* and that Texans were reading his appeals. Nor did he know that the politicians in Washington-on-the-Brazos were questioning his information. Some said that Travis was manufacturing a crisis to promote his own career, that his letters were more political documents than accurate assessments of his military position. Sam Houston, his mind fogged by alcohol in what was far from his finest moment, told a friend that Travis's report was "a damned lie, and that all those reports from Travis & Fannin were lies, for there were no Mexicans forces there and that he believed that it was only electioneering schemed [by] Travis & Fannin to sustain their popularity." Listening to Houston and other Travis detractors, many reached the conclusion that there was no crisis or that it was exaggerated, and there was even the suggestion that the Travis letters were forgeries.[55]

On March 3, a fine, clear day, Travis's eyes were focused on the activities taking place in Béxar. There were wild celebrations, punctuated by cheers, artillery fire, and military songs. Soldiers cheered loudly, "Santa Anna! Santa Anna!" Travis had no way of knowing that the outburst of joy was a reaction to the news of Urrea's victory at the battle of San Patricio and the realization that Fannin was not on the road to the Alamo with reinforcements. All Travis saw was the celebrations, and even more ominous, the long, seemingly endless lines of soldiers marching into Béxar. It was General Antonio Gaona's First Brigade and Cavalry Regiment in full dress regalia, more than a thousand men strong. Travis correctly estimated the numbers but failed to identify the unit. Actually, he had discounted rumors that Santa Anna was already in Béxar and assumed that the celebrations signaled his arrival. The Alamo defenders now faced 2,590 Mexican troops in the Army of Operations. To show that there were still fighting men in the Alamo, Travis ordered a few cannon rounds and some gunfire. But the odds were getting long.[56]

The arrival of Mexican reinforcements did not sink Travis's hopes entirely. Just hours before Urrea's men marched into Béxar, Colonel James Butler Bonham and perhaps two other Texans had skirted the Mexican defenses and ridden into the Alamo. This broad-daylight foray, as dramatic in its conception as in its execution, was so like the dashing Bonham, a tall, thin, gray-eyed adventurer. Decades later Enrique Esparza still recalled Bonham through a child's eyes. The Mexicans had fired at the South Carolinian, Esparza said, but could not hit him. And then he was inside the walls, "a white handkerchief tied to his hat; this handkerchief was a sign that he had seen Fannin." Esparza noted that his mother dropped to her knees "and said her beads and thanked the good God" for Bonham's safe passage.[57]

Not only did the sight of Bonham lift the defenders' spirits, he carried with him hope for their deliverance. A letter from R. M. Williamson to Travis dated March 1 indicated that Texans were rushing to the Alamo. Sixty men had departed Gonzales, three hundred soldiers under Fannin's command had left La Bahía, perhaps another three hundred were coming from Washington-on-the-Brazos, Bastrop, Brazoria, and San Felipe—all headed for the mission. "[N]o time will be lost in providing you assistance," Williamson had written. And in a postscript: "For God's sake hold out until we can assist you. . . . Best wishes to all your people and tell them to hold on firmly by their 'wills' until I go there."[58]

Writing to the convention later in the afternoon, Travis gave a clear-headed assessment of the Alamo's position. The Alamo was surrounded—that was the crucial military fact. The Mexicans had set up a battery on the west side of the river four hundred yards away, and they shelled the fort regularly. They had also established entrenched encampments on all sides—"in Bexar, four hundred yards west; in la Villita, three hundred yards south; at the powder house, one thousand yards east by south; on the ditch, eight hundred yards north." Still, as the Gonzales men and Bonham demonstrated, it was possible for reinforcements to get in, and his troops had not given up hope. "The spirits of my men are high, although they have had much to depress them."[59]

Travis was no Pollyanna. His letters evince careful organization and clarity of thinking—a lawyer's mind, not a dreamer's. As much as he wanted to believe Williamson's letter, he saw too many problems with it. Most important, he had repeatedly sent messages to Fannin and not gotten one in return. "Col. Fannin is said to be on the march to this place with reinforcements," he wrote, "but I fear it is not true." He placed what hopes he had in the arrival of new colonists and the support of the new government. If the Council sent five hundred pounds of cannon powder, two hundred rounds of cannonballs, and ten kegs of rifle powder, all under a strong guard, he felt he could defeat the force outside the Alamo's walls and win a "great and decisive battle." After all, he argued, it was better to fight in the plains of west Texas than in the Anglo settlements of the east.

But no matter if anyone or no one came, if supplies were sent or withheld, he planned to stay and fight. "I feel confident that the determined valor and desperate courage, heretofore evinced by my men, will not fail them in the last struggle, and although they may be sacrificed to the vengeance of a Gothic enemy, the victory will cost the enemy so dear, that it will be worse for him than a defeat." Writing while Mexican troops massed in Béxar, firing cannons and shouting greetings, Travis still thought about honor and liberty, not in the abstract but as palpable, eternal truths.

In several other letters written the same day he even more clearly and personally expressed his reasons for fighting. On the political level, he wrote friend Jesse Grimes that the convention should declare independence so that his men and the world would know why he was fighting. "[U]nder the flag of independence, we are ready to peril our lives a hundred times a day, and to drive away the monster who is fighting us under a blood-red flag, threatening to murder all prisoners and make Texas a waste desert." But even more personally, he was fighting for his and his family's future. He asked another friend, Davis Ayres, to take care of his son, Charles, if he died. "If the country should be saved, I may make him a splendid fortune; but if the country should be lost and I should perish, he will have nothing but the proud recollection that he is the son of a man who died for his country."[60]

✯

The timing of the defenders' deaths was the topic the next day in Santa Anna's headquarters in the Yturri house, an undistinguished flat structure on the northwestern corner of the Main Plaza. The house had served as military headquarters for Spanish, Mexican, and Texan officers and it was only fitting that Santa Anna had taken it over. In the windy but mild afternoon of March 4 he summoned his leading general and colonels to decide on the best moves to make in the endgame of his chess match with Travis.

Such meetings usually bored him, since "the discussions," he later wrote, "which such councils give rise to have not always seemed to me appropriate." But he felt obligated to go through the motions, even if they did not really matter. On February 27, Santa Anna had informed Minister of War José María Tornel that the assault on the Alamo would occur "at least with the arrival of the First Brigade." Now with the First Brigade in place and surrounded by his most important officers, Santa Anna sought consent, not advice. Clearly, he wanted to take the Alamo, and he was tired of waiting. In this contest, strenuous opposition was a politically dangerous course of action.[61]

Among the assembled officers were Generals Joaquín Ramírez y Sesma, Martín Perfecto de Cos, and Manuel Fernández Castrillón and Colonels Juan Almonte, Agustín Amat, Francisco Duque, and Manuel Romero. When Santa Anna announced his intention to assault the Alamo, Castrillón and Cos expressed concern. De la Peña remembered that they "were of the opinion that victory over a handful of men concentrated in the Alamo did not call for a great sacrifice." Instead, they urged *el presidente* to postpone the assault for a few days until his heavy artillery had arrived. Once installed, the twelve-pounders could pummel the adobe walls of the Alamo and open large breaches through which infantry could pour. Climbing over high walls defended by a determined foe would wreak terrible, unnecessary losses. "Had it [artillery] been judiciously employed, it would have saved many lives." After all, de la Peña argued, "The soldier's glory is the greater, the less bloody the victory and the fewer victims sacrificed." Concern for wounded troops also dictated delay. "There were no field hospitals or surgeons to treat the wounded, and . . . for some it would be easier to die than to be wounded."

Nor was there any need for haste. Throughout much of the siege, Santa Anna had worried whether Sam Houston or James Fannin would reinforce the Alamo. He had deployed elements of Ramírez y Sesma's force east of Béxar to intercept an invading army, and Mexican cavalry patrols diligently worked the banks of the San Antonio River and the Goliad highway to detect any troop movements. But they came up with nothing. The Mexicans in Béxar also knew full well that General José Urrea's troops, after their victory at San Patricio, had all but cut Fannin off. "There was no need to fear that the enemy would be reinforced," de la Peña concluded, "for even though reinforcements had entered because of our lack of vigilance, we were situated so as to do battle with any other possible arrivals one by one."

Finally, the Mexicans knew that inside the Alamo, morale might be slipping, not so much because of inadequate supplies and ammunition, or doubts about the righteousness of their cause, but because eleven days of psychological warfare—martial music, noise, and constant fire from field cannon and howitzers—and ongoing disappointments from the lack of major reinforcements might have taken their toll. "The enemy was in communication with some of the Béjar townspeople who were their sympathizers," de la Peña remembered, and Santa Anna was fully aware of the situation. As the Tejanos filtered out of the fort, the Mexicans heard about the grumblings inside.[62]

But there was a good case to be made for an earlier attack. While Santa Anna listened, Ramírez y Sesma and Almonte argued that there was no need to wait for the large guns. They agreed with Santa Anna in principle if not language that the Alamo was "an irregular fortification hardly worthy of the name." It was equipped with artillery, a double wall, and "courageous" defenders, and therefore could not be ignored, but it did not demand the energies of the entire army. In Santa Anna's mind, the Texans, while undoubtedly brave, were little more than a poorly organized, badly trained rabble, and to have to wait for further reinforcements would show weakness on his part. An assault now, he reasoned, "would infuse our soldiers with that enthusiasm of the first triumph that would make them superior in the future to those of the enemy."[63]

Santa Anna listened, but he probably heard selectively. The Napoleon of the West fancied himself a tactical genius, and his subordinates refused to press their case. "Some, though approving this proposal in the presence of the commander in chief," de la Peña wrote disgustedly, "disagreed in his absence . . . others chose silence, knowing that he would not tolerate opposition, his sole pleasure being in hearing what met his wishes, while discarding all admonitions that deviated from those wishes." Santa

Anna discounted their misgivings, and the meeting broke up after several hours without a final decision. Santa Anna agreed to mull over the tactical issues and reconvene the next day.[64]

As a last order of business, Castrillón raised the issue of how to treat prisoners of war, particularly if Travis surrendered before the assault. Santa Anna probably reminded his men of Congress's December 1835 edict that the insurgents were all pirates worthy of extermination, and he then cited a memory of his youth, when he had served as a cadet under Spanish general José Joaquín de Arredondo and had fought against another insurgent army in Béxar. "The example of Arredondo was cited," de la Peña remembered. "[D]uring the Spanish rule he had hanged eight hundred or more colonists after having triumphed in military action, and this conduct was taken as a model." Castrillón and Almonte countered with reminders about the demands of professional military conduct, how gentlemen soldiers treated the vanquished, about the humane treatment of prisoners, but Santa Anna dismissed them out of hand. The Army of Operation would take no prisoners.[65]

★

That night several Tejana women departed the Alamo with scraps of vital information. Precisely what they said and to whom is unknown, but the essence of their intelligence was that the garrison inside the Alamo was still relatively small, though they might have added that there was talk of many more Texan reinforcements on the way. For Santa Anna, here was one more reason not to delay the assault. When he fell asleep that night, he had probably stopped wrestling with the timing of the attack on the Alamo. What need was there for siege guns when the enemy numbers were so small?[66]

INTERLUDE

———— ✦ ————

ANDREA CASTAÑÓN VILLANUEVA'S skin was like parchment paper, yellowed and wrinkled. The clothes hanging off her shoulders seemed attached to a clothes hanger. By the end of the century she had become almost as famous a fixture in San Antonio as the Alamo itself, and visitors traipsed to her small adobe house on South Laredo Street to listen to her tales of Texas long ago. Speaking in soft, musical Spanish, her body swaying back and forth, she shut her blind eyes and remembered. Better known as Madam Candelaria, she claimed that she had been inside the Alamo during the siege and the battle, that she had known Travis and Crockett, and that she had nursed poor Bowie, deathly sick with typhoid, during his last days. "Colonel Bowie died in my arms only a few minutes before the entrance to the Alamo of the soldiers. I was holding his head in my lap when Santa Anna's men swarmed into the room where I was sitting." Though Bowie was dead, the soldiers stuck him in the head with a lance anyway. She also claimed that she had been born on November 30, 1785. Most historians, then and now, question both claims. And quite frankly, Madam Candelaria did not help her case much by occasionally changing the date of her birth or the last few moments of Bowie's life. She was like a novelist, not a historian, seeing truth in the whole, not the details.[1]

She remembered that on March 5, 1836, Travis addressed his troops. She forgot exactly what he said but recalled vividly that "he drew a line on the floor with the point of his sword and asked all who were willing to die for Texas to come over on his side." All but two stepped over the line. One of the two "sprang over the wall and disappeared." The other was Bowie, and he was just too weak to step at all. "He made an effort to rise, but failed, and with tears streaming from his eyes he said: 'Boys, won't none of you help me over there?'" Crockett and a few others came to his aid. "At the time," she commented, "we all knew that we were doomed, but not one was in favor of surrendering."

Madam Candelaria was not the only person—or even the first—to mention Travis's last speech to his men. William P. Zuber, who at the time of his death, in 1913, was the last surviving member of General Sam Houston's army, told a similar story. Zuber claimed that shortly after the fall of the Alamo, Moses (or Louis) Rose had shown up at his parents' home with a remarkable tale. Rose said that he had been at the Alamo and had fled rather than fight to the death. A veteran of the Napoleonic wars, he had seen enough of death to realize that he preferred life, so rather than wait for the Mexicans to attack he had slipped out of the Alamo the night before the final battle.[2]

But Rose too remembered that Travis had made a stirring speech—or at least that was what Zuber swore his parents had told him. Rose said that the night before the fateful assault Travis had gathered his men together and told them that their plight was hopeless. Addressing his soldiers as "my brave companions," Travis said, "Our fate is sealed. Within a few days—perhaps a very few hours—we must all be in eternity. This is our destiny, and we cannot avoid it. This is our certain doom." He had hoped for reinforcements but few had come. "I have evidently confided too much in the promises of friends," he said. Then he told his followers that the choices remaining were few but distinct: "[W]e must die! Our speedy dissolution is a fixed and inevitable fact. Our business is not to make a fruitless effort to save our lives, but to choose the manner of our death." They had three options: surrender and face certain execution;

make a run for open country and be butchered; or remain and fight, taking as many Mexicans as possible into eternity with them. Only by selling their lives dearly could they help their families, friends, and country. But it was each man's decision. "My own choice is to stay in this fort, and die for my country, fighting as long as breath shall remain in my body. This I will do even if you leave me alone."

Travis then drew his sword and traced a line in the ground, saying, "I now want every man who is determined to stay here and die with me to come across the line. Who shall be the first?" And the men, some briskly, others more slowly, crossed the line. The sick got out of their cots and crossed the line. Bowie asked to be carried over the line. In the end only Rose remained on the other side, and shortly afterward he left the Alamo with his life and a story.

Did Zuber invent the Rose story? Perhaps. Even he later confessed that he had invented some of Travis's speech, though he insisted that the story was true and his rendition of the address was faithful to the actual one. In truth, there probably had been a Louis Rose at the Alamo, and he undoubtedly did depart the mission before the final battle. But historians have traditionally regarded the Rose-Zuber account of the line episode with hearty skepticism, charging that it is too melodramatic and too improbable to be true. The idea that Rose told Zuber's parents, they told him, and he waited until 1873 to tell the world seemed far-fetched at best, a damn lie at worst. And the critics might just be right.

But they also just might be wrong. The idea of clarifying a choice by scratching a line in the dirt and then asking men to cross to one side or another was hardly novel. Southerners often voted in this method, and Ben Milam supposedly rallied Texans to take Béxar in December 1835 with just such an action. Certainly it was a melodramatic gesture, but it was a melodramatic age and Travis was far more melodramatic than most. His letters are filled with dramatic excesses and lofty hyperbole. He courted the notion of death as avidly as he wooed females—thinking about it, speculating about it, writing about it. In several letters he considered how people would think about him after he died, seemingly more concerned with his posthumous reputation than his chances of survival. One senses, reading his letters, that death probably did not frighten Travis as much as the idea that in death he would be forgotten or considered a fool. Not only was Travis capable of tracing a line in the sand, the action would have been a perfect expression of his character.[3]

Certainly Travis must have known by the night of March 5 that the Alamo's plight was virtually hopeless. Santa Anna had methodically surrounded the fort, cutting off the roads to Laredo, Goliad, Gonzales, and Nacogdoches. To be sure, some reinforcements had been able to get to the Alamo; the Gonzales men arrived on March 1, and perhaps another group fought their way into the fort a few days later, though this is by no means certain. But with the arrival of more Mexican troops the chances of more Texans arriving were slim. Looking outside the fort, the defenders, numbering somewhere between 180 and 250, saw the inevitable. They were badly outnumbered; almost twenty-four hundred Mexicans surrounded their compound. Water was in short supply, and the food resources were dwindling. And there was always the chance that more Mexican troops were on their way. Calculating the mathematics of survival was a simple process.

It is difficult to imagine the conditions inside the Alamo. For two weeks the defenders had been crammed into a relatively small space with inadequate washing and latrine facilities. Added to this, they were hemmed close to a horse corral and a cattle pen. The stench, a cross between stockyard and outdoor latrine, must have been hideous, but the health problem was even more serious. Poor sanitation, monotonous diet, contaminated drinking water, and improperly cooked food created ideal conditions for diarrhea, dysentery, consumption, and typhoid. Bowie was not the only man who had succumbed to the bacterial wonderland. At least 20 percent of the Alamo garrison were "ineffectives," a not uncommon number for besieged forces. All things considered, the invisible enemies inside the Alamo's walls were almost as deadly as the visible ones outside the walls.

Yet in the few letters Travis wrote during the siege he did not linger too long on physical hardships. His troops needed supplies, yes; and he needed more troops. But the twin characteristics of the letters were bravery and bitterness. Repeatedly Travis stated that he intended to remain at the Alamo and fight for Texas. He did not want to die, but if that was the price of his command he was determined to pay it. He would not betray Texas (which, given the unstable nature of its government, must have seemed like a distant abstraction). But he also expressed a nagging feeling that Texas had somehow betrayed him and his men. Where was Fannin?

Where were the reinforcements? Where were the citizen soldiers like himself determined to fight the enemy in a forward position? Did they plan to wait until Santa Anna reached Anglo Texas? Did they intend to wait until their towns were sacked, their wives violated, and their families slaughtered? The Alamo was the place to meet the enemy, but Texas had not responded to Travis's urgent pleas.

In the Mexican camp the troops and the guns were quiet. Santa Anna had made his decision. At noon on March 5, he had reassembled the general staff and announced his decision to attack early the next morning—even though the big guns would arrive in a matter of days, the Alamo defenders were becoming weaker by the hour, and the threat of reinforcements had largely dissipated. He had determined that it was time to end the siege and demonstrate to Béxar and Texas the price of rebellion. Santa Anna's closest associates suspected he wanted combat for combat's sake, blood for blood's sake, glory for glory's sake, and feared an Alamo surrender that would rob him of battlefield victory. For de la Peña, "It was for this reason that he precipitated the assault, because he wanted to cause sensation and would have regretted taking the Alamo without clamor and without bloodshed, for some believed that without these there is no glory."[4]

At two in the afternoon, Santa Anna issued operational instructions. To his brother-in-law General Martín Perfecto de Cos he offered redemption, an opportunity to avenge his December humiliation in Béxar. Cos would take a column of troops consisting of the Aldama Permanent Battalion (six *fusilero* and one *cazador* company) and the San Luis Active Battalion (the 1st, 2nd, and 3rd *fusilero* companies)—a total of three hundred men, carrying ten ladders, two crowbars, and two axes—and attack from the north against the northwest wall of the Alamo. At the same time, also from the north, Colonel Francisco Duque would lead four hundred troops from the Toluca Battalion (six *fusilero* and one *cazador* company) and the San Luis Active Battalion (4th, 5th, and 6th *fusilero* companies) against the northeastern wall. Like their counterparts under Cos, they would be equipped with ten ladders, two crowbars, and two axes. From the northeast, Colonel José María Romero's three hundred men from the permanent Matamoros and Jiménez Battalions (six *fusilero* companies), with six ladders, would attack the outer east wall, to the rear of the Alamo chapel and the convent, or long barracks. Colonel Juan

Morales, at the head of a column of one hundred *cazadores* from the Matamoros, Jiménez, and San Luis Battalions, bearing two ladders, would attack from the south, sweep the southern wall, and enter the compound after breaching the vulnerable palisade and penetrating the lunette and main gate. Santa Anna would remain in the rear, commanding a reserve column of four hundred troops, consisting of the *zapadores* battalion (*granadaro* companies from the Matamoros, Jiménez, Aldama, Toluca, and San Luis Battalions). Finally, General Ramírez y Sesma's cavalry—composed of the Dolores Regiment, the Veracruz Platoon, the Coahuila Company, and the Rio Grande Presidial Company—would be stationed near the alameda, a grove of cottonwoods, to cut off escape routes to the south and east.

Santa Anna ordered his column commanders to position their men within one hundred yards of the first entrenchments, musket range for the Brown Bess. Slavishly devoted to Napoleonic tactics, he decided to have his infantry attack in linear formation, line after line of men moving toward their objectives. It was understood that the Mexican troops in the first lines would suffer frightful casualties. Grapeshot and cannonballs would slice through the Mexicans like a scythe moving through wheat. "If our soldiers are driven back," *el presidente* assured his commanding officers, "the next line in their rear must force those before them forward, and compel them to scale the walls, cost what it may."[5]

Late in the afternoon of March 5, Santa Anna gathered Cos, Duque, Romero, and Morales together and they jointly reconnoitered the battlefield, making sure to stay out of range of the long rifles, even though, in the darkness, they would be far less effective than usual. He reiterated his orders, pointing out the lines of attack and talking of a glorious victory. The assault would commence just before dawn with the sound of bugles. At dusk, Santa Anna ordered his men to bed. They would need their sleep, and failing that, at least rest.[6]

The officers rousted their men just after midnight on March 6, 1836, with orders to keep their mouths shut. Santa Anna hoped to catch the exhausted Alamo defenders asleep at their posts and insisted that his own troops move into position as quietly as possible. In every respect, his orders were specific. Regardless of the weather, the Mexican troops were to wear no overcoats or blankets, nothing that might slow them down or trip them when scaling the ladders. Chin straps were to be tightly secured to keep shakos and helmets from falling off, making noise, and slowing down the assault, and all soldiers were ordered to wear shoes and sandals. Santa Anna did not want any troops yelping in pain because of rocks and cactus thorns or splinters from the ladders. Since hand-to-hand combat would be a certainty at such close quarters, bayonets were to be fixed in place. Smoking was strictly forbidden, lest the Alamo sentries catch wisps of burning tobacco in the air. But the defenders were in a dead sleep, sentries probably included, and at 1 A.M. Santa Anna's four columns crossed the San Antonio River undetected and assumed their positions. Ramírez y Sesma's cavalry rode their mounts quietly to the Alameda.[7]

The Mexicans had several hours to contemplate destiny. Many clutched rosary beads and crucifixes and whispered Hail Marys. Others fondled Indian charms made of bones, feathers, and dried flowers. Thoughts drifted to homes, wives, lovers, parents, and children and whether they would ever be seen again. De la Peña remembered that "night came, and with it the most sober reflections. . . . Each one individually confronted and prepared his soul for the terrible moment." Captain José Juan Sánchez wrote in his diary what many other Mexican soldiers spent that dark morning pondering: "Why is it that Santa Anna always wants to mark his triumphs with blood and tears?" Later, in the early morning hours, de la Peña again considered mortality. "The moon was up," he remembered, "but the density of the clouds that covered it allowed only an opaque light in our direction, seeming thus to contribute to our designs." In the odd darkness everything seemed slightly out of whack. De la Peña solemnly remembered:

> This half-light, the silence we kept, hardly interrupted by soft murmurs, the coolness of the morning air, the great quietude that seemed to prolong the hours, and the dangers we would soon have to face, all of this rendered our situation grave; we were still breathing and able to communicate; within a few moments many of us would be unable to answer questions addressed to us, having already returned to the nothingness whence we had come; others, badly wounded, would remain stretched out for hours without anyone thinking of them, each still fearing perhaps one of the enemy cannonballs whistling overhead would drop at his feet and put an end to his suffering.

Battle, many of the experienced soldiers knew, was more glorious as an abstraction than as a reality.[8]

While his troops obsessed about life and death, a nervous Santa Anna paced back and forth inspecting the preparations, worrying more about that abstraction than about his men. General Vicente Filisola knew Santa Anna's attitudes intimately. More than once, *el presidente* had argued that the "first object of a general who gives battle . . . is the glory and honor of his arms. . . . [T]he safety and consideration of his men is only secondary." Around midnight, over a chicken dinner, General Castrillón allegedly proposed, for one last time, a postponement of the assault until the twelve-pounder siege guns had arrived. Otherwise, the Army of Operations would sustain terrible losses. Holding up a chicken leg, Santa Anna smirked. "What are the lives of soldiers more so than many chickens? I tell you, the Alamo must fall, and my orders must be obeyed at all hazards." At 1 A.M., Santa Anna and Colonel Juan Almonte returned to headquarters, where over a cup of coffee Almonte spoke casually of the costly fight ahead. Santa Anna silenced him: "It doesn't matter what the cost is; it must be done."[9]

Out in the field, with the outlines of the Alamo clear, officers and soldiers waited for the order. By two o'clock they were in position. By three o'clock many were cold and wet from resting in the damp grass. By four o'clock many had begun to grow impatient. They were ready; come what may, they were ready. Wisps of light streaked the eastern sky when, sometime between 5 and 5:30 A.M., Santa Anna ordered bugler José María González to sound the call to arms, and the shrill notes ended rest, cutting short dreams, nightmares, Hail Marys, and silent prayers. Buglers in other units picked up the tune and filled the air with the sounds of a bitter brass symphony. The Mexican band then struck the chords of the *degüello*, announcing to the enemy one last time that there would be no quarter. "We soon heard that terrible bugle call of death," de la Peña recalled, "which stirred our hearts, altered our expressions, and aroused us all suddenly from our painful meditations. . . . Seconds later the horror of this sound fled from among us, honor and glory replacing it." Shouts of *"Viva Santa Anna"* and *"Viva México,"* mixed with the bugle calls and the "Degüello," filled the night. Inside the Alamo, some Texans also heard *"Muerte* [death] *a los Americanos."*[10]

Long after one of the sentinels should have sounded the alarm, officer of the day John J. Baugh ran into Travis's west wall quarters shouting,

"The Mexicans are coming." Travis immediately grabbed a shotgun and saber and rushed to the gun emplacement on the north wall, followed closely behind by his slave Joe. All around them was confusion. Mexican fire flashed in the night. Voices called out in Spanish and English, mixing curses and oaths in the cacophony of battle. Men ran to their posts and began shooting. Cannons roared, spitting out fire and smoke.

Texans rushed to their positions on the walls and palisades, but they had few targets. Musket and artillery fire filled the air with clouds of acrid smoke, and noise crowded the senses. Along the east wall, with the sun still well below the horizon but the skyline just beginning to brighten, the attackers stood out a bit, casting long shadows, but at the north, south, and west walls they were, at best, opaque objects scurrying about in dim moonlight. The early morning attack had rendered the Kentucky long rifle all but useless. They were accurate up to two hundred yards, but the Texans' field of vision was only a few feet deep.

Travis's slave Joe later said that Travis shouted encouragement to the soldiers on the wall: "Come on, boys, the Mexicans are upon us and we'll give them hell." Looking out into the darkness, illuminated only by flashes of cannon and rifle fire, Travis saw that Duque's Toluca Battalion was close to the wall, and he discharged his shotgun into a mass of Mexicans. Then, perhaps only seconds or minutes after the fighting started, it all ended for Travis. A bullet from a Mexican gun hit him in the head. Joe would later give several versions of Travis's death. In one account he said that Travis was hit and fell back bleeding, but when a Mexican general tried to behead the Alamo commander, "the dying Colonel raised his sword and killed him!" This is doubtful. The impact of a bullet from a .753 caliber Brown Bess smoothbore musket, traveling at around eight hundred feet per second, would have resulted in a blunt-force trauma roughly equivalent to getting hit on the forehead with a sledgehammer. It certainly knocked Travis down and out, and probably killed him instantly. In any case, Joe ran for cover as soon as Travis fell.[11]

Dozens from Colonel Francisco Duque's Toluca Battalion soon joined Travis in death. Under strict orders of silence, the Mexicans had quietly crept in close to the north wall, but a cocktail of nervous energy, adrenaline, and testosterone bubbled up and fogged their judgment; they could not suppress loud cheers once the bugles sounded. Near the northeast corner of the Alamo, the Toluca troops hailed Mexico, praised Santa

Anna, and cursed the Texans, but the screams revealed their positions. De la Peña was aghast. "The officers," he wrote, "were unable to repress this act of folly, which was paid for dearly." Texans on the north wall pointed a cannon in the direction of the screams and unleashed a wall of grapeshot, killing and maiming dozens in an instant. A pile of bodies and body parts began accumulating at the north wall.[12]

Once the defenders reached their posts they sent a punishing storm of lead in every direction. Romero's forces, moving toward the east wall, were torn apart by enfilade fire from the cannon positions at the church, corral, and cattle pen. The church battery destroyed the left flank of the attack and the remaining forces shifted toward the northeast corner of the Alamo in an instinctive act of self-preservation. The Texans' northwestern battery delivered two blasts of grapeshot into General Cos's Aldama Battalion, butchering forty Mexican soldiers. Remembering Cos's assault at the northwest corner, one of his soldiers said, "We ran to the assault. . . . Although the distance was short, the fire from the enemy's cannon was fearful. . . . One can but admire the stubborn resistance of our enemy, and the constant bravery of all our troops. It seemed every cannon or ball or pistol shot of the enemy embedded itself in the breast of our men who without stopping cried: 'Long live the Mexican Republic! Long live General Santa Anna!' I can tell you the whole scene was one of extreme terror." In the prevailing confusion, Cos's and Romero's columns converged amidst the bloody pools at the north wall. "All united at one point," de la Peña recalled, "mixing and forming a confused mass." The Alamo's north wall assumed the look of a slaughterhouse. "Our columns," de la Peña added, "left along their path a wide trail of blood, of wounded, and of dead."[13]

What had seemed like a well-organized plan of attack the afternoon before had turned into a mob action. Ladders were dropped or buried under dead bodies, separated units began to merge and change directions, and undoubtedly chin straps came unsnapped and sandals disappeared in the wild, horrible fighting at the base of the walls. Even worse, friendly fire brought down hundreds of Mexican soldiers. In the dark, with grapeshot, canister, and cannonballs creating utter confusion and terror, many Mexican troopers fired at random, aiming, when they bothered to aim, at anything that moved. Too often their own comrades in forward infantry lines became the targets. "Since they attacked in close column," General Filisola remembered, "all the shots, the direction of which was turned somewhat downward, aimed the bullets toward the backs of those ahead of them." The Mexican infantry found themselves dodging grape and canister ahead and musket balls from the rear. Enemy and friendly fire exacted a terrible toll. "Thus it was that most of our dead and wounded . . . were suffered by this misfortune. It may be said that not a fourth of them were the result of enemy fire."[14]

Watching the action from the north battery, Santa Anna must have sensed that the defenders' fire was slowing the advance of his soldiers. If the result of the attack did not exactly hang in the balance, the assault had reached a critical stage. Duque had been hit in the thigh and was down; the Toluca Battalion had been ripped apart by the Texan fire; what was left of Cos's, Duque's, and Romero's forces had degenerated into a melee below the north wall. De la Peña later wrote that from where Santa Anna stood it looked like the Texans were repulsing the attack, so he sent Colonel Agustín Amat to the north wall with the reserves, a crack *zapadores* battalion and a provisional *granadaro* battalion. Santa Anna's reserves then massed in the killing field below the north wall with the surviving elements of Cos's, Duque's, and Romero's columns, a total of thirteen to fifteen hundred men trying to negotiate their way through four to five hundred dead and wounded men and over the barrier. "A quarter of an hour had elapsed," a stunned de la Peña later wrote, "during which our soldiers remained in a terrible situation, wearing themselves out as they climbed in quest of a less obscure death than that visited on them, crowded in a single mass." What resulted was a terrific push against the weak north wall.[15]

The Mexican attackers found the north wall the easiest to climb, even if they had misplaced their ladders. A weak link in the chain of Alamo fortifications, the crumbling north wall had been reinforced by an elaborate wood outerwork cribbing, with the open space between the wood and wall filled with dirt. The cribbing provided footholds up the wall. "There was therefore a starting point," observed de la Peña, "and it could be climbed, though with some difficulty." Brave Mexican troopers went up the facing of the woodwork, but according to de la Peña, "a lively rifle fire coming from the roof of the barracks and other points caused painful havoc, increasing the confusion of our disorderly mass." The initial wave at the top encountered bayonets, hatchets, axes, and small arms fire. "The

first to climb were thrown down by bayonets already waiting for them behind the parapet, or by pistol fire," remembered de la Peña. But the Mexicans kept coming, undaunted by the carnage. Often using the hung-up
bodies of their own comrades as stepping-stones, they ascended the wall.
Horrific carnage and confusion filled de la Peña's vision of the north wall.
"The sharp retorts of the rifles, the whistling of bullets, the groans of the
wounded, the cursing of the men, the sighs and anguished cries of the dying, the arrogant harangues of the officers, the noise of the instruments of
war, and the inordinate shouts of the attackers, who climbed vigorously,
bewildered all. . . . The shouting of those being attacked was no less loud
and from the beginning had pierced our ears with desperate, terrible cries
of alarm in a language we did not understand." The defenders managed
to repulse a wave or two of attackers, but they were soon overwhelmed,
unable to reload rifles, pistols, and muskets in time to fire at the next
group of attackers. Lieutenant Colonel Sánchez Navarro remembered the
moment of truth when the Mexicans conquered the north wall. "Our
jefes, officers, and troops, at the same time, as if by magic, reached the
top of the wall." Only twenty minutes had passed since the first bugle had
sounded.[16]

While the north wall was being breached, Colonel Juan Morales, with
his small contingent of one hundred *cazadores,* attacked the south wall
and palisade, where Davy Crockett and the defenders fought them off.
The *cazadores* retreated into the *jacales* outside the southwest corner,
where they faced the wrath of the Alamo's big gun, the eighteen-pounder.
Luckily for Juan Morales and the *cazadores,* it was too big. The cluster of
jacales was positioned below the cannon's angle of declination, and the
shots whistled well over the soldiers' heads. The breaching of the north
wall provided Morales a second chance. Many defenders of the south
wall, perhaps including Crockett, abandoned the palisade to reinforce the
Texans at the north wall, and when Morales attacked the second time, the
cazadores encountered less resistance.

At the same time, General Cos ordered his columns off the north wall
for an attack along the Alamo's west wall. One eyewitness remembered
that "several companies of soldiers came running down the street with
heavy bridge timbers" and proceeded to use them as battering rams. Also
armed with crowbars and axes, the *soldados* broke through barricaded
windows, doors, and posterns along the west wall or ascended it, finding

the Texan resistance surprisingly light. With so much activity along the north wall, many of the defenders had probably abandoned those positions to engage the Mexicans attacking from the north. Cos's men poured into the compound, and the Texans at the north wall soon found themselves taking fire from the front and the rear.

As the Mexicans poured in from the north and west, the defenders fell back, fighting and firing as they moved. Some defenders moved toward the south wall, others ran into barracks along the east wall. About the same time, Morales's *cazadores* gained a foothold on the southwest corner of the Alamo, captured the eighteen-pounder, and began blasting away at barricaded doorways and Texan artillery batteries. They targeted the chapel and long barracks, where some defenders had taken cover. Enrique Esparza, a Tejano child huddling in the chapel, remembered the artillery assault and attack. "Suddenly there was a terrible din. Cannon boomed. Their shot crashed through the doors and windows and the breeches in the walls. Then men rushed in on us. They swarmed among us and over us. They fired on us in volleys. They struck us down with their escopetas."[17]

De la Peña recalled how his troops "turned the enemy's own cannon to bring down the doors to the rooms or the rooms themselves; a horrible carnage took place. . . . The tumult was great, the disorder frightful; it seemed as if the furies had descended upon us. . . . In the midst of this thundering din, there was such confusion that orders could not be understood." The first Mexican troops into the compound found themselves in a withering cross fire. Not only were Texans shooting at them, but they were also being brought down by friendly fire from Morales's troops, who were firing at the defenders from the south. The deadly cross fire sent hundreds of Mexican soldiers scrambling for cover at the bottom of a dry streambed running through the compound.[18]

Cowering in the Alamo chapel, clutching her twenty-month-old daughter, Susanna Dickinson acted as hostess at a reception for the doomed. As soon as the north wall fell, her husband, Almaron, burst into the chapel, ready to say a final good-bye. "Great God, Sue!" he shouted. "The Mexicans are inside our walls! All is lost! If they spare you, save my child!" Dickinson stole a kiss and returned to the battle. Galba Fuqua, Susanna's teenage friend from Gonzales, then stormed into the chapel. He wanted to tell Susanna something, but a musket ball had blown apart his jaw. Fuqua tried to hold the bones together and speak, but blood gurgled out, not words. He then shrugged, shook his head, and raced back into the compound. Crockett, according to Dickinson, showed up as well, kneeling in the chapel and making his peace with God before taking up his rifle and hurrying off. Several Mexican soldiers then chased Jacob Walker, a father of four and a friend of the Dickinsons, into the chapel. They went after him with bayonets. "Drunk on blood," Susanna recalled later, "they lifted him up like a farmer does a bundle of fodder on his pitchfork," raising and lowering him several times.[19]

Once again, in the dark and confusion, defenders and attackers alike shot at moving shapes, shadows streaking across their line of vision. For fifteen or so minutes the fighting continued. Overwhelmed at the northern and western walls, the Alamo defenders fell back, retreating to defensive positions in the rooms and buildings of the inner east wall, especially into the long barracks. Colonel José María Romero's troops, who had entered the compound by climbing the outer east wall and running through the cattle pen and horse corral, then entered the long barracks, where defenders held out in pitch black darkness, forcing the Mexicans to negotiate a deadly catacomb. "Our soldiers, some stimulated by courage and others by fury, burst into the quarters where the enemy had entrenched themselves from which issued an infernal fire. Behind these came others, who, nearing the doors and blind with fury and smoke, fired their shots against friends and enemies alike, and in this way our losses were most grievous." It took nearly an hour of room-to-room, hand-to-hand combat to wipe out the resistance. At one point, several defenders holding out in the long barracks, according to de la Peña, "poked the points of their bayonets through a hole or a door with a white cloth, the symbol of cease-fire, and some even used their socks." The Mexican troops entered expecting surrenders, but the Texans had set a trap. The white flags were a ruse. "Among those pleading for mercy," de la Peña wrote, "stood men determined to kill until they were killed. Treating the white flags as mere bait, they bled the Mexican soldiers with pistols, knives, and bayonets." In an enraged fury, the Mexicans "rekindled their anger and at every moment fresh skirmishes broke out with renewed fury."[20]

In the hand-to-hand fighting in the courtyard and barracks, the sheer numbers of the Mexicans overwhelmed the Texans. In the barracks the

Mexican soldiers moved from room to room, smashing down the doors and killing the Texas troops inside. They killed the sick inside the hospital as well as the defenders fighting for their lives. In a room near the main gate they found the dying Bowie and hastened his end. They moved into every part of the Alamo—cattle pen, horse corral, convent, church, barracks. A few women and children and Joe they spared.[21]

Some of the defenders raced instinctively toward the open space outside the Alamo, dropping over the south wall and moving in the general direction of the alameda and the Gonzales Road or climbing over the stockade walls and moving toward the east. But the safety of the open territory was an illusion. Ramírez y Sesma's cavalry road down and killed the Texans. The Texans fought hard for their lives, but they were no match for experienced cavalrymen. Once again, it was a case of few against many, odds too great to overcome.[22]

Between 6:30 and 7:30 A.M., as fighting in the long barracks died down and gunfire became more sporadic, the dawn revealed an Alamo littered with upwards of eight hundred corpses. With nobody else to kill but adrenaline still pumping, Mexican troops marched from body to body, ferreting out the Anglo and Tejano rebels, engaging in an orgy of violence, firing musket rounds and sticking bayonets into the living and the dead, mutilating and stripping the bodies. It was a dirty business, embarrassing many Mexican officers. "There were deeds that we refrain from relating," wrote General Vicente Filisola, "because of the sorrow that the account of the events would cause." Santa Anna's soldiers also captured a handful of defenders alive. They were quickly dispatched as well.[23]

In an hour the battle was over. The sun was just beginning to rise in the eastern sky. As the women and children were led out of the Alamo church, they saw the bodies, many horribly mutilated. So many dead brave men. Travis was dead near the north wall. Bowie was dead in his room in the south wall. And Crockett was dead—somewhere.

6

━━━━ ✦ ━━━━

IN SEARCH OF
DAVY'S GRAVE

AT 4 O'CLOCK IN THE AFTERNOON of March 11, less than a week after the final assault on the Alamo, Anselmo Bergara and Andrés Barcena, two Tejanos, rode into Gonzales, the town that separated the Anglo east from the Latino west. They rode past the unfamiliar frame houses, down the muddy street to where a clump of men huddled around General Sam Houston. They rode heavy with bad news. The Alamo had fallen, they reported. All the defenders, including the brave men from Gonzales, were dead.[1]

Most of the report, Barcena noted, was decidedly secondhand. Bergara had wandered the streets of San Antonio undisturbed during the siege but, like so many other Tejanos, had left the city on the Saturday night before Santa Anna's troops attacked. He had returned, however, on Sunday night and spoken with a Mexican soldier who had fought in the battle. The soldier said that 521 Mexicans had died in the assault, but so had all the defenders of the Alamo. The two Anglo commanders, Travis and Bowie, had died ignominiously. Travis had killed himself, and Bowie had died "lying sick in bed." Lieutenant Dickinson had fought with "desperate courage" until the end was near, then had tied his child to his back and had leaped from the top of a two-story building. He and his child died together. Seven others had surrendered and asked for quarter but had been "murdered" on the order of Santa Anna.

Exactly how Barcena and Bergara presented their information, and in what language or combination of languages, is unknown, and at least one listener was dubious of the entire story. Barcena said all he knew was what Bergara told him, and Bergara said all he knew was what the Mexican soldier had told him. "The contradiction of these two men makes me suspect that they are spys [sic] of Santa Anna," wrote E. N. Gray, "because, why should Bergara fly from Bejar after remaining so many days there undisturbed and enjoying himself?"

Sam Houston didn't buy the spy story, though he placed them in custody as spies. He sent the news in a letter to James Fannin at Goliad, adding that while the report was only rumor, "I fear a melancholy portion of it will be found too true." Houston knew that the numbers and small details made sense. Bergara had said that twenty-five hundred Mexicans had stormed the Alamo, taken it just before sunrise, and suffered 521 deaths and about as many wounded. But they had killed all 187 men inside. After the "massacre" Santa Anna had ordered the lifeless defenders burned "in alternate layers of wood and bodies." Based on these details, Houston concluded, "I have but little doubt that the Alamo has fallen. Whether the above particulars are all true may be questionable."

During the next few days reports from Béxar reaffirmed the fate of the Alamo but added layers of rumors and suppositions about what had happened—or might have happened—to the Texas leaders. Houston was chattier in a letter to his friend Henry Raguet. "Our friend Bowie, as is now understood, unable to get out of bed, shot himself as the soldiers approached it." Others followed his example, fighting until all hope was lost and then robbing the Mexicans of the satisfaction of a kill. "Travis, 'tis said, rather than fall into the hands of the enemy, stabbed himself."[2]

The news that reached Gonzales, a mixture of fact and fiction, was the starting point of the great mystery story of the Texas Revolution. It would spur new controversies and has troubled Alamo historians ever since. During the following months, through the sad fate of Goliad and the great news of San Jacinto, the battle of the Alamo remained on the lips and minds of Texans and Americans. So many questions remained unanswered, so many pieces of the puzzle were missing. What had happened?

That the soldiers who had manned the walls and palisade were all dead was fairly certain. But how had they died? Had Travis and Bowie killed themselves? Had Dickinson leaped to his death with his child tied to his back, a scene straight out of an epic romantic novel? And what of Davy Crockett? How had he met his end? Bravely, no doubt, but how? These were no idle questions, for in the age of Lord Byron, Sir Walter Scott, and Samuel Coleridge, in a country where the exploits of Napoleon, the duke of Wellington, and Andrew Jackson had been followed in detail, how a man died was as important as how he lived, sometimes more so. Dying bravely counted.

Beyond this, there were the loved ones left behind who waited for news. No detail was unimportant to them; every morsel of information was greedily consumed. They wanted to know that their fathers and brothers, husbands and friends had died well, sacrificing their lives in a noble cause. Did not fighting and dying for freedom matter? Did it not join the ashes of the dead with Patrick Henry and with the patriots of the past who had died for liberty, or even with Byron himself?

Benjamin Goodrich, a member of the Washington convention, wrote his brother Edmund about their brother John Camp Goodrich, who like Crockett had made the trip from Tennessee to Texas. "Texas is in mourning," he noted, "and it becomes my painful duty to inform my relations in Tennessee of the massacre of my poor brother John." Their brother was murdered with other "brave countrymen, gallantly defending" the Alamo against an army of "8,000" Mexicans. Benjamin had heard the same rumors as Houston, and he even added a few new details. Travis stabbed himself in his heart, dying instantly. Bowie was murdered in his bed. Seven men surrendered but were summarily shot. Crockett and other men from Tennessee also sacrificed their lives, but they "died like men" and "posterity will do them justice." Benjamin ended by promising to be "another victim" or "see Texas free and Independent."[3]

As weeks passed, stories of bravery benefited from natural inflation. As the tales passed from ear to ear they took on a life of their own. By the end of March one man wrote his parents in Sudbury that Travis and his band had died like tigers. Travis was "found dead grappled with a Mexican Officer with a sword through his body." And Crockett, who had brushed near Sudbury on his Eastern tour just two years before, exacted the greatest cost for his life. He was found "with about 20 of the enemy with him and his rifle was broken to pieces." Some claimed that he had "killed at least 20 or 30 himself."[4]

By April the defenders had passed into immortality, at least among freedom-loving Texans. "Brave, chivalrous, heroic, patriotic band! yee sleep in death but 'still are not free,'" wrote Thomas J. Chambers, who was charged with raising recruits in the United States. "Your names shall be inscribed in the proudest and the brightest pages of history with those of Leonidas, Warren and others who have offered themselves as sacrifices upon the alter [sic] of their country. The foundation of the temple of liberty and independence about to be erected by your fellow-citizens, have been laid deep by you, and the corner stone rests upon your consecrated ashes." For Chambers, the defenders were Texas's "first glorious martyrs in a holy struggle," and he was certain posterity would "repeat hymns of praise" to them. For at the "Thermopylae at Béxar" Texas manhood was defined, and Santa Anna should expect nothing less from the rest of its citizens. The dictator "will find in the plains of Texas a Marathon and a Plataea. The bones of the barbarians shall bleach upon the fields they desolate!"[5]

Chambers thought, wrote, and spoke the language of the romantic age. Like Byron, Shelley, or thousands of other classically educated Englishmen and Americans, he interpreted the events of the day in the light of history. No allusion seemed more apt than Thermopylae, the 480 B.C. battle where Leonidas's Spartans and his Greek allies sacrificed their lives to stall the march of Xerxes' Persians. All but one Spartan was killed, but their deaths gave their countrymen time to organize. Eventually at the battles of Salamis (480 B.C.) and Plataea (479 B.C.), the Greeks drove the Persians out of Greece, presumably striking a blow for civilization and against barbarism and for liberty against autocracy.

In the aftermath of the Alamo, journalists repeatedly mentioned the story of Thermopylae, insisting that now Texas had heroes made of the same mettle as the ancient Greeks. The defenders, wrote a resident of Nacogdoches, Texas, "died martyrs to liberty; and on the altar of their sacrifice will be made many a vow that shall break the shackles of tyranny. Thermopylae is no longer without a parallel, and when time shall consecrate the dead at the Alamo, Travis and his companions will be named in rivalry with Leonidas and his Spartan band." Or as another Texan later observed, "Thermopylae had her messenger of defeat—the Alamo had none."[6]

Thermopylae helped Texans place their independence movement in a stark, apocalyptic context. At the Alamo, worlds had collided. The early Texans, historian Paul Andrew Hutton has pointed out, viewed the battle "as a contest of civilizations: freedom vs. tyranny; democracy vs. despotism; Protestantism vs. Catholicism; the New World Culture of the United States vs. the Old World Culture of Mexico; Anglo-Saxons vs. the mongrelized mixture of Indian and Spanish races; and ultimately, the forces of good over evil." Placed in such a context, the question of how the defenders died seemed as important as Socrates' last words.[7]

Yet the comparison to Thermopylae did not move Americans one inch closer to learning how Travis, Bowie, Crockett, and the rest died. The Alamo desperately needed what the Greek battle had had: a survivor. In fact, the Alamo had several. On March 20, Susanna Dickinson, her daughter, Angelina, and Travis's slave Joe straggled into Gonzales. Since the Mexicans found Susanna in the Alamo church sacristy and Joe in a room hiding, the two had experienced numbing emotional swings. They had witnessed the horrors of battle without quarter, seen people they knew and loved shot and stabbed, dead bodies scattered about like the detritus of war. And what would be their fate? Death? Worse?

Santa Anna treated them kindly. The Napoleon of the West assured Joe that his country did not sanction slavery and that Joe would be a slave no more. He asked only that Joe identify the bodies of Travis and Bowie. Joe did so. Then before releasing him the dictator treated Joe to a review of his troops, telling him that there were eight thousand in all and that he would bring Texas to its knees. Santa Anna promised to send Susanna and her daughter to Mexico City, a place more civilized than the plains of Texas. Susanna pleaded against the idea, and Santa Anna relented. She could leave then, and go to Gonzales with word of his strength and ruthlessness. Santa Anna assigned Ben, Almonte's black manservant, to escort her. And so, on March 11 she departed, meeting up by chance with Joe along the way.[8]

Susanna carried messages of doom. One was the images in her memory, what she had seen and heard during those fateful hours on the morning of March 6. The other was an English proclamation in Almonte's handwriting but dictated by Santa Anna. Addressing the inhabitants of Texas, Santa Anna claimed that the problems in the territory were the work of "audacious adventurers, maliciously protected by some inhabitants of a neighboring republic," and he promised to "check and chastise such enormous daring." But though he was "bound to punish the criminal," he was just as determined to "protect the innocent," and he called on all citizens to remain loyal. "Fulfill always your duties as Mexican citizens, and you may expect the protection and benefits of the laws," he told Texans.[9]

Deaf Smith, Houston's invaluable scout, discovered the small messenger party when he was on his way to the Alamo in search of information, and he guided Susanna and the rest back to Gonzales. After telling Houston what they had witnessed, Susanna and Joe moved farther east. Eventually they shared their story with the leading politicians of Texas, but not in Washington-on-the-Brazos, where the convention had only recently finished the new Texas constitution. By mid-March, the mood of the convention—and of Texas—was as bleak as the cloudy, drizzly weather. The Alamo was lost. Santa Anna was marching east, with rumors rippling outward. Texas, William Fairfax Gray noted in his convention journal, was an "invaded, unarmed, unprovisioned country, without an army to oppose the invaders, and without money to raise one." Convention members were scurrying out of Washington, mostly in an eastward direction. "A general panic seems to have seized them"—one they shared with thousands of fellow citizens. "A constant stream of women and children, and some men, with wagons, cars and pack mules, are rushing across the Brazos night and day." Washington storekeepers were joining the exodus, packing up what they could haul and hotfooting it east. Most politicians departed as well, bumping into one another on the road to the temporary capital at Harrisburg or to Galveston Bay. It was as if some invisible hand had picked up Texas at San Antonio and tilted it, causing everything to roll toward the southeast—women and children in the front, followed by land speculators, politicians, Houston and his army, and Santa Anna and his forces. Texans soon referred to the wholesale flight as the "Runaway Scrape."[10]

On March 20, Susanna, Joe, and the Texas politicians met at Jared Groce's plantation, the primary point for crossing the Brazos River. Gray, a handsome Virginia land dealer with cold, calculating eyes, recorded the meeting in his journal. He wrote that Joe recounted his tale "with modesty, apparent candor, and remarkably distinctly for one of his class." Joe said that the garrison was bone-tired when the Mexicans attacked. Everyone was asleep—picket guards, sentinels, Travis, Joe, and the rest. When the alarm came, men rushed to their posts, including Travis, with Joe following behind. Travis discharged his rifle. Joe fired his. Then Travis was down, slumped against the wall. Joe ran back into the barracks. Perhaps with more imagination than actual memory, Joe told how the Mexicans finally poured over the walls "like sheep," turning the battle into a melee of gun butts and pistols and knives.

Joe said that Travis recovered enough to run his sword through the body of General Mora before dying. Like Travis, the rest died fighting, except for "a little, weakly man named Warner, who asked for quarter. He was spared by the soldiery, but on being conducted to Santa Anna, he ordered him to be shot, and it was done." Bowie died in his sickbed, died bravely and was mutilated. Crockett and his friends died together; they were found "with twenty-four of the enemy dead around them." "Negroes" like himself and women like Mrs. Dickinson were spared. After the battle, Santa Anna, dressed "like a Methodist preacher," questioned Joe and eventually released him.[11]

Susanna Dickinson did not contradict Joe's story. In fact, the tales of Joe and Susanna had become intertwined during the period they spent together traveling and talking. What she saw became part of the fabric of his account, and what he saw became part of hers. Gray did not record Joe's exact words, nor Susanna's, and his passive voice dulls precision. When Gray notes that Joe claimed that "Crockett and a few of his friends were found together," the identity of the finders is unclear. Did Joe see Crockett's body? Or did Susanna see the body as she departed the Alamo church (which she later claimed) and tell Joe? There was a regrettable absence of grammarians at the interview with Susanna and Joe, and no alert prosecuting attorneys to separate who saw what where and when.[12]

Certainly the men who listened to the tales at Groce's plantation accepted them as a single, factual entity. Politician George Childress heard the tales and carried away the impression that Crockett fought with "heroic desperation to the last, and was one of the last that perished, almost burying himself with the slain." That day, and the days and years after, Susanna and Joe continued to tell how the Mexicans paid dearly for Crockett's life and how Travis stopped dying long enough to impale General Mora. Brave men who died gloriously was the message. Susanna even told John Smith and Andrew Ponton that in death "the countenance of Crocket [sic] was unchanged: he had . . . that freshness of hue, which his exercise of pursuing the beasts of the forest and the prairie had imparted to him."[13]

By the time Susanna and Joe reached Groce's plantation, however, other stories had begun to eclipse theirs. Events in Texas had become a mass of spilled mercury, changing shapes constantly. Militarily, after the fall of the Alamo the primary theater of the war shifted southeast, where in Goliad James W. Fannin's troops lingered, waiting for Texas's most indecisive man to make a decision. Free of Fannin's emotional constipation, General José Urrea was moving toward Texas's Hamlet, determined to force a decision upon him. Initially Santa Anna had deployed Urrea to Matamoros to intercept a rumored Texas move on that city, but in February the Generalissimo had sent new orders to his aggressive commander. Urrea was to cross the Rio Grande and sweep north across the coastal prairies of south Texas, crushing insurgents wherever he found them. Leaving two hundred men of his army of 550 in Matamoros, with orders to rejoin him later, Urrea crossed the Rio Grande on February 16 and moved up the coast. During the next month, he battled rebel forces at San Patricio and Los Cuates de Agua Dulce, on the way to Goliad and Refugio. In case Urrea's approach was not enough to move Fannin to action, after the battle of the Alamo, Santa Anna ordered Colonel Juan Morales's Jiménez and San Luis Battalions—approximately five hundred men—to march southeast and link up with Urrea.[14]

When General Sam Houston arrived in Gonzales on March 11 and learned of the Alamo's fate, he sensed that Fannin was in danger's path and ordered him to pull back to Victoria, where the Guadalupe River afforded a sound defensive line. Take what artillery you can, Houston wrote, and sink the rest in the river. As for Goliad, "You will take the necessary measures to blow up that fortress." In case Fannin had any doubts about Houston's intention, General Sam ended his message as clearly as possible: "The immediate advance of the enemy may be confidently expected, as well as a rise in the water. Prompt movements are therefore highly important."[15]

Unlike Goliad, where most residents had tired of rebel troops who abused local Tejano ranchers and businessmen by taking what they wanted and paying what they chose, Victoria remained friendly and supportive of the cause. But Fannin, being Fannin, delayed his retreat and seemed not to have taken the enemy seriously. Dr. J. H. Barnard, a military surgeon, wrote in his journal that Fannin's "former experience in fighting Mexicans had led him to entertain a great contempt for them as soldiers, and led him to neglect to take such precautionary measures as were requisite, from their great numerical superiority."[16]

Not until Fannin saw the advance portion of Urrea's force did he begin to stir. On the foggy morning of March 19 he began his long-delayed and badly planned retreat. His force, traveling heavy with cannons and arms and light with food, moved sluggishly east. At a moment when time was everything, Fannin treated it as if it were nothing. When a cart broke down and fell in the San Antonio River, his party stopped to haul it out. More time was lost when he ordered everyone to stop to allow the oxen to graze. Several of his officers protested that they were in a vulnerable position, that they were out in the open with no means of defense. Fannin was calm; Mexican soldiers did not worry him.[17]

Although the oxen were "wild and contrary" and some men grumbled over the absence of a noon meal, other soldiers took time to joke and admire the landscape. The road snaked across narrow prairies and through oak woods, over fields of rich, soft grass, past "droves of deer" that gazed on "in wonder." From time to time, they spied wild horses, which "fled shyly."

Urrea arrived at Goliad soon after Fannin's lazy exit, and he did not stop to eat or admire the scenery. Two hours behind his prey, he moved fast to close the gap. Early in the afternoon Urrea's cavalry overtook Fannin's force. One mile short of Coleto Creek, whose timbers offered a strong defensive position, Fannin finally made a quick decision. He ordered his men to form a skirmish line. They would fight the Mexicans out in the open, taking on a larger force from a weaker position. Even with the safety of the timbers in sight, they would fight out on the prairie. Fannin's decision was as bad as it was quick.

Urrea took advantage of the natural cover and deployed his men on the high ground surrounding the Texas position. Urrea attacked; Fannin, his men formed into a hollow square, defended. The Texans fought ferociously and bravely, but everything was on the Mexicans' side. Their sharpshooters picked off the Texan gunners and killed the Texan oxen. From the cover of high grass, the Mexican infantry shot into the Texan square. Fannin took a bullet in the thigh, but he kept fighting, demonstrating at least that if he lacked judgment he did not want for courage.

The Texans' position was perilous. They lacked water to cool their guns and quench their thirst. They lacked cover from the sun and Mexican bullets. But most of all, they lacked viable choices. Nightfall would end the day's fighting, but unless they received reinforcement it would not change their predicament. Night came. Nine of Fannin's men were dead, fifty-one bleeding from wounds. Little food. Almost no water. The enemy, moving under the cover of darkness, had encircled them. That cold night it rained, which took a toll on gunpowder and drenched the soldiers. Fannin ordered the construction of breastworks. His men dug a three- or four-foot ditch and surrounded it with overturned carts and dead horses and oxen, listening all the while to the blare of Mexican bugles and the shrill cries of Urrea's troops.

Dawn came with no reinforcements, at least for the Texans. Reinforcements did come for the Mexicans. What had been perilous twelve hours before was now hopeless. Fannin raised a white flag and limped out to meet his Mexican counterpart. Urrea would accept Fannin's surrender, but it had to be without terms. "If you gentlemen wish to surrender at discretion, the matter is ended, otherwise I shall return to my camp and renew the attack," Urrea said. After conferring with his officers—and perhaps misleading them about the nature of the surrender—Fannin accepted Urrea's offer, hoping, perhaps assuming, that he would be treated as a prisoner of war and not a soldier of fortune. Under guard, his force walked back to Goliad. There they were incarcerated in the chapel at La Bahía. Urrea, not Fannin, finally occupied Victoria.[18]

"Fannin was a gentleman, a man of courage, a quality which makes us soldiers esteem each other mutually," Urrea later wrote. "If it had been in my hand to save him, together with his companions, I would have gladly done so. All I could do was to offer him to use my influence with the general-in-chief, which I did from Guadalupe." No doubt, Urrea's attitude raised Fannin's hopes. In his memoir of the war, José Enrique de la Peña would later comment, "Fannin and his comrades surrendered with the understanding that their lives would be respected, [but] Urrea had given them no [such] guarantee. . . . [T]hey did, nevertheless, trust our overrated generosity in the belief that the intercession of the victor could not be ignored." John C. Duval, a soldier under Fannin's command, later wrote, "I have always believed myself that Gen. Urrea entered into the capitulation with Col. Fannin in good faith." A man of his word, Urrea wrote Santa Anna from Victoria and recommended clemency. "A gesture of generosity after such a hard-fought battle is most worthy of the most singular commendation, and I can do no less than to commend it to your Excellency." Even Urrea later admitted that Fannin surrendered "confident that Mexican generosity would not make their surrender useless, for under any other circumstances they would have sold their lives dearly, fighting to the last."[19]

Santa Anna saw the matter differently, viewing Urrea's humanity with lofty contempt. He replied immediately, reminding Urrea of the government's December 1835 decree that "any foreigners invading the Republic be treated and tried as pirates whenever found armed" and adding his own opinion that any "Mexican who engages in the traitorous act of joining adventurers, as described, loses his rights as citizen according to the laws . . . [and] should be treated likewise." Santa Anna sent his instructions in triplicate, dispatched an aide to go to Goliad to witness the executions, and sent separate orders to Colonel José Nicolás de la Portilla, the Mexican commander in Goliad, to carry them out. Portilla received the courier at 7 P.M. on March 26. An hour later, he received a message from Urrea to "treat the prisoners with consideration, and particularly their leader, Fannin."[20]

De la Peña, who grew to despise Santa Anna, had nothing but scorn for Portilla, characterizing him as a "blind and willing servant." Actually, Portilla hated his assignment, and he spent a sleepless night pondering the contradictory orders. "What a cruel contrast in these opposite instructions," he noted in his diary. At dawn the prisoners were divided into four groups. The sick and wounded were left behind in the chapel, and three other groups were escorted under guard out of La Bahía. There the three groups parted ways—one headed up the Béxar Road toward San Antonio, a second southwest along the San Patricio Road, and a third east on the Victoria Road.

It was spring, a time for hope. The prisoners undoubtedly hoped for the best. Had not Urrea actually allowed Fannin to travel under guard to Copano Bay, where he had tried unsuccessfully to charter a vessel? Fannin had returned less than forty-eight hours earlier, talking about plans for a safe passage home. Arrangements were made, he said. While Portilla contemplated his terrible orders, the Texans amused one another with jokes, tall tales, and reminiscences. Better times were ahead, they thought as they sang "Home Sweet Home." The next morning many believed they were being sent off on a work detail, perhaps to herd cattle or gather wood. Or maybe they were being taken to Copano Bay or Matamoros for a boat to New Orleans. Why else would Portilla have them carry knapsacks?

The men had not marched long before they were ordered to stop. Then the singing and the planning and the hoping stopped, replaced in a moment of recognition with praying and waves of fear. Some men pled for their lives, other encouraged their comrades to "die like brave men." The Mexican guards opened fire. Lancers cut off the men who avoided the first volleys, and infantrymen butchered the wounded. Back in the presidio, in the shadows of the chapel, the wounded who had been too weak to march were slaughtered. An officer told Fannin, "For having come with an armed band to commit depredations and revolutionize Texas, the Mexican government is about to chastise you." Fannin asked only that he be shot in the chest, given a Christian burial, and his watch sent to his family. Unable to stand, he tied on his own blindfold and sat in a chair to await the end. The commanding officer of the execution party shot Fannin in the face and kept the watch, then ordered him burned with the other Texans. Some 342 Texans died that morning, and twenty-eight managed to escape. It was Palm Sunday—March 27, 1836.[21]

The extermination—a "crime against humanity," observed de la Peña—discredited Santa Anna among many of his officers and demonized him in the eyes of Texans and Americans. Urrea sank into a depression when he heard the news. "I never thought that horrible . . . massacre would take place in cold blood and without urgency." On the day of the slaughter, Portilla wrote Urrea recounting his own horror at executing the terrible orders. The Alamo, they both knew, was warfare. But Goliad was something else, a badge of shame, a national disgrace. It "tarnished our glory," wrote de la Peña, "took away the fruits of victory, and . . . prolong[ed] the war and ma[d]e its success doubtful, because it provoked the enemy and placed him in the difficult position of vanquishing or dying." Had Santa Anna simply imprisoned Fannin's men, or deposited them penniless in New Orleans, the Texas Revolution might have evaporated, or at least attenuated. Instead, Texas had 342 martyrs to add to the Alamo's pantheon.[22]

Davy Crockett (above) *and Jim Bowie* (below) *were two of the most famous defenders at the Alamo. By the time of the Mexican attack, Bowie was lying sick in bed. Crockett was active among the defenders—but the precise facts surrounding his death remain a mystery. Did he die fighting, with Mexican victims all around? Or did he, as some rumors then and now suggest, surrender at the end, only to be executed?*

William Barret Travis was in charge at the Alamo. Before the battle, he begged for reinforcements in two famous letters that were published in several papers. In one he vowed, "Victory or death!" Whether or not he also drew the famous line in the sand with his sword is another Alamo mystery.

General Sam Houston, commander of the Army of Texas. A few weeks after the Alamo fell, he decimated Santa Anna's army while urging his troops to "remember the Alamo."

Antonio López de Santa Anna. An accomplished politician and inveterate schemer, he survived several regime changes in Mexico only to emerge as president in 1833. After centralizing power, he led an army to the north, to put down rebelliousness among the Anglos and Tejanos.

Above: *the Alamo as it appeared in an 1849 sketch by Edward Everett. For years after the battle the Alamo was little used. In that year, the U.S. army rented it from the Catholic church for $150 per month, turning it into a quartermaster's depot. Major E. B. Babbitt supervised a renovation in which the convent was rebuilt and a new, gabled roof was put on the chapel. To close in the open west end of the roof, he erected the now-famous Campanulate, or bell-shaped façade, atop the front wall. The picture below shows the Alamo on the eve of the Civil War, just before a fire that brought down the chapel's roof.*

Alamo survivors Susanna Dickinson (top left), *Enrique Esparza* (top right), *and Angelina Dickinson* (below). *On March 20, 1836, Susanna and Angelina, along with a former slave, Joe, reached Sam Houston at Gonzales, carrying a proclamation from Santa Anna and some of the first reports of the massacre. They claimed that Crockett fought to the death, surrounded by twenty-four Mexican dead. Meanwhile, some papers reported that Crockett was still alive, and others that he had surrendered.*

The Alamo in 1866 (top) and 1888 (bottom). In 1886 the fiftieth anniversary of the battle passed without notice, though it prompted the San Antonio Daily Express to suggest "that a society be formed, whose duty it shall be to see that the prominent anniversaries of Texas histories are observed." In 1892 the Daughters of the Republic of Texas was formed; in 1905 the society became the official custodian of the chapel and convent.

Adina De Zavala (left) *and Clara Driscoll* (right) *soon waged the "Second Battle of the Alamo" (1911–12). Earlier, Driscoll had helped save the site by raising money to purchase the Hugo & Schmeltzer building, to the left of the chapel, and then by purchasing the chapel itself. De Zavala had helped push through legislation for the state to remunerate her and grant custodianship to the Daughters of the Republic. Yet a few years later, Driscoll wanted to tear down the Hugo & Schmeltzer building (on the site of the old barracks) and De Zavala did not. Driscoll formed a new, rebel chapter of the DRT and got her way.*

Above: *The Alamo courtyard in 1911, in the midst of the "battle."* Below: *The Hugo & Schmeltzer building in its full glory, from 1890.*

Above: *The Alamo in 1912 after the dismantling of the Hugo & Schmeltzer building.* Below: *The compound before the 1913 destruction of the second-story walls.*

The Alamo and Fort and Menger Hotel, San Antonio, Tex

Madam Candelaria in 1896. She claimed she had been inside the Alamo during the siege and battle, and that she had nursed Bowie during his last days, though most historians dispute both claims. She became a famous fixture in San Antonio by the end of the century, telling and retelling the story of Travis drawing a line on the floor with the point of his sword.

John Wayne on the set of his film The Alamo. *He played Crockett, and spent lavishly on an advertising campaign to link the Alamo story to the presidential election of 1960.*

Franklin and Eleanor Roosevelt had campaigned at the Alamo as early as 1936, on the centenary. John F. Kennedy (bottom) also visited the Alamo while campaigning in 1960.

Left: *The cover of a 1955 Dell comic book, part of the licensing campaign associated with Disney's Crockett.* Right: *Another Disney license produced novelizations of the script.*

A scene from the climactic show.

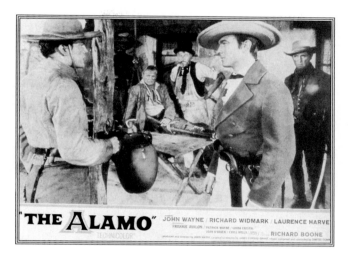

Above: *A poster for John Wayne's 1960 movie.* Below: *A scene from the siege, before the battle.*

The making of the film Viva Max *in 1969.*

Quite a few forgettable Alamo movies have come and gone, including The Man from the Alamo (left) *and* Man of Conquest (right).

Top: *Arizona Governor Bruce Babbitt* (center) *during his controversial 1979 visit to San Antonio.* Bottom: *A delegation from the Ku Klux Klan demonstrates in front of the Alamo on May 1, 1986.*

American popular culture, with games (top) and *novels (bottom), helps keep the Alamo alive for young and old.*

Fannin's men were dead only a day when stories of the fall of the Alamo started to appear in American newspapers. It had taken three weeks for the news to travel to the Gulf Coast and then by ship to New Orleans. From there it booked passage on riverboats up the Mississippi and ships bound for Charleston, Philadelphia, New York, Boston, and Portland. It was the news of the day, relegating every other story to a distinctly secondary status. The Seminole war in Florida paled next to the heroic stand at the Alamo. And stories of mere murders, land swindles, and ambitious plans for national expansion were not fit to be mentioned in the same breath as the Alamo.

The Alamo changed how all Americans viewed the Texas Revolution. Before the fall, newspaper editors generally treated the conflict in Texas as foreign news. After the fall, they were more likely to include it in their national news columns. Where once politics and the debate over slavery colored Americans' attitude toward the Revolution, now everyone seemed to think with one mind and speak with one voice. Whig and antislavery editors increasingly joined the Democratic and Southern legions in support of Texas independence. The once neutral *Frankfort Argus* now implored that Santa Anna be taught "the virtue of American rifles and republicanism." Not to be outdone, the *Memphis Enquirer,* long opposed to Texas's independence movement, had a change of heart: "We have been opposed to the Texas war from first to last, but our feelings we cannot express—some of our own bosom friends have fallen in the Alamo. We would avenge their death and spill the last drop of our blood upon the altar of liberty." A poem published in the *New Orleans Commercial Bulletin* captured the new mood:

> Vengeance on Santa Anna and his minions,
> Vile scum, up boiled from the infernal regions . . .
> The offscouring baseness of hell's blackest legions,
> Too filthy far with crawling worms to dwell
> And far too horrid and base for hell.[23]

The early newspaper stories, like the first verbal reports of the fighting, were filled with sensational and inaccurate details. They were products of a series of word-of-mouth exchanges, chains that began with

Andrés Barcena and Anselmo Bergara or Susanna Dickinson and Joe, were passed along by intermediaries, and eventually found their way, by letter or verbal report, to a newspaper. There were no war correspondents at the Alamo, nothing even approaching objective journalism. Yet these first, dubious stories, reprinted across the nation in paper after paper, were all Americans learned about the tragic event.

In this jumble of solid information and wild speculation the fate of Davy Crockett attracted the most interest. As the only national figure at the Alamo, he became more important than Travis or Bowie, rivaled in newspapers only by Santa Anna himself. In fact, newspapers transformed the fall of the Alamo into a perfect melodrama, complete with a noble, Byronic hero (Crockett), a ruthless, satanic villain (Santa Anna), and a fine cast of secondary characters. A poem in the *New York Star,* which was widely reprinted, captured the American story of Crockett:

> Tho' sad was his fate, and mournful the story,
> The deeds of the hero shall never decay;
> He fell in a cause dear to freedom and glory,
> And fought to the last like a lion at bay.

> When rang the loud call from a nation oppressed,
> And her vallies with slaughter of brave men were red;
> 'Twas the pride of poor Crockett to help the distressed
> And the watchword in Texas was heard, Go Ahead.

> His death-dealing rifle no longer shall shower
> Its unerring balls on the proud haughty foe.
> Cut down in the spring-time of life's budding flower—
> His tomb stone, alas, are the walls, Alamo.

> Then may we not hope, since valor has crown'd him,
> And o'er him bright fame her mantle has spread;
> In the soul's parting hour good angels were round him,
> Did his spirit arise to the skies "Go Ahead."[24]

In death Crockett became what he never was in life—a politician who transcended party squabbles and represented an American ideal. There were even some reports that Crockett had not died at all, though he had suffered near-mortal wounds. In late April, the *Cincinnati Whig* noted that a gentleman brought word from Texas "that Col. CROCKETT is still living. It is said, that he had been left for dead on the battle ground at San Antonio; but some acquaintances who happened to visit the scene of action, after the departure of the Mexicans, discovering that he still breathed, had him removed to comfortable quarters, where his numerous wounds were dressed; and he 'was doing well' when the gentleman in question . . . left San Antonio." But this report came to light after earlier stories of Crockett's death and the burning of all the corpses, and even the hopeful editor warned his readers to be cautious about the latest news.[25]

Far more common were reports that Crockett died "fighting like a tiger." A story in the *New Orleans Bulletin* commented that Crockett's "conduct on this occasion was most heroic; having used his rifle as long as possible by loading and discharging, and the enemy crowding upon the walls, he turned the britch of his gun, and demolished more than twenty of the enemy before he fell." Along the same lines, the *Richmond Enquirer* reported that "David Crockett (now rendered immortal in glory) had fortified himself with sixteen guns well charged, and a monument of slain encompassed his lifeless body." In report after report, tales of Crockett's heroic fighting and epic glory escalated.[26]

But there were also reports of surrenders and executions. Most papers used the Barcena and Bergara number of seven rebels who gave up a lost cause, though there were different versions of what exactly happened. One widely reported version noted that the Texas garrison fought until only seven men remained alive, and that they "cried for quarters but were told that there was no mercy for them—they then continued fighting until the whole were butchered." Another said that some men did surrender, only to be "dragged through hot embers, and their flesh cut off previous to being burnt in a pile." Occasionally reports said that Crockett was one of the last to die, and that he and a few of his comrades were the ones who asked for quarter, but when none was forthcoming they

fought on to the death. The confusion offered fertile ground for an un-
solvable mystery.[27]

✷

Concern over the fate of Crockett was probably more intense in the
United States than in Texas. Of more immediate concern for Texans was
the success of their own Revolution and their own survival, although not
necessarily in that order. The situation was critical. The Revolution dangled by a few thin threads, which Santa Anna was anxious to sever. And
on both sides there was a creeping sense that time was running short.

Santa Anna knew that the Alamo had settled nothing. He exaggerated
when he told Captain Fernando Urizza that "it was but a small affair," but
in the context of his mission he did not exaggerate much. After the battle
he did not tarry in Béxar, where his welcome, never very deep, was wearing even thinner. Many Tejanos regarded him as capricious and malignant,
and stories about the sack of Zacatecas circulated throughout the town.
In addition, the Army of Operations was living off the land, or as Béxar
residents saw it, off them. Santa Anna knew all this, though he cared little.
More important to him was the fact that the army of Sam Houston was
not in Béxar, and to win the war he had to catch and destroy that force.[28]

Destruction, he believed, would be the easy part of the equation. The
trick was catching General Sam. But he had a plan. On March 11, 1836, he
ordered General Antonio Gaona to lead several hundred troops northeast
to Bastrop, on the Colorado River, and from there to move up the Old San
Antonio Road to Nacogdoches. At the same time, he sent General Joaquín
Ramírez y Sesma with eight hundred men due east to Beason's Crossing
with orders to ford the Colorado and invade and destroy San Felipe de
Austin, on the Brazos. Santa Anna himself, with the main army, would follow in Ramírez y Sesma's path. A third force, under General José Urrea,
was to move south and east to seize Goliad, crush the insurgency throughout the coastal prairies, and establish a supply depot at Matagorda Bay. A
simple plan, but also highly unorthodox. Without knowing the size,
strength, or deployment of his enemy, Santa Anna divided his own forces.[29]

By almost every military measurement, it would have been difficult to
underrate Houston's army. It was small, hungry, and unorganized; poorly
disciplined, badly armed, and insufficiently trained; equally ready to launch

off on some wild-goose chase, go home, or fight. Sitting in the mud and muck of Gonzales, drunk and grumbling, his soldiers risked being out-flanked by Gaona and Urrea or hit head-on by Ramírez y Sesma and Santa Anna. On March 13, after hearing Susanna Dickinson's account of the Alamo, Houston decided to fall back to the Colorado.

The decision was prudent, but unpopular. His soldiers had just heard about the brave stand of their fellow Texans, they cried for revenge, and yet Houston ordered them to fall back. Houston's troops were not the kind that accepted orders blindly. They were partial to debate and to airing their own opinions. Nor were the residents of Gonzales struck dumb. One Texan later recalled, "There were over thirty Gonzales victims who had fallen at the Alamo, and the screams and lamentations of the mothers, wives, children and sisters of these brave men who gave their lives for Texas liberty will ring in my ears so long as memory liveth." Yet over the protests of his men, who pitied the Gonzales women and nurtured, in the words of one veteran, "a blood grievance against Mexicans" and the ability "to whip ten-to-one of the carrion-eating convicts of Santa Anna," Houston abandoned the settlement and withdrew to Burnham's ferry, on the Col-orado. To try to hold Gonzales, he thought, "would have been Madness." His army reached Burnham's ferry on March 17. Early the next morning, when his scouts reported that a Mexican infantry column was only fifteen miles away, Houston destroyed the ferry and moved his men down the Col-orado to Beason's Crossing, where he waited for Fannin's brigade.[30]

The torrential rains that made Houston's retreat a slow, muddy busi-ness also bought him time, swelling the Colorado River and leaving it im-passable. On March 21, Ramírez y Sesma pitched camp at Beason's Crossing on the west bank of the Colorado, and the two armies watched the flicker of each other's campfires and listened to each other's songs. The more aggressive soldiers urged Houston to attack, but once again he was cautious, loath to surrender a good defensive position for a risky as-sault across a swollen river into a wall of canister, grapeshot, and small arms fire. No, General Sam would wait.

On March 23, 1836, Houston learned that the Mexican army had at-tacked Fannin's force, though he was uncertain of the outcome. In a let-ter to Secretary of War Thomas Rusk, he lamented, "You know I am not easily depressed, but before my god, since we parted, I have found the darkest hours of my past life." When he learned Fannin's fate, he concluded that the Colorado was no longer defensible. "Urrea," he surmised, "could . . . cross the Colorado at Wharton, about forty miles below the Texan camp, with his 1500 men and attack [our] left flank. Gaona with his force of about 750 could cross the Colorado at Bastrop, about 60 miles above the Texan camp, and attack our right flank, while Sesma could attack the front." Anxious to avoid getting trapped with a river at his back, he ordered another retreat, this time to San Felipe de Austin, on the Brazos River. Critics howled. "Thirteen hundred Americans retreating before a division of 800 Mexicans!" veteran Robert Coleman later wrote. "Can Houston's strong partizans [sic] presume to excuse such dastardly cowardice under the pretence [sic] of laudable prudence?"[31]

Houston ignored the barbs and continued the retreat. From his camp near San Felipe de Austin, on March 29 he wrote Secretary of War Rusk, "Had I consulted the wishes of all, I should have been like the ass between two stacks of hay. Many wished me to go below, others above. I consulted none—I held no councils of war. If I err, the blame is mine." Again the spring rains aided Houston's cause, turning roads into quagmires, widening creeks, and flooding rivers. General Eugenio Tolsa's troops arrived from San Antonio and joined Ramírez y Sesma's at Beason's Crossing but could not ford the Colorado. Nor could Gaona get out of Bastrop and across the Colorado to march on Nacogdoches. And Urrea's army was stymied by the flooding Brazos at Matagorda. For a moment, the war had stopped.[32]

After only a night in San Felipe de Austin, Houston was on the move again, this time twenty-five miles north to Mill Creek on Jared Groce's plantation. Why? his soldiers asked one another. Why not fight? Why not here? Why not now? One of Houston's men later wrote that the general could do nothing more than "tuck his tail and run from the Colorado, from half his own number and from the Brazos, it was a total want of military capacity." As before, Houston stayed tight-lipped, explaining himself and his actions to no one. But he knew that his troops needed training and his army needed ordnance. The weather made it difficult to acquire artillery, but he did order close-action drills in an attempt to drum some military expertise into his grumbling army. At Groce's he received a stinging communication from Texas president David Burnet: "Sir: The enemy are laughing you to scorn. You must fight them. You must retreat no further. The country expects you to fight. The salvation of the country depends on your doing so."[33]

Houston had little use for Burnet, let alone for any thoughts or military instructions the politician might have. He went about his job of turning a mob into a disciplined army. Drenched by rain, chilled by northers, plagued by dysentery, his men drilled—form a line, fire a volley, advance; form a line, fire a volley, advance. Caked with red mud, filthy beyond the imaginable, coughing and sick, his men responded—complained and swore, but responded. Although some died and some deserted, the rest became an army. Silent, suspicious, sleepless, often sick himself, Sam Houston was accomplishing part of what he had set out to do. But there was much left undone.

Santa Anna's job was similarly incomplete. On April 8, he joined Ramírez y Sesma's brigade at Beason's Crossing. When he learned that the fledgling government of Texas had relocated to Harrisburg, he picked 950 men from the Matamoros, Guerrero, Mexico, and Toluca Battalions and set out at the head of his own troop column. Hearing of Santa Anna's move, Houston force-marched his men through sixty miles of mud and rain, reaching the outskirts of Harrisburg in two days on April 18. Late in the day, a Texan patrol intercepted two Mexican couriers. One had saddlebags with *Travis* stamped into the leather. The Texans wanted to lynch him, but Houston wanted to harness the rage. It was not a lynching he was after, it was victory.

"Victory is certain!" he told his men in the early hours of April 19. "The army will cross [Buffalo Bayou] and we will meet the enemy! Some of us may be killed and must be killed; but soldiers remember the Alamo! The Alamo! The Alamo!" The troops took up the refrain: "Remember the Alamo! Remember Goliad!" An officer who heard Houston's remarks later recalled, "After such a speech, but damned few will be taken prisoner—that I know."[34]

If the captured saddlebags gave Houston a psychological advantage, they also provided him with an intelligence edge. Messages inside revealed that Santa Anna and a force of about eight hundred soldiers was just in front of the Texas army. Reinforcements were expected, but for the moment the Mexican leader was in a vulnerable position. For Houston it was a stroke of pure, blind luck. He was at the right place, with the right force, at the right time; for once the stars of his star-crossed career were in line.

On the morning of April 19, he wrote Colonel Henry Raguet, "[W]e are in preparation to meet Santa Anna. It is the only chance of saving Texas. . . . We go to conquer. It is wisdom growing out of necessity to meet the enemy now; every consideration enforces it. No previous occasion would justify it. The troops are in fine spirits, and now is the time for action." Though Houston still believed the odds were against him, he knew he would never find a better opportunity. "I leave the result in the hands of a wise God, and rely upon his providence."[35]

On the morning of April 20, Houston's army was on the move again. Few had slept much the night before. Another norther had blown in and chilled them to the bone. But they were ready, and there was little grumbling as they set out for Buffalo Bayou. That day they saw Mexicans, and many Texans wanted to fight then and there. Sidney Sherman, always impetuous, even led a foolhardy and unsuccessful attempt to capture a Mexican cannon, and a few of his men got bloodied for their efforts. Other soldiers wanted to rush out and help Sherman and his volunteers, but General Sam said no. They would have to fight their way back. He wasn't going to risk his army to save some hotheads. He would remain secure in his fortress of dense oak trees with Buffalo Bayou at his back.[36]

By that evening the two sides camped about a thousand yards from each other. The Texans occupied the elevated bank of the bayou, mostly hidden by the cover of oak trees. The San Jacinto River was on their left and the New Washington–Lynchburg Road on their right. Santa Anna took position in a wooded area bordered by the road and a marsh. Peggy's Lake was to his rear. Both positions were seriously flawed; both invited a battle of annihilation. But in the minds of the leaders and soldiers, strengths became flaws and flaws became strengths.

Once again Houston hesitated, and as usual he told no one what he was thinking. He was going to fight, but how? Should he attack, picking the moment? Or should he defend, allowing Santa Anna to dictate the timing? An attack had more inherent risks; defense was safer. But what of Santa Anna's reinforcements? Houston knew from the captured documents that General Cos was close by, but he had no idea where Ramírez y Sesma, Filisola, or Urrea were. These were all things to ponder. There was no right or simple answer.

The next morning Houston learned that Cos had arrived. That brought the Mexican force to some 1,250 men, compared to Houston's army of somewhere around nine hundred men. Houston made one dramatic move that morning: he ordered Vince's Bridge, which led directly to his and Santa Anna's position, destroyed. This severed the line between Santa Anna and more reinforcements; it also cut the Texan path of escape. That pretty much said it all. There would be no more running. He would fight and win—or die.

But when would he fight—and how? For once, he asked his officers. They favored fighting from a defensive position. Sitting behind his tree line, Houston thought about that. Across an open field of high grass Santa Anna's thoughts were as mysterious as Houston's. Santa Anna had a marsh to his back, the Texas army to his front, and dreams of glory between his ears. He had expected Houston to attack the day before; then that morning. He had supervised the construction of breastworks for just such an attack. But it had not come, and by early afternoon, he was tired. Some would later say that he idled away his time with a mistress; others insisted that he was lost in an opium-induced dreamworld. Undoubtedly he did not expect Houston to attack in the afternoon—after the past month and a half, who could blame him? He told General Cos to rest his weary men. They would attack Houston the next day. Fatally overconfident, Santa Anna did not even order a guard to be posted.

It was then that Houston acted. Somewhere between 3:30 and 4:30 P.M., he ordered an assault. The Texans fanned out over about nine hundred yards, with Houston, astride his stallion Saracen, twenty yards to the front. To provide a cadence beat to keep the columns aligned, three fifes and a drum struck up "Will You Come to the Bower I Have Shaded for You," a popular song of the day. The Mexicans—sleeping, chatting, and playing cards, many recuperating from near-starvation rations and bouts of dysentery—were utterly unprepared and allowed the enemy to march within two hundred yards of them before buglers sounded the troops to their stations. The Texans charged, and the orchestrated assault quickly disintegrated into a bloody melee, with the Texans screaming "Remember the Alamo!" and "Remember Goliad!" and the Tejanos bellowing *"Recuerden el Alamo!"*[37]

The assault turned into pure carnage as the Texans exacted a terrible revenge. The months of cold and wet weather, frustrating retreat, and tales of Mexican brutalities had not bent them toward thoughts of mercy. This was their moment. A Mexican officer remembered seeing "our troops flying in small groups, terrified, and sheltering themselves

behind large trees. I endeavored to force some of them to fight, but all efforts were in vain . . . they were a bewildered and panic-stricken herd."
With Texans "thirsting for gore," according to veteran Noah Smithwick,
the slaughter continued long after the engagement was decided. Criss-
crossing the battlefield, Houston tried to stop the butchery. At one point,
while his troops chased down and killed fleeing Mexicans, he tried to appeal to their finer instincts: "Gentlemen! Gentlemen! Gentlemen! Gentlemen! I applaud your bravery, but damn your manners." But the ghosts
of the Alamo and Goliad were more powerful than Houston's words,
and the soldiers continued their grim work. Capturing the mood of his
comrades, one soldier told an officer, "[I]f Jesus Christ were to come
down from heaven and order me to quit shooting Yellowbellies, I
wouldn't do it sir!"[38]

The battle lasted eighteen minutes, the homicides much longer.
Wounded Mexicans were dispatched with a shot or a rifle butt to the
head. Some were scalped, many mutilated. Some Mexicans fled into the
marsh, tripping over bodies and using the dead as stepping-stones, trying
to reach Peggy's Lake to escape into the waters and beyond. To Texan riflemen the running, sliding, tripping, swimming Mexicans amounted to
little more than a turkey shoot. Mexicans cried, *Me no Alamo!*" and
"Me no Goliad!" but their words were met with more fire. Nicholas
Labadie, an army physician, remembered witnessing "acts of cruelty
which I forebear to recount." More than 650 Mexicans died within an
hour; another two hundred were wounded. The Texans suffered nine
dead and thirty wounded.

The Mexicans who managed to get across the lake were rounded up
during the next two days, and Houston found himself with approximately five hundred prisoners. Santa Anna was one of them. He had managed to get away on horseback and change into common clothes, but he
did not know the land and was a poor escapee. When he was captured,
he tried to hide his identity, but the diamond studs on his dirty silk shirt
suggested that he was something more than a humble enlisted man, as did
the shouts of *"El presidente! El presidente!"* when his soldiers saw him.

Hauled before Houston, who was wounded and reclined against a
tree, Santa Anna begged for mercy, asking for himself what he had denied
others. "That man may consider himself born to no common destiny who
has captured the Napoleon of the West; and it now remains for him to be

generous to the vanquished!" he said through an interpreter. Houston asked why *el presidente* had not himself been generous to the vanquished at the Alamo and at Goliad. Santa Anna answered that he had only been following the orders of his government, but since he *was* the government, Houston was decidedly unimpressed with the explanation. Houston, however, was both a soldier and a politician, and the politician in him knew that Santa Anna was more useful alive than dead. Filisola and the body of the Mexican army were still at large. Without a negotiated peace, the Revolution might still be lost.

In return for his life, Santa Anna agreed to a withdrawal of the Army of Operations to south of the Rio Grande River and to never again take up arms against Texas. He even said he would promote the cause of Texas independence in Mexico City. On May 14, 1836, he and President David G. Burnet signed the Treaty of Velasco, which formalized those terms. Santa Anna then left Texas, as did Filisola. The Mexican Congress, no longer enamored with *el presidente*, denounced the treaty. But that last point hardly mattered. Texas, for all practical purposes, had won its independence.[39]

✳

While the major issue was being decided, some Texans were still searching for answers to several questions, the most important of which was what exactly had happened in the last moments of the battle of the Alamo. On the subject of David Crockett's death, they now had more witnesses. They had Santa Anna, as well as a number of his officers and men. After their defeat at San Jacinto, most of the Mexican soldiers were incarcerated on Galveston Island. There they waited while Burnet and the Texas cabinet negotiated final terms with Santa Anna, and their captors decided what to do with them. Many feared for their lives, and most nursed deep resentments toward Santa Anna, who may have become simultaneously the most unpopular man in Texas and Mexico. While on Galveston Island they passed their time like prisoners of war from other wars, chatting, engaging in wild speculations, reliving the past, and worrying about the future. In this uncertain, charged atmosphere, far-fetched stories grew into facts, and rumors blossomed into POW gospel.

One thing the prisoners knew for certain: Texans remembered the

Alamo and Goliad. Ramón Caro, Santa Anna's secretary, believed that the Goliad murders in particular were "the chief cause of the infinite hardships and sufferings we endured as prisoners and of the dangers to which we were exposed." During their incarceration, the prisoners had to answer repeated questions about the chain of orders that culminated in the brutalities at the Alamo and Goliad, and most readily gave Santa Anna credit for every terrible thing that happened. He, the prisoners said, ordered the executions of prisoners in both the Alamo and Goliad. He, they claimed, was the cause of their misfortunes and the shame of their country. He was the Mexican equivalent of the god that failed.[40]

The story that received the most attention involved the Texans who had surrendered and been executed at the Alamo. The story itself was nothing new, of course; it had been passed on by word of mouth and in the newspapers for several months. What the Mexicans added was more details. George M. Dolson, an orderly sergeant who had joined the Texas army after San Jacinto, wrote to his brother in Detroit that he had been called upon to act as an interpreter for Colonel James Morgan, commandant of Galveston Island, in an interrogation of a Mexican prisoner. Dolson noted that Texas was in an agitated state. Rumors were circulating that Santa Anna had cut a deal for his own liberty and passage back to Mexico, and the news reached the army "like an electric shock." How, Dolson wondered, could such an evil tyrant—"a cold-blooded murderer, and worthy only of the sympathy of cowards and the scorn of great men"—be allowed to leave the very land he had "stained with blood"?[41]

As proof of the dictator's evil, Dolson offered the Mexican officer's statement, given "according to a promise" (an intriguing phrase that is not explained). The officer stated that on the morning the Alamo was taken, General Manuel Fernández Castrillón discovered six Texans in a back room of the Alamo. They had fought bravely, but the battle was decided and continued bloodshed was useless. Castrillón offered them hope. Placing his hand on his chest, he said, "Here is a hand and a heart to protect you; come with me to the general-in-Chief, and you shall be saved." One of the men, the officer claimed, walked to the rear of the rest, "his arms folded, and appeared bold as the lion." Santa Anna's interpreter identified him as Crockett. When Castrillón presented the "brave prisoners" to Santa Anna, the dictator demanded, "Who has given you orders to take prisoners, I do not want to see those men living—shoot them." In a flash, "the hell-hounds of the tyrant" killed the six prisoners.

Dolson's letter, which appeared in the *Detroit Democratic Free Press* on September 2, 1836, and was reprinted in other newspapers, echoed another account, by an unidentified letter writer, that had appeared in the *Frankfort Commonwealth* on July 27. The details of the two letters, evidently, circulated widely among the Mexican prisoners and were undoubtedly picked up in several Mexican newspapers. Taken as a whole, the story conforms to the dictates of nineteenth-century melodrama. There is the valiant victim, Crockett; the noble victor, Castrillón; and the bloodthirsty fiend, Santa Anna. And since Crockett died at the Alamo, Castrillón fell at San Jacinto, and Santa Anna's word was without value, no one could really challenge the story. Throughout Texas, America, and Mexico, it played well and often.

Of course, as a sound narrative it has problems. In his letter Dolson identifies the officer in parentheses, as "(Almonte)," presumably Juan Nepomuceno Almonte, one of Santa Anna's aides-de-camp. This very well might have been an error made by the typesetter, however. What appeared in the *Detroit Democratic Free Press* was: "Colonel Crockett was in the rear, had his arms folded, and appeared bold as a lion as he passed by my informant (Almonte). Santa Anna's interpreter knew Colonel Crockett, and said to my informant, 'the one behind is the famous Crockett.'" Perhaps the passage should read: "Colonel Crockett was in the rear, had his arms folded, and appeared bold as a lion as he passed my informant. Almonte, Santa Anna's interpreter, knew Colonel Crockett, and said to my informant, 'the one behind is the famous Crockett.'" But in Almonte's private journal the execution of Crockett is not mentioned. Almonte briefly discusses the assault on the Alamo, noting that at 6 A.M. "the enemy attempted in vain to fly, but they were overtaken and put to the sword, and only five women, one Mexican soldier (prisoner) and a black slave escaped from instant death." Furthermore, although Almonte had spent considerable time in the United States, he probably had never met Crockett, never seen Crockett in person, and expressed little if any interest in Crockett. To suppose that he would have recognized Crockett after the long siege and intense fighting strains belief. Adding further to the implausibility of the entire story is the testimony of Francisco Antonio Ruíz, alcalde of San Antonio, that when the battle ended, Santa Anna called on him to identify the bodies of Travis, Bowie, and Crockett. If Santa Anna had ordered Crockett's execution, why would he need Ruíz to identify the famous American?[42]

The same rumors of Santa Anna's cruelty and Crockett's death that floated through the prisoner of war camp on Galveston Island followed the repatriated Mexican soldiers back to their capital. Just as American newspapers reprinted Dolson's letter and other reports of Crockett's execution, Mexican newspapers spread the story. Brisk newspaper traffic between New Orleans and Vera Cruz ensured that any story of even marginal interest to Mexicans that was printed in the Crescent City found its way into Mexico. The Vera Cruz *El Censor* carried news of surrenders and executions at the Alamo, and the Mexico City *La Lima de Vulcano* soon picked up the story. Undoubtedly, from there the reports spread to other newspapers throughout Mexico.[43]

The time was right in Mexico for any fanciful flight of anti–Santa Anna propaganda to take wing. The campaign in Texas had left the dictator's career in shambles. While Santa Anna was still imprisoned in Velasco his government had already begun the process of disowning him. In May it had decreed that any treaty the general signed in Texas was null and void and would have no "value or effect" on the Mexican government. And when the government learned that by a secret treaty Santa Anna had promised to lobby the Mexican cabinet to receive a Texas commission, grant Texas independence, and set the boundary between the two nations at the Rio Grande, his stock dipped even lower. For once intellectuals, liberals, nationalists, and even a few centralists discovered common ground. Seldom had a politician fallen so quickly and completely from grace. Although from his estate at Manga de Clavo he attempted to talk and write his way back into favor, for the moment he was persona non grata.[44]

Santa Anna no doubt sensed what was waiting for him back in Mexico while he was still a prisoner. Even some of his closest supporters deserted him. Ramón Martínez Caro, Santa Anna's secretary, gained his own release by telling Texas authorities about *el presidente*'s plan to escape, after which he stole Santa Anna's diamond shirt studs. The Mexican Congress, noted the American chargé d'affaires in Mexico City, considered Santa Anna's return as a "curse to the nation." Even Santa Anna wrote that "the end of my public career has arrived." The end would last only eighteen months.[45]

Santa Anna's critics went after him with their pens, carefully recon-
structing the Texas campaign and enumerating his many careless and
heartless mistakes. Between 1836 and 1838, Ramón Martínez Caro, Vicente Filisola, José Urrea, and José María Tornel wrote accounts of what
they witnessed and knew about Santa Anna's activities in Texas. Far from
impartial, these were desperate attempts to salvage the writers' own reputations and careers. Any tactical mistake, any ruthless inhumanity, any
ill-advised decision that could be attributed to Santa Anna readily was.
The critics retraced their former leader's path to defeat and shame, ex-
posing the poor planning that dogged the campaign, the bad decisions
made in the battle of the Alamo, the inhumane order to execute the cap-
tives at Goliad, and the various inept choices made on the road to San
Jacinto.

The story of the surrenders and executions at the Alamo played a part
in several of the critical accounts. Caro, for example, notes that General
Castrillón did discover five Texans hiding after the assault and took them
to Santa Anna. But His Excellency "severely reprimanded [him] for not
having killed them on the spot, after which he turned his back upon Castrillón while the soldiers stepped out of their ranks and set upon the prisoners until they were all killed." Caro comments that what he describes
"is a cruel truth, but I cannot omit it." The story in its essential points is
the same one that Andrés Barcena and Anselmo Bergara described to Sam
Houston a week after the event, and the same one that George Dolson
told on Galveston Island. Unlike Dolson, however, Caro does not say that
David Crockett was one of the executed defenders.[46]

Nor do the other major accounts mention the execution of Crockett,
even though the detail would have further stained Santa Anna's name.
Only a few minor Mexican sources refer to the execution of Crockett,
and most of those had odd, involved histories. In 1859, for instance, the
Texas Almanac published Nicholas Labadie's account of Colonel Fernando Urizza's experiences at the Alamo. Labadie claimed that he was a
physician who treated Urizza's wounds after the battle of San Jacinto and
that in the course of their conversations Urizza discussed the Alamo assault. When the battle was over, Urizza said, he saw Castrillón lead "a
venerable looking old man by the hand" out of the Alamo, and he overheard a Mexican soldier refer to the man as "Coket." Urizza also said
that he was Santa Anna's secretary, which he wasn't; and taken as a

whole, his and Labadie's account lacks any sense of reliability. The Labadie-Urizza account mentions only one execution and does not in any way explain how any of the Mexican soldiers knew Crockett. Nor does it illuminate how the healthy forty-nine-year-old Crockett had become a venerable old man.[47]

Even less sound is Francisco Becerra's version. Becerra claimed to have been a sergeant in Sesma's command, and in the 1870s he told Texan antiquarian John Ford that he well remembered the death of David Crockett. He asserted that he personally had killed a sick man who fit Bowie's description and then discovered Travis and Crockett sitting on the floor of the church. There followed a friendly meeting between Crockett, Travis, Almonte, and General Cos. Then Cos took Crockett and Travis to Santa Anna, who ordered the leaders shot. No Castrillón, no other prisoners. In all likelihood, no truth. Becerra's account, like other Tejano accounts of the period, was probably crafted with the Alamo tourist in mind. They told thrilling stories. By the 1870s and 1880s the Alamo had long since passed into memory.[48]

But the tourists of the late-nineteenth century, the antiquarians, and the Texan hagiographers were tied to Sam Houston and the early citizens of Gonzales by one burning question: what had been the end of Davy Crockett? The question was put to the few Texan survivors, formed part of the central story of the meaning of the Alamo, became hopelessly confused in the political debates in Mexico over the personality and actions of Santa Anna, then passed quietly into folklore. Scores of people had an answer to the question, but their answers banged against one another, knocking silly any hope of discovering the truth. And in the end, what remained of David Crockett was a long list of "he said's" and "she said's." Crockett died surrounded by twenty or more Mexicans. Crockett hid, surrendered, and was executed. Only two things are certain. Crockett fought—and died. But for many those two facts would not be enough.

7

━━━ ✦ ━━━

RETRIEVING THE BONES
OF HISTORY

THE FIRST BIG STEP in the postrevolutionary life of the Alamo legend was taken by a matron of Texas several generations after the event. Adina De Zavala's thick black hair, streaked with wisps of gray, bore witness to Tejano ancestry, but her dark blue eyes reached back to Ireland. A round, benign face with rosy cheeks camouflaged a fierce determination. Her paternal grandfather, Lorenzo de Zavala, was a certifiable Texas hero, a native of Yucatán who loathed Antonio López de Santa Anna, helped lead the rebellion against Mexico, and became the first vice president of the Republic of Texas. Adina was born in 1881 at the family homestead in Harris County, Texas, at the mouth of the San Jacinto River, in sight of the famous battlefield. Like her father, she nursed a near-religious love for Texas and its heroes, spending her life—as a teacher, preservationist, and feminist—promoting Lone Star history.[1]

Now that history was under siege. At dusk on February 10, 1908, she made a statement that she had "learned on good authority that a syndicate, which had an option on the property back of the Alamo, intended to seize the chapel itself and tear it down [and] to use the space as a sort of front yard to the hotel, or amusement palace, they expected to erect." To prevent desecration of the shrine, she broke the law. "My lawyers were out of town, but I had heard that 'possession is nine-tenths of the law.' Something had to be done, and quickly. So I took possession." She barricaded herself inside. When the county sheriff tried to serve an injunction, she "refused to accept the copy . . . and when an attempt was made to read it . . . she stopped her ears with her fingers." She stayed put for three days. Finally, on February 13, she marched out on an Alamo Plaza crowded with journalists and cheering supporters. Across the country, newspapers and magazines picked up the story, publishing file photos of the famed Alamo chapel and its savior.

Actually, her occupation of "the Alamo" was all grandstand, a staged media event by a woman playing politics long before most women contemplated such ploys. Better than anyone else, she knew that no syndicate threatened the Alamo. The state of Texas had title to it, and the Daughters of the Republic of Texas maintained it. The so-called evil syndicate had about as much chance of dismantling the chapel as Davy Crockett and Jim Bowie had of returning to life. And press reports had the story all wrong. De Zavala had not occupied the Alamo chapel; she had locked herself inside the neighboring Hugo & Schmeltzer building, a grocery warehouse that had once been part of the old Alamo mission. The state owned that building as well, as she knew, since she had lobbied for its purchase. What Adina De Zavala feared was not an ethereal Eastern syndicate but the state of Texas itself. She was not so much fighting to save the Alamo as to salvage her own vision of what the Alamo ought to be.[2]

*

For years, almost brick by brick, the Alamo had been dying. The events of March 6, 1836, had provided Texas a pantheon of martyrs and a source of inspiration and celebration. Less than three weeks after the battle, the editor of San Felipe de Austin's *Telegraph and Texas Register* put it best, urging Texans to "consecrate to future generations the memory of our heroes who perished at the Thermopylae of Texas. Such examples are right ones and should be held up as mirrors, that by reflection we may catch the spirit and learn to fashion our behavior. . . . That event, so lamentable and yet so glorious . . . is of such deep interest and excites so much our feelings that we shall never cease to celebrate it."[3]

Celebrate it they did. As news of the slaughter reached the rest of the country, it became a rallying cry. And in no time the Alamo entered popular culture as the stuff of legend in romantic novels and epic poems. In Texas it became much more, the heart and soul of a people, a holy grail of patriotic nationalism. It represented, as novelist Anthony Ganilh wrote in a preface to the second edition of his 1838 *Mexico Versus Texas,* a "crusade in behalf of modern civilization."[4]

For months, Tejano residents of Béxar approached the Alamo with superstitious caution, as if spirits of the dead lurked behind walls and hid in crevices. When locals crossed the river and walked toward it, they hushed their voices, clutched rosary beads, and instinctively crossed themselves. They had seen too much not to consider the Alamo sacred ground. Hundreds of men had died there. As soon as the shooting stopped, mission priests had moved from body to body, administering last rites. Desperate *soldaderas* had searched the grounds, wailing with grief when they located husbands and fathers. Mexican soldiers spent two days lugging their dead to the local cemetery, sometimes just dumping the bodies in the river. The funeral pyres of the Texan dead, ignited late in the afternoon, burned for two days, filling the air with the scent of singeing flesh, staining the ground with rendered fat, and darkening the skies. One of Santa Anna's soldiers remembered how "the air was filled with the fumes of the roasting flesh." Another eyewitness recalled, "I saw an immense pillar of flame shoot up . . . and the dense smoke from it rise high in the clouds. . . . I . . . watched the vultures in their revel and shuddered at the sickening sight. [A] crowd was gathered around the smouldering embers and ashes of the fire. . . . I did not need to make inquiry. . . . Fragments of flesh, bones, and charred wood and ashes revealed it in all its terrible truth. Grease that had exuded from the bodies saturated the earth for several feet beyond the ashes . . . the odor was more sickening than that from the corpses in the river."[5]

Ignorance of the final resting place of the charred bones deepened the mysticism. Santa Anna insisted that the bones and ashes remain untouched and for weeks attracted hungry dogs and vultures. Juan Seguín claimed to have returned several months after the final assault, laid the bones in a flag-draped coffin, and placed it with a ceremonial rifle and sword in the San Fernando Church. Several weeks later, a contingent of local citizens and Texas mounted troops supposedly escorted the ashes back across the river and buried them. San Antonio alcalde Francisco Ruíz claimed that he had buried some of the ashes. But nobody knew exactly where they were. R. M. Potter, who visited San Antonio several times between 1841 and 1861, noted in 1878 that the "place of burial was a peach orchard . . . outside the Alamo . . . and a few hundred yards from the fort. When I was last there in 1861, it was still a large inclosed open lot, though surrounded by the suburb which had there grown up, but the rude landmarks which had once pointed out the place of the sepulture had long since disappeared. . . . [I]t is now densely built over, and its identity is irrevocably lost. This is too sad for comment."[6]

Santa Anna's refusal to bury the defenders was a perfect ingredient for the recipe of mythology, particularly among those who had witnessed the siege, the assault, the corpse-littered convent, and the funeral pyre. Many concluded that the spirits of the dead Texans, denied eternal access to their own bodies, had no place to go, neither to heaven nor to hell, and remained on the battlefield, angels of righteousness charged with defending the Alamo against future enemies. Rumors of ghosts and haunted hallways, of spirits lurking in the shadows, kept most San Antonians away from the Alamo after dark. Eternally armed with swords of fire, so the legend went, the dead heroes would forever stand watch.[7]

But ghosts cannot fight neglect. Texans revered the memory of the dead, but the Alamo itself got less respect, deteriorating into a ruin more than a shrine. In the days before the final assault, Santa Anna's artillery had blasted huge chunks out of the mission walls. The chapel, its roof long before collapsed, was cluttered with debris. After San Jacinto, General Juan Andrade, whose cavalry had occupied the Alamo since the final siege, was ordered to spike the cannons and raze the fortress. An Anglo prisoner of war later wrote that Andrade's men tore down much of the walls and set fires throughout the complex. "The Alamo was completely dismantled," he recalled; "all single walls were leveled . . . and the pickets torn up and burnt."[8]

Over the years, tourists pilfered rubble and chipped off souvenirs. Local entrepreneurs collected rocks and stones from the chapel and hawked them. As early as 1840, the town council allowed citizens to haul away Alamo stone for $5 a wagonload. Occupation troops took a toll. Republic of Texas soldiers occupied what was left of the Alamo in December 1836 and again in January 1839, and Mexican troops did so in March 1841 and September 1842. Both groups carved names into the Alamo's walls, dug musket rounds out of the holes, and knocked off stone carvings for souvenirs. Some statues were used for target practice. Anglo and Tejano boys used the walls for playing war and refighting the battle. The further threat of destruction again rose after Texas's statehood was realized in 1845, provoking the Mexican-American War. In 1846 a member of the Second Illinois Voluntary Infantry, deployed to San Antonio during the war, described the Alamo as "the place where Colonel Crockett and his little band of heroes fell . . . defending it. . . . [It is now] an old building—and was once, no doubt, a handsome one, but it has mostly crumbled down now." One San Antonian remembered the shrine at the time of the Texas annexation. "It was a veritable ruin. No doors or windows shut out the sunlight or storm; millions of bats inhabited the crevices in the walls and flat dirt roofs and in the twilight the bats would pour forth in myriads. It was a nesting place for owls; weeds and grass grew from the walls." Several years later, a traveler noted that the Alamo "stood in ruins as it was left by the Mexicans, and was occupied by a few hundred soldiers, and as many thousand chattering swallows, forever passing in and out like bees around a hive."[9]

In 1849 the U.S. Army rented the Alamo from the Catholic church for $150 a month and converted it into a quartermaster's depot. During the next two years, army engineers rebuilt the convent, or long barracks, and cleared the grounds. Major E. B. Babbitt, who supervised the project, put a new, gabled wooden roof on the chapel. To close in the open west end of the roof, he erected the now famous Campanulate, or bell-shaped facade, atop the front wall of the chapel. Edward Everett, a U.S. Army soldier, was stationed at the Alamo in 1847 with the First Regiment of Illinois Volunteers and worked on the remodeling. "We had the debris cleared away from the interior [of the chapel] in which process we found several skeletons and other relics of the siege." Using original stones that littered the grounds, Babbitt's men partially rebuilt the mission walls. But a fire in 1861 brought down the chapel's roof, and when Fort Sam Houston was established in 1876, the army abandoned the Alamo.

The Catholic church then sold the convent to businessman Honoré Grenet, who quickly framed up a large, two-story arcaded wooden building, with crenelated cornices, using the remaining walls as a foundation. Until his death in 1882, Grenet operated a wholesale grocery business from the building and ran horses in the patio. Next, the mercantile firm of Hugo & Schmeltzer bought the convent. During these years, it hardly resembled sacred ground. One tourist expressed "amazement and disgust upon this my first visit to the old church fortress of the Alamo at finding the structure, so famous not only in the history of Texas but the annals of liberty . . . filled with sacks of salt, stinking potatoes, odorous kerosene and dirty groceries. . . . [How can] . . . the great state of Texas . . . permit a historic building like the Alamo, once consecrated to deity and latterly baptized in blood of heroes like Travis and Crockett, slain in the cause of liberty and democracy, to become a grocery warehouse." Another remarked that the Alamo was a "reproach to all San Antonio. Its wall is overthrown and removed, its dormitories are piled with military stores, its battle-scarred front has been revamped and repainted and market carts roll to and fro on the spot where flames ascended . . . over the funeral pyre of heroes."[10]

In 1883, the Catholic church sold the chapel to the state of Texas for $20,000. Texas then hired Tom Rife to manage the chapel. An eloquent man given to patriotic excess, he toured visitors through the chapel, but he had little sense of history. Graffiti had long been a problem, but he did nothing about it. During the 1850s, the army had let a Masonic lodge use a room in the long barracks, and ink-painted square-and-compass Masonic emblems appeared in several places, even on statues venerating Roman Catholic saints. In 1886 E. I. Coyle, a devout Roman Catholic, asked Rife to remove a Masonic emblem from the St. Theresa statue. Rife considered Coyle an irrational zealot and, in his own words, "took no notice of the affair." Not about to be ignored, Coyle asked the governor for help. He too ignored Coyle, who was prepared to "blow up the Alamo with dynamite rather than . . . [see] such an outrage . . . exist." In May 1887, Rife heard a commotion in the chapel, and "when I got there I found Coyle breaking the statue, which is stored on the ground floor, in pieces. As I advanced he raised the sledge-hammer he was using. I drew my pistol and commanded him to drop the hammer, telling him . . . if he did not I would kill him . . . he dropped the hammer, and I arrested him." The editor of the *San Antonio Express* considered Coyle mentally unbalanced. "If Mr. Coyle expects to go about the world smashing with sledge-hammers, or blowing up with dynamite, everything his fervid imagination construes to be offensive to Catholicism, he will find plenty of trouble on his hands. . . . [He] got down the wrong chute."[11]

In addition to the rubble, trash, graffiti, bat guano, and swallow droppings, real estate development crowded the shrine. During the 1850s, new construction in San Antonio penetrated the east bank of the San Antonio River. Samuel Maverick, a veteran of the Texas Revolution and a San Antonio land developer, purchased property on the Alamo side of the river and subdivided it into plots. By the 1860s, he had sold most of the lots. After the Civil War, a construction boom of warehouses, saloons, real estate offices, title companies, livery stables, attorneys' offices, hotels, and homes all but swallowed up the Alamo. An 1890 history of the city lamented the "wanton mutilation . . . by thoughtless relic hunters."[12]

✯

But that was about to change. Late in the nineteenth century, like prospectors scouring a streambed for nuggets, Americans became prospectors of their own history in hope of fashioning a national identity. While Europe had been shaped by a thousand years of recorded history, the United States was in its infancy, less than a century old, too young to appreciate the past, too naive to worry about the future. Without national monuments, religious shrines, and great cathedrals, and bedeviled with fractious ethnic diversity, nineteenth-century America took pride instead in nature, finding in Niagara Falls or Yellowstone an identity that could not yet be found in history. When Samuel Bowles, editor of the *Springfield Republican,* first caught sight of Yosemite's granite peaks in 1866, he wrote, "Such tide of feelings, such stoppage of ordinary emotions comes at rare intervals in any life. It was [like seeing] God face to face. . . . All that was mortal shrank back, all that was immortal swept to the front and bent down in awe." After an 1858 visit to Mammoth Cave, Bayard Taylor confessed, "What are the galleries of the Vatican, the Louvre, Versailles, and the Crystal Palaces of London and Paris to this gigantic vault hewn in living rock? [The cave] is like a visit to a just created and more brilliant planet, where God has not yet said, 'let there be light.' "[13]

After the Civil War, as the frontier closed, natural beauty failed to satisfy Americans' hunger for sacred places. Americans had long worshiped the frontier. If it helped perpetuate the values of freedom, individualism, and self-reliance, it also elevated nature over history. The Civil War—with its more than nearly one million dead, wounded, and missing people—then turned hearts to the past. The blood-drenched landscapes of Shiloh, Gettysburg, Antietam, Vicksburg, and Chancellorsville testified to the willingness of so many to sacrifice so much for competing traditions. President Abraham Lincoln had said it best of Gettysburg: "The brave men, living and dead, who struggled here, have consecrated [this ground], far above our poor power to add or detract." The Civil War killing fields constituted man-made shrines, the sites of reunions, rhetoric, and reconciliation, sacred ground where Americans could, in the 1929 words of Governor Angus W. McLean of Virginia, celebrate "a joint and precious heritage" and catch a glimpse of the "golden mist of American valor."[14]

Rapid economic change also triggered a nostalgia for simpler times. The industrial revolution altered the rhythms of life and left Americans wondering whether rural virtues could survive commercialism and urbanization. The rise of big business and its elite, and their insatiable appetite for money, seemed to threaten bedrock values. By cultivating an appreciation for history, argued Louis Napoleon Parker in 1905, society could block "the modernising spirit which destroys all loveliness and has no loveliness of its own to put in its place."[15]

Finally, demographic change created a need for public history. Improved transportation systems and giant factories drew farmers out of rural villages and into larger towns, where they confronted recent immigrants from Europe and Canada. Citizens were less likely than ever before to share a common set of values, and civic leaders hoped to find in history the glue of collective identity. During the early 1900s, America witnessed an explosion of pageants in which towns and cities reenacted critical historical events, all to strengthen civic pride, boost the local economy, and inculcate traditional values. "Nothing is more likely to cement the sympathies of our people and to accentuate our homogeneity," wrote the editor of *Century* in 1910, "than a cultivation of pageants."[16]

Americans also began to construct historical monuments in earnest. Within weeks of the July 1863 battle, the Gettysburg Battlefield Memorial Association was founded "to commemorate the heroic deeds, the struggles, and the triumph of [the] brave defenders." By 1900, more than two hundred thousand tourists visited Gettysburg each year. More than a hundred thousand people descended on Lexington, Massachusetts, in April 1876 to celebrate the centennial of the "shot heard round the world." Within a few months of General George Armstrong Custer's

1876 debacle at the Little Bighorn, tourists were sifting through the bones of horses and men. The Custer Monument Association was formed, the bodies reburied, and in 1878 a thirty-six-thousand-pound granite monument was erected on the site.[17]

If anything, Texans were even more determined than most states to recover their past. No other region of the country had experienced such a convoluted history. In less than a half century, the flags of five sovereign nations had flown over Texas: those of Spain (until 1821), Mexico (1821–36), the Lone Star Republic (1836–45), the United States of America (1845–61), and the Confederate States of America (1861–65). During Reconstruction, Texans had experienced military occupation by a conquering power and the reimposition of United States sovereignty. Not surprisingly, given such shifting loyalties, they developed an overpowering, almost jingoistic state patriotism, complete with a pledge of allegiance to Texas and the right to fly the Lone Star flag level with the Stars and Stripes.[18]

The outcome of the Civil War also helped shape Texas identity. Texans could distance themselves from the Lost Cause of the South by embracing their own unique—and triumphant—history of the Texas Revolution and conquest of the West. Texas, alone among the Southern states that seceded from the Union, trafficked in memories of being both conquerors and members of a vanquished people, and they preferred remembering victory rather than defeat. The wellspring of the Texas Revolution flooded them with pride and kept them from wallowing in "Lost Causism" like other Southern states. In rediscovering their past, Texans put the Civil War behind them.

In the 1880s and 1890s, in particular, the national economy squeezed Texas and made the contrast between the present and the glorious past all the more stark. While merchants and industrialists in the Northeast seemed to be accumulating fabulous riches, farmers and ranchers in Texas suffered. Beef and commodity prices fell steadily, but costs seemed to rise just as inexorably, and Democrats and Populists demanded that the federal government prevent a takeover of America by "syndicates," "plutocrats," and "monopolies."

The time was ripe for Texans to rescue their past. In 1873 the Texas Veterans Association was formed to promote Texas history, and Guy Bryan, a nephew of Stephen F. Austin and leader of the group, encouraged his daughter to form a women's association. At the time, all over the country, women were organizing into clubs. In an age when they could not vote or hold public office, they nevertheless exercised considerable power at the local level. At first the clubs focused on cultural activities and self-improvement. Over time, however, they became more overtly political. Club women demanded improvements in water quality, schools, and municipal services; protested political corruption; lobbied against child labor and for laws protecting working women; pushed for pure food and drug laws and conservation; and in what can be called early forms of urban planning and environmentalism, clamored for the protection of historic sites from commercial development. In 1910 the General Federation of Women's Clubs had a membership of 1.1 million.

In San Antonio, Adina De Zavala led the preservationist crusade. In 1886, the fiftieth anniversary of the fall of the Alamo had passed without a formal ceremony, prompting the editor of the *San Antonio Daily Express* to suggest "that a society be formed, whose duty it shall be to see that the prominent anniversaries of Texas histories are observed." An organizational meeting was held in 1891, and in 1892 the women named themselves the Daughters of the Republic of Texas (DRT) and adopted the motto "Texas, One and Indivisible." The DRT's mission was the "acquisition, preservation and proper adornment of the historic spots . . . associated . . . with those deeds of heroism . . . [and to] implant in the minds and hearts of succeeding generations a desire to emulate the example and maintain the high principles of patriotic devotion bequeathed them by their ancestors."[19]

At the top of the preservationist list was the Alamo. After completing her education in 1887 at Sam Houston Normal Institute, Adina De Zavala accepted a teaching post in San Antonio. Dismayed at the condition of the Alamo and four other missions south of the city, in 1889 she began meeting with other interested women, hoping to "keep green the memory of the heroes, founders, and pioneers of Texas." In 1893, they affiliated with the DRT as the De Zavala Chapter. But the women had more hope than resources. Local artist Pompeo Coppini remembered his wife, Lizzie, and Adina going "out every day with our horse and buggy, calling on all the merchants of the town for some contributions of bricks, lumber, cedar posts, or wire to repair fences. These articles, in lieu of money, were to be used in repairing all the missions, the chapel of the Alamo included." A construction boom in San Antonio had the women worried. Title to the Alamo chapel rested with the state, but the convent, where much of the fighting had occurred in 1836, remained in the hands of the Hugo & Schmeltzer Company. Property values were skyrocketing. Worried that a real estate developer might make Hugo & Schmeltzer a lucrative offer, De Zavala persuaded Gustav Schmeltzer to grant the DRT first option to purchase it.[20]

In 1903, the *San Antonio Express* complained that although "Friday was the . . . sixty-seventh anniversary of the fall of the Alamo, there were no ceremonies carried out at the historic structure. . . . Above the building the Texas flag floated at half mast. Nothing else was there to indicate the day." Hugo & Schmeltzer also announced its decision to sell the property to a buyer who planned to demolish the building and replace it with a modern hotel. Coming up with the $75,000 purchase price was out of reach for a schoolteacher, so De Zavala visited the nearby Menger Hotel, hoping they would put up the money to forestall the competition. The owners were out of town, but De Zavala learned that Clara Driscoll, heir to a cattle, railroad, and oil fortune, was a guest at the Menger.

Three years before, Driscoll had returned to San Antonio after several years in Europe. The state of the Alamo had stunned her. Comparing the neglect of the Alamo with the reverence Europeans paid their shrines, she wrote in 1901 to the *San Antonio Express* calling on Texans to repent of their neglect. "There does not stand in the world today a building or monument which can recall such a deed of heroism and bravery, such sacrifice and courage, as that of the brave men who fought and fell inside those historic walls. Today, the Alamo should stand out, free and clear. All the unsightly obstructions should be torn away." By "unsightly" she meant the Hugo & Schmeltzer building.[21]

De Zavala could not believe her good fortune. She had an ally, and a rich one at that. Born in 1881 in St. Mary's, on the Gulf Coast, Clara Driscoll came from one of south Texas's founding Anglo families. The Driscolls—along with the Klebergs, the Kenedys, and the Kings—pioneered the Anglo settlement of the Rio Grande Valley. Clara's grandparents, paternal and maternal, had settled in Refugio and Goliad Counties, building cattle and cotton kingdoms on tens of thousands of acres. Clara's father, Robert Driscoll, a unique man as comfortable in chaps, boots, and bandannas as he was in a double-breasted suit, had amassed nearly 170,000 acres in Nueces, Refugio, Bee, and Goliad Counties.

Clara was raised on stories of Texas heroes. Both grandfathers fought at San Jacinto, and at family gatherings in subsequent decades, the two veterans recollected their exploits again and again, regaling children and grandchildren with tales of the battle, of Santa Anna's stupidity and Mexican perfidy, of carnage and victory, and of the brave men of Goliad and the Alamo. The military tradition continued into the next generation. Clara's father, Robert, and her uncle Jerry spent four years killing Yankees during the Civil War, surviving combat at Fredericksburg, Chancellorsville, Petersburg, and the Wilderness. The Driscolls understood what it meant to shed blood for a cause.[22]

De Zavala convinced Driscoll to join the DRT and chair the De Zavala Chapter's Alamo fund-raising committee. The two women negotiated with Charles Hugo, who offered them a thirty-day option on the property for $500. At the end of thirty days, if they came up with another $4,500, he would extend the option for a year. On February 10, 1904, the DRT would have to make a $20,000 payment. The remainder of the purchase price would be paid in five annual installments of $10,000. On March 17, 1903, Driscoll secured the option with a personal check for $500. The committee then called on Texans to remember the Alamo, mailing tens of thousands of copies of "A Plea for Texas" and asking each recipient for a fifty-cent donation. The appeal resonated with love of country.

Too long . . . have we left [the Alamo] neglected and unhallowed. . . . [T]oday its grim old walls, scarred and battered in that heroic struggle of liberty, stand threatened by vandalism and menaced by the hand of commercialism. . . . The Daughters of the Republic, in whose veins runs the blood of the men who fought and died for the salvation of their country's honor, are now making a struggle for the preservation of the surroundings of the Alamo. . . . So I ask you one and all to join us in rallying around the Lone Star flag as it floats over the Alamo, and assist us in uniting the honor for the flag and its sacred building as they should be.

Confident that all Texans shared their passion, the two women expected "the money," as Driscoll later recalled, "to come pouring in, but it didn't." In fact, it barely trickled in. On the eve of the option's expiration, the DRT had raised only $1,021.75. Ready to fill the breach herself, Driscoll sought her father's counsel. He told his daughter, "If you've really got your heart set on this thing, it looks like you'll have to put up the money yourself to complete the deal." On April 17, she wrote out a check for $3,478.25.[23]

At the same time, the two women lobbied the state legislature for $5,000 to purchase the Hugo & Schmeltzer building. Driscoll appeared personally and chastised the politicians for neglecting their heritage. Early in May 1903, the lawmakers passed the bill, but on May 15, 1903, Governor Samuel W. T. Lanham vetoed the measure, arguing that it "was not a justifiable expenditure of the taxpayers' money." He also doubted whether the DRT could come up with the next $20,000 payment. The Daughters tried to prove him wrong, setting up a collection booth outside the Alamo, putting on a patriotic ball during Battle of the Flowers week in April, sponsoring a special restaurant during San Antonio Fair week in October, and blanketing the state with pleas for financial support. But as February 1904 approached, they had raised only $5,666.23. Rather than lose the option, Driscoll decided to buy the building herself. On February 10, 1904, she wrote another check for $14,333.77 and agreed to pay another $50,000 in five annual installments.

News of her generosity as "Savior of the Alamo" spread quickly, and political pressure mounted. At the county courthouse in Mason, Texas, for example, a resolution was passed claiming that the state of Texas "owes a debt of gratitude . . . to the memory of our departed heroes" and calling on the state legislature to assist the DRT in "the proper care, protection and preservation of the old Alamo mission." In January 1905, the legislature appropriated money to reimburse Driscoll. The bill, largely drafted by Adina De Zavala and sponsored by Samuel Ealy Johnson, also guaranteed that once Driscoll transferred title to the state, the DRT would be named custodian of the Alamo. Driscoll passed to Texas the title to the Hugo & Schmeltzer building on September 5, 1905, and one month later, Governor Lanham conveyed the property—the chapel and the convent—to the DRT.[24]

✳

That victory, however, set the stage for the "second battle of the Alamo." No sooner had the Hugo & Schmeltzer building been handed over than an epic struggle developed inside the DRT. Driscoll and De Zavala had competing visions for the Alamo. Even as a child, Driscoll had enjoyed art and architecture, and in Europe and India she developed a love for historical monuments and religious shrines. She had noticed that the most spiritually evocative sites, such as the Taj Mahal in India, the Waterloo monument in Belgium, and Mont-Saint-Michel and the cathedral of Chartres in France, dominated surrounding landscapes. Unencumbered vistas inspired reverence. She also realized that the best monuments centered the towns and cities surrounding them. Notre-Dame, Westminster Abbey, the Brandenburg Gate, St. Peter's, the Alhambra in Seville, St. Basil's Cathedral in Moscow—each throbbed with so much moral authority that surrounding buildings seemed to have backed away and bowed to them. Finally, she appreciated how Europeans buried their famous dead within their monuments. Cathedrals in England housed crypts with the remains of veterans of Waterloo, the Crimea, the Hindu Kush, the Zulu wars—wherever the empire had sent young men to die. In France and Spain, the prelates of the church were buried in great cathedrals.

For Clara Driscoll, the Hugo & Schmeltzer building was an eyesore, dominating Alamo Plaza and crowding out the chapel, which people all over the world identified as "the Alamo." She insisted that "this building should be torn away at the earliest possible moment. The daughters are not in favor of keeping anything ugly on this ground and are always in favor of things beautiful." Driscoll nursed a European vision of downtown San Antonio—a city center opened by a large plaza and anchored by an ancient chapel.[25]

For De Zavala, tearing down the Hugo & Schmeltzer building was unthinkable. The building had been constructed on the ruins of the Alamo mission's convent, which had once housed nuns and priests and had been later known as the long barracks. De Zavala was a preservationist at heart. "The proposition to demolish the Hugo & Schmeltzer building cannot be considered," she insisted. Instead, the Daughters would remove the building's roof, rip off the external woodwork, and restore the exterior to its original condition. The first floor would become home to a historical museum and library, while the second story would serve as a "hall of fame to the heroes." The fighting and dying on March 6, 1836, after all, had taken place in the long barracks. Little blood had been shed in the Alamo chapel.[26]

But Adina De Zavala underestimated Clara Driscoll, considering her little more than a rich, immature coquette. An interviewer once described Driscoll as "small, dainty, gracious always, with sensitive mouth and eyes that twinkle on the slightest provocation." Driscoll was, to be sure, young and rich, but she was hardly a coquette. She knew what she wanted. It was clearly indicated in the deed to the Hugo & Schmeltzer building. De Zavala chose not to argue the point; she was too desperate to get the young woman's money and too confident that once the DRT controlled the property, she would have her way with it.[27]

The state of Texas owned the Alamo chapel and the Hugo & Schmeltzer building, and the DRT managed both, but when De Zavala insisted on preservation of the Hugo & Schmeltzer building, Driscoll and her supporters seceded from the De Zavala Chapter and established the Alamo Mission Chapter. Determining which chapter served as official custodian soon became a legal matter. San Antonio business interests sided with Driscoll. In 1906, hotel promoters out of St. Louis had resurrected a proposal to demolish the Hugo & Schmeltzer building and replace it with a high-rise hotel. The developers insisted, however, that "the old building must go or the hotel will not come." Most businessmen agreed. "The building should have been torn down years ago," commented a member of the Business Men's Club. "Its walls are decorated with unsightly signs directing the people of San Antonio to use various and sundry varieties of cigarettes, chewing tobacco, and quack nostrums. Surely . . . there is nothing about all this to suggest a memorial to the heroes who spilled their life's blood."[28]

In February 1908, the pro-Driscoll statewide executive committee of the DRT decided to lease out the Hugo & Schmeltzer building until the issue of control was resolved. With the court case pending to determine which DRT chapter had custodial rights, Adina De Zavala staged her three-day occupation, accusing Driscoll of "pandering to the rabid desires of the money-getters, who for business reasons only, want to tear down 'unsightly walls.'" A frustrated Governor Thomas Campbell, hoping to defuse the controversy, on February 12 had the state superintendent of public buildings and grounds take control of the property, and the next day De Zavala "surrendered" to him. De Zavala had garnered public acclaim, but in the end, the court decided in favor of the Driscoll faction, declaring them the official custodians. The Alamo Mission Chapter eventually took over the Alamo. De Zavala unsuccessfully appealed. The

DRT, meanwhile, expelled her and her followers. For De Zavala's friends, the decision was "shameful . . . against a poor woman who had worked so hard to save all that was a memento of sincere, true patriotism."[29]

In the middle of the controversy, San Antonio businessmen had gone too far, raising the wrath of Driscoll and De Zavala, and giving both women, temporarily at least, common cause. Intoxicated with commercial development and the prospects of attracting a luxury hotel, businessmen attacked the preservationists. At a June 19, 1908, meeting of the Publicity League of San Antonio, held at the Business Men's Club, a number of prominent developers ridiculed the DRT's reverence for the Alamo and their opposition to development. "We do not want to appear sacrilegious," said businessman L. J. Hart, "but we realize that the time has come to stop mentioning the Alamo in the same breath with San Antonio. This has and is still being done to a most harmful degree for by doing it we are advertising San Antonio not as a modern and enterprising city . . . but are associating her with a name that carries with it the idea that San Antonio is still a Mexican village. . . . Let's let the people abroad forget the Alamo." T. L. Conroy, chairman of the Publicity League, then characterized the DRT as "mossbacks [who should] come and catch the proper spirit by mingling with us. . . . We have progressed to the point that insures success and can afford to pat the mossbacks on the head and tell them how bright the future looks." For all the acrimony within the DRT, the Publicity League's paternalistic dismissal of their concerns triggered an immediate backlash. Word of the resolution spread through San Antonio like a grass fire, and within hours the Publicity League backpedaled for shelter. In a press release the next day, it denied any intention to "forget the Alamo" and extolled the site as "sacred" and a "shrine to heroism" and promised to highlight the Alamo in its advertising campaign.[30]

Clara Driscoll wasted no time moving ahead, offering at her own expense to raze the Hugo & Schmeltzer building, surround the Alamo property with a stone wall, and convert the interior into a park. At the DRT convention in San Antonio, Rachel Fisher, a Driscoll ally, reiterated the need to "have the Alamo protected from the intrusion of other buildings. . . . The Alamo must stand there alone. . . . Any other building . . . would detract . . . and would be an insult to those blood stained walls."[31]

The battle quickly shifted from San Antonio and the courts to Austin, where a decision about the Hugo & Schmeltzer building had to be made. The *San Antonio Light* aptly described the controversy, which had "torn Texas from Texarkana to El Paso and from where the Rio Grande winds its way to the muddy banks of the Red River. . . . Erstwhile friends have become sworn enemies and those who formerly drank tea and exchanged small talk together are arrayed in a warfare quite as determined as the defense of the Alamo [in 1836]." The governor and members of the state legislature considered the controversy no-win politics, certain to make them more enemies than friends. Regardless of what they decided, they were going to end up having a group of very angry, very politically active women aligned against them. So they stalled and postponed making any decision until after the 1910 elections.[32]

In 1911, newly elected governor Oscar Colquitt tried to settle the matter. On December 28, he convened a meeting at the St. Anthony Hotel in San Antonio for "all persons interested, and who had any information they could give me, about the Alamo as it stood at the time of the butchery of Travis and his men." The governor listened to several people, including Adina De Zavala and Clara Driscoll, toured the property, and took the matter under advisement. In March 1912, he canceled DRT custodianship of the Alamo on the grounds that the Daughters had done nothing in six years to improve the site. He then announced his own plans to rebuild the long barracks. De Zavala felt vindicated, but Driscoll was livid. In the spring of 1912, Colquitt demolished all of the Hugo & Schmeltzer building except the two-story west and south walls. Under the direction of the state architect, government contractors began to restore the convent, but the legislature's $5,000 appropriation for the project ran out before the job could be finished. Driscoll kept up the pressure. On April 22, 1912, at a meeting of the Alamo Mission Chapter of the DRT, she renewed her demand: "It is the desire of the Daughters of the Republic to convert this property into a beautiful Park, filled with swaying palms, tropical verdure and native flowers, enclosed by a low wall, with arched gateways of Spanish architecture. In the wall will be placed any original stones that may be found. They do not approve of the erection of a modern building which would have no historic or sentimental value, but on the contrary be incongruous and inartistic and overshadow that sacred edifice so sacred to the heart of all Texans—the Chapel of the Alamo."[33]

In crossing swords with Driscoll, Colquitt had picked the wrong enemy. Savvy, wealthy, and fiercely determined, she was an even better politician than De Zavala. When rumors surfaced that Colquitt was considering a run for the U.S. Senate, Driscoll threw down the gauntlet. "The Daughters [of the Republic of Texas]," she told the *New York Herald Tribune*, "desire to have a Spanish garden on the site of the old mission, but the governor will not consider it. Therefore, we are going to fight him from the stump, for we understand that he intends to run for the United States Senate this year. We attempted to get a resolution passed in the Texas Legislature . . . but Governor Colquitt defeated its passage. We also are going to make speeches in the districts of State Senators who voted against and killed the amendment." Colquitt knew when, and how, to give in. The last thing he wanted was Clara Driscoll organizing women to harass him everywhere he went. He left Texas, ostensibly on state business, and while he was gone Lieutenant Governor William Harding Mayes let San Antonio officials demolish the upper-story walls. The one-story west and south walls were all that remained of the original convent.[34]

Some historians would later treat the second battle for the Alamo as an example of avaricious Anglos, in the form of Clara Driscoll, overwhelming innocent Mexicans, embodied in Adina De Zavala. One historian wrote that in "modern eyes, the contest is between the Anglos and the Hispanics as to who will be the descendent of the Alamo's heritage; in this fight, as in the 1836 Alamo battle, the Hispanics became the disenfranchised kin." Another wrote that De Zavala's vision for the Alamo was doomed because "such a vision could not sustain the social and racial cleavages necessary for the continued reorganization and stratification of a class society; a society of 'brothers and sisters' would not only undermine class differentiation but thwart racial divisions as well." And another insisted that the controversy reflected "divergent visions of the Alamo and its role in Texas. The groundswell in favor of creating an Alamo shrine was predominantly an Anglo-American movement. . . . In legend, as in fact, the enshrinement of the Alamo had become an Anglo-American crusade."[35]

To be sure, Santa Anna's viciousness at the Alamo and at Goliad had poisoned ethnic relations and precipitated a bitter struggle for the soil, and the soul, of south Texas. Forgotten were the Tejanos who died defending the Alamo as well as the Tejano volunteers under Juan Seguín who fought beside Sam Houston. At San Jacinto, long after the battle had been decided, the Texans had kept hacking away at wounded Mexican soldiers, finishing them off one by one to bloodcurdling yells of "Remember the Alamo" and "Remember Goliad." During the Mexican-American War, still seething with hatred over the Alamo and Goliad, many Texan soldiers lost the capacity to distinguish between Mexican soldiers and noncombatants or even between local Tejanos and citizens of Mexico. One historian wrote that "they felt a contempt for all things Mexican." All Mexicans, the prevailing racism held, bore at least some responsibility, by virtue of their heritage, for the Alamo and Goliad. Among the Texas volunteers during the Mexican-American War, Sergeant Edward Everett noted, a "frequent exploit was the plunder and outrage of defenceless villages or ranches. . . . The usage of the Mexican population by these men . . . was shameful. Shooting or robbing them was of frequent occurrence, and little was thought of it, and no redress was to be had." General Zachary Taylor, upon learning after his victory at Monterey in September 1847 that the Texas volunteers had been mustered out, was reported to have heaved a sigh of relief and "thanked God that the last Texas Ranger was discharged."[36]

✷

But the Driscoll–De Zavala fight was not simply an ethnic one. In the twentieth century, Texas history was told from the Texas point of view, which both women shared. There had been too many decades since 1836 for a Mexican point of view to survive. The Treaty of Guadalupe Hidalgo of 1848 had ended the Mexican-American War, but fighting continued in the Rio Grande Valley, not between American and Mexican troops but between Tejano natives and incoming Anglo settlers. The Tejanos remained in control of the land until the mid–nineteenth century, when global economic changes generated insatiable appetites for land. The industrial revolution stimulated demand for cotton and wool and for the land to run the sheep and grow the plants. At the same time, improving standards of living in Europe and the Eastern United States increased demand for beef, just when railroads and steamships made its delivery possible. The most accessible chunk of land in North America was the great trapezoid running from San Antonio southwest to Laredo, down the Rio Grande to Brownsville, up the Gulf Coast to La Bahía, and back up the river to San Antonio. Anglo-American settlers poured into the region.

Although the treaty had awarded U.S. citizenship to resident Tejanos and guaranteed land titles, many Anglo immigrants behaved cavalierly, as if they enjoyed a right to settle wherever they wanted. They also possessed overwhelming political power. By 1850 they outnumbered Tejanos ten to one, and immigration during the decade increased the ratio. Race relations, which had been poor ever since the Alamo and Goliad, took a decided turn for the worse as besieged Tejanos struggled to protect their land. Throughout south Texas, the state legislature and local counties imposed heavy taxes on Tejano property, and when foreclosures inevitably followed, title was transferred to the Kings, the Kenedys, the Klebergs, the Stillwells, and the Driscolls. All too often, Texas Rangers exercised heavy-handed justice, helping dislodge Tejanos from their own land. Even Walter Prescott Webb, a historian sympathetic to the Rangers, summarized the struggle in this fashion: "After the troubles developed the Americans instituted a reign of terror against the Mexicans and . . . many innocent Mexicans were made to suffer."[37]

South Texas periodically slipped into guerrilla warfare, with insurgent Tejanos trying to hold off the Anglo onslaught. During the late 1850s, Juan Cortina, a Mexican who owned land on both sides of the Rio Grande, protested Anglo treatment of Tejanos. "Mexicans!" Cortina proclaimed. "My part is taken; the voice of revelation whispers . . . that to me is entrusted the work of breaking the chains of your slavery. . . . [T]he Lord will enable me, with powerful arm, to fight against our enemies . . . to the improvement of the unhappy conditions of those Mexican residents . . . exterminating their tyrants, to which end those which compose it are ready to shed their blood and suffer the death of martyrs." He fled back to Mexico in 1859, but when Texas seceded from the Union in 1861, Cortina led another invasion, attacking the town of Carrizo in Zapata County. In the 1870s and 1880s south Texas ranchers accused him of heading up a large cattle-rustling ring. Among Tejanos, on the other hand, he became a gringo-fighting folk hero.[38]

By the late 1880s and early 1890s, the mantle of Tejano authority had passed to Catarino Garza, a native of Matamoros, Mexico, who twice married American women, worked as a traveling salesman for Singer sewing machines, and published such newspapers as *El Bien Público* in Brownsville and *El Comercio Mexicano* in Eagle Pass and Corpus Christi. He crusaded against the loss of Tejano land in Texas and insisted that the Rio Grande should not be recognized as a national frontier. He encouraged the establishment of *sociedades mutualistas* (mutual aid societies), which raised money to assist wrongly accused Tejanos and campaigned for voting rights and an end to segregated schools. When he died, in 1895, Garza had already become, like Juan Cortina before him, a hero to all Tejanos.[39]

Soon after Garza died a new folk hero appeared. On June 12, 1901, Gregorio Cortez was at work on rented land near the town of Kenedy in Karnes County when Sheriff W. T. "Brack" Morris showed up investigating a horse theft case. Cortez was not even a suspect, but he did not speak English. Morris did not speak Spanish, and the interpreter hardly spoke either. Cortez mistakenly assumed that he was going to be arrested, and in the ensuing misunderstanding, Morris pulled out a handgun and fired it, wounding Cortez's brother Romaldo and turning it on Gregorio. Cortez then shot and killed Morris, precipitating a ten-day manhunt followed closely by every newspaper in the state. Tejanos regarded Cortez as a hero, while Anglos viewed him as vicious killer. *Sociedades mutualistas* raised enough money to provide Cortez with good attorneys who saw him through four trials, several changes of venues, and three conviction reversals. In April 1904, Cortez was convicted yet again and sentenced to life in prison. Leading Tejano newspapers still lobbied for his pardon, and many influential Anglos agreed that Cortez had probably acted in self-defense. In July 1913, Governor Oscar Colquitt pardoned Cortez, prompting spontaneous fiestas throughout south Texas.[40]

All this was but one act in a much larger American drama. As immigration patterns changed in the early 1900s—white Protestants from western Europe giving way to Catholics and Jews from eastern and southern Europe—millions of Americans worried about the future. Racist notions escalated the growing sense of alarm. Madison Grant's best-selling *The Passing of the Great Race* in 1916 captured the public mood: "The cross between a white man and an Indian is an Indian; the cross between a white man and a Negro is a Negro; . . . the cross between a . . . European and a Jew is a Jew. . . . The Nordics are, all over the world, a race of . . . rulers, organizers and aristocrats. . . . [They] are domineering, individualistic, self-reliant and jealous of their personal freedom both in political and religious systems. . . ."[41]

American popular culture tended to view the Alamo through the same racist lens, reducing the battle to a clash between the upstanding forces of a Protestant Anglo-Saxon culture and the dissolute representatives of a Catholic Latin culture. In *Mexico Versus Texas* (1938), the first novel to consider the Alamo, Mexico gets top billing but comes out a distant second in every other category. Slightly changed and reissued in 1842 as *Ambrosio de Letinez,* its dedication page announced the theme: "The Texians may be considered as leading a crusade in behalf of modern civilization, against the antiquated prejudices and narrow policy of the middle ages, which still govern the Mexican Republic." And so it continued in such novels as *Inez* (1855), *Remember the Alamo* (1888), *The Lost Gold of Montezuma* (1906), *Guy Raymond* (1908), *La Belle San Antone* (1909), and *The Texan Star: The Story of a Great Fight for Liberty* (1912). Sadistic priests, corrupt officials, cruel leaders, and depraved soldiers characterize the Mexicans, while strong men, pure women, and noble ideals denote the Americans.

Early filmmakers readily adopted these racist themes. Though now lost, *The Immortal Alamo* (1911) at least suggested that the honor of American women was at stake at the Alamo. *The Martyrs of the Alamo* (1915) continued along the same line. Directed by William Christy Cabanne under the supervision of D. W. Griffith, the film bears an eerie resemblance to Griffith's *The Birth of a Nation.* Skin color, the film suggests, is what mattered to most Texans; that and virginal Anglo women. To reinforce the racial theme, Cabanne/Griffith cast Walter Long, who had portrayed the leering black rapist Gus in *Birth of a Nation,* as Santa Anna. Santa Anna's arrival in Texas is like the coming of a barbarian hoard. Not only is "honor and life of American womanhood . . . held in contempt," the public streets and private homes are unsafe. Drugs, "shameful orgies," and massacres occupy Santa Anna's attentions, and he clearly sets the agenda for his soldiers, who kill unarmed children and women, at least those whom they do not have sexual designs upon. In contrast, the Anglo-American Texas defenders are irredeemably virtuous, brave men willing to sacrifice their lives on the altar of liberty so that decent settlers can live without fear.[42]

But to filter the second battle for the Alamo through such a lens is to demonize Clara Driscoll, victimize Adina De Zavala, and trivialize both. Clara Driscoll was hardly an advance agent of Anglo civilization. Raised on the Driscoll ranch, she had spent much of her young life around Tejanos, attending their baptisms, confirmations, marriages, and funerals, and at mass accepting the wafer and wine from the hands of Mexican priests. She had ridden the range, branded cattle, and eaten meals with Tejano cowboys, and she spoke fluent Spanish. A friend recalled how fond she was "of Mexican and Spanish songs." At the Driscoll home a friend remembered "liking to sing . . . because there was a tiny balcony above the drawing room. . . . The railing was covered with a handsome Spanish shawl. . . . [S]he was a woman of quick sympathy, with little tolerance for stupidity or bigotry." And at the Alamo, Clara Driscoll wanted to preserve Mexican heritage. "All this improvement," she told an interviewer, "has modernized San Antonio . . . and while I was glad to see the place had gone so far ahead in every way, I could not help feel that it was a great pity to let all this advancement crowd and push out the really unique features of the Alamo City, and the one that is of the greatest interest to strangers, and that is the foreign—the Mexican—element, that has clung to the place for so many years."[43]

Nor was Adina De Zavala a defender of Mexico. She loved Texas, hated Antonio López de Santa Anna, and revered Davy Crockett, Jim Bowie, William Travis, Juan Seguín, and her grandfather. She defined herself as a "student and jealous lover of Texas history." The Alamo, she told anyone and everyone, was "an example of unselfish heroism" and should "be sacred to every man in whose heart throbs one iota of patriotism and respect for the heroic dead." Pompeo Coppini, a close friend, described De Zavala as a woman "who had an almost fanatical devotion to all that was connected with the history of Texas."[44]

Driscoll and De Zavala had much in common. Born to prominent Texas families and afforded abundant opportunities, they were accustomed to getting their way. Each had deep roots, by ancestry, in Roman Catholicism and had received parochial school educations. Driscoll was full-blooded Irish, and De Zavala, with three Irish grandparents, could trace most of her roots back to Ireland as well. Both women had made a religion out of Texas history and built their lives around it. And both were feminists and reformers, politically active in the women's club movement. But De Zavala was a historic preservationist in the strictest sense of the word, while Driscoll was an artist and city planner. And Clara had more money and played a better game of politics. Her victory in the second battle of the Alamo was far more political than ethnic.

★

With control of the Alamo and its future shape settled, Clara Driscoll set out to portray the Alamo as a fountain from which Texas, and the rest of America, could continually regenerate the values of sacrifice and patriotism, and where, during times of crisis, countrymen could find the courage to persist and prevail. Steadily during the 1900s and 1910s, the annual celebration on March 6 became more elaborate, and the Alamo became a setting for Texans and Americans to measure themselves against the past. On March 6, 1917, as the United States edged closer to entering the conflagration in Europe, the Alamo celebrations took on special meaning. At 10 A.M., delegations from the DRT and the Texas Landmarks Association unveiled on Commerce Street, between Blum and Bowie, a plaque marking the spot of the funeral pyre Santa Anna had ignited to consume the fallen Texans. Thousands lined Commerce Street, where an honor squad of U.S. troops from Camp Travis fired a three-shot salute to the dead and an army bugler played taps. Adina De Zavala lifted the veil from the tablet, which read: *On this spot bodies of the heroes slain at the Alamo were burned on a funeral pyre. Fragments of the bodies were afterward buried here.* Major Charles Barnes attended, bearing the Lone Star flag that Lorenzo de Zavala had once owned. (During the Spanish-American War, Adina had loaned the flag to a unit of San Antonio soldiers, who carried it into battle. On July 10, 1898, after Spain capitulated, Barnes raised the flag over Morro Castle, a Spanish battery overlooking Havana harbor.) Finally, a message from General Henry T. Allen, commander of the army's Ninetieth Division, was read. "It is only fitting," he said, "that the men who had enjoyed the liberties for which the defenders of the Alamo gave their lives are now preparing to cross the seas as allies of France; for France was the first of the European countries to give national recognition to the Republic of Texas."[45]

No sooner had World War I ended than the United States faced a new identity crisis. In the middle of the Red Scare and the xenophobia that swept the country, Texans used the Alamo as a symbol of capitalism, democracy, and individual rights—of Americanism. At the 1920 Alamo anniversary, General James A. Harbord noted that to defend America against the "Red Terror," there is "no better evidence of the patriotic spirit than the sentiment that prompts the citizens of a nation to honor the undying memory of their heroic dead, and to cherish the monuments associated with their supreme sacrifice. . . . Every civilized country has its shrines and the strength of national spirit is largely to be measured by the care of its shrines and battlefields. . . . The Spirit of the Alamo . . . must become the inspiration of the Nation, of a new regenerated Americanized America."[46]

During the 1930s, Driscoll worked locally, on Alamo Plaza, and nationally to project the Alamo to a broad public. As chairman of the DRT's Alamo Acquisition Board, as early as 1926 she had convened a meeting of hundreds of influential women at the Menger Hotel to promote the purchase of property surrounding the Alamo, and she discussed the matter with city officials and local businessmen. Her annual donations of $25,000 to the Democratic National Committee throughout the 1920s had given her a high profile outside the state and rendered her one of the most powerful women in Texas. In 1928 she was named to the Democratic National Committee, an appointment that cemented her growing influence. In 1931, she pushed through the state legislature a bill to purchase two tracts of land between the chapel and Crockett Street. One year later, she negotiated a purchase price of $220,000 for several vacant lots bordering the Alamo, but the state legislature appropriated only $150,000, and once again Driscoll stepped in, making up the difference out of personal funds. When Houstonian multimillionaire and Democratic Party mogul Jesse Jones heard the news, he wrote Governor Ross Sterling, "We all knew what ought to be done regarding the creation of a setting for the Alamo, but it remained for Clara Driscoll Sevier to do it. I suggest to Governor Sterling and all State legislators that an appropriation be made to commemorate the fall of the Alamo during our centennial observance of Texas independence." Driscoll eventually got her money.[47]

Other battles had to be fought. In 1933, at the urging of downtown merchants, city officials suggested purchasing some Alamo property to widen Houston Street, which would provide more efficient traffic flow. Driscoll would have none of that sort of progress. She announced that she and the DRT would not "approve any plan or anything that would release or exchange any Alamo property," and she threatened a "bitter political controversy" if the city persisted. City engineers backed down. Two years later, she talked the city out of putting a fire station in a building that bordered the Alamo on Crockett Street. The building eventually became the DRT library.[48]

In 1936, the centennial celebration provided Driscoll an opportunity to give the Alamo a national profile, to transform the most important shrine of Texas into an American monument as well. To avoid any repeat of the internecine warfare that had wracked the DRT three decades before, she sought and won the 1935 election to head the Daughters. While Adina De Zavala led the state's centennial celebration committee, Clara Driscoll, as she had for decades, remained in charge.[49]

The centennial observances began at 10:30 P.M. on March 5, 1936, with a reenactment of Colonel William Travis drawing the famous line in the sand and brave men solemnly crossing the line and committing their lives to history. San Antonio Mayor C. K. Quin paid his respects to the dead and delivered rhetoric of regeneration. "We stand with bowed heads in our historic shrine," he said, "which in the early hours of morning ran red with martyrs' blood. Let us resolve anew, as did the heroes of Texas and 20 other states, to stand for right against wrong and thus be worthy of the heritage they vouched to us." Early the next morning, humbled by how the Alamo must have looked just after the battle on March 6, 1836, the Daughters gathered in the Alamo chapel for a memorial service.[50]

For Driscoll, the highlight of the centennial began next. She had decided that the Catholic church, because of its central role in Alamo mission history and its place in the hearts of Mexican Americans, would play the lead role in the observance. On Alamo Plaza, in front of the chapel, she constructed a large platform and draped its sides with green cloth and its front with red-white-and-blue bunting. An altar flanked by stained-glass windows occupied center stage. From one corner of the platform waved the Stars and Stripes; from the other the papal flag of yellow and white. At 9 A.M. a solemn procession brought to the stage hundreds of Roman Catholic nuns, novices, priests, monks, and altar boys, many of them dressed in purple, yellow, and white robes. Among them were eighteen bishops. At 9:30 A.M., Archbishop Arthur J. Drossaerts of San Antonio celebrated a pontifical high mass with more than twenty thousand people, who filled the plaza and surrounding streets.

At 2 P.M., a delegation of Masons gathered at the shrine to hear remarks by Attorney General William McGraw. A Masonic band played patriotic music, and at the appropriate moment several thousand Masons bowed in homage to the Masons who had died at the Alamo. "[W]ithin them," McGraw said, "burned the love of governmental freedom, love of justice, love of the privilege of pursuing one's individual inclinations so long as they did not infringe upon the rights of their neighbors. These things are Americanism."

Catholics and Masons were not the only rivals Driscoll brought together. The Alamo, she believed, was for everybody a symbol of courage and sacrifice that transcended time, space, and ethnicity, and she went to great lengths to make the celebration inclusive. "Though they may not have been fortunate enough to have been born with the ermine upon them by direct ancestry, they are all Texans." To celebrate the heroic sacrifice, she invited Baptist pastors to preach, Jewish rabbis to pray, and Episcopal priests to read biblical passages. She brought labor leaders and businessmen together and put the Sons and Daughters of the Confederacy, the Grand Army of the Republic, and the Daughters of Union Veterans on the same platform, where they could together celebrate the Alamo's ideals. Protestant choirs sang "The Old Rugged Cross," "Onward Christian Soldiers," and "When the Roll Is Called Up Yonder, I'll Be There," while a Jewish choir chanted Kaddish to honor the dead.[51]

Throughout the rest of the day, high school marching bands and cheerleaders, drill teams, pep squads, columns of Boy Scouts and Girl Scouts, military honor guards, and the rank and file of Kiwanis, Rotary, and women's clubs marched through Alamo Plaza. At 6 P.M., bombers out of Kelly Field showered the Alamo with twenty-five thousand red-white-and-blue "Lone Stars." At six-fifteen, a message from Franklin D. Roosevelt was read. The president proclaimed the Alamo "a victory for the principles of liberty" and expressed his convictions that "those who died at the Alamo became deathless in their dying." Late in the evening, Governor James Allred of Texas and Governor Hill McAlister of Tennessee presided over a ceremony in which the flags of fifty states and nations—representing the homes of the defenders—paraded into Alamo Plaza. "There has never been a greater shrine of liberty than this building and these grounds," extolled Governor Allred. Governor McAlister insisted that "this is not a celebration of a military victory, but in sentiment and significance the Fall of the Alamo was one of mankind's greatest victories. . . . Here was written an imperishable message. . . . I sometimes think that Texas herself does not realize the proud destiny she has achieved." A roll call of the dead was solemnly read. Finally, taps sounded for the dead and an honor guard fired a salute.[52]

Three months later, Clara Driscoll capped the Alamo centennial with the visit of Franklin D. Roosevelt and first lady Eleanor Roosevelt. The Democratic Party owed Driscoll, and the president paid the debt by coming on June 12, 1936. Despite cloudy skies and showers, tens of thousands of people lined the downtown streets, shouting in English and Spanish and applauding FDR. The president looked particularly tired, drained perhaps by too many hours on the road and the sticky June weather. One reporter described him as "physically and mentally tired. There were lines in his face and he moved with the movement of a man who had been sawing logs all day." The president and first lady were ushered into the chapel and given a brief tour before FDR paid homage to the heroes. "[T]he Alamo stands out in high relief as our noblest exemplification of sacrifice, heroic and pure. . . . Without the inspiration of the cry—'Remember the Alamo'—the great Southwest might never have become a part of the nation. . . . It is with a feeling of deep reverence and humble veneration that I place a wreath on this shrine where the blood of a hundred and eighty-two Americans was shed." Reporters then described the Alamo's regenerative powers, noting that FDR "was a different man when he came out . . . after he had communed with the spirits of the 182 heroes who died here that Texas might become the Empire of the Southwest."[53]

Adina De Zavala sounded the only sour note. Keeping up her vigil to restore the long barracks, she warned Texans that a "crime against patriotism is being attempted." That Franklin and Eleanor had been ushered through the chapel only made matters worse. "Would any other place in the world," she complained, "have permitted the Alamo history to be misstated and camouflaged for so many years? And would any other place have permitted the main building of the Alamo, where our heroes died, to be dismantled and unroofed and desecrated? . . . No visitor really sees the place where our heroes died. . . . The president did not see it. He was ushered into the . . . [chapel] . . . which was full of stones and debris in 1836 . . . the Texans could not occupy it and did not occupy it."[54]

But few people listened to Adina De Zavala anymore. Once the president's visit was concluded, Driscoll moved ahead with the final work on Alamo Plaza. Because of her connections in the Democratic Party and her support of the New Deal, she managed to garner more than San Antonio's fair share of Works Progress Administration (WPA) and National Youth Administration (NYA) money. Texas NYA head Lyndon B. Johnson, whose father had helped usher Driscoll's original save-the-Alamo bill through the legislature in 1905, loosened the NYA purse strings for the remodeling. WPA and NYA workers razed several old buildings on recently purchased Alamo property, constructed a wall around the entire Alamo block, and built a museum facing Houston Street. Clara Driscoll's thirty-five-year-old dream of an uncluttered, uncrowded Alamo chapel surrounded by a beautiful park had become a reality.[55]

★

For all the rhetoric of blood, sacrifice, and death in San Antonio, a spirit of isolationism prevailed across the United States. The rise to power of Benito Mussolini in Italy, Joseph Stalin in the Soviet Union, and Adolf Hitler in Germany threatened another world war, and most Americans wanted nothing to do with it. At the 1934 anniversary of the Alamo, the Reverend H. Bascom Watts had said, "This is a memorial to the redemption of blood. While it seems we have to climb upward over the graves of our predecessors, we are inclined to pray for universal peace, so that no more human sacrifice will have to be made for human liberty." During his own 1936 visit to the Alamo, President Franklin D. Roosevelt cloaked his praise for the Alamo heroes with an appeal for world peace. "We, too, are ready and willing to stand up and fight for truth against falsehood, for freedom of the individual against license by the few. . . . Unlike them, we do not need to take up arms; we are not called upon to die; we can carry on a national war for the cause of humanity without shedding blood." Before Eleanor Roosevelt left San Antonio that day, she promised to return to "Texas and give a talk on the importance of world peace." And in October 1939, just a month after the outbreak of World War II in Europe, Clara Driscoll herself was asked if the United States should become involved. "We have too much common-sense for that," she told a reporter.[56]

But events in Europe soon undermined Americans' isolationism, and they began looking to the Alamo in a different way, to locate in its hatred of dictatorship a lens for viewing Adolf Hitler and the Nazi conquest of Europe. Between September 1939 and June 1940, Germany had crushed Poland, Belgium, the Netherlands, Norway, Denmark, and France, and few Americans knew where the juggernaut would stop. An October 1940 article in *The Reader's Digest* hailed the Alamo as "an example of deathless courage; of such stuff is our history made. . . . Today one hears that Hitler is making promises down in Mexico—as the Kaiser did in 1917. He tells them that when the United States falls apart—as a decadent democracy must—he may help Mexico to get back its lost province of Texas. . . . It's hard for a dictator to learn some things."[57]

Pearl Harbor, of course, turned the tide. Back in November 6, 1914, at a special ceremony on the Alamo grounds, a five-foot-high granite marker had been dedicated. Professor Shigetaka Shiga of Waseda, Japan, had visited San Antonio and had been touched by the story of the Alamo because it so resembled Japan's 1575 battle of Nagashino. He had also become concerned about rampant anti-Japanese sentiments in the United States. As a gesture at improving relations, he commissioned the marker—*To the Memory of the Heroes of the Alamo*—and had it inscribed with classical Chinese characters, extolling the virtues of the Alamo and Nagashino defenders. A DRT spokesman had praised Shigetaka: "On the subject of patriotism, love of country, home, friends, kindred and family there can be no difference between us—we meet on common ground. . . . You . . . have journeyed more than six thousand miles . . . attracted by deeds of patriots of foreign blood; and to their honor we bless you and thank you for the sacrifice." But in the early morning hours of December 8, 1941, patriotic vandals made their way into the Alamo compound and desecrated the marker.[58]

Throughout the war, the Alamo inspired a new generation of Texans to risk their lives in the name of liberty. In the early summer of 1942, after a series of Japanese victories in the Pacific, Texas historian Charles Jeffries sent Texas boys into battle with this message: "What kind of soldiers will these men . . . make? When the baptism of fire comes, can they stand it? The chances are they can. They will be properly imbued for the ordeal.

As they have shone on men of the Lone Star land for a hundred years, the lights of the Alamo will shine on them too." On March 6, 1943, with the war going better, Evelyn Carrington of the DRT told listeners that the "children and grandchildren of the Daughters of the Republic of Texas are in every branch of the service. . . . Many have left the boundaries of their beloved Texas, but Texas still holds them close to her heart and asks that God in His mercy will keep them safe. . . . If [they] should fall— and lives will be lost—Texas knows that such sacrifice will have its roots . . . in the faith of their fathers who dreamed and labored that liberty, honor and justice would be a part of every life." One year later, with Allied forces preparing the invasion of Europe and the assault on the Philippines, Samuel Terry, pastor of the Madison Square Presbyterian Church, hailed the Alamo's heroes as the men who made America a great country. He also proclaimed that during times of trial "we must go back to the original foundation from which we sprang." And when President Franklin D. Roosevelt died suddenly on April 12, 1945, Texans wondered if, during his 1936 visit to San Antonio, the Alamo had endowed him with special gifts to fight the war. "Could it be possible," wrote the editor of the *San Antonio Evening News,* "that the President of the United States carried back to Washington, D.C. with him the spirit of the Alamo? . . . Was his sacrifice in the glorious struggle against the forces of evil that would usurp the freedom of the world comparable with that of the heroes of the Alamo?"[59]

When the United States won the war, Clara Driscoll was not alive to see it. She died a month before the Japanese surrender, and San Antonio gave her a heroine's burial. In the early hours of July 20, 1945, before the morning sun appeared in the eastern sky, a black Cadillac hearse quietly backed up to the famous shrine in downtown San Antonio. Morticians lifted out an elegant bronze casket and carried it inside, where a committee of the Daughters of the Republic of Texas reverently opened the chapel's heavy wooden doors. The coffin was carefully placed on a raised bier bordered with dark blue drapes. Florists soon arrived with elaborate arrangements of pink daisies, gladiolas, and carnations. Outside, a Texas flag hung at half-mast, limp in the still, humid summer air. Not since March 6, 1836, when Mexican and American corpses littered the compound, had the body of a hero graced the Alamo. Inside the casket rested the remains of "Miss Clara," the matron of matrons, the "Savior of the

Alamo." Like a fallen president, she would lie in state that day, receiving in death the accolades of Texas patriots.

Lines began forming soon after the hearse pulled away—elderly men and women in mourning clothes, housewives in their Sunday best, chamber of commerce types in gray flannel suits, blue-collar workers in ill-fitting sports coats, cops in uniform, and hushed children tightly gripped by somber parents. The lines lengthened, winding out to the Menger Hotel and down Crockett Street. Some mourners, in the predawn darkness, may have remembered Miss Clara's description of the Alamo. "Watch it," she had written in 1906, "in the silence of the eventide, when the glow of a departing day throws its radiant color like a brilliant crimson mantle about the old ruin. . . . [G]o and stand before it on a night when the moon throws a white halo over the plaza; when the lights of the city are darkened, the winds of heaven hushed."

The doors to the chapel swung open at 11 A.M., and mourners shuffled single file by the open casket, some whispering to their children that she had "saved the Alamo." San Antonio policemen in dress uniforms guarded the bier, as did honor guards from the Daughters of the Republic of Texas and the Texas Federation of Women's Clubs. The honorary pallbearers were a who's who of the Democratic Party—former secretary of state Cordell Hull, former vice president John Nance Garner, Senator Thomas Connally, former postmaster general and party boss James A. Farley, Congressman Lyndon B. Johnson, and Speaker of the House Sam Rayburn. Adorning the walls were portraits of Davy Crockett, Jim Bowie, James Bonham, and William Barret Travis, whom some said Miss Clara had now joined.[60]

Thanks to Clara Driscoll, the Alamo had become sacred ground to Texans, but her dream of making it a truly American shrine remained unfulfilled. To be sure, four sitting presidents had visited the Alamo—Benjamin Harrison in 1891, William McKinley in 1901, William Howard Taft in 1909, and Franklin D. Roosevelt in 1936—but the stops had been brief, photo-op visits. Visitors to the Alamo peaked at one hundred thousand annually during the late 1920s, but the vast majority were Texans out to see what they had heard about in school. The number of visitors declined drastically during the Great Depression, when money was so tight; gas rationing during World War II made visiting even more difficult. Transforming the Alamo into a truly national shrine would require more, much more, than Clara Driscoll had been able to give.

Adina De Zavala survived Clara Driscoll by ten years, but late in the afternoon of February 14, 1955, at the age of ninety-three, she collapsed in her San Antonio home, the victim of a broken hip. Adina had spent the day, as she always had, writing letters to influential Texans, urging them to promote Texas history and to support restoration of the convent. An ambulance rushed her to Santa Rosa Hospital. She rallied at first, but pneumonia set in, and several days later she slipped into a coma. At 6 P.M. on March 1, the eve of Texas Independence Day, Adina De Zavala died. Four days later, a hearse took her remains, draped in the Lone Star flag, for a final visit to the Alamo.

In some ways, the cortege was anticlimactic. Perhaps in her coma during the previous week, Adina had dreamed of the Alamo, hoping to make sure that Texans would never forget. But how could they? Six days earlier, to a huge television audience, ABC had broadcast the final episode in its Davy Crockett trilogy, in which Walt Disney's Davy Crockett died in Clara Driscoll's Alamo. Perhaps a chattering television in the nurses' station penetrated the fog cloaking Adina's mind, letting her know that the Alamo was about to become an American obsession, the ultimate shrine to courage, sacrifice, and freedom.[61]

8

━━━ ★ ━━━

KING OF THE
WILD FRONTIER

THE NATIONALIZATION OF THE ALAMO by Walt Disney's famous 1954–55 broadcasts—the event that transformed it from a Texas shrine to an American one—was spurred by the Cold War and by Disney's sense that America needed heroes who represented liberty and the rights of man. Disney was less concerned with superpower conflicts in Turkey, Greece, or Iran than with a much tamer version of left versus right in his own company.

Even before Pearl Harbor, as far back as May 1941, less than six months after his fortieth birthday, Disney had begun to experience labor trouble. By then, he had made it, literally—made money, made an industry, made a universe. Bumping out of the Midwestern poverty and straitjacket piety of his father, he had tied his artistic and entrepreneurial talents to the relatively new field of animation. He formed his first company in his early twenties; by his early thirties Oswald the Rabbit and Mickey Mouse had made him famous. Step by step, through the conversion to sound, color, and feature-length animated cartoons, he stayed ahead of the pack, pioneering new techniques and demanding the highest-quality productions. Even during the Depression, Walt and his studio stood tall, proud of such hits as *Snow White and the Seven Dwarfs, Pinocchio,* and *Fantasia,* secure in the profits generated by Mickey

Mouse, Donald Duck, Minnie Mouse, Goofy, and Pluto. But now, long before there was a Magic Kingdom, there was trouble in the house of Disney.

The origins of what would become a nasty labor dispute were deep and muddy, products of Disney's labor practices, union infighting, and the special nature of the times. After the passage of the Wagner Act in 1935, unions, now protected by the federal government, won converts in many of the country's major industries. In Hollywood, the Screen Cartoonists Guild (SCG) formed in 1936 and allied itself with the International Alliance of Theatrical Stage Employees (IATSE), belonging to the powerful American Federation of Labor (AFL) fold. Throughout that turbulent period, however, Disney workers stayed on the sidelines, watching the battles at Metro-Goldwyn-Mayer and other studios. And as far as Walt Disney was concerned, there was no need for unions or any other kind of government interference in his studio. He insisted his workers call him Walt, paid them well, gave ample opportunity for ambition and innovation, and rewarded the most able. His new studio in the flatlands of the lower San Fernando Valley, he thought, was more of a home than a factory. How many factories had corridors painted in various soft colors to provide visual variety, a theater, a first-class commissary, a gymnasium, and a roofed parking lot? Wasn't that proof that he was more of a father than an employer?[1]

Disney, however, did not stand outside the gravitational pull of history. Some workers complained that wages varied wildly, that the merit system was unevenly applied, and that the lack of bureaucratic structure made it difficult to gauge how to get ahead in the company. The main problem was that Disney's studio had grown too large and successful to be run as a family business. Increasingly, Walt appeared aloof and distant to the lowly animators, painters, and inkers at his studio, and his paternalistic approach struck them as hopelessly behind the times. They wanted change, looking forward to the day when the Disney studio adopted the same labor policies as U.S. Steel and General Motors.[2]

Many younger, more radical workers also thought that IATSE was out of step with the times. The union, they thought, was corrupt, dominated by mob wiseguys, transplanted racketeers from Chicago whose heavy suits looked out of place in Hollywood. More to their liking was Herb Sorrell's Conference of Studio Unions (CSU), which opposed IATSE's policies. Sorrell, a former boxer whose nose looked like a caved-in mine, was considered a worker's labor leader, though his politics were decidedly leftist. But in an era when the idea of a popular front was still alive in Hollywood, many of Disney's employees were as politically charged as Sorrell. In the late 1930s, the Screen Cartoonists Guild (SCG) organized a large faction of Disney's workers and prepared for a showdown with the great man himself.

The stage was set. Disney despised unions. The SCG despised Disney's mom-and-pop managerial policies and hired Herb Sorrell as its "business agent." Sorrell quickly upped the rhetoric of the dispute by threatening to turn Disney's plant into a "dust bowl," words that did not endear the SCG to the creator of Mickey Mouse. Sorrell's loosely organized CSU also backed the SCG. And as so often happened in the years after the passage of the Wagner Act, when enough acronyms joined together there was always the potential for a strike.[3]

It started on May 28, 1941, but it did not just happen to Disney; he provoked the strike by laying off leading SCG activists. At first the strikers demonstrated an undeniable flair. They were, after all, cartoonists, artists with quick minds and light touches. One carried a sign of Jiminy Cricket with the caption "It's not cricket to pass the picket." Another sign showed Pluto asserting, "I'd rather be a dog than a scab." Their jokes were funny, their speeches well crafted, and their props the best in the business. As strikes go, this one had great production values. There were plenty of laughs during the day, and during the night a local musicians union supported them with sing-alongs. Even the normally staid *New York Times* got in the act when it announced that other AFL unions would blacklist Mickey Mouse.[4]

But the jokes soon got stale, and as calluses began to form on the placard carriers' hands, their strike took on a harder edge. The strike divided the studio—about one-third of Disney's twelve hundred employees struck—and engendered hard feelings. Both sides soon swore like sailors, calling former friends and associates every name in the big book of profanity. It was like "a civil war," said one nonstriking animator. "Friends whom you had worked beside the day before were snarling and spitting on your car as you drove on the lot." Strikers used screwdrivers to scratch the nonstrikers' cars and puncture their tires. Men went after one another with their fists, and a few shots were fired. It was an ugly period.[5]

Disney did not escape the bitterness. On one summer morning as he slowly drove into his studio, smiling and waving to his former workers, striker Art Babbitt gripped a bullhorn and shouted twice, "Walt Disney, you should be ashamed of yourself." Babbitt had been one of Disney's most talented animators—the artist who had developed and animated Dopey and the Wicked Queen for *Snow White,* Geppetto for *Pinocchio,* as well as key scenes for *Fantasia* and *Three Little Pigs.* Even more important, without Babbitt, Goofy would never have had a fully developed personality. But now Babbitt was humiliating Disney, in front of Walt's own studio and former employees. Disney hit the brakes and threatened to punch Babbitt before he had second thoughts and drove on.[6]

Disney knew what was happening, but he was vague about why. More than anything else, the strike assaulted his worldview. Just before the strike, but when discontent was so thick at the studio that it was palpable, he had delivered an odd, highly personal speech to his employees. He admitted that the studio faced financial problems; the war in Europe had cut deeply into industry profits, the studio had cash problems, its creditors were nervous, and the federal government was milking corporate profits. But the studio had faced other troubles, overcoming them with hard work, imagination, unselfishness, and faith in animation. If everyone at the studio, including himself, would work together, increase productivity, and cut costs, they would weather the economic storm.[7]

Sounding every bit like John D. Rockefeller or Andrew Carnegie, Disney shared his grand notion of how the world worked. Success was not the product of union grumblings or bureaucratic quick fixes; it was the fruit of hard work. If anyone has a problem, he should "do something about it. I would suggest that you talk to yourself first, complain to yourself first, be honest with yourself, and if you're at fault, give yourself a good kick in the fanny and do something about it." "Don't forget this," he concluded, "it's the law of the universe that the strong shall survive and the weak must fall by the way, and I don't give a damn what idealistic plan is cooked up, nothing can change that."

Before the dispute, he was known as Walt—just plain Walt—with a soft spot in his heart for the underdog and a gentle and optimistic approach to life. In 1933 his eight-minute cartoon *Three Little Pigs* captured the mood and attention of a nation chilled by the huffing and puffing of the big, bad winds of unemployment and hunger. Pull together, the short suggested, and everything would turn out well. And so it was in Walt's little world. From *Snow White and the Seven Dwarfs* and *Pinocchio* to *Dumbo* and *Bambi,* Disney's populist parables of spunky little guys—and little animals—lightened Americans' hearts at the same time as they proved inspirational. Certainly no studio head in Hollywood enjoyed the universal love of Disney. Louis B. Mayer and Harry Warner were moguls, Harry Cohn was nasty—but Disney was Walt. In September 1941, after the intervention of the National Labor Relations Board, Disney settled the strike, caving in to many of the strikers' demands. He extended official recognition to the union; agreed to standardized pay scales, written merit pay raise guidelines, vacation time, and severance pay; and implemented seniority guidelines for future layoffs.

Disney's world darkened after the strike, which he insisted was the work of communists. In a published communication to his striking employees, he wrote, "I am positively convinced that Communist agitation, leadership, and activities have brought about this strike, and have persuaded you to reject [a] fair and equitable settlement." Privately, he wrote journalist Westbrook Pegler that the "entire mess was Communistically inspired and led" and that Sorrell "is dirty, sneaky, and as foul as they come and there is no doubt but he is a tool of the Communist group." But, he added, the strike had awakened him politically. There was a war in America, and democracy was under siege. What happened at his studio was a minor skirmish, and though he lost that fight he was determined not to surrender. Drawing his own line in the political sands, he told Pegler, "I'm not licked. I'm incensed. . . . The dirty, foul means used against me in this fight cannot be easily forgotten. I was called a rat, a yellow-dog employer, and an exploiter of labor. . . . My plant and methods were compared to a sweatshop and above all, I was accused of rolling in wealth."[8]

Walt's frustration and disillusionment took different forms. At the most basic artistic level, a new animal emerged as Disney's doppelgänger. If gentle, sweet, optimistic Mickey Mouse was the Disney of the 1930s, Donald Duck was the Disney of the 1940s. Impatient, quick tempered, easily frustrated, often angry, Donald took Disney and America to war. As critics noted, Donald resisted the modern bureaucratic world. "He resents authority and refuses to submit meekly," wrote one Donald interpreter. "He revolts. He storms. He rages. He breaks dishes, furniture, heads." Though it is difficult imagining Mickey Mouse getting Adolf Hitler in the crosshairs of a rifle and pulling the trigger, it takes no great leap to envision Donald taking the shot.[9]

Disney also took a more active interest in politics. During the 1930s, the popular front united Hollywood liberals and radicals. For the Hollywood left, there was always a cause to champion, a project to support: the Scottsboro boys, the victims of the dust bowl, the strikes and struggles of organized labor, the plight of the Jewish refugees, the fight against fascism, aid to the Republican forces in Spain—an endless breadline of just causes. In Hollywood there were always leagues to join, petitions to sign, and fund-raisers to host. "We're up to our necks in politics and morality just now," boasted Hollywood screenwriter Mary McCall in 1937. "Nobody goes to anybody's house any more to sit and talk and have fun. There's a master of ceremonies and a collection basket, because there are no gatherings now except for Good Causes." To be sure, the Nazi-Soviet nonaggression pact made almost everyone left of center question the honorable intentions of the Soviet Union, but even that storm eventually passed as Russia and America joined forces during World War II.[10]

Never comfortable with the unions and the causes of the left, the Hollywood right became more outspoken toward the end of the war. Their rallying cry was anticommunism. In February 1944, members of the right wing of the film community organized the Motion Picture Alliance for the Preservation of American Ideals, whose Statement of Principles boldly announced, "We believe in and like the American way of life." All they asked for was the freedom "to speak, to think, to live, to worship, to work and to govern ourselves, as individuals, as free men" and "the right to succeed or fail as free men, according to the measure of our ability and our strength." The organizers of the Alliance were admittedly and proudly reactionary. "We have no plan to offer," they claimed. "We want no new plan, we want only to defend against its enemies that which is our priceless heritage." Their only reason for existence was to fight the "un-American" influence of Hollywood communists.[11]

MGM director Sam Wood was the driving force behind the Alliance. He had directed several of the Marx Brothers' finest comedies, worked on *Gone With the Wind*, and directed such hits as *Goodbye Mr. Chips*, *Kitty Foyle*, *The Pride of the Yankees*, and *For Whom the Bell Tolls*, but he believed that he had been denied the credit he deserved. Blaming Hollywood communists for his not having won an Oscar, and considering Soviet communists as a greater threat than even Hitler, he had passionately embraced anticommunism, going so far as placing a stipulation in his will that all his heirs, save his widow, could not inherit a penny until they affirmed under oath that they "were not now, nor ever have been, Communists." The cause became his raison d'être, and fittingly he was elected as the first president of the Alliance.[12]

Disney had won an armful of Oscars, so he could not charge that communists had robbed him of professional glory, but he was convinced that they had caused the strike and smeared his reputation. Members of the Alliance elected Disney one of the three vice presidents, and he supported the ideals and goals of the organization, though he was probably not very active in its day-to-day operations. Like Gary Cooper, Spencer Tracy, King Vidor, and several other highly visible members of the Alliance, Disney lent his name more than his energies to the cause, and his interest in it seemed to decrease as his memories of the strike became less painful. But his attitude toward communism did not soften. It threatened "all of the good, free causes in this country, all the liberalisms that really are American," he said, and he felt "if the thing can be proven un-American it ought to be outlawed."[13]

As in his populist phase in the 1930s, Disney enshrined his politics in his films. As he himself aged, his country's past, as well as his own, became increasingly sacred. History was a gift to be cherished and guarded, something pure to be passed down hand to hand, generation to generation. His vision of history, however, assumed oddly idiosyncratic dimensions.

The landscape of his past, its physical presence and psychological vistas, shrank. Simply put, he miniaturized history. On a personal level, in the mid-1940s he developed an absolute passion for miniature railroads. He carefully plotted and constructed a half-mile track in his backyard, a one-eighth-scale world of his own, complete with bridges, tunnels, trestles, and communities. When he was assaulted by critics or plagued by anemic quarterly reports, he trudged to his private world, where all trains ran on time and workers silently stood frozen at their tasks. A *New York Times* film critic visited the Disney studio during this period and "came away feeling sad." Walt, he noted, had lost his zest for animated movies and seemed obsessed—"almost weirdly concerned"—with his miniature railroad world.[14]

He may have lost some of his zest for animation, but perhaps that was because he was dreaming of bigger smaller things. Disneyland was the outward expression of this paradox. The idea took hold of Disney in the late 1940s, and although the plans for the amusement park became bigger, bolder, and more costly, Disney's grand conception for the park remained small. The houses and shops on Main Street in Disneyland, for instance, looked normal sized, but they were not. First stories were built at nine-tenths scale, and second stories at eight-tenths. The railroad running around the park was five-eighths scale, as were all the bricks, shingles, and gas lamps. Main Street set the tone for the entire park and underscored Disney's idea that the past was something comfortable and knowable, smaller and more intimate, neat and safe.[15]

Disneyland was, of course, a statement about America and its history. From turn-of-the-century Main Street and Frontierland to the roboticized President Lincoln and the miniaturized architecture, there was, Disney told a journalist, "an American theme behind the whole park." "I believe in emphasizing the story of what made America great and what will keep it great." And he believed that keeping the country small and manageable should do that nicely. No heavy Stalinist architecture and art, oversized to the point of shrinking the individual to insignificance, for Disney. Just wide walkways, elysian green spaces, and enough rides to breed perfect satisfaction. Tyrants, he observed, constructed massive edifices to glorify themselves. Disneyan architecture aimed to make people feel good about themselves.[16]

Disney's dream of and search for a usable past also led in more cinematic directions. Although he never abandoned animation, beginning in 1950 he did shift increasingly to live action films. Some critics dismiss such movies as *Treasure Island* and *Twenty Thousand Leagues Under the Sea* and such television series as *The Swamp Fox* and *Zorro* as harmless—and mindless—escapism, or perhaps even good, wholesome family entertainment. But Disney biographer Steven Watts disagreed, arguing that in the Cold War Americans engaged in "attempts to explain the nature of the American people, American history, the American character, and the bedrock values that supported the whole. Walt Disney engaged his enterprise to grapple with these broad issues and emerged as a key figure in the process of national self-definition."[17]

As early as 1948 he was planning to move into historical dramas. As he told columnist Hedda Hopper, a fellow member of the Alliance, it was "time to get acquainted, or renew acquaintance with, the robust, cheerful, energetic and representative folk heroes." Johnny Appleseed, John Henry, Pecos Bill, Paul Bunyan, and other legends, figures of American mythology, "were all working men," laborers who "earned their keep riding herd, planting trees, felling timber, building railroads, pounding a steel drill, poling keelboats, taming nature." They were connected to the present by the sweat of work and a sense of accomplishment, and separated only in the level of exaggeration. But Disney had no doubt that they were representatives, as connected to the present as a man's arm is to his hand.[18]

They were the builders of America. Other Disney heroes, from Francis "the Swamp Fox" Marion and Don Diego "Zorro" de la Vega to little Johnny Tremain and Texas John Slaughter, were the fighters for America. Some battled for independence, others struggled to maintain freedom. Pitted against British redcoats, Hispanic tyrants, frontier outlaws, or corrupt landowners, they showed a willingness to give their lives for independence and freedom. And freedom won was jealously guarded. Governments, Disney's films and television shows suggested, might exceed their mandates, and people were not perfect. There would always be a need for Slaughters and Zorros to safeguard citizens against rapacious governments and greedy individuals.

In Disney's evolving pantheon, no civic god stood above Davy Crockett. Backwoods philosopher, loyal friend, public servant, and freedom fighter, Davy was the American prototype, pure of intention, of the world but untainted by it. The origins of Disney's Davy are tied to Disneyland and television. In 1953 nothing was more important to Walt Disney than his dream of Disneyland, but without outside financing, it would remain in the dream stage. Most bankers and investors scurried away in horror after meeting with Disney. To them an amusement park meant many things—waiting in long, inching lines while sweat sealed their shirts to their backs; listening to the buzzing machines, clanking rides, the screaming barkers; looking for lost, frightened children and cleaning up after dizzy sick ones; dealing with one tough-looking, grimy carny type after another—none of them very appealing. They told Disney that outdoor amusement parks were about as modern as swimming holes. "Even with his plans laid before them," Richard Schickel observed, "the bankers could not see what Disney was talking about."[19]

One investor, however, believed in Disney's name if not actually in Disneyland. The American Broadcasting Company (ABC) shared a common uphill fight with Disney. ABC was so far below NBC and CBS that it did not even seem in the network race, and an alliance with Walt Disney seemed a fair way to obtain some instant credibility. In 1953 the network made a deal with Disney. Under two separate but clearly related agreements, it consented to purchase 34.48 percent of the shares of Disneyland, Inc., and broadcast seven years of weekly, one-hour television programs for a show called *Disneyland*. On his show, Disney could hype his amusement park and his movies. In return, ABC could hype its affiliation with the Disney studio—the first studio to make a production agreement with a television network—and air Walt's television shows. Altogether a nice quid pro quo that would pay off handsomely for both parties.

Out of the deal came a compelling need for Disney to generate product to fill his program commitments, and out of that came Davy Crockett. *Disneyland* the television show was structured like Disneyland the amusement park. Initially it was divided into four rotating segments with the same names as the theme areas of his park—Frontierland, Fantasyland, Tomorrowland, and Adventureland. Since Disney turned to ABC for venture capital more than any artistic motive, he developed *Disneyland* along a loose anthology format. But early in its first season it discovered its mission: to give Americans heroes.

Davy Crockett, of course, became Disney's first and biggest star, creating overnight a frontier and merchandising craze. Yet when Disney and his producer began to discuss their first Frontierland episode, the choice of Crockett was far from inevitable. In early 1954, David Crockett was relatively obscure, remembered by Texans for his stand at the Alamo and by Tennesseans for his frontier wit and failed political career. There were few serious historical articles about Crockett, no major biography, and outside of Texas hardly any interest in him. In Arthur M. Schlesinger Jr.'s Pulitzer Prize–winning *The Age of Jackson* (1945), the most important book about America in the 1830s, Crockett barely warrants a mention. On one page Schlesinger refers to Crockett as "the picturesque if somewhat phony frontiersman," and on another suggests that he was a dupe of the Whigs, a tall-tale flimflam man who turned on Jackson but died "heroically" at the Alamo. In short, he did not seem to fit Disney's needs.[20]

And when aides first proposed Crockett, Disney expressed reservations. "All he did was fight Indians," Disney told his producer. "How can you say anything new about that?" But if not Crockett, who? Disney wanted a primarily historical figure, effectively eliminating Paul Bunyan, Johnny Appleseed, and John Henry. And he refused to glorify an outlaw, ruling out Jesse James, Billy the Kid, the Daltons, and the other famous western bad men. Daniel Boone was an option—he was more famous and an authentic frontiersman—but his life lacked Hollywood sex appeal. The film industry had never done much with America's early frontier experience, and Revolutionary War movies had often died at the box office. Besides, Boone died peacefully at an advanced age, which was nice for him but lacked drama. As one authority on the subject commented, "Boone's wilderness was too early, too arcane, too closed-in, and too mysterious; too uprooted in any pre-existing popular format to be readily understood and appreciated, especially by child viewers." In the final analysis, Crockett's association with Texas linked him to the frontier of cowboys and wide open spaces, to a Western genre that yielded successful novels and films.[21]

Unearthing no one better, the Disney studio went to work on Crockett, quickly discovering that his life was perfect for their project. The reality of Davy's life had always been less important and less interesting than the thick web of legend that cocooned his memory. Yes, he had been born in the backcountry. And yes, he told tall tales, fought in the Indian wars, served in Congress, and died in the Alamo. But except for his death, the rest of his life was eminently malleable. Starting with the basic essentials, screenwriter Tom Blackburn and producer Bill Walsh shaped a three-episode life for their hero: *Davy Crockett, Indian Fighter; Davy Crockett Goes to Congress;* and *Davy Crockett at the Alamo.* The shows starred an unknown but likable actor named Fess Parker and aired on the Wednesday evenings of December 15, 1954, January 26, 1955, and February 23, 1955. By the end of the three shows, Fess Parker would be very well known, the power of television would be fully recognized, and Davy Crockett would be the most famous frontiersman in American history.

The first and second shows established Davy's character. As a Western actor, Parker was more of a Jimmy Stewart than a John Wayne. Radiating sincerity, truthfulness, and a quiet dignity, he led by example, always pushed forward by others and motivated by a keen sense of public duty.

In truth, he was neither the David Crockett of history nor the Davy Crockett of legend, neither the politician on the make nor the canebrake buffoon. His sidekick, George Russel, was more like the Davy of the autobiographies and almanacs; Buddy Ebsen played Georgie broadly, contrasting nicely with Parker's underplayed Crockett. It is Georgie who tells fanciful tales about Davy, Georgie who spreads Davy's fame, Georgie who gets the cheap laughs. Although Parker's Davy is not above a brief speech or a flurry of bombast, he seems more comfortable with silence than words, resembling the popular image of Daniel Boone or James Fenimore Cooper's Natty Bumppo. In the one letter Crockett receives in the show, Georgie reads while Davy listens.

Davy is clearly portrayed as a Cold War hero, and the three episodes are framed by war. In *Davy Crockett, Indian Fighter,* Davy is fighting in the Creek War under the command of General Andrew Jackson. The enemy is not so much Indians as one specific Indian named Red Stick, who insists upon fighting despite the desires of the older chiefs. Davy literally fights for peace, which the episode suggests can be won only from a position of greater strength. In the episode's central scene, Davy outfights Red Stick but stops short of killing him, saying that honorable peace is the only way to end and prevent conflicts. Red Stick argues that governments break treaties, that "white government lies." "Davy Crockett don't lie," Davy responds. No speeches, no promises, just "Davy Crockett don't lie." That settles the conflict. The two men shake hands and end the war.

The idea that "Injuns got rights, they're folks like anyone else" carries into *Davy Crockett Goes to Congress*. Historically, of course, the central event in Crockett's congressional career was his split with Jackson and alliance with the Whigs. Disney, however, did not want to elevate Crockett at Jackson's expense. Although Jackson is shown to be a plantation and slave owner, he is still portrayed as a fatherly man of the people, always ready to kick back and share a sip of corn mash with a neighbor from the West. Essentially, neither Jackson nor Crockett is viewed as a politician, and it is the politicians, the Tobias Nortons of Washington, who dress finely, break treaties with the Indians, and line their own pockets. They come between the honest Crockett and the well-meaning Jackson, causing an unnatural rift. The second episode ends with Davy praising expansion, but not at the sacrifice of Indian treaties. Congress, he lectures, has a duty to make Americans live up to their ideals, and should not become involved in greedy land grabs.

In *Davy Crockett at the Alamo*, Davy enlists in yet another war. After sacrificing his political career on the altar of truth, Davy takes a river cruise with Georgie. One night Georgie asks where they are going, and Crockett hands him a newspaper, filled with stories about Texas moving toward independence and General Santa Anna vowing to "expel colonists." "Texas," Georgie explodes. "There's nothing there but a mess of trouble." "Americans in trouble," Davy quietly adds. Georgie ponders the hopeless plight of the Texans, people too far from the United States to expect any help and too close to Mexico to anticipate anything more than the worst. "Bunch of rock-headed idiots that won't quit because they think they're right," he concludes, rephrasing one of Davy's favorite aphorisms. Then he says, "How soon ya reckon we'll be headed out that way?" Davy smiles, knowingly.

To viewers of the 1950s, Davy's world was not much different from their own. It was a place where liberty was under siege, where freedom-loving citizens, who knew they were right, were battling against incalculable odds. It was Greece and Turkey in 1947, Berlin in 1948, Korea in 1950, or any one of the other flash points of the Cold War. Davy was a visible expression of the Truman Doctrine, and his mission in Texas was to fight the encroachment of an evil empire, in this case Santa Anna's forces. Disney consciously turned the Alamo into freedom's last stand. Davy, Georgie, and the Indian and gambler who go with them become representative Americans determined to preserve freedom. They meet Travis's challenge, cross the line, and die "fighting for liberty." Davy's decision to head south is accompanied by a verse from "The Ballad of Davy Crockett":

> [He] heard of Houston an' Austin an' so,
> To the Texas plains he jest had to go,
> Where Freedom was fighting another foe,
> An' they needed him at the Alamo.
> Davy—Davy Crockett,
> The man who don't know fear.[22]

The final scene is especially telling. Neither Santa Anna nor any member of his army is given any individuality. They are simply a horde—

nameless and faceless, indistinguishable one from another. They attack in human waves, like some sort of biologically driven insects, swarming toward the walls of the Alamo, finally winning by sheer numbers. Their style of warfare resembled what Americans believed had happened near the Yalu River in North Korea, or even Stalingrad during World War II. Americans had read newspaper accounts of night battles lighted by flares when wave after screaming wave of Chinese had attacked American positions in Korea—a "bottomless well" of manpower, General Douglas MacArthur had said. Now here was Davy Crockett, fighting in the dark, facing similar odds.

Long before Davy's television death, however, something odd had happened. What was supposed to have been a simple television program—part of the bill for the Disneyland loan—started to take on a life of its own. *Davy Crockett, Indian Fighter* was broadcast on Wednesday, December 15, 1954, on about forty stations in the ABC network. The remaining eighty to ninety stations had to wait for prints and broadcast the show in the following week. This delayed broadcast contributed to the building momentum for the episode, and by the end of the week it was clear that the show was a very big hit. Across America, children pretended to be Davy Crockett in their games of cowboys and Indians, and the refrain "Davy—Davy Crockett / King of the Wild Frontier" was sung or whistled by children morning, noon, and night until it was as familiar as the opening notes of Beethoven's Fifth Symphony. The reception caught Disney by complete surprise. "We had no idea what was going to happen to Crockett," he later recalled. "Why, by the time the first show finally got on the air, we were already shooting the third one and calmly killing Davy off at the Alamo. It became one of the biggest one-night hits in TV history, and there we were with just three films and a dead hero."[23]

The second episode, *Davy Crockett Goes to Congress,* aired January 26, 1955, and created even more of a buzz. Series producer Bill Walsh was mystified: "ABC couldn't believe it. [Fess] Parker couldn't believe it. Neither could Walt or I. After the second aired . . . there was no mistake. We had a hit show." And the third episode, *Davy Crockett at the Alamo,* which aired February 23, 1955, only confirmed the obvious. By then the country was full stride into a merchandising craze of epic proportions.[24]

Practically overnight, in a miracle of capitalism, everything that had to do with Davy Crockett was on sale—and things that had nothing to do with Davy Crockett were for sale with his name attached to them. Any American boy with enough money or willing parents could wear a buckskin Davy Crockett jacket, cotton Davy Crockett shirt, denim Davy Crockett pants, and stylish Davy Crockett underwear. He could carry a wood or plastic Davy Crockett rifle and load it with a Davy Crockett powder horn. If he anticipated serious fighting he could strap on a Davy Crockett holster, complete with a pair of Davy Crockett guns, and stick a Davy Crockett rubber knife in his belt. After several hair-raising adventures, he could go home to a meal served on Davy Crockett plates, drink milk from a Davy Crockett mug, bathe with Davy Crockett soap, dry off with a Davy Crockett towel, slip into a pair of Davy Crockett pajamas, watch television for a while on a Davy Crockett bearskin-looking rug, then go to bed between Davy Crockett sheets to dream Davy Crockett dreams. Davy Crockett's picture or name could be put on just about anything, from T-shirts, raincoats, and boots to wallets, balloons, and lunch boxes; from dolls, purses, telephone sets, and baby shoes to tipis, rocking chairs, ukuleles, and swimming pools. *Everything*—saddlebags, bicycles, tricycles, face powder, ropes, jigsaw puzzles, ice cream cups, athletic equipment, panties, toy logs, dart games, books, trucks, wagons, board games, rings, and on and on—as far as mechandisers' imaginations could stretch.[25]

But one item stood out from all the rest—the Davy Crockett coonskin cap. The cap was something special. Historically it tied Davy to Daniel Boone and a long line of frontiersmen, but even more deeply it linked him to America itself. In 1776 when Benjamin Franklin had journeyed to France he had donned a coonskin cap instead of a powdered wig. Franklin was making an eloquent statement about the cultural difference between aristocratic Europe and republican America, and the cap became a symbol of the new nation. Disney's appropriation of the cap, and its revival in the 1950s, was a nice gesture.

The cap, furry and tailed, was omnipresent in 1955. A *Life* magazine article in April of that year contained picture after picture of boys and girls cavorting in caps, many armed with rifles, smiling, laughing, lost in their Davy world. They proudly wore their caps outside Davy Crockett Elementary School in Dallas, Texas, but no less proudly in Chicago, Denver, Englewood, New Jersey, and Washington, D.C. They were "brother[s]-in-arms of almost every American of both sexes from the age of 2 to 12."

No popular fad or craze had ever embraced so many impressionable youngsters.[26]

The mania must have made a dent in the raccoon population because the demand for tails seemed inexhaustible. The price of a pound of tails started at twenty-five cents, then doubled, tripled, quadrupled, and kept climbing until it reached $6, even $8 in a few places. Raccoon coats from the 1920s, symbols of another age of crazes, were slaughtered to make caps. Producers turned wolf and fox pelts into coonskin, and rabbit and skunk fur into coonskin. "Anything with hair on it moved," said one furrier. Even caps made of cardboard and crepe paper bounced out of stores on the heads of happy kids.[27]

If Disney did not anticipate what happened, he certainly scrambled to capitalize on it. Unfortunately for him, a man named Morey Swartz owned a patent for a "Davy Crockett, Frontiersman" line of clothing, and he made a fortune licensing to other manufacturers for 5 percent of net sales. But Disney merchandised his own "Walt Disney's Davy Crockett" line. In a successful attempt to prolong the life of the craze, Disney rebroadcast the three episodes in April and May 1955, then combined the segments into a feature-length movie that he released in the summer. He also sent Parker and Ebsen on a forty-two-day, twenty-two-city tour. Parker accepted keys to cities, dedicated ballparks and playgrounds, spent hundreds of hours in department stores, and met with politicians, as well as making speeches, singing "The Ballad of Davy Crockett," and shaking hands. Next, Disney sent Parker on tours of Europe and Japan.[28]

In the process Davy Crockett became the most profitable figure in history. By May, Americans had purchased more than $100 million of Davy Crockett merchandise, and by the end of the craze that figure exceeded $300 million, or over $2 billion in current dollars. To put these figures in perspective, the 1950–51 Hopalong Cassidy craze did about $1 million a year and the 1958–59 Zorro spending spree amounted to slightly more than $20 million. One estimate judged that Davy Crockett merchandise accounted for 10 percent of all children's wear sales during 1955. Not even the *Star Wars* bonanzas of the 1980s and 1990s were as pervasive as the mania for Davy.[29]

Social critics and cultural commentators were even more surprised than Disney with the enormous success of the Crockett series, but that did not prevent them from ascribing meaning to the phenomenon. Some advanced complex explanations. Dr. Evelyn Mills, former executive secretary for the National Council on Family Relations, said that "due to the restiveness of our society, children today . . . require tangible evidence of human beings able to battle the problems of their time." The new frontier, she claimed, was a social one, and Davy showed children how to hack their way through it.[30]

Other commentators simply stated the obvious. Television, they boldly asserted, was a powerful medium; or, as Leo Rosten would later call it, a "marvelous, exciting, depressing, promising, wonderful, deplorable miracle." It emerged as a viable entertainment source in the late 1940s and was accepted with "surprising suddenness." In the 1950s it was like a dye that was poured onto a map of the United States, spreading out of the cities until it covered the entire country. In 1950, only 7 percent of American households had television. That figure climbed to 47 percent in 1952, and 58 percent in 1955. Disney must have wondered if the Crockett craze could have been bigger outside the cities if this figure had been higher. By 1957, television was close to ubiquitous, at 82 percent, and 89.4 percent in 1960. Increasingly, noted Eric Goldman, an early historian of the decade, home "was where the TV set was located." By the year that Davy Crockett first aired, not only did more than one out of every two American homes have television, but members of those families could eat TV dinners while watching their sets.[31]

In the mid-1950s watching television, like eating dinner, was a shared experience. Not only would parents and children watch programs together, but often they invited guests to share their viewing pleasure. Television advertisements emphasized this communal experience, sometimes picturing children and adults huddled around sets, other times illustrating a group of well-dressed adults watching a program. Together they watched, sharing the character's failures and triumphs. And unlike sitting in a darkened theater where talking was frowned upon, television had commercials that almost encouraged relaxed discussions.

More than any other programs, the Davy Crockett series demonstrated the commercial and educational power of the new medium. From its inception in America, television was transcendently a moneymaking enterprise. Its raison d'être was to hawk products. The program was the hook; the commercial was the point. In the 1960s television authority David Karp would wisely answer the many critics of the tube by returning to the essence of the matter: "TV is not an art form or a cultural channel: it is an advertising medium." Its purpose was to push cars and detergents and to increase revenues for manufacturers. "Obviously," Karp wrote about the leading network executives, "if their object is to make money—and they do make money—it seems a bit churlish and un-American of people who watch television to complain that their shows are so lousy. They are not supposed to be any good. They are supposed to make money."[32]

The genius of Disney was to employ television to advertise himself, to combine the roles of producer and advertiser. The Davy Crockett series only incidentally sold some nonrelated commercial product; it primarily sold the world of Walt Disney. Without actually using the designated commercial space, it sold Disneyland, coonskin caps, buckskin coats, and Walt Disney's view of America past and present. It trafficked in myths of the past and dreams of the future, all glued together by hundreds of millions of dollars. Nothing even remotely like the Davy Crockett craze had happened before, and its impact was incalculable. Something important happened in America between Davy's fight with the Creeks in the first episode and his death at the Alamo in the final one. Some unknown, if perhaps only dimly perceived, cultural gear shifted. The television generation was born.

This, of course, entailed a subtle transition in cultural power. Certainly America had never been fully governed by a cultural elite. Historian Neal Gabler has cogently traced the skirmishes between high and low culture. High culture educated and uplifted; low culture entertained or (according to its high culture critics) lowered and degraded. It was a war between the intellect and the senses, reason and emotion. Although vendors of a middle-class culture showed a middle way, and Hollywood occasionally satisfied both intellect and senses, highbrow critics often failed to distinguish between *Gone With the Wind* and bearbaiting. These elites were not the aristocrats of Franklin's day; no longer did they dress in aristocratic waistcoats and powdered wigs, or even wear clerical collars. They had become the liberal, educated elite, writers for the *Saturday Review* and the *New Yorker*, university professors and psychologists, the social engineers of a better tomorrow.[33]

In television, they saw the ultimate threat, the furthest extension of the "graphic revolution" that threatened to replace words with images.

In the nineteenth century, editor E. L. Godkin had fretted that a visual culture was driving out an authentic, word-based culture like some sort of Gresham's law. His twentieth-century counterparts have worried about the same problem, magnified by the power of television. Historian Daniel Boorstin feared that the graphic revolution was undermining higher aspirations by offering up bloody slices of debased reality. Cultural critic Neil Postman has charged that television is only low entertainment. "No matter what is depicted or from what point of view, the overarching presumption is that it is there for our amusement and pleasure." To him, television is a placebo for a culture that suffers from a serious cancer.[34]

Television, however, can also educate, sometimes factually, sometimes mythically. Educator Max Rafferty would later call Disney "the greatest educator of [the twentieth] century." Davy Crockett was not Pinocchio; he was a historical figure who had been born in what would become Tennessee, elected to the United States Congress, and died defending the Alamo. The question was, did Disney's Crockett capture the essence of the Alamo, or was it a distortion that did more harm than good?

There were some initial defenses of the TV Davy. Kenneth S. Davis, writing in the *New York Times Magazine,* noted in a backhand compliment that "the most remarkable thing about this now vastly commercialized legend is that it accords well with the known facts of Davy's life and character." Crockett was "an authentic hero . . . as attractive in appearance as he was magnetic in personality," and if Disney got a few points wrong—like suggesting that he had died fighting at the Alamo—he had done no serious harm. In fact, he had served educators by turning the attention of American youths away from the deplorable "vogue of comic-book supermen."[35]

Davis thus recognized that some aspects of the graphic revolution were better than others. In the mid-1950s, such cultural critics as psychiatrist Frederic Wertham were blaming comic books for everything from juvenile delinquency and racism to fascism and homosexuality. In his 1954 book *Seduction of the Innocent,* Wertham waxed hysterical on the Nazi meaning of Superman's *S* and the secret perversions in Batman's cave. Compared to the mind-bending damage of comic books, Disney seemed a positive public servant, reminding Americans of their true mythic heroes.

But as the Crockett craze boomed, the cultural elite sharpened their knives, or at least their pencils. Both E. J. Kahn Jr. in the *New Yorker* and John Haverstick in the *Saturday Review* executed flanking attacks on Crockett by assaulting the books written about him. Since the vast majority were older reprints or slapdash juvenilia, this was a bit like going after a flea with a howitzer. Surprise—Kahn discovered that his selection of tomes was inconsistent about when Davy shot his first "b'ar," the age his dog died, the name of his wife, and how exactly he died at the Alamo. Surprise—Haverstick unearthed the fact that the Davy Crockett of children's literature is a sanitized version of the historical David Crockett.[36]

Not content to just review the books, both Kahn and Haverstick felt compelled to unmask the real Davy Crockett. "David, as distinct from Davy, Crockett," wrote Kahn, "emerges from his own story as a barely literate backwoodsman with a parochial view of the world, an engaging, if somewhat windy, storyteller, a legislator who was far more of a politician than a statesman, and a man of scant humility." Haverstick was less kind, asserting that Crockett's adventures were not "precisely as Mr. Disney describes them." Then he turned to historian Vernon L. Parrington's short, sharp sketch of Crockett, perhaps as slanted a source in its own way as Disney, but with the authoritative weight of "real history." "Strip away the shoddy romance that has covered up the real man," Parrington wrote and Haverstick quoted, "and the figure that emerges is one familiar to every backwoods gathering, an assertive, opinionated, likable fellow, ready to fight, drink, dance, shoot, or brag, the biggest frog in a very small puddle, first among the Smart Alecks of the canebrakes." In the end, Crockett was little more than a wag who fooled citizens into voting, then tricked "posterity" into "swallow[ing] the myth whole."

Bernard Kalb in a *New York Times Magazine* essay also accepted Parrington as the final word on Crockett, quoting many of the same passages as Haverstick and concluding that there was not enough reality in the Davy legend to make him really worth remembering. Kalb's main concern, however, was Disney's impact on historical canonization. He had seen the future, and it disturbed him terribly. Crockett had died "in high style" in 1836 and, outside of Texas, gradually slid to the margins of history, a figure more like Paul Bunyan or Pecos Bill than such historically important frontiersman as Daniel Boone. He was then "disinterred one night last winter by two of the mid-century's most formidable influences—Walt Disney and television, or vice versa—and that was that. The next morning, the Crockett saga was up and around, doing nicely." And Boone, an authentic American pioneer and hero, "was still in his grave, undisturbed, though possibly whirling."[37]

It had all happened so suddenly, and that was the soul of the problem. In the past, heroes and heroines earned their greatness over time. "[G]reat men, like famous men," Daniel Boorstin noted, "came to the nation's consciousness only slowly." Noteworthy deeds, singular accomplishments, important feats—these added up over a lifetime, culminating in fame, or at least notoriety. Then historians went to work, separating the chaff of fame from the wheat of greatness. But Disney had used television to shortcut the process, and in a few nights Crockett had amassed more fame, garnered more attention than he had during his lifetime and the next century. But did that instantly revived fame add up to greatness? Quite frankly, that was a matter for the cultural elite to debate, for Disney and his legions could have cared less. The graphic revolution had introduced a new cultural currency.[38]

Davy Crockett, then, represented something larger than an historical individual or even a mythical character. He symbolized a cultural break, a major turn on the road to Andy Warhol's fifteen minutes of fame. Though few on either side of the cultural divide understood the full implications of the Crockett craze, some sensed that something important was at stake. Certainly John Fischer, a transplanted Texan and editor of *Harper's Magazine*, accused Disney of corrupting America's children. Six months before, he romanticized, American kids were loyal Space Cadets or aspiring Hopalong Cassidys. "Then, almost overnight, two million clean, patriotic youngsters were seduced into switching allegiance. . . . [T]hey turned—within the course of a single television program—into Davy Crocketts. Crowned with coonskin, they now infest the trash-can forests and parking-lot prairies from coast to coast, brandishing their Old Betsies in an endless war for the kingship of The Wild Frontier." The words are telling: "seduced," "switching allegiance," "infest," a vague sense that something unclean has taken place.[39]

"The historic truth," Fischer confidently informed his readers, was that the real Davy Crockett was a "juvenile delinquent" who ran away from home, married, and "deserted" his family. He was "an unenthusiastic soldier" who "weaseled his way out of the army"; "a poor farmer, indolent and shiftless"; a justice of peace "who boasted about his ignorance of the law"; "an unsuccessful politician; a hack writer . . . ; and . . . a violinist." All things considered, "He never was king of anything, except maybe the Tennessee Tall Tales and Bourbon Samplers' Association. When he claimed that he had shot 105 bear in nine months, his fellow tipplers refused to believe a word of it, on the sensible grounds that Davy couldn't count that high." Contrary to the "Simonized, Disneyfied version of history," Davy Crockett was a lout and a bore.

Not content just to assault Crockett's life, Fischer proceeded to trash his death. The defense of the Alamo was a waste of time, as is all the "steamy, impassioned" oratory Texans expend on the event. The battle was "in fact, the worst military blooper in American history, short of Pearl Harbor." Fischer suggested that the defenders formed a motley crew of "hotheads" and military incompetents, mostly lazy, drunken, and prejudiced. The only one with any sense was Louis Rose, a French mercenary who slipped out of the Alamo before the Mexicans attacked. As for the rest, "They died well. From a military standpoint, that is about all that can be said for them; and it is the only solid fact about the Alamo which most Americans ever hear."

So much for Disney's Crockett. Fischer's point was that Disney and television should leave the history business to more judicious minds. But that was not an opinion universally held. Hundreds of angry letters poured into the offices of both the *Saturday Review* and *Harper's Magazine*. Some pointed out the sloppy historical work of Haverstick and Fischer. Haverstick confused the *Southern Review* for the *Southwest Review* and overlooked several important studies of Crockett. But Fischer's historical sins were much greater. For a Texan, his knowledge of the history of the Texas Revolution and the role of the Alamo was remarkably thin. To be sure, he knew enough to hold several radical opinions, but not nearly enough to adequately support them. His brief foray into Alamo history robbed the event of all its complexity and terrible significance. As one letter writer showed, Fischer's discussions of what the "main Texas army" needed, what the Alamo's engineers did, and how the defenders behaved was about as wrong as an educated Texan's could be.[40]

Most letter writers, however, did not quibble with the facts as much as they did with Fischer's attack on American heroes, especially Davy Crockett. "Every bit of information you quoted may be true," wrote a person from Tennessee. "I am not questioning it, but I would like to ask you what you have gained by the attack on the man?" For American children, Davy "represented a frontiersman of the highest caliber and a fighter for the good of the country." Why shred his reputation? Maury Maverick Jr., descendant of an old Texas family with a deep love for the state, was more to the point. He treated Fischer like a rattlesnake, a creature impervious to rational argument or explanation. His four-word letter probably spoke for millions: "Damn you, Jack Fischer."

Disney had scratched a line in the ever shifting cultural sands, and Americans stepped to one side or the other. Disney gave television watchers a brave, decent, stalwart hero. Fischer said Davy was an ignorant, lazy slob. One's politics determined where he stood on the issue. Brendan Saxton, educational director of the United Auto Workers, commented in a radio address that Davy was nothing more than an "ordinary backwoodsman, who probably spat on the sidewalk, chewed tobacco, certainly didn't know any grammar . . . not at all an admirable character." In a show of solidarity, labor columnist Murray Kempton wrote a four-part series in the then liberal *New York Post* on Crockett, suggesting that the King of the Wild Frontier was a coward, a Republican hack, and "a fellow purchasable for no more than a drink."[41]

Legions defended Disney's Davy. They wrote letters to *Harper's Magazine* and San Antonio newspapers condemning Fischer. They picketed the *New York Post*'s offices carrying placards reading, "Davy killed a b'ar at 3—What did Murray Kempton ever shoot—except the bull???" and, "Who you gonna expose next!—Santa Claus?" Even the conservative writer William F. Buckley joined the debate on the *State of the Nation* radio show. Buckley expressed no concern for the survival of Crockett's heroic status: "The assault on Davy is one part a traditional debunking campaign and one part resentment by liberal publicists of Davy's neuroses-free approach to life. He'll survive the carpers."

For over half a year the debate raged. In Congress Representative Martin Dies of Texas debated the wisdom of Davy Crockett. On the campaign trail Estes Kefauver wore a coonskin cap like Davy Crockett. Millions of words joined the hundreds of millions of merchandized dollars. Then, in the summer of 1955, it ended. *Variety* commented, "Davy was the biggest thing since Marilyn Monroe and Liberace, but he pancaked. He laid a bomb." A student at Public School 40 in Manhattan put it another way: "It was a lot of cheap publicity. I'll bet Disney made a fortune."[42]

Though the fad passed, the cultural divide did not heal, and Crockett was now firmly planted as a symbolic seed between the two sides. A few years after the end of the craze, historian Richard Hofstadter in *Anti-Intellectualism in American Life* used Crockett as a prime example of the appeal of egalitarianism and anti-intellectualism to Americans in the nineteenth century. But the twentieth-century context was more important. Americans, locked in a Cold War, had responded to Davy's Americanism, his appeal to the country's highest characteristics and ideals. Truth, justice, defense of a noble cause. The ribbon on the package was the Alamo. Disney had given the central event in Texas's history to the nation; he had made Texas's battle America's battle.[43]

9

———— ✦ ————

ONLY HEROES,
ONLY MEN

In 1960, the Alamo became the stuff of presidential politics. It began innocently enough on September 12, 1960, a stormy morning in the middle of a presidential campaign, when John Fitzgerald
Kennedy awoke early thinking about a speech he was scheduled to deliver that night in Houston, Texas. The address, he hoped, would bury
the controversy over his Catholicism. Before a gathering of Protestant
ministers, Kennedy planned to turn on all his Boston Irish charm and assure his listeners as well as the rest of the country that he was an American first and foremost, and a Catholic only by birth and faith.

The religious question was less a question than a problem, and it
had always lurked just under the surface of Kennedy's campaign, a
cancer of unknown severity, perhaps benign, perhaps malignant, but
there all the same. Months earlier during the West Virginia primary,
he had attempted to use his military record to trump the bogeyman.
"Nobody asked me if I was a Catholic when I joined the United States
Navy," he said in a speech in Morgantown. He couldn't believe that
40 million American citizens had forfeited their right to run for president because they attended mass and took Communion in a Catholic
church. "That wasn't the country my brother died for in Europe," he
observed, "and nobody asked my brother if he was a Catholic or a

Protestant before he climbed into an American bomber to fly his last mission."

That should have been that, but it wasn't. No matter how often Kennedy talked about the sacred ideal of separation of church and state, regardless of how many times he intoned that he did not take orders from any pope, any cardinal, any bishop, or any priest, despite his soulful references to his dead brother, the question of his religion followed him like a foul odor, raising doubts about his fitness to hold the highest office in the land. Indeed, earlier in September, the Reverend Norman Vincent Peale, the popular lecturer and author from New York City, had asserted, "It is inconceivable that a Roman Catholic president would not be under pressure by the hierarchy of his church to accede to its policies with respect to foreign relations in matters, including representation to the Vatican."

And so Kennedy turned his eyes toward Houston, where once again, maybe even for the last time, he would say in so many words that being president of the United States meant a damn sight more to him than his mother's rosary beads. But nothing in an election year is ever that simple. Before Houston, his staff had scheduled stops in El Paso, Lubbock, and San Antonio. The stop in El Paso passed uneventfully, but an angry thunderstorm in Lubbock grounded all air traffic. By the time Kennedy reached San Antonio, he was an hour behind schedule.

If any part of Texas was Kennedy country, heavily Catholic San Antonio was it. Several thousand people crammed into Alamo Plaza, spilling out into the street beyond and sweating in the afternoon heat. By noon the temperature had already passed ninety degrees, and it seemed even hotter to the Massachusetts-bred Kennedy crowd as their man climbed aboard the swaying platform. Appropriately enough, he talked about heroism and Latin America, much to the delight of the cheering crowd. By the time he had finished, he was further behind schedule. It was time to escape, but Kennedy faced a minor crisis. Security was in short supply, and he dreaded the idea of wading into the gridlocked courtyard. Instead, he retreated into the cool inner sanctuary of the Alamo. Turning to his host, a full matron of the Daughters of the Republic of Texas, he asked to be led to the rear exit of the Alamo.[1]

"Senator," she coolly replied, "there are no back doors at the Alamo. Only heroes."

The dig soon became the talk of Texas, but it was not the first Alamo-inspired insult aimed at Kennedy. Only a few months before, actor John Wayne had taken a shot at Kennedy in an advertisement for his upcoming film, *The Alamo*. Publicly, Wayne believed that Kennedy was the victim of wrongheaded—that is, leftist—politics and the absence of a moral vision. Personally, Duke considered the Massachusetts senator "a snot-nosed kid who couldn't keep his dick in his pants." He had heard rumors that Kennedy's Pulitzer Prize–winning *Profiles in Courage* had been ghostwritten by Theodore Sorensen, and he had been told by several close and trusted friends that when the senator came to Hollywood, the morality of the town dipped a notch. Yet because of his "daddy's money" most reporters considered Kennedy's private life untouchable, and many politicians and academics treated him like an oracle. For Wayne, it was all a trifle too much. Feeling abundantly patriotic—he had, after all, just finished making a movie about the siege of the Alamo, which he considered one of the centerpieces of American history, and he had played its coonskinned-capped hero—he took dead aim on the Democratic politician.[2]

Duke fired his salvo a week before the Democratic and Republican conventions. In a three-page, red-white-and-blue advertisement in the Fourth of July edition of *Life* magazine, he hyped the release of *The Alamo* and delivered civic lectures to his fellow countrymen. "Very soon the two great political parties of the United States will nominate their candidates for President," the ad began. "One of these men will be assigned the awesome duties of the White House. . . . [I]n this moment when eternity could be closer than ever before, is there a statesman who for the sake of a vote is not all things to all men; a man who will put America back on the high road of security and accomplishment, without fear or favor or compromise; a man who wants to do the job that must be done and to hell with friend or foe who would have it otherwise; a man who knows that the American softness must be hardened; a man who knows that when our house is in order no man will ever dare to trespass. In short, a Man. . . . There were no ghost writers at the Alamo. Only Men."[3]

In a single line Wayne's publicity writer had managed to include "ghost writers," "Alamo," and "Men" in a manner singularly harmful to John Kennedy. Now one of the Alamo's Daughters was brandishing the phrase "Only heroes" like a moyle's knife. What was it about the shrine that so inflamed passions in 1960? And why was John Wayne using it as his own personal weapon?

✯

John Wayne discovered patriotism only in midlife, and the Alamo even later. Some critics of Wayne have suggested that his sense of country amounted to something of a midlife crisis. Some men turn to fast red sports cars and mistresses, they intimate; John Wayne's tastes simply fancied the American flag and conservative ideologies. To the critics, Duke was little more than a Midwestern joiner transplanted in southern California, a Hollywood Babbitt, fodder for any bombastic message wrapped in red-white-and-blue, a fake, more humbug than cowboy or soldier. The critics, however, missed the point of Wayne's life and misunderstood the message and importance of his epic film *The Alamo*.

To be sure, Wayne was undoubtedly plagued by about his own failure to stand and fight. Just when his career was taking off, World War II had also arrived, presenting him with a ticklish dilemma. Should he enlist, or not? Should he follow John Ford, Henry Fonda, Jimmy Stewart, Clark Gable, Ronald Reagan, and so many others? He was thirty-four, married, with four children, and enjoying a career that might not withstand the hiatus. He was an aging leading man still better known in small towns than big cities.

Presented with a choice between patriotism and careerism—between doing what he knew was right and what he sensed was smart business—Wayne opted out of the "big show." For the next four years he talked endlessly about enlisting, wrote letters about and flirted with the idea of enlisting, but he never took the fateful step. Always there was another film to make, another reason not to step forward. He received deferments in 1942, 1943, 1944, and 1945. The war made Wayne a bigger star than ever. During the conflict he starred in twelve films. He battled for freedom as a soldier, sailor, and pilot, in Europe, Asia, and America. He gave substance to the most cliché-ridden role: the rock-hard American who through individual effort ensures the victory of good over evil. Perhaps because he always played one form or another of the same character, he was believable; and Americans so wanted to believe in the values he represented. By the end of the war he had become an idealized figure—soldier, sailor, cowboy. At no time in the country's history did so many people go to the movies so frequently; at no time in his career did John Wayne make so many feature films. Neither his draft status nor the divorce scandal that plagued his private life seemed to matter to his audience. On the silver screen he was what they needed most.[4]

Before World War II Wayne had expressed little interest in politics. As a young man he had flirted very briefly with the left, recalling many years later, "When I was a sophomore at USC I was a socialist myself—but not when I left." And during the 1930s he probably thought of himself as a New Deal Democrat, which meant that like most other Americans he was willing to give Franklin Roosevelt a chance to straighten out the national economic mess. During long trips on director John Ford's yacht, the *Araner,* Duke had listened to Ford and liberal screenwriter Dudley Nichols debate reactionary actor Ward Bond about the strengths and weaknesses of Roosevelt. Ford and Nichols emphasized the good job FDR was doing; Bond warned—without ever being too specific—about the dangers of big government. Wayne might have added his two cents but mostly just laughed at Bond's excesses. And he did star in the openly pro–New Deal *Stagecoach.*[5]

But as Wayne began to think for himself, he moved right. During the war he discovered that Bond's conspiratorial rants no longer seemed so excessive. Big government existed, and he was one of its victims. Just as he was beginning to make serious money, Congress passed the 1944 Revenue Act, significantly raising tax rates on the wealthy. People with incomes more than $100,000 owed 68 percent to the federal government; people who earned more than $500,000 owed 88.6 percent. Meanwhile the left's popular front remained strong in Hollywood.

When the Motion Picture Alliance was formed in 1944, Wayne was still on the political sidelines. And he remained there for most of the next five years—years that saw the House Committee on Un-American Activities investigate Hollywood, witnessed the martyrdom of the Hollywood Ten, unveiled the beginnings of the blacklist. In the mid-1940s the Alliance tried to recruit Wayne to their cause, but he resisted, bothered not so much by their stridency as by their practice of having famous actors read speeches written by someone else. That might be acceptable to Gary Cooper or Clark Gable, but not John Wayne. "Christ, I wouldn't have done it for anybody," he later said. But by the late 1940s Duke found neutrality an untenable position. In 1948 he was elected to the executive board of the Alliance, and in 1949 he was chosen president of the organization. By then Wayne was the biggest star in the industry, and he was willing to lend that power to the Alliance's cause even if it was a risk to his career. As he said in his short inaugural speech, Hollywood and America faced a crisis, and he saw no reason why either should tolerate a political party controlled by their Cold War rival.[6]

Why did Wayne risk his career for his political beliefs? It was a question he never fully answered. Certainly he advanced part of the answer. Communists, he told biographer Maurice Zolotow, "were rotten and corrupt and poisoned the air of our community by creating suspicion, distrust, and hatred." The Alliance, he added, "were the real liberals. We believed in freedom. We believed in the individual and his rights. We hated Soviet Communism because it . . . trampled on the individual, because it was a slave society." In discussing his motives, he tended to emphasize the times—the Cold War, the Berlin blockade, the communist victory in China, the Soviet detonation of an atomic bomb, the Hiss and Rosenberg trials.[7]

But Duke's motives were like an iceberg, the most important part of which was submerged and unexpressed. Though he seldom even mentioned his failure to answer his country's call during World War II, it helps to explain why he became so involved in the Cold War. "He regretted not serving," his personal secretary recalled. "He was not the kind of man to dwell on it or talk about it, but you knew he did. You could see it in his face when anyone asked him about his war record. He would tell them that he had not served, and it made him feel like a hypocrite." Perhaps he concluded that he had made a mistake. Perhaps he recognized that his screen reputation was a product of playing the sort of hero he had failed to be during the great national crisis. Perhaps he even wondered if he were a real man, or just a reel man. Whatever the case, he stepped across the line in the Cold War.[8]

As the president of the Alliance between 1949 and 1953, he labored to purge Hollywood of communists and movies of communist influences. Typical of Wayne's brand of Americanism was his reaction to the script of Robert Penn Warren's Pulitzer Prize–winning novel *All the King's Men*. Filmmaker Robert Rossen bought the rights to the novel about the Louisiana politician, a thinly disguised Huey Long, and began casting the film. Wayne's agent, Charles Feldman, sent Duke the script in hopes that he would play the lead role of Willie Stark. The script outraged Wayne, and he immediately wrote Feldman an angry letter. Not only did he categorically reject the role, he noted that before Feldman sent the script to any of his other clients he should ask them if they wanted to star in a film that "smears the machinery of government for no purpose of humor or enlightenment," that "degrades all relationships," and that is populated by "drunken mothers; conniving fathers; double-crossing sweethearts; bad, bad, rich people; and bad, bad, poor people if they want to get ahead." The script sickened Wayne; it tore at the very fabric of "the American way of life," smearing family life, human dignity, and ambition. If Feldman had clients anxious to subvert their country, then he should "rush this script . . . to them." If not, Duke had another idea: "You can take this script and shove it up Robert Rossen's derriere."[9]

For John Wayne, the letter was a manifesto. A movie was not merely entertainment. It was a weapon, a cultural grenade capable of altering the way people imagined and constructed reality. Duke felt that writers, directors, and producers on the left, men like Robert Rossen and his friends, wanted to insert their messages into their films because they were preparing the way for a revolution. Demonstrating the need for radical change was the first, critical step toward radical change. Not that Wayne disagreed with the methods of the left; he didn't. All he wanted to do was to deny his political enemies the cinematic weapon and to enlist it in his own cause—the cause of freedom.

It was about this time that Wayne got the idea for an epic film about the struggle for freedom and liberty against an oppressive regime, a movie that would encapsulate all that he believed was wrong with the world and right with America. A history buff, he had long been interested in the Alamo story. Here, he believed, was not just a Texas story but an American story, a tale of brutal oppression and the struggle to be free, a piece of history that held examples for the present. If ever there was a story that had never lost its relevance—a part of the past that had never become the past—the thirteen days at the Alamo was it. Shortly before he died, in 1979, Duke said that he first began thinking to make an Alamo film in 1945, about the same time he began considering setting up his own production company.[10]

At Republic studios in Los Angeles, Duke took his first steps toward making *The Alamo* when he gave Jimmy Grant the task of preparing an initial script. Historian Garry Wills aptly described Grant as a "poor man's Ben Hecht." Both began careers in Chicago as reporters, knocked off short stories between assignments, and migrated to Hollywood to write screenplays. Both were noted for their ability to write fast and get the job done. The difference was that Hecht had style and Grant was a hack. But Wayne liked Grant, liked his gangster argot and his Mickey Spillane, crew-cut swagger. In addition, both were big drinkers—Grant, in fact, an alcoholic—and intoxicated with Hollywood. Duke would later remark that Grant's writing "just fits my pistol," but the truth was that Wayne was a far better actor than judge of good writing.[11]

Wayne and Grant seldom had a drink or conversation that did not include a discussion of *The Alamo*. They traveled to San Antonio together, researching the history of the battle, and Grant began the long process of producing an acceptable script. They got Republic to hire John Ford's son Pat to work on the project as a research assistant. Pat Ford pored over the material Wayne and Grant had amassed, taking notes and cataloguing information. He even interviewed legendary Texas historian J. Frank Dobie. Although Republic eventually fired Ford, it did not dampen Duke's enthusiasm for the project.[12]

By 1951 Republic boss Herb Yates was clearly on the defensive. He had allowed John Wayne to plan the film, listened to Duke's proposals for a budget, even paid some preproduction costs. Grant had produced a script, Wayne had discovered an ideal location in Panama to shoot the film, and Yates had lined up some outside financing. But Yates, a man who threw around nickels like manhole covers, continued to blanch at Wayne's proposed budget. Duke was ready to go, but all he had from Yates was a fistful of promises. Now he wanted commitments, firm commitments on paper with neatly typed dollar amounts—and no more crawfishing.

High noon came in the fall of 1952, shortly after the successful release of *The Quiet Man*. Wayne's position in the industry had never been stronger, and he wanted $3 million to make an epic drama in Panama. Yates balked, claiming that $3 million was too much money. Couldn't the film be made more inexpensively on the Republic lot? Couldn't they trim the number of extras? How about shooting in black-and-white? When it came to ways to slice a budget Yates considered himself something of a genius. Duke believed he was something closer to a "cheap son of a bitch." The more they talked, the angrier and louder they became. Sitting at her desk just outside Wayne's office, Mary St. John, Wayne's secretary, over- heard the "terrible shouting match" that concluded when Yates "stormed" out.[13] A few minutes later, Duke stormed out after him, never to return. The Alamo had cost Herbert Yates the biggest box office draw in Hollywood.

*

Wayne departed Republic with his dream of the Alamo, but tangibly lit- tle else. Grant had written his script as an employee of Republic and it be- longed to Yates, who was in no mood to give, sell, or otherwise transfer the property back to Duke. A few years later Republic had Grant's script rewritten and made an Alamo film sans John Wayne. *The Last Command* centered on Jim Bowie, played stiffly by Sterling Hayden, and dealt less with the siege of the Alamo than with Bowie's growing sense of political awareness. In an age of epic films, *The Last Command* seemed little more than an above-average television production, suffering from mediocre acting, tepid direction, and poor production values. Most of the film was shot on Republic's soundstage and back lot. The Alamo set constructed on the Louis Hobbs Ranch outside Brackettville, Texas, looked—and in fact was—prefab. It had only two walls, a short wooden palisade, and no chapel. An Alamo film without the famous chapel and north wall was like a racehorse with only three legs.[14]

While Republic made its Alamo film, Wayne and Robert Fellows estab- lished their own independent production company and named it Batjac, distributing its films through Warner Bros. They produced anticommunist films and airplane films, Western, adventure, and football films, but noth- ing with a humpbacked Alamo in it. Executives at Warners showed even less interest in the Alamo than had Yates. But Duke, like a man itching for a woman of his dreams, was still obsessed with the project. It was a dream that survived his second sloppy divorce scandal, Grant's fight with alco- holism, Wayne's break with Fellows, and his fallout with Grant. Through- out the 1950s Wayne and Grant—when they were talking to each other—continued to work on the script (now Grant's second), make plans, and dream of the day when all the stars and planets in the universe were aligned just right.

The problem with John Wayne's Alamo movie was that the longer it remained in the planning stage, the bigger it became. In Duke's mind it outgrew a Republic picture, outgrew a Warner Bros. picture, and damn near outgrew Hollywood. It assumed Homeric proportions, something bigger than *Birth of a Nation,* more sweeping than *The Big Parade,* grander than *Gone With the Wind.* In the Alamo story he saw elements of all the great American epics—the desire for peace and liberty, the willingness to fight for it, and the lure of the West. Grant's script evolved to match Wayne's vision. Yates had done Bowie, done him small and cheaply. Walt Disney had done Crockett, done him tiny for a television screen. Duke would do Bowie, Crockett, *and* Travis on a Texas-sized screen. He would talk to Americans about their past and their future, about their problems and their dreams. As the project grew larger, Wayne realized that he could not trust it with any producer or director. They could not possibly share his vision. He would raise the money himself, produce the film himself, and direct it himself. And perhaps play a small cameo role.

Financing entailed compromises. In 1956 he signed a multipicture deal with United Artists, which agreed to distribute Wayne's Alamo film and to invest $2.5 million in the picture. But there was a catch: Batjac, Wayne's own company, would have to invest $1.5 to $2.5 million in the film, and Duke would have to star in the picture. United Artists was not interested in investing millions in a John Wayne film that did not feature John Wayne.

With United Artists' promise, Wayne expanded his search for more money. He estimated that the film would cost $7.5 million to make, and he was still $3 to $4 million short. It did not take much for him to sell his dream to influential and rich Texans. He flew to Austin and had talks with Governor Price Daniels, who put him in touch with such Texas oilmen and businessmen as Clint W. Murchison and I. J. and O. J. McCullough. They liked Wayne, his politics, and the idea of a Texas epic, but they were not particularly interested in wagering millions without a fair chance of a return. They too wanted Wayne to play a major role in the film, and they wanted it shot in Texas, not out of the country, in Mexico or Panama. Duke saw their point. So what if he could make the film less expensively south of the border? Any story of Texas this big should be made on Texas soil. This point settled, the McCullough brothers invested

$3 million and Murchison $2.5 million, and the Yale Foundation added another $1.5 million.[15]

By 1958 preproduction on *The Alamo* was well under way. Wayne had a script that still needed work, but that was not unusual. He also had a site. After meeting with James T. "Happy" Shahan of Brackettville, Texas, he decided to build a replica of the Alamo on Shahan's twenty-two-thousand-acre ranch. It was a perfect location, far enough away from civilization to look like the west Texas of the early 1800s but close enough to have an airstrip and enough facilities to house a large cast and crew. Furthermore, Shahan assured Wayne that he had a general contractor named Chatto Rodriquez who could build the Alamo in Duke's mind.

Work started on several fronts. In Brackettville, Chatto prepared the way for the film industry. He and his workers drilled six deep wells to guarantee a daily supply of twelve thousand gallons of water, laid fourteen miles of tarred roads between Brackettville and the set, put in miles of water and sewage lines, and constructed five hundred acres of corrals. Then he worked with art director Alfred Ybarra to build the most authentic set in the history of the movies. Chatto imported craftsmen from Mexico to make hundreds of thousands adobe bricks and hired 150 laborers to construct the set, following Ybarra's drawings and models. He did not build a perfect Alamo—the courtyard was smaller than the original and there were a few minor design flaws in the facade. But after a year of work Chatto had come as close as anyone—even John Wayne—could have hoped.

In Hollywood, Wayne's pace matched Chatto's. He wanted to lure two of the industry's leadingest leading men to play Travis and Bowie, and at one time or another the trade papers linked Clark Gable, Burt Lancaster, William Holden, Charlton Heston, and Rock Hudson to the project. But the stars Duke wanted most—actors of his generation—were committed to different films. He turned to younger actors with solid professional reputations. The role of Travis went to Laurence Harvey, an English actor better known at the Old Vic than in the United States, who had earned an Academy Award nomination for his work in *Room at the Top*. Richard Widmark agreed to play Bowie. Like Harvey's, Widmark's talent was obvious. Handsome and athletic, he could play a clean-cut leading man or go against type, as he did in *Kiss of Death*, for which he was nominated for an Oscar as best supporting actor for his performance as a psychopathic killer. He could play a cowboy or a sailor, a marine or a gangster, but the word "actor" fit him better than "star." Again like Harvey, Widmark represented the best of the new Hollywood, where tight, well-acted films aimed at more select audiences had become the norm. Neither man had the mass audience appeal of Gable, Hudson, or Wayne.

Still, Duke was satisfied. No sooner did Widmark sign to do *The Alamo* than Wayne took out an advertisement in the trade papers announcing, "Welcome Aboard, Dick. Duke." Widmark, however, was nobody's Dick, and he told Wayne the next time he saw him. "Tell your press agent that the name is Richard," he said. The comment infuriated Wayne, but he showed unusual restraint. All he said was, "If I ever take out another ad, I'll remember that, Richard."[16]

Soon the secondary roles were filled. Richard Boone, star of the popular television Western series *Have Gun, Will Travel*, signed to play a cameo role as Sam Houston. Frankie Avalon, a heartthrob crooner from Philadelphia whose string of hits included "Dede Dinah," "I'll Wait for You," and "Venus," was cast as the messenger Smitty. The hope was that Avalon would attract young female viewers. Similarly, the small part of Lieutenant Reyes went to Carlos Arruza, a famous Mexican matador and friend of Duke's, with the hope that Arruza would attract a South American audience. Other roles went to Duke's family and actor friends—Patrick Wayne as James Butler Bonham, Aissa Wayne as Lisa Dickinson, Hank Worden as Parson, Denver Pyle as Gambler, Ken Curtis as Captain Dickinson, Chill Wills as Beekeeper.

Female roles plagued the project from the start. The story of the Alamo was a man's tale. Men crossed the line, men defended the walls, and men died. This was probably one of the reasons the story appealed to Wayne. But successful films, and especially successful historical epics, involved strong female leads. What was *Birth of a Nation* without Lillian Gish or *Gone With the Wind* without Vivien Leigh? The primary female role in *The Alamo*—and it was really only a secondary part—was Flaca, Davy Crockett's rather bloodless love interest. Wayne gave the part to Linda Cristal, an Argentinean-born actress who had a fine reputation in the Mexican film industry but almost none in Hollywood. The choice of Cristal announced to the industry that Duke was making a picture fashioned to suit him, not Hollywood. Maybe it was hubris, the belief that his name was all a theater owner needed to sell tickets. Perhaps it was just that Duke did not want any fictional part to detract from the historical content of the film.

✴

At 8 A.M. on September 9, 1959, Father Peter Rogers of San Antonio's St. Mary's Church gazed for a moment at the 321 members of the cast and crew and then began to pray. "O, Almighty God, centuries ago, Thou raised a magnificent mission—a harbor for all, of peace and freedom. This was the Alamo. Today, we ask Thy blessings, Thy help and Thy protection as once again history is relived in the production. . . . We ask these things so that the film 'The Alamo' will not only be the world's outstanding production, but will also be a tribute to the spirit of the men who built it, who lived in it, who died in it."[17]

Duke did not write the prayer—but he might have. It expressed his mission, a mixture of patriotism and commerce, part George Washington and part P. T. Barnum. He wanted to glorify America and make money, and he saw not the slightest contradiction between the two impulses. That was the beauty of America, the chance to succeed by dint of imagination and hard work.

No one doubted Wayne's capacity for labor. He had made a career out of being the hardest-working actor in Hollywood, the one who day in and day out, picture after picture, never missed a morning call and never came unprepared. He could drink with his friends until 2 or 3 A.M. and still be on the set at 5 A.M. for makeup. Sleep seemed an afterthought, something of a nice luxury if he had the time, but not really a necessity. Black coffee and cigarettes—those he needed, but not long nights of sleep. Once shooting began on September 9, 1959, Duke moved into his work mode—about a hundred cigarettes a day, washed down with gallons of coffee. Supplied with the necessities of life, he confronted the difficulties of shooting a huge epic in a land temperamentally unsuited to it.

For the next three and a half months Wayne battled to keep the project on schedule. On a budget of about $60,000 a day, he simply could not afford to lose control of the pace. Some things, however, were outside his powers. He was fortunate with the weather; though it was brutally hot in the afternoons and chillingly cold at night, he lost only a day and a half to rain. Varmints and microbes were less kind. Thousands of rattlesnakes, skunks, rabbits, coyotes, and deer called Shahan's ranch home, and the boldest frequently asserted their squatters' rights. This was especially true of the snakes, which evidently wanted to watch the making of a Hollywood film close-up. The set had to be cleared every morning, and as the temperatures lowered, the snakes liked to stretch out on the warm, new asphalt roads. For some of the old Western actors, snakes were nothing new. But for a few of the young actors raised in cities, rattlesnakes were no joking matter. Wayne's secretary recalled that Frankie Avalon moved about the set as if he had been "personally targeted" by Texas's reptile population.[18]

Crickets bothered Wayne more than rattlesnakes. They were everywhere, threatening no one and nothing, except the budget. They ruined some takes by jumping on an actor's shoulder during close-ups, others by chirping in the background. "God dammit! Shut those crickets up," Wayne would occasionally shout at no one in particular. Insisting on as much realism as possible, Wayne shot his night scenes at night, instead of using the popular "day-for-night" process that made sunny shooting look dark. But the late-night crickets were no more subject to Duke's art of persuasion than the day crickets.

The cast added to the director's worries. Most worked hard under difficult conditions, but there were a few personality clashes. Friends of Wayne, and even members of the crew, considered Widmark aloof. "Widmark enjoyed his own company best," was the way Happy Shahan remembered it. That may have been so, but Widmark had a hearing problem and occasionally missed conversational remarks. His troubles with Wayne ran deeper. The two got off on the wrong foot and never got back in step. A few days after shooting began, Widmark told Wayne that he felt miscast and wanted out. Threats of lawsuits mixed with a dab of flattery convinced Widmark to stay, but the two men dealt with each other as little as possible. "[J]ust chemically, we were two guys who didn't like each other," Widmark recalled. Wayne was well known for quick flare-ups—and equally swift apologies—and on one occasion he verbally tore into Widmark in front of members of the cast and crew. Widmark responded in kind. "I told him: 'You no talent sonofabitch, don't ever talk to me that way.' But I didn't say it before I had an iron bar in my hand, because if he had come at me, I was a goner. I didn't really think he had no talent, but I knew that would set him off." Whether it was the iron bar or his desire to restore a touch of harmony to his set, Wayne let the incident pass, and the two men established an uneasy peace.[19]

Nothing could patch up the problems between LeJean Ethridge and Charles Harvey Smith, however. The two lovers signed on as extras in the film, and Wayne was so impressed with Ethridge that he decided to give her a larger role. Perhaps Smith was jealous; undoubtedly there were other problems between the two. Whatever the case, on the evening of October 11 they had an argument that ended with Smith plunging a butcher knife into Ethridge's chest. She died, he went to jail, and Wayne worried that he might have to lose a day of shooting to testify at a hearing. Duke's reaction was hardly the most sensitive, but by October he had so many other problems—so many physical and emotional demands—that all he could think about was the film.

Murder, personality conflicts, unprofessional insects and reptiles, heat, and a few fires and accidents taxed the rookie director. But in the end, Wayne handled them better than his directorial duties. Sadly, he was a competent but not outstanding director. He had a beautiful eye for composition, knew what would make a great shot, and he had a fine sense of detail in set design. But he was not particularly good at script development or handling actors. Grant's script was too preachy, and Wayne—a gifted nonverbal actor—allowed it to remain that way. And he demonstrated a lack of nuance in directing others. Ken Curtis, a fine Western actor, said, "Duke was great at action. But directing actors, I was not that pleased with him. All he told you to do was his mannerisms." Harry Carey Jr. agreed: "Duke sometimes forgot that there was only one John Wayne, that the way he played a scene might not work for a guy who was five-six and scrawny. Try walking like John Wayne in a seven and a half shoe."

Duke was under intense pressure to get the job done. Each evening after dinner he worked on his own lines and toyed with the script, then viewed rushes and made notes. Each day he made decisions on individual shots and camera angles, budget details and publicity issues, stunt ideas and second-unit arrangements. In his head he balanced the demands of actors, crew members, moneymen, and studio executives. Dressed in a leather outfit, he poured sweat, lost weight, became dehydrated, and suffered from leg cramps. He lost his temper often. When some offscreen chatter ruined one shot, he exploded, "Jesus-fucking-Christ! Shut up back there." Turning around he saw the culprits were a group of nuns. One actor recalled, "After the outburst, you could have heard a rat cough." Duke just apologized and went back to work. There was nothing else he could do. It was his picture. He had to finish it.[20]

By the second week in December all that remained were the death scenes and the closing sequence. On the ninth Wayne shot Crockett's death, and on the tenth Bowie's and Travis's. On the eleventh he filmed the survivors departing the Alamo. On the fifteenth he finished a few shots of a battle scene and said, "Cut." He had shot some 566 scenes— over 560,000 feet of film—and completed the project only three weeks over schedule. All things considered, it was an amazing effort. When the editing was completed and the music and score added, he had the three-hour-and-thirteen-minute patriotic epic he had long dreamed about.

✶

The Alamo moves on various levels, sometimes successfully, other times unsuccessfully. As a historical drama, the story had problems that Wayne and Grant were unable to solve. Simply put: The story involves a relatively short, thirteen-day siege followed by a battle that lasted just over an hour. The battle, fought mostly before daybreak, was intense and bloody. The siege, while psychologically interesting, lacked significant dramatic action. To make matters worse for the long film, every viewer knew in advance how it would end. Undoubtedly a director like Otto Preminger, Stanley Kramer, or Fred Zinnemann would have used the siege to focus on character development and build psychological tension. But that was not Wayne's style. His approach was part John Wayne, part John Ford, with a touch of Jimmy Grant—a combination of action, physical humor, and preachy, stilted dialogue.

Most of the first three hours of *The Alamo* is concerned with pointless raids into enemy ranks and drunken humor, with an occasional song mixed in to break the tedium. Crockett gets drunk; Crockett's men get drunk. Bowie gets drunk; Bowie's men get drunk. Crockett and Bowie get drunk; Crockett's men and Bowie's men get drunk. Only Travis and his closest aides resist the bottle, and this very act of sobriety seems to separate them from the rest of the Texans. Throughout these exchanges, characters remain static—Bowie the hotheaded, moody patriot; Travis the priggish, prickly skinned patriot; Crockett the wise, fatherly patriot. For three hours they talk, they posture, they sulk, they get drunk; they fight, they shoot, they ride, they raid. And in the end they die.

The beauty of the film is in its details. William Clothier's spectacular cinematography and Dimitri Tiomkin's eulogistic score rightly deserved the Academy Award nominations they won. If Wayne did not exactly capture the essence of the Alamo, Clothier touched the soul of west Texas, from its burned-over land to its rivers and trees. The second-unit scenes of the Mexican army approaching the Alamo are equal to some of the best landscape footage produced by John Ford. And the Alamo itself is rendered in its three-dimensional fullness. The front of the chapel, the location and look of the palisade, long, low barracks, and defensive positions, even the pecan trees and La Villita—Wayne, Ybarra, and Chatto Rodriquez had done their research and work well. No set had ever been so faithfully re-created. It would have made Adina De Zavala proud.

But the concern for authentic historical detail is more the product of antiquarianism than inquiry. The world Wayne re-created in *The Alamo* is jarringly familiar to the one he inhabited. It is a land under siege, where free men are confronted with difficult decisions. The film begins with a prologue stating the plight of Texans in 1836: "Generalissimo Santa Anna was sweeping north across Mexico toward them, crushing all who opposed his tyrannical rule. They now faced the decision that all men in all times must face . . . the eternal choice of men . . . to endure oppression or to resist." Wayne makes almost no attempt to explain the causes of the conflict because he has little interest in the specific problems between the central government in Mexico City and the province of Texas. The part of Santa Anna reinforces this theme. The Mexican dictator, played by Wayne's friend Ruben Padilla, is virtually faceless. Other characters read letters and an ultimatum from him that give a rough idea of his personality, but none of the communications can be trusted to give a true sense of the man. He is simply a dictator—perhaps even a just one. A defender of the Alamo comments after one attack that the Mexicans must believe they are fighting in a good cause. But for Wayne, the question of just or unjust is ultimately pointless. A man must resist any infringement upon his freedom.

The guiding principle in *The Alamo* is Wayne's notion of republicanism, which shades closer to classical liberalism or libertarianism than anything endorsed by Dwight Eisenhower. In a crucial political scene Crockett tells Travis, " 'Republic.' I like that word. Means that people can live free, talk free, go or come, buy or sell, be drunk or sober, however they choose. Some words give you a feeling. Republic is one of those words that makes me tight in the throat. Same tightness a man gets when his baby takes his first steps, or his first baby shaves and makes his first sound like a man. Some words can give you a feeling that makes your heart warm. Republic is one of those words."

Several commentators have attempted to place too much of a Cold War emphasis on Crockett's/Wayne's words. To be sure, the script evokes parallels between Santa Anna's Mexico and Khrushchev's Soviet Union, as well as Hitler's Germany. All three demanded lines in the sand and resistance to death. Wayne could have been talking about Texas in 1836 or Munich in 1938 or Vietnam in 1959 when he had Crockett say, "Talk about whose ox is gettin' gored. Figure this. A fellow gets in the habit of gorin' oxes, it whets his appetite. He may come up north and gore yours." But Wayne also opposed domestic evils, ranging from heavy taxes to government regulation of lifestyles. He tells Flaca that he plans "[t]o hit a lick at what's wrong, or to say a word for what's right." It's his only choice, he adds. "There's right and there's wrong, you gotta do one or the other. You do the one and you're living, you do the other and you may be walking around but you're as dead as a beaver hat."

"I think making *The Alamo* became my father's own form of combat," his daughter Aissa later wrote. "More than an obsession, it was the most intensely personal project in his career." Wayne's friends and associates agreed; making *The Alamo* was his war, Crockett's statements in the film his political platform. Never the subtlest of men, he drove home his message with hands of lead. And to make sure that no one in America missed a chance to be exposed to his philosophy, he hired Russell Birdwell to orchestrate the film's publicity campaign.[21]

A native of Texas who had worked for a Dallas newspaper, Birdwell was the P. T. Barnum of Hollywood advertising. He had become famous as the publicity agent of *Gone With the Wind,* was notorious for marketing Jane Russell's breasts in *The Outlaw,* and boasted that he could make anyone famous for the right price. His central credo was that any publicity agent with a couple of hundred thousand dollars could buy space in an entertainment section to advertise a film; the great publicity agent obtained free space outside the entertainment pages by turning a feature into a pseudo event. In short, Birdwell aimed at making news, whether he was hawking Margaret Mitchell's vision of the Old South, running the "search for Scarlett" campaign, or creating a controversy over Jane Russell's cleavage.

Wayne shared Birdwell's philosophy, reasoning that a personal statement like *The Alamo* deserved front-page publicity. Warming to the task, in early 1960 Birdwell wrote Roger Lewis, vice president in charge of publicity at United Artists, that *The Alamo* was not just another Hollywood movie. It represented fourteen years of John Wayne's life and was "an inspiring film document about the greatest single event, perhaps, that has transpired since they nailed Christ to the cross. . . . *The Alamo* affords us the opportunity of prying open new channels of selling, new avenues of publicizing, new roads of exploitation, new paths of infiltration of every sort."[22]

Forget about the Crusades, the Hundred Years' War, and the two great world wars; about Columbus, Copernicus, Newton, and Einstein; about the printing press and sliced bread—only the crucifixion of Christ overshadowed Texas's stand at the Alamo, and the way Birdwell was beginning to see things, the most important event since the Alamo was *The Alamo*. Birdwell's vision set the agenda for selling the film. It was not a movie just about history. It was about America, as fresh as the day's headlines, that also happened to tell the story of some brave patriots. In a Birdwell press release entitled "*The Alamo* Shows No Price Is Too Great for Freedom," Wayne commented on the film's message: "I want to remind the freedom-loving people of the world that not too long ago there were men and women in America who had the guts to stand up and fight for the things they believed in. . . . The people of the Alamo realized that in order to live decently a man must be prepared to die decently. There were no namby-pamby pussy-footers, malingerers or skedaddlers in that brave band."[23]

Birdwell's plans for the promotion of *The Alamo* resembled a political campaign. His hope was to mobilize the local, state, and federal governments, as well as schools and churches, behind the film. To this end, he convinced seven governors to officially proclaim an "Alamo Day," prepared Alamo kits to be used in elementary and secondary schools, and approached congressmen and senators about joining his promotional crusade. He even proposed that some future summit conference of the major world powers be held at the Alamo, an idea that offended Texas governor Price Daniel, who chafed at the notion that Khrushchev might step foot into the sacred shrine.

The *Life* magazine gatefold spread was Birdwell's boldest publicity stunt. It tied the film directly into the 1960 presidential campaign and suggested that any American interested in his or her country would do well to go see the movie. There were few words in the three-page advertisement, but what was there expressed a weariness about corporate, modern America and called for a return to the country's frontier greatness, a time when a man spoke his own words and backed them up through his actions. Americans, the advertisement asserted, were tired of "the handiwork of the opinion molders. They have had a bellyful of payola, influence peddling, quiz show rigging, the ghost-writing of political speeches—symptoms of a pallid public morality." They long for "a return to the honest, courageous, clear-cut standards of the frontier days—the days of America's birth and greatness; the days when the noblest utterances of man came unrehearsed."[24]

The layout, a brilliant piece of publicity, aroused an immediate reaction. If *The Alamo* was entertainment, the *Life* advertisement was news, and it was treated as such on the front pages and in editorial sections of newspapers across the country. John Kennedy was asked about the ad in a press conference; he gave an evasive answer. Publisher Henry Luce was "really impressed—and inspired" by the ad. Most editorialists agreed with the sentiments expressed in the ad, and none delved too deeply into the irony of a ghostwritten advertisement condemning political ghostwriting. Months later Wayne wrote Birdwell that he was entirely satisfied with the *Life* spread: "[W]e expected big results from our Alamo ad but we did not anticipate that it would create a continuing dividend of news and editorial impact over a six-month period—not only throughout the United States but a large part of Europe. I've been told by experts that our gatefold ad has brought us more than five million dollars worth of editorial recognition—influential, selling space in newspapers, magazines as well as over network television and radio shows."[25]

But Birdwell's and Wayne's campaign—the advertisements, political tie-ins, and promotional stunts—did not guarantee the success of the film. It was still a long, preachy melodrama, back-loaded with action. United

Artists, however, decided to gamble on a road show release. The road show scheme had been around for years—*Gone With the Wind* had been released on that basis—and had become popular in the 1950s. It was, in effect, a limited release designed to capitalize on a film's epic quality. Instead of the film being released on the same day to thousands of theaters, it was released to only a small number of carefully selected showcase theaters in major markets. The idea was to turn the film into a major event, which entailed more publicity, higher ticket prices, reserved seating, and limited runs. Normally road show films were long enough to have intermissions, and many were wide-screen spectaculars. The hope was that the film would create a sensation and a wave of anticipation for its general release. Of course, if it generated more yawns and negative reviews than thrills, an expensive film was in trouble. Road-showing, in short, was a serious roll of the dice, and Wayne was not that comfortable with the choice.[26]

The Alamo was scheduled to premiere on the evening of October 24, 1960, at the Woodlawn Theatre in San Antonio. For two days before the opening, San Antonio and Team Wayne enjoyed a love fest of square dances, sing-alongs, autograph sessions, parades, and as Davy himself would say, speechifying. The afternoon before the premiere the skies darkened and it began to rain, lightly at first but harder as the day wore on. That night the spectators outside the Woodlawn dripped water waiting for the stars, but their spirits were not dampened. And the people who paid $50 a seat for the premiere—many of whom had been involved in the project—expressed complete satisfaction.

Similar scenes, minus the square dances and rainfall, were repeated when the film premiered in New York City, Los Angeles, Houston, Dallas, San Francisco, Philadelphia, Chicago, Tulsa, Oklahoma City, London, Montreal, and Toronto. First-night crowds loved *The Alamo;* they loved John Wayne, the rest of the cast, the battle scenes, and the intermission; they loved everything about everything that had to do with the film. But that was the nature of the first-night beast. What was less predictable were the reviews and the word-of-mouth response.

Reviewers were less kind. As in their response to Walt Disney's Davy Crockett, liberal reviewers harped on Wayne's message and historical inaccuracies. One reviewer commented, "If he is saying that what America needs is about 10 million men with the courage and determination of

Davy Crockett, Jim Bowie, and Colonel Travis the point is well taken. It may also occur to some he is suggesting that the easy answer to today's complex problems is to pit this raw courage against Russia's 10 million Santa Annas, the result of which may well be a worldwide Alamo and instead of a shrine we may have only a cosmic incinerator full of ashes." The film critic of the *New Yorker* agreed, accusing Wayne of having "turned a splendid chapter of our past into sentimental flapdoodle. . . . Nothing in *The Alamo* is serious . . . nothing in it is true. . . . [It] is a model of distortion and vulgarization." Even *Newsweek* and *Time* panned the movie. *Newsweek:* "*The Alamo's* place in history will probably be that of the most lavish B picture ever made. . . . B for banal." *Time:* "*The Alamo* is the biggest Western ever made. Wayne & Co. have not quite managed to make it the worst."[27]

Even the normally generous trade press took a few shots at the film. For all its fine production values, *The Alamo* was just too long and too slow. *Variety* suggested that the birthday scene featuring Aissa Wayne was "embarrassing . . . the film momentarily seems on the verge of dissolving into a family musical." Even John Ford's puff for the film was used against *The Alamo*. After previewing the film Ford announced, "It's timeless, it's the Greatest Picture I have ever seen. It will last forever—run forever—for all peoples, all families—*everywhere!*" Another previewer responded, "May I humbly suggest to Mr. Ford that the film only *seems* to last forever."[28]

Birdwell and Wayne responded to the negative and mixed reviews by increasing the political content of their promotional campaign. One advertisement for the film warned, "THE ALAMO WILL REMIND A FORGETFUL WORLD WHAT KIND OF PEOPLE AMERICANS REALLY ARE . . . savagely cruel against injustice, willing to carry their share of disaster—*and at all times on the side of God-fearing people!*" Put in that context, any criticism of *The Alamo* smacked of the unpatriotic. Taking the moral high road, Wayne added that his film was not just patriotic, it was clean family entertainment in an age when Hollywood had become mired in filth. "I have been in pictures all my adult life," he said, "and I deplore the garbage now being splashed on the screen . . . it is giving the world a false, nasty impression of us. . . . I don't like to see the Hollywood bloodstream polluted with perversion, and immoral and amoral nuances. Filthy minds, filthy words and filthy thoughts have no place in films."[29]

Unquestionably the controversy generated interest in *The Alamo,* but that interest did not translate into box office receipts. The film did well, but not by blockbuster standards, and Birdwell and Wayne looked to the Academy Awards as a chance to save the film. If it got a few major Oscars it might still make money. Once again, Birdwell and Wayne appealed to patriotism. In one attempt to influence Academy voters Birdwell ran an advertisement with the question "What Will Oscar Say to the World This Year?" next to the famous Alamo facade. And Wayne added, "This is not the first time 'The Alamo' has been the underdog. We need defenders today just as they did 125 years ago."[30]

Many reporters objected to Birdwell's campaign. They insisted that aesthetic tastes and political inclinations were different and independent, and that thinking *The Alamo* was boring did not make them communists or security threats. In the end, the critics won the day. The only Oscar *The Alamo* won was for best score.

The campaign and the movie had fused the memory of the Alamo with the image and politics of John Wayne. A criticism of Wayne or his film became an attack on Davy Crockett, Jim Bowie, William Travis, and the other heroes of the Alamo. In some quarters, it even became an assault on the state of Texas. For a generation of Americans *The Alamo* combined with Walt Disney's version to define who Davy Crockett was, what he believed in, and how he died. To call any part of that into question was a dangerous challenge.

But the challenge would come.

10

---- ✦ ----

DE LA PEÑA'S REVENGE

JOHN WAYNE WAS NOT INVITED. Nor was Walt Disney. In 1965 when the invitations to the White House Festival of the Arts went out, neither of the men who had reintroduced Americans to Davy Crockett and the Alamo received one. The exclusion was doubly odd. First, it was difficult to conceive of the arts in any popular sense without thinking of Duke and Walt, two giants in the film, television, and entertainment industries. Second, the host of the festival was President Lyndon B. Johnson, a Texan for whom the Alamo was no distant abstraction. His great-great-grandfather, Johnson often said, had died defending the Alamo and giving birth to Texas. And his own father, Sam Ealy Johnson Jr., had introduced the Alamo Purchase Bill into the Texas legislature at the urging of Clara Driscoll and the Daughters of the Republic of Texas, a successful measure that prompted a local newspaperman to write, "Santa Anna took the Alamo—that was 1836. Sam Johnson saved the Alamo—that was 1905." Still, nobody connected with the Alamo—not Wayne, not Disney, not historian Walter Lord, whose Alamo book, *A Time to Stand,* had been a 1961 best-seller—was deemed important enough to get invited to the Festival of the Arts.[1]

Even without Wayne and Disney, however, the event soon turned into an Alamo farce. A group of radicals and liberals, recognized leaders in the fields of painting, sculpture, literature, music, dance, cinema, and photography, decided to use the White House festival to draw their own line in the sand and make, if not their last, at least *a* stand against the Vietnam War. Actually, the stand began even before the festival commenced. Poet Robert Lowell, who had received an invitation, had earlier declined it loudly in a public letter to Johnson published in the *New York Times*. "We are in danger of imperceptibly becoming an explosive and suddenly chauvinistic nation, and may even be drifting on our way to the last nuclear ruin," he wrote. "I feel that I am serving you and our country best by not taking part in the White House Festival of the Arts." As politically savvy as any president ever to occupy the White House, Johnson sniffed a political disaster in the making, but it was too late to cancel the affair. All he could do was circle the wagons and hope for the best.

Others, evidently, felt that they were serving Johnson and their country by churlishly taking part. John Hersey read a passage from his book *Hiroshima*, but only after remarking, "We cannot for a moment forget the truly terminal dangers, in these times, of miscalculation, of arrogance, of accident, or reliance not on moral strength but on mere military power. Wars have a way of getting out of hand." Cultural critic Dwight Macdonald added to the awkwardness by treating the festival like a political rally, criticizing Johnson, working to get signatures on a pro-Lowell petition, and verbally assaulting guests who took exception to his behavior. At one point, actor Charlton Heston told Macdonald, "Having convictions doesn't mean that you have to lack elementary manners. Are you really accustomed to signing petitions against your host in his own home?" Although Johnson exited before the fireworks started, he knew what was going on. Loud enough for the press to hear, he remarked, "Some of them insult me by staying away and some of them insult me by coming." At least, he later added to a friend, "nobody pissed in the punch bowl."

✳

Originally, President Johnson had not given much thought to the notion of a White House Festival of the Arts. It was something that Jack and Jackie Kennedy had done so well, a sort of spring fling, a cross-pollination of culture and politics where everyone could be witty, fashionable, and charming, an event more typical of the East than of the Texas hill country, where Johnson preferred to take guests deer hunting and fill them with beer and barbecue. Still, a Festival of the Arts seemed to Johnson like a "nice thing" to do, and he probably did not think much more about it. The problem, as Wayne and Disney might have warned him, was that the line between politics and the arts had blurred, and political battles were being fought on cultural fronts. Everything was text and subtext, layers of bubbling subterranean meaning beneath a seemingly tranquil and harmless surface. Before the term "cultural war" came into general usage, combat had broken out. And Johnson, like Disney and Wayne, made sure that the Alamo was part of the conflict.

The Alamo was ingrained in Johnson's intellectual makeup, central to the way he made sense of world events. On one level, the defense of the Alamo and the fight for Texas independence helped him to define manhood. He was raised on stories of his great-great-uncle John Wheeler Bunton, who had emigrated to Texas from Tennessee in 1835, crossed the line in the sand with Ben Milam in Béxar, and fought with Sam Houston at San Jacinto. Bunton, like Lyndon, was a tall man with a powerful presence and abundant ambition. In addition to his military exploits, Bunton was one of the signers of the Texas Declaration of Independence, helped draft the Texas constitution, was often credited with leading the party that captured Santa Anna, served several terms in the republic's Congress, and entertained heroic-sized dreams—dreams whose retelling cut a scar in Lyndon Johnson's psyche. Lyndon's mother used to tell him that if he ever amounted to half of what John Bunton had been, his life would be a success.

Then there was his father, Sam Johnson Jr., another dreamer who never quite achieved the visions of success that filled his head. But Sam had helped to keep the legend of the Alamo alive, working with Clara Driscoll to preserve and enshrine the site. In 1917, the year America entered the Great War, Sam Johnson and Driscoll were honored in the state capitol as saviors of the Alamo. Although Lyndon was not yet ten years old, he already knew what the Alamo meant to Texans. Many times his father had taken him from their home in the hill country to San Antonio to visit the site and to instruct him on what it meant to be a Texan.

John Bunton and San Jacinto. Sam Johnson and the Alamo. Probably, in Lyndon's fertile imagination, he conflated and then reformed his family's and Texas's history until he could publicly assert that his great-great-grandfather had died on the Alamo's walls. When a fact-checking reporter refuted his claim, Johnson exclaimed, "God damn it, why must all those journalists be such sticklers for detail? Why, they'd hold you to an accurate description of the first time you ever made love, expecting you to remember the color of the room and the shape of the windows. . . . The fact is that my great-great-grandfather died at the battle of San Jacinto, not the Alamo." Of course, that ancestor—the one who had not died at the Alamo—had also not died at San Jacinto. The president could not even resist putting his own spin on the Alamo Purchase Bill, giving his father all the credit for saving the Alamo, including "convincing a woman [Clara Driscoll] to put up enough money long enough to hold the structure until the legislature could pass the bill to preserve the Alamo." Regardless of the "details," what Johnson really meant was that no matter whose great-great-granddaddies died at the Alamo, they had died like real men, and all Texans and all Americans should admire them and be equally ready to lay down their lives in defense of liberty.

This was not simply a position Johnson took after being sworn in as president. In 1940–41, while Germans were marching into Paris and then toward Moscow, he told Texans that they might soon have to "step over the line" again for liberty. From then on he tended to view all important foreign policy decisions in light of the Alamo experience. As a senator, when Great Britain and West Germany refused in 1954 to back any allied attempt to rescue France at Dien Bien Phu, he opposed sending U.S. troops to Vietnam: "Would you tell us who will go in with old Ben Milam?" And during his first days as president he talked about Vietnam as if it were a county in Texas: "Hell, Vietnam is just like the Alamo. Hell, it's just like if you were down at that gate and you were surrounded and you damn well needed somebody. Well, by God, I'm going to go—and thank the Lord that I've got men who want to go with me, from McNamara right on down to the littlest private who's carrying a gun." For Johnson, World War II, Korea, Vietnam—it was all the same: men defending their homes and "nailing the coonskin to the wall."[2]

During the Vietnam War, the Alamo became Johnson's touchstone. Whereas Munich and the appeasement policy had provided John Kennedy a lens for viewing the present, the Alamo and the Texas Revolution served Johnson. Repeatedly he talked about drawing a line in the sand, manning a wall, making a stand, and being a man. He told *Life* writer Hugh Sidey that he had "gone into Vietnam because, as at the Alamo, somebody had to get behind the log with those threatened people," and he compared the siege of Khe Sanh to the siege of the Alamo. One London *Times* reporter recalled Johnson talking about the two sieges. "It seemed an unfortunate parallel," he thought. "Colonel William Travis and the 150 defenders were annihilated, but one could hardly point that out to the Texas President. In any case, he remembered only the grim courage of his brother Texans, the ruthless fighting, and Mexican duplicity." For Johnson, the soldiers in Vietnam were descendants of the Alamo, and he, at least in spirit, was William Barret Travis.[3]

On several occasions—sometimes with just a person or two in a room with him, other times before White House dinner guests—Johnson would without warning begin to recite a poem his mother had taught him when he was a child. With a low, solemn rumble he would begin:

> Santa Anna came storming, as a storm might come;
> Here was a rumble of cannon; there was a rattle of blade;
> There was cavalry, infantry, bugle and drum—
> Full seven thousand in pomp and parade,
> The Chivalry, flower of Mexico;
> And a gaunt two hundred in the Alamo!

> And thirty lay sick, and so were shot through;
> For the siege had been bitter, and bloody, and long;
> "Surrender, or die!"—"Men, what will you do?"
> And Travis, great Travis, drew sword, quick and strong,
> Drew a line at his feet . . . "Will you come? Will you go?
> I die with my wounded, in the Alamo!"

Eventually, as a politician, Johnson died on the walls of Vietnam.[4]

Like John Wayne in *The Alamo,* Johnson employed the earthy patois of Texas to make his point, reducing war and defense of liberty to simple questions of manhood and sexuality. To show weakness was worse than cowardly—it was unmanly. And nations, like men, could not afford to be unmanly. Johnson displayed his lack of respect for a man by comparing him or his behavior to a female. He cast aspersions on the Kennedy crowd by saying that they vacationed on that "female island"—Martha's Vineyard—and he criticized foreign policy positions that seemed to be compromising. "If you let a bully come into your front yard one day," he said, "the next day he will be on your porch and the day after he will rape your wife in your own bed." Johnson's imagery reveals a heightened concern with personal honor and bravery. Johnson's language toward American involvement in Vietnam carried an eerie echo of Travis's 1836 letters to the citizens of Texas.[5]

Given the president's constant references to the Alamo, it is not surprising that it assumed even greater national symbolic power during the Vietnam era. In the debate that separated Americans into hawks and doves, the Alamo became the high hawk shrine. In 1965 a patriotic rally staged by the United Veterans' Council supporting America's involvement in the war was held in front of the Alamo. Three hundred people listened to resolutions of support from San Antonio mayor Walter W. McAllister and Governor John Connally, sang "God Bless America" and "The Star-Spangled Banner," and cheered speeches supporting the country's efforts to "save" Vietnam. In 1967 a similar prowar rally was held in front of the Alamo. Posters announcing "Down with Protestors" and "Better Dead Than Red" captured the mood of the affair. The Alamo, the rallies suggested, stood squarely for a strong, proud America, a country willing to pay the price for freedom, even if the fight was on the other side of the world.[6]

By the 1970s the association of the Alamo with a forceful American foreign policy had seeped into popular culture. Any picture or image of the humpbacked chapel was enough to suggest strong, proud nationalism. And not only Americans in favor of the country's stand in Vietnam capitalized on the Alamo's iconography. In the mid-1970s, Liggett & Meyers Tobacco Company used the Alamo chapel as the backdrop for an L&M advertisement. "The proud smoke," the ad announced. "Product of a proud land. Tobacco. It's as proud a part of the American tradition as the Alamo." The impact of Walt Disney, John Wayne, and Lyndon Johnson on American culture had been profound. The Alamo had transcended Texas and had become a vital American symbol.[7]

The symbol evinced a singular lack of nuance. It was, like the defenders themselves, strong, aggressive, defiant, and masculine. It aroused an equally strident backlash. Groups protesting American militarism, imperialism, and brutality regularly marched in front of the Alamo. In one August 1971 march, protestors commemorated the bombing of Hiroshima in 1945, smashed plastic weapons, threw service medals onto the Alamo grounds, and passed out invitations to a gay liberation function. One speaker shouted at a group of servicemen, "If you don't go to Vietnam, there won't be any damn war!" On other occasions, protestors decried America's foreign policy, history of racism, and failure to create a just society. "The Alamo itself is offensive," declared a spokeswoman for the Maoist Revolutionary Party, "not only to Chicano people but to people all over the world. It is a decrepit old monument . . . a symbol of oppression, not freedom; slavery, not liberation."[8]

For liberals and radicals in the 1960s and 1970s, the Alamo, if it was remembered at all, was recalled as a warning more than an ideal. America, they suggested, was the sum total of the dreams and illusions of its founders. Freedom and slavery, independence and oppression, equality and racism—they coursed together through the nation's history. "If Americans must remember the Alamo," commented a *New York Times* editorial, "let's remember that gallant men died needlessly in that old mission and that their sacrifice eventually led to a war that reflects little credit on the United States. . . . To persevere in folly is no virtue. To dare to retreat from error can be the highest form of courage."[9]

To join the words "retreat" and "the Alamo" struck many Texans and other Americans as blasphemy. At its core, the Alamo signified the refusal to retreat, the willingness to fight to the end. For Americans of the post–World War II generation, the Alamo had become a living symbol both of everything that was great and worthy and of everything that was terrible and false. Defending or attacking the Alamo clearly delineated a social and political philosophy. Across the country the line had been drawn—for or against, right or left, "God Bless America" or "The Draft Dodger's Rag." In such a broiling cultural atmosphere it was impossible to discuss the Alamo without crossing to one side or the other of the line.

✶

Lyndon B. Johnson clearly stood on one side of the line, and a new generation of liberals viewed him as a political dinosaur, like Davy Crockett a combination of the frontier ethos and the virtues of the common man, notions that seemed to be losing resonance in the modern world. Ever since the age of Jackson, in the early nineteenth century, liberalism and populism had staked out common ground, and in the twentieth century, progressivism and the New Deal fused them. President Theodore Roosevelt, for example, had founded the Boone and Crockett Club, a men's organization committed to conservation and the development of masculine virtues. During the years of the Great Depression, WPA muralists found Davy Crockett, Daniel Boone, Jim Bowie, Buffalo Bill Cody, and other Western heroes perfect icons for the walls of post offices and government buildings. Immortalizing nineteenth-century Western heroes had never seemed inconsistent with liberal tradition. Quite the contrary. They epitomized egalitarianism.

After World War II, however, the American left experienced a sea change when liberalism and populism parted company in a divorce whose repercussions would redefine politics and culture. The old left—with its roots in the labor movement, socialism, the big cities, and the Eastern intelligentsia—had little use or respect for rural values, folksy aphorisms, or rugged individualists bent on defying communal expectations. And when liberalism dumped populism, President Lyndon Johnson became its most high-profile victim. Raised in a region where the frontier was still visible and its values still paramount, Johnson looked almost as if he had just walked barefooted out of the hill country and put on his first suit and tie. The handlebar ears, the baboonlike nose, the slicked-back, Brylcreemed hair, and the Texas twang contrasted too sharply with the Kennedy celebrity, with Jack's perfectly coiffed, air-dried hair, and with Jackie's impeccable style. While Kennedy would not have been caught dead shredding a lobster in front of photographers, Johnson wore barbecue sauce on his lips as a badge of honor.

Both men wanted to be all things to all people, but Johnson never felt understood. The intellectuals like Robert Lowell, Dwight Macdonald, and John Hersey who criticized him, Johnson insisted, did not understand the real world of politics. "They never take the time," he once said, "to think about what really goes on . . . because they've never been involved in persuading anyone to do anything. They're just like a pack of nuns who've convinced themselves that sex is dirty and ugly and low-downed and forced because *they* never have it. And because they never have it, they see it all as rape instead of seduction and they miss the elaborate preparation that goes on before the act is finally done." The two sides might as well have been speaking different languages. In the battle of East versus West, Massachusetts versus Texas, Boston versus Johnson City, and Harvard versus Southwest Texas State Teachers College, Lyndon Johnson lost.[10]

John F. Kennedy's assassination all but guaranteed the defeat. The image of Jacqueline Kennedy, her pink woolen suit stained with JFK's blood, standing to the side on *Air Force One* while Johnson took the oath of office seared into the national consciousness. Kennedy and Camelot died in Dallas on November 22, 1963, and many Americans somehow held Texas responsible, attributing the killing to nests of right-wing, John Birch fanatics infesting the rich suburbs of north Dallas. Easterners had long tolerated

Texas—with its big landscapes, big money, and big mouths—as a parent tolerates a rowdy, rambunctious child. But Lee Harvey Oswald's bullets transformed tolerance into dislike, paternalism into disdain, and grudging respect into grinding resentment. A New Yorker acknowledged those feelings in a letter to the *San Antonio Express:* "Texans have reason to feel shame and guilt but please don't erect any more monuments to our late president's memory. He wouldn't have wanted that. He would rather see [Texas] utilize [its] energy and money to eradicate ignorance, bigotry and narrow-mindedness." Some suspected that perhaps even LBJ had conspired in the assassination—to prevent Kennedy liberalism from sweeping the country, to keep the United States in Vietnam, to guarantee more government money to Texas defense contractors, or just to get LBJ in the White House without having to rely on voters. The theories, of course, were specious and without merit, but they had staying power, finding expression again and again over the years in such films as *Executive Action, JFK,* and *Nixon.*[11]

In the wake of the assassination, a telling letter-writing war erupted in the Texas press. Some critics responded to the renaming of airports, schools, and public sites after the slain president. "With no guilt such as ours," a resident of Lubbock wrote the *San Antonio Express,* "New York has its Kennedy Airport, Florida has Cape Kennedy and even Mexico has its Kennedy Observatory. [Isn't it time to] put into effect a change of name for your Alamo to include the greatest hero of any fallen in Texas? I suggest the John F. Kennedy Alamo Memorial. This may help erase our shame." Other Texans disagreed. "No Alamo name change, please," wrote a Texan. "We need to be as proud of our past as ashamed of our present."[12]

But for every Texan suffering guilt over the death of the president, even more refused to accept such a burden. "I, for one, fail to see how Texas is guilty or bears the shame of the assassination. . . . Since when are the scene of the crime and the spectators to the crime guilty of the crime?" Many Texans were outraged at the very notion of changing the Alamo's name. "Treason! Treason! Treason!" wrote another. "The affrontery, the audacity, the sacrilege of . . . proposing that the glory of our shrine of freedom, our cradle of liberty . . . be transferred to one who neither he nor his ancestors shared in, is shameful. . . . Why deify Kennedy?" One writer put it in simple terms: "John F. Kennedy had nothing to do with the Alamo. In fact, he wasn't even [alive then]. . . . I think Travis, Crockett and others are worth as much as any of the Kennedy dynasty. I am a Texan."[13]

The name remained the same, but the Alamo began to come under siege. Like Lyndon Johnson, the Alamo could not escape anti-Texas zeal. When the producers of the film *Viva Max* showed up in San Antonio in 1969 for location shooting, the Daughters of the Republic of Texas took umbrage. The film starred British actor Peter Ustinov as an incompetent Mexican general who leads an army across the Rio Grande River, invades modern-day San Antonio, and reoccupies the Alamo for twenty-four hours. Iconoclastic and sarcastic, the script had a tongue-in-cheek, Monty Python–like, nothing-is-sacred irreverence. After one look at the script, the DRT launched a crusade against the film, refusing to cooperate in any way with its producers. They declared the Alamo grounds off-limits to actors, cameramen, and scriptwriters, and a DRT delegation even marched on City Hall, demanding that the mayor and City Council ban the film crew from using streets adjacent to the compound. If the film ever reached the screen, the Daughters argued, the reaction would "lead civilization down the twilight trail to oblivion." Unmoved by DRT hyperbole, the City Council let the filming proceed.

That hardly ended the fireworks. The DRT turned to the legal system, trying and failing to secure court injunctions against the producers. One columnist wrote that the Daughters "did everything but pull out their muskets and Bowie knives to thwart the film effort." Peter Ustinov, anxious to generate free publicity for the movie, let no opportunity pass to tweak the Daughters, strolling around the grounds at will, picking verbal fights with guides, intentionally offending sensibilities. The Daughters were particularly outraged when, during the shooting of one scene, a white flare landed atop the Alamo chapel. Completely unrepentant, Ustinov remarked that one "act of war deserves another. . . . The problem is that [the Daughters] aren't wearing sunglasses and we can see the whites of their eyes." The standoff generated publicity throughout the United States and Europe and guaranteed box-office success for *Viva Max* when it was released in 1970.[14]

✶

Viva Max was not the only assault on the Alamo during the 1970s, or even the most important. In October 1975, only months after the communist victory in Vietnam, Texas A&M University Press published a firsthand account of the Mexican campaign against Texas entitled *With Santa Anna in Texas: A Personal Narrative of the Revolution*. Written by José Enrique de la Peña, a lieutenant in the *zapadores* battalion, and translated by Carmen Perry, it recounted how Mexico lost Texas and, more specifically, who was responsible. De la Peña argued that Mexico had been betrayed by greedy, vicious, incompetent officers led by Generals Antonio López de Santa Anna, Vicente Filisola, and Joaquín Ramírez y Sesma, as well as officials in the war and treasury departments. As a whole the document is a product of the turmoil of late-1830s Mexico, an age of social decay, political chaos, and emotional unrest, a time of pointing fingers. Behind all of de la Peña's discussions of the strategy, logistics, and geography of war is the desire to affix blame for Mexico's sad condition.[15]

Mexico's problems in the late 1830s were not even a fleeting American concern, and *With Santa Anna in Texas* would certainly have been ignored by everyone save a few historians if it had not been for one paragraph. After recounting the horrors of the attack on the Alamo, the senseless deaths and avoidable suffering, de la Peña turned his attention to Santa Anna. He noted that the general's victory speech lacked the "magic" of Napoleon, and that from his "crippled battalions" only a few icy *viva*s broke the silence. It was a grim scene—"an unbearable and nauseating odor," blackened faces contorted in death, friends searching through the dead for friends, groans of the wounded and dying. The best of the Mexican officers were surfeited with the fighting and dying. General Manuel Castrillón even disobeyed Santa Anna's order of no quarter and offered protection to seven Alamo survivors.[16]

Among the seven, de la Peña wrote, "was one of great stature, well proportioned, with regular features, in whose face there was the imprint of adversity, but in whom one also noticed a degree of resignation and nobility that did him honor. He was the naturalist David Crockett, well known in North America for his unusual adventures, who had undertaken to explore the country and who, finding himself in Béxar at the very moment of surprise, had taken refuge in the Alamo, fearing that his status as a foreigner might not be respected." Castrillón asked Santa Anna to show mercy on the survivors, but with a few words and a "gesture of indignation" the general ordered their executions. Instantly, several of Santa Anna's lackeys "thrust themselves forward, in order to flatter their commander, and with swords in hand, fell upon these unfortunate, defenseless men just as a tiger leaps upon his prey. Though tortured before they were killed, these unfortunates died without complaining and without humiliating themselves before their torturers."[17]

At no point does de la Peña explain how he recognized Crockett, or how he learned the details of the former congressman's excursion to Texas and the Alamo. Did Crockett concoct the story of his innocence in an attempt to save his life? Which of the Mexican officers at the scene translated Crockett's words? So many questions unanswered. Still, de la Peña gave such graphic detail and his account of the entire battle of the Alamo was so powerful that his "eyewitness" story seemed to carry a rough if melodramatic truth. And as editor and translator Carmen Perry noted, de la Peña's manuscript was published in Matamoros, Mexico, in September 1836, just months after the end of the war in Texas, when the officer's memory and campaign notes were still fresh. In the assertion of the publication date, Perry was following in the footsteps of Alamo historian Walter Lord and noted Texana bibliographer John Jenkins.[18]

De la Peña's brief aside on the death of David Crockett created an immediate controversy. No matter that rumors that Crockett surrendered—or was captured—and was then executed had begun within weeks of the end of the battle and were published in newspapers and books, and as late as the 1940s in the *Biographical Directory of the American Congress, 1774–1927.* No matter that the *Columbia Encyclopedia* continued to retread the rumors as if they were well-established fact. The de la Peña diary was harder to dismiss.[19]

Even taken at face value, the smoking guns in de la Peña's account of the execution of Crockett were hardly historical smoking guns. To take just one problem, de la Peña also discusses the death of William Travis, saying that he fell after the Mexicans had forced their way inside the Alamo. "Travis was seen to hesitate, but not about the death that he would choose. He would take a few steps and stop, turning his proud face toward us to discharge his shots; he fought like a true soldier. Finally, he died, but he died after having traded his life very dearly." This story differs radically with other accounts of Travis's death and is almost certainly not true. Michael Lind put the problem well:

> If we are to believe the account in *With Santa Anna in Texas,* we must believe that either De la Peña himself, or some informant in the Mexican army, was able to distinguish Travis from the other Texans, while looking up from below the wall and being fired upon, in the darkness before daybreak. If De la Peña was the alleged eyewitness, then we must further believe that, after witnessing the death of Travis on the

north wall, he providentially made his way to the other side of the fortress—just in time to see David Crockett executed by Santa Anna.

Only saints and fanatics have such power of belief.[20]

But there were more problems with de la Peña's narrative than just his seeming ability to be at every important scene. Most important, his account was not published in September 1836—or September 1936 for that matter. In an earlier, now lost manuscript, de la Peña said that he planned to publish his diary, vindicating the honor of the nation and the army. He mentioned several of the outrages Santa Anna committed during the campaign, including the execution of a "few unfortunates who had survived the catastrophe" of the Alamo. "Among those had been a man who pertained to the natural sciences, whose love of it had conducted him to Texas, and who locked himself up in the Alamo not believing it safe by his quality of [being a] foreigner, when General Santa Anna surprised Béxar." There was no mention of Crockett in the pamphlet, though clearly this "man who pertained to the natural sciences" became "naturalist David Crockett" in his later account.[21]

De la Peña's longer account of the war was first published in Mexico in Spanish in March 1955, the month after millions of Americans watched Fess Parker's Davy Crockett die on the set of Walt Disney's Alamo. The narrative, edited by Jesús Sánchez Garza, went unnoticed in Mexico and the United States. In fairness to de la Peña, he never claimed that his book was published in 1836—nor did Sánchez Garza—but the fact of publication was important. It meant that his story was not constructed immediately after the war but rather written and rewritten over a period of years, during a time when other Mexican officers were publishing their accounts and de la Peña was languishing in prison for opposing the centralist regime. Although the diary is almost certainly not a forgery, it is a highly charged political document, aimed at discrediting the centralists and defending the federalists. As a whole, de la Peña's description of the look, smell, and feel of the campaign is unsurpassed; his grasp of grand strategy, his description of leaders, and his sympathy for the plight of the soldiers is outstanding. But in many cases he clearly drew from a deep pool of rumors, details, and stories that suited his overarching interpretation of the campaign and Mexican politics.

Translated into English, *With Santa Anna in Texas* attracted immediate attention. "Students of American history and John Wayne fans take note," commented a journalist for the *Denver Post*. "The legendary story of the Alamo may need revision." "Has the King of the Wild Frontier been relieved of his coon-skin crown?" wondered a writer for the *Jackson* (Tenn.) *Sun*. "Naturally, it will be hard for a generation that grew up singing 'Born on a mountain-top in Tennessee' to accept the mental image of a cowardly Crockett groveling in the Alamo corner." Throughout America, de la Peña was news. *People* ran a story, complete with pictures of Carmen Perry and John Wayne and the headline DID CROCKETT DIE AT THE ALAMO? CARMEN PERRY SAYS NO. And the *Texas Monthly* presented the diary with one of its 1975 "Bum Steer" awards.[22]

"We don't believe Davy Crockett ever surrendered," responded Mrs. Charles Hall, chair of the Alamo Committee of the Daughters of the Republic of Texas. "We feel he went down fighting. And by 'we' I mean all Texans." After publication of the book, Perry received angry phone calls and harassing anonymous letters condemning her efforts. But not all Texans stayed on the DRT's side of the line. The Sons of the Republic of Texas gave the book a prize, and the Movimiento Estudianil Chicanos de Aztlán of El Paso applauded it. Many people accepted it as a clear case of myth versus scholarship, Walt Disney and John Wayne versus dispassionate historical research. Commenting on the de la Peña controversy, Perry said, "People don't believe his account because they don't want to believe it. We prefer to live by legend."[23]

Yet as Crockett's most persistent defender, Bill Groneman, observed, "The image of Crockett clubbing away at hoards of swarthy men was not that attractive in 1975 after so many Americans had been 'clubbed' by other hoards of swarthy men in Vietnam just a few years earlier." It was the time of the sly political manipulator and the antihero. Richard Nixon had been awarded a pardon for all his sins, and *One Flew over the Cuckoo's Nest* won the Academy Award for best picture. The game, it seemed to many Americans, had been fixed by the coldblooded Nurses Ratched of the country, and anything that smacked of the heroic or the authentic had probably been produced by some political adman. That Crockett was a "sly Politician" and his heroic death at the Alamo was so much claptrap seemed only natural. Weren't all wars false and all gods dead?[24]

Three years after the appearance of *With Santa Anna in Texas*, Texas A&M University Press published *How Did Davy Die?*, Dan Kilgore's brief examination of the death of Crockett. The book was the outgrowth of Kilgore's controversial presidential address to the Texas State Historical Association. Simply and dispassionately, he asserted that Crockett "either surrendered or was captured near the end of the assault and was immediately killed by Santa Anna's order." Then with lawyerlike efficiency, he constructed his case, examining the various documents that supported his contention and charging "that a preponderance of the evidence" virtually proves the execution story. Although Kilgore does not thoroughly examine the historical context of each document, he admits that the earlier accounts "have a ring of folklore instead of history." But the reappearance of such important documents as the de la Peña diary and the 1836 George M. Dolson letter, originally published in the *Detroit Democratic Free Press,* convinced him that Crockett had been executed.[25]

Kilgore's detached conclusions set off another storm of protest. THEM'S FIGHTING WORDS; DAVY'S LEGEND SMUDGED ran the headline in Kilgore's hometown *Corpus Christi Caller-Times.* "Any Texan worth his lizard skin boots and Willie Nelson albums knows better than to smear the legend of Davy Crockett." The more popular than accurate *World Weekly News* editorialized, "Some smarty-pants historians now claim Davy didn't die fighting at the Alamo—but instead surrendered when he ran out of ammo and was then executed." Fittingly, the writer added that John Wayne, not Crockett, must be rolling in his grave. Newspapers in countries as far from Texas as Canada and Great Britain carried stories of the controversy, and Kilgore was even accused of fostering a communist plot to destroy American heroes and spreading damnable lies. What was worse as far as he was concerned, his critics failed to buy and read his book. He suffered more from what journalists said he wrote than from what he had actually written.[26]

Some Crockett defenders were convinced that the de la Peña diary was a cleverly crafted forgery, and scandals among Texas bibliophiles fueled the rumors. Artifacts of Texas history were becoming big business. For most of the nineteenth and twentieth centuries, Texans had manifested a lofty disregard for their own history. Although the DRT labored to keep the Alamo from becoming an adjunct of a department store or hotel, other Texans were not as vigilant. Even into the 1950s, Texans continued to ignore the tangible objects of their past. In 1957, for example, Thomas Streeter, a New Jersey oilman who had amassed the finest private collection of Texana, offered to sell his priceless documents, rare books, and singular artifacts to the University of Texas. The university declined the offer, the collection went to Yale, and Streeter's *Bibliography of Texas 1795–1845* was published by Harvard University Press.[27]

That unofficial policy of benign neglect began to change in the 1960s and 1970s. In the age of oilmen and real estate developers, relics of the state's proud past dramatically increased in value. Had Streeter waited a decade, his collection of letters, books, and broadsides would have fetched a fortune. But Streeter was gone and a new generation of bibliophiles and book traders, most born in or close to Texas, began to assert their power. Three in particular—John Jenkins, William Simpson, and C. Dorman David—emerged as the most impressive dealers of Texana. More likely than not, if a buyer was searching for rare broadsides of the Texas Declaration of Independence or William Travis's "VICTORY or DEATH" letter, either Jenkins, Simpson, or David had one to sell.

All three were characters. Simpson had been a friend of Ezra Pound, wore a white goatee, and sold or traded items ranging from crystal and rugs to art and furniture, with a document business on the side. Working out of Houston, he struck some people as charming and others as merely curious. But he was a sedate conformist compared to Jenkins and David. Before Jenkins was out of high school, he had edited a book of his great-great-grandfather's memoirs and earned a reputation as a sharp coin trader. After graduating from the University of Texas, he set up shop in Austin and dealt in books and manuscripts. He also took frequent trips to Las Vegas, where he played poker under the name of Austin Squatty. David, whose father had made a fortune in oil, ran the Bookman in Houston, an establishment so refined and expensive that it often intimidated buyers. Not that David was overly concerned. Through a succession of wives, addiction to heroin, and a life lived on the razor edge, he generally seemed oblivious to the fact that merchants went into business to make money. Buy high and sell low appeared to be his business motto.[28]

Novelist Larry McMurtry knew Jenkins and David and had a fine sense of their characters: "Both were frontier snake-oil salesmen who *liked*—indeed, gloried in—being frontier snake-oil salesmen. The notion that either of them would have sunk to his knees, rending the air with mea culpas, because he had sold some chump a Texas Declaration of Independence that had just been peeled off the Xerox machine is absurd: their whole practice as tradesmen was a hearty 'up yours!' to the genteel canons of the trade, which, after all, are still the canons of a northern European men's club." And that was the problem. Just as a market in Texana emerged—or perhaps because a market emerged—the two snake-oil salesmen opened their wagons for business. You want rare documents, they seemed to say, we got your rare documents. Oh yes, caveat emptor. David even entitled his 1964 catalogue *The Bookman Offers for Sale Texas Books from a Recent Robbery,* and on the cover of another catalogue he put a wanted poster with his picture.[29]

The combination in the 1960s and 1970s of Texas nostalgia and Texas money created an open range for stolen and forged documents, an unfenced land where the word "provenance" was seldom heard. Rare documents disappeared from libraries and archives in Mexico and Texas and found their way to David's establishment. Other rare documents appeared out of nowhere. Before 1970, for instance, only five copies of the Texas Declaration of Independence broadsides were known to exist; fifteen years later there were at least twenty. Most were, of course, forgeries, the work of C. Dorman David, who did good enough work to fool most of the people most of the time. But not all of the time, and in the summer of 1972 a police raid forced him out of business. He sold many of his forged and stolen documents, however, to Jenkins and Simpson, who continued to do a brisk and lucrative trade in them. It was no wonder that traditionalists like Bill Groneman were skeptical about the de la Peña diary.

In the late 1980s, the entire Texana world would be shaken by a series of scandals. Experts had identified more than fifty forged documents. Jenkins lost his holdings, including the forgeries, in a providential fire, though the Travis County district attorney believed God had nothing to do with it. Two years later, Jenkins died of a shotgun blast, ruled suicide, but a very suspicious one. Some Texans and non-Texans believed that the forgeries, scandals, and violence symbolized the history of the state. The fact that one of the most important Alamo documents—Isaac Millsaps's March 3, 1836, letter to his blind wife, in which he mentioned that Travis was going to address the defenders—was almost certainly a forgery cast doubts on other crucial pieces of the Alamo story. "Because of me, everyone is having to look at Texas history a lot more closely," David gloated.[30]

Everybody did just that. Journalists transformed their stories of the de la Peña controversy into simple morality plays—objective historical researchers, uncontaminated by any sort of bias, versus defenders of the faith, blind to all evidence to the contrary. It was "The truth will set you free" versus "America, right or wrong," the sterility of the historical petri dish versus the emotional patriotism of John Wayne and the flag. Not a good reason to conclude that Davy surrendered, but a reason nonetheless.

11

════ ✦ ════

THE THIRD BATTLE
OF THE ALAMO

WHEN LYNDON JOHNSON departed the White House in 1969, he left behind in official Washington a legion of Texas politicians who remembered the Alamo as if it were recent history. Each of them, like Johnson, had heard the story again and again, watched school plays, memorized poems, visited the shrine, acted out the battle in boyhood games, and thrilled to the cinematic efforts of Walt Disney and John Wayne.

The strength of the Alamo's grip on the Texas imagination manifested itself repeatedly at Senator John Tower's annual Texas Independence Day party. A political scientist who knew more about early Texas than most professional historians, Tower nurtured a patriotic, almost jingoist devotion to his state. In March 1962, soon after winning his first term in the Senate and relocating to Washington, D.C., he invited several friends over to his home to celebrate Texas Independence Day. Tower fondly remembered the celebrations of his youth, when public schools let out and local communities hailed the Alamo and San Jacinto and staged festivities matched in grandeur only by July 4 celebrations. The senator decided to re-create the fun for Texas expatriates in the capital. At the end of the first party, he delivered a pious lecture on the meaning of Texas independence and read aloud a copy of William Barret Travis's "VICTORY or DEATH" letter.

Over the years, the party grew steadily in size, as did Tower's power in

Washington, and the reading became even more dramatic. Dripping in heartfelt sentiment, Tower described Travis's letter as "the most moving document in military history, an ode to courage, liberty, and sacrifice." Over the years, the annual celebration of Texas independence attracted more and more visitors. The guest list read like a who's who of Texas politics, and included such luminaries as Lyndon Johnson, George Bush, and Lloyd Bentsen. By the late 1970s, when Tower had become chairman of the powerful Armed Services Committee, the annual gathering had to be moved to the Senate Caucus Room on Capitol Hill, where it drew defense contractors, Texas journalists, congressional committee staff members, and politicians of every stripe. Invitations to the party were among the most sought after in town.

Lone Star flags adorned the walls and Lone Star bunting covered the tables, beneath barbecued beef and pork ribs, brisket and sausage, and nachos with *chili con queso*. As beer and bourbon coursed through the room, businessmen negotiated government contracts, politicians leaked stories to the press, and deals were made. At the end of the evening, a somber John Tower hushed the crowd. With a seriousness that only native Texans could fully appreciate, he reminded everyone that they had gathered to pay homage "to what is probably the greatest event in human history—Texas independence." Removing his glasses and speaking without notes, Tower eulogized the heroes and martyrs, described the Alamo and San Jacinto, and reminded everyone of Travis's line in the sand and invitation to stay, fight, and probably die. "To a man," Tower said at the 1984 gathering, "they died because they resolved they would rather die as free men than live as slaves." He then read Travis's letter—"*I shall never surrender or retreat. . . .* I am determined to sustain myself . . . & die like a soldier who never forgets what is due to his own honor & that of his country. . . . VICTORY or DEATH." When the celebration concluded with a rendition of "Texas, Our Texas," journalists noted few dry eyes in the room.[1]

Yet not even all politicians stood on the same side of the Alamo line anymore. During a 1979 visit to San Antonio, Arizona governor Bruce Babbitt exposed the raw nerve of culture politics. Politically ambitious and anxious for national office, he came to Texas hoping to expand his political base. Taking a few verbal shots at Republican governor Bill Clements, Babbitt thought, might drum up support among Hispanics.

For a venue, he chose a luncheon of the Mexican American Unity Council. Speaking as the voice of the future, Babbitt lectured: "We are on the threshold of a new era with Mexico who is finally emerging from the Third World as a developing nation. We must forge a new relationship based on recognition of Mexico as an equal." So far, so good, but Babbitt continued. "The Alamo is a symbol of the problem in our relationship with Mexico, a sacred symbol to Texans and an extension of the American ideal. But to Mexico, it's a symbol of territory lost, a nation plundered by overbearing gringo neighbors." Mexican American activists hailed Babbitt. "Texas suffers from an Alamo mentality," said Ruben Bonilla, a League of United Latin American Citizens leader. "As a result of that, Mexican Americans have been denied access to political and social systems of this state and country."[2]

In courting of Mexican American activists, Babbitt generated ill will among Texas traditionalists, and the Democratic Party establishment abandoned him in a flash. "The heroes of the Alamo don't need defending against a politician two states away," commented Texas attorney general Mark White, and Speaker of the House Bill Clayton warned that "it's not going to help for a governor from some other state to come over here and try to fire up emotions." Governor Bill Clements, on tour in Europe, remarked, "It appears that the honorable governor never learned to mind his own business. He's got enough problems in Arizona to worry about."[3]

Babbitt put up with the heat for several days before waving the white flag. In an open letter to all Texans, he said, "It was not my intention to offend anyone. I share your pride in Texas history. I share the pride of all Americans in the heroic deeds of Travis, Bowie, Crockett and their followers. But I also believe that we honor history best if we appreciate how those events are viewed by others, in this case by Mexico." Babbitt's wife, a native of Texas, heaved a sigh of relief. "I have relatives in Hondo and San Antonio," she said, "and they've been writing and calling me since Wednesday. It's gotten to the point I'm afraid to come visit."[4]

By the 1980s, the Alamo was one of the most hotly contested symbols in the nation. The Ku Klux Klan continued to show up every May 1 to wage war against invisible communists bent on "desecrating a shrine to freedom and sacrifice," and abortion opponents incensed with *Roe* v. *Wade* found in the Alamo a "beacon of life," a perfect setting to promote their convictions that, in the words of one Roxanne McKnight, "abortion is murder and we're not going to put up with it." Vietnam veterans used the Alamo as a backdrop to plead their cause. The so-called Last Patrol, a column of hundreds of Vietnam vets dressed in fatigues and carrying rucksacks, arrived at the Alamo on November 8, 1985, singing "When Johnny Comes Marching Home Again" and proclaiming, "Remember the Alamo! . . . [R]emember the POWs, remember the MIAs." Almost any cause would do. To protest the triumph of conservative resolutions at the 1988 Southern Baptist Convention, alienated moderates showed up at the Alamo and shredded their convention ballots. When Alamo security removed them, they cited their First Amendment rights. "This is not a demonstration," one Baptist remarked. "Rather, it is a gathering of tourists who are here this afternoon to praise the word of God."[5]

Critics mounted an enormous offensive against Alamo symbolism during the 1980s, challenging the foundations of Texas history and the westward movement. The Alamo was the perfect Cold War metaphor for American innocence and willingness to die for important beliefs. As such, it became an obvious target for anyone who doubted the pristine foundation of the American experiment or the justness of its cause. Even rock stars flouting convention were drawn to the Alamo. In 1975, during a Rolling Stones concert tour of the United States, the *London Daily Mirror* asked Mick Jagger and the Stones to stage an irreverent pose in front of the Alamo. Jagger wrapped himself in the Union Jack and the others donned Davy Crockett coonskin caps. A Daughter later confronted Jagger, informing him that leaning against the Alamo's walls was disrespectful. Somewhat bewildered, and completely ignorant of the shrine's place in Texas culture, Jagger later remarked, "I don't know what the Alamo is or where it is, but we'll never play it again."[6]

With so much at stake, every incident involving the Alamo assumed larger significance. In 1982, San Antonio's police arrested iconoclastic British rock star Ozzy Osbourne for public intoxication and urinating on a monument at the Alamo. Osbourne, who was known for biting the heads off bats and chickens, represented the radical extreme of popular culture. For him, the object of music and life was to disrupt conventions and challenge authority. In reports after the incident, Osbourne supposedly commented that the act fulfilled one of his life's goals, the most important being to urinate on the steps of the White House. At the police station an officer asked him, "How would [the British] like it if I came over and pissed on Buckingham Palace?" "They probably would cheer you," he answered.[7]

*

By the 1980s the cultural wars over the Alamo had a new intellectual underpinning that was far more powerful than any activist's gesture. Among professional historians, significant change was under way. Back in 1893, historian Frederick Jackson Turner had launched a theory that dominated American thought for nearly a century. Conquest of the Western frontier, Turner argued, generated a spirit of freedom, democracy, egalitarianism, and equal opportunity that became quintessentially American. Although Turner's "frontier thesis" had been refined by several generations of Western historians, most still agreed in the 1970s that westward expansion represented a heroic chapter in American history. Minority historians laboring in the wake of the civil rights movement, of course, dissented. In 1972, Chicano Rodolfo Acuña, a historian at California State University, Northridge, wrote, "Racism . . . is at the heart of colonialism. . . . Anglo-Americans have failed to recognize that the United States committed an act of violence against the Mexican people. . . . The violence was not limited to the taking of the land; Mexico's territory was invaded, her people murdered, her land raped, and her possessions plundered." Another Hispanic historian described Manifest Destiny as "a peculiarly Anglo-American version of the chosen race theory. . . . [T]he Mexican American found his lands gone, his religion seriously challenged, and himself a citizen of a country whose language, laws, and social customs he did not understand."[8]

But until the early 1980s, such views were confined to a radical fringe; most historians were still wedded to Frederick Jackson Turner. But at Yale University historians were forging a new synthesis. Under the tutelage of historian Howard Robert Lamar, graduate students exposed the dark side of the frontier thesis. They despised old-fashioned "gunsmoke and horseshit" history. Patricia Limerick, whose *The Legacy of Conquest: The Unbroken Past of the American West* (1987) made her the revisionist leader, later remembered that a "younger generation, shaken by Vietnam and other national disgraces—poverty, racism, environmental degradation—could not pretend that the only story that mattered in the West was one of stagecoach lines, treasure hunts, cattle brands, and wildcatters. . . . What was missing was a frank, hard look at the violent imperialistic process by which the West was wrested from its original owners. . . . It was time for historians to call such violence and imperialism by their true names."[9]

They rewrote history from the angle of the conquered, the colonized, and the oppressed. Donald Worster insisted that Western development had been "plagued by racism, ethnocentrism, brutality, misunderstanding, and rage on the part of the majority and minority peoples alike, but especially marred by oppression and exploitation on the part of those holding the whip hand." And the list of victims extended beyond Native Americans and Hispanics. The environment succumbed as well. "The economic development of the West was often a ruthless assault on nature and has left behind it much death, depletion, and ruin." Historian Richard White reinforced that perspective. "Old Western Historians," he wrote, "looked past the garbage and saw 'nature.' . . . Many New Western Historians—particularly environmental historians—see the garbage first."[10]

The debate spread beyond ivory towers in 1989 when Patricia Limerick headed a National Endowment for the Humanities symposium in Santa Fe, New Mexico, entitled "Trails: Toward a New Western History." The press jumped on the term. Limerick remembers that the conference "started off an improbable rush of media coverage. A variety of news organizations picked up the story," and "the New Western History had come to exist." Articles about the conference appeared in the *Arizona Republic,* the *Los Angeles Times,* the *San Francisco Chronicle,* the *New York Times,* and the *Washington Post.* Historical conferences erupted in acrimony over Western themes, and university presses and professional journals readily published books and articles revolving around the new ideas. The so-called Old Western Historians—represented by Frederick Jackson Turner, Ray Allen Billington, and Walter Prescott Webb—became targets of derision and scholarly abuse, some of it deserved but much of it ideological hyperbole.[11]

The New Western History caught many Americans off guard and inspired a backlash. Larry McMurtry claimed that "there's a new land rush in the history departments, a new Wild Bunch thundering out of New Haven, racing through the academies, shooting out streetlights, roping barber poles, and telling everyone who will listen that the West was actually being lost while a befuddled nation thought it was being won." He labeled the New Western History "Failure Studies" and accused revisionists of "rarely do[ing] justice to the quality of imagination that constitutes part of the truth." Critics accused revisionists of pushing political agendas. One claimed that "the rhetoric of 'new' and 'old' seems simply a way of distinguishing between arguments one does and does not like. Alternative approaches to the history of the American West have existed among historians since the reconsideration of the frontier thesis began in earnest, and contrasting interpretations have less to do with 'generations' than with social theory, moral values, and angle and breadth of historical vision."[12]

The debate over the nature of the Western experience was rich with invective. Traditional historians, alienated by the crusading zeal of the revisionists, accused them of examining the past from a neo-Marxist perspective and seeing only class conflict, imperialism, and racial tension. Trained in the wake of the Vietnam War and the civil rights protests, the New Western Historians had fallen victim to pessimism and nihilism, and in the process, according to traditionalists like Gerald Nash of the University of New Mexico, they fixated on white men as the culprits of American history, conquerors who "despoiled the land, ravaged the environment, and oppressed ethnic and racial minorities and, of course, the poor."

Accusing intellectual rivals of bias and myopia was hardly new; each new generation of historians builds its reputation on the carcasses of predecessors. What particularly galled traditionalists was the not so tacit assumption that loyalty to older views was tantamount to racism, sexism, and ethnocentrism. For some traditionalists, the New Western Historians had bulldozed the profession, formulating a party line that brooked no opposition and tolerated no dissent. Such methods, according to Nash, bore "striking similarity to the *modus operandi* of Nazi, Fascist, and Communist academicians in their heyday." He also accused New Western Historians of spading for deconstructionists. During the 1970s and 1980s, Yale was a hotbed of deconstructionism because of the pervasive influence of (among others) literary critic Paul de Man. As a founding father of European deconstructionism, de Man enjoyed extraordinary cachet among Yale's arts and humanities faculty. But during World War II, de Man had supported Adolf Hitler, penning pro-Nazi and anti-Semitic articles for Belgian newspapers. Even when his racism was exposed, according to Nash, "many good Yalies—like good Germans in the 1930s—kept their silence." As a result, the New Western Historians "are attempting proselytization for what in essence are totalitarian ideologies."[13]

Heroes do not die quietly, and the West had long been a land of heroes. A columnist for the *San Antonio Express-News,* reacting to a meeting of the National Association for Chicano Studies, wrote, "The school of the politically correct has been in session here the past few days, its teachers and students taking to the streets to protest and denounce Eurocentric, white, male, heterosexual versions of world history. . . . It doesn't really take much to ignore the adolescent mental masturbation of the politically correct." Another defender of tradition warned that "political correctness is beating at the door of the Alamo. . . . [F]or the 60s generation which now dominates much of academia, history is yet another theater in the fight for radical social and political change. . . . Many of today's scholars see history simply as a struggle between oppressor and oppressed, and their duty is not to discover truth, but to decide who is who and then distort accordingly."[14]

Academic theories tend to trickle down into the public sphere, and in this case certain interest groups were already primed for battle. No target pleased revisionists more—intellectually, culturally, and politically—than the Alamo. The opening salvo of the "third battle of the Alamo" was fired in 1988 when San Antonio's Imax theater premiered the film *Alamo . . . The Price of Freedom.* Hyped as a technological marvel, with its eighty-five-foot-wide, six-story-high screen, the Imax anchored the city's new Rivercenter mall. The Alamo attracted 3 million tourists a year, and Imax owners were certain that hundreds of thousands would make their way to the theater. The forty-minute-long movie made demigods of Bowie, Crockett, Travis, and the other defenders—no doubt what most ticket buyers expected to see—but Mexican American activists found the script offensive. It all but ignored, they insisted, the contributions of Tejanos in the creation of Texas history. San Antonio city councilman Walter Martinez stormed out of the premiere, insisting that the film "had no redeeming social value" and would be "damaging to ethnic progress in San Antonio." He called on Imax owners to scrap it, find a new script, and start over. They refused but did agree to edit out the most egregiously anti-Mexican comments. When the film debuted, protestors demonstrated along Crockett Street, and the League of United Latin American Citizens (LULAC) threatened a nationwide boycott of Luby's cafeterias and Pace Foods, the Imax sponsors. For one San Antonio city councilman, the film was "one more effort to perpetuate a myth that has no basis in fact."[15]

The Imax controversy prompted Hispanic activists to demand that control over the Alamo be transferred from the Daughters of the Republic of Texas to LULAC. Resentment over the Alamo had long simmered in the Hispanic community. A few radical activists took up the New Western History banner, condemning the Alamo as a symbol of white racism and the DRT as an agent of Anglo oppression. The Daughters reminded listeners that 6 percent of its membership was Hispanic, a number consistent with Texas's ethnic composition in 1836. Not that radicals listened. Chicano Marxists insisted that the defenders of the Alamo and their descendants "have sucked the blood of the Chicano people, driving them into the ground, destroying their language and culture and trying to force them to live on their knees." Others, like LULAC's Ramón Vásquez y Sánchez, claimed that "not all Tejanos of Mexican descent have felt truly at ease when entering the walls of this edifice. The bias and overemphasis of the Anglo-Saxon defenders project a negative portrayal of Tejano-Mexicanos." He wanted the DRT to acknowledge the sacrifices of Santa Anna's troops. "What is totally disregarded are the thousands of lives lost by defenders of the mother country. What did they sacrifice? Where is their history on the display walls of the Alamo? . . . The fact is that the Tejanos were the only Texans there and the rest were new arrivals interested in self-gain and land."[16]

Some observers noted a disconnect in the Hispanic critique. Although many Hispanic intellectuals condemned the Alamo as an icon to imperialism, most activists complained that the DRT had not given Tejano defenders of the Alamo *enough* credit for their role in the defense of liberty. Ironically, although a handful of radicals trumpeted the rhetoric of racism, imperialism, and oppression, most Mexican Americans just wanted in on the glory. They argued that such names as Juan Abamillo, Juan Antonio Badillo, Carlos Espalier, José Gregorio Esparza, Toribio Losoya, Andrés Nava, Juan Seguín, and Damacio Ximénes should get equal billing on Alamo marquees, along with Travis, Bowie, Crockett, Bonham, and the Anglo heroes. "The traditional attitude of the Alamo needs to be changed," argued LULAC leader José García de Lara, "so our children may grow up with the pride that they were part of the fight for freedom." The Daughters were just as touchy. "They are not at the Alamo for any particular race, creed or color," argued a DRT attorney. "They're down there to preserve the heritage."[17]

LULAC had less chance of securing control of the Alamo in 1988 than the defenders had of keeping it in 1836. The very suggestion offended many Texans. Newspapers bristled with indignation. In Houston, one critic asserted that handing the Alamo over to LULAC "makes about as much sense as giving control of the Pearl Harbor memorial to the Japanese." Another Houstonian added that the LULAC proposal was "a major attempt by liberal historians and Hispanics to discredit the history of the battle and to paint the Mexicans in a better light, taking away from the ultimate sacrifice of the men who gave their lives so Texas could become the great state it is today." Charles Edgren of the *El Paso Herald-Post* sarcastically suggested that in addition to letting LULAC have the Alamo, perhaps the Ku Klux Klan should take over Harpers Ferry, Virginia, site of John Brown's legendary 1859 raid against slavery. Better yet, Mexico should award to the United States custody of Chapultepec Hill—where brave Mexican boys in 1847 had battled General Winfield Scott's troops during the Mexican-American War. An editorialist for the *Houston Post* added, "Face it, man, about 188 men died defending the Alamo, and they came from many places. At least 10 of the defenders were Tejano men, and at least seven of them died there. But that means Tejanos played a relatively small role in the battle. . . . We don't need another battle of the Alamo. The Anglos have it and aren't going to give it back—to the Tejanos any more than to the Mexicans."[18]

LULAC's defeat did not end the third battle for the Alamo. State representative Orlando García, San Antonio Democrat, opened legislative hearings into DRT finances, hinting at irregularities in the administration of a reserve fund totaling $1.7 million. "If money is being derived from state property, an accounting of those processes should be made," he insisted. "To do otherwise would be to give a license to do as one willed. And a government ought not to operate in that way." A DRT spokeswoman insisted that the money was earmarked as a hedge against possible declines in future revenues and for the production of new Alamo films. Historian Richard Santos lambasted the Alamo gift shop, the heart and soul of the DRT budget. "I fail to see what coonskin caps—made in Taiwan or wherever—have to do with Texas during its Republic. . . . [It is] a glaring example of what could be construed as a misuse of public funds." He backed García's demand for state controls of DRT spending. José García de Lara suggested that the DRT surplus be transferred to other state agencies to fund needy programs. "They're making the money with state property. Why should they keep the money?"[19]

History mattered in Texas, and no leading politician wanted to offend the DRT. García's not so veiled threat—"We're serving notice that the Alamo isn't their [DRT] exclusive shop"—may have resonated with liberal activists, but it made little headway in the political backrooms of Austin. Attorney General Jim Mattox agreed that the DRT was subject to the state's open records and open meetings act, but that its revenues should be secure as long as they were "used exclusively for the maintenance and repair of state property in your custody." State comptroller Bob Bullock, one of the most powerful politicians in Texas, went on record that DRT funds were not under his jurisdiction, and Governor Bill Clements again raised the specter of a veto. The Daughters kept control of the purse strings but agreed to make public their financial records. "I'm satisfied with the outcome," García reported. "The Daughters have committed to making their records available."[20]

The DRT's enemies then moved the battle to a different front. Jerry Beauchamp, a San Antonio Democrat in the state legislature, proposed transferring jurisdiction over the Alamo from the DRT to the state Department of Parks and Wildlife, a move that quickly received the endorsement of other minority legislators, including Frank Tejeda, a state senator from San Antonio, and Ron Wilson, an African American Democrat from Houston. "It's one of the most important history structures in the state," Wilson insisted. "It belongs to everybody, or at least it should. . . . [It] shouldn't be managed by any private group—I don't care if it is the Daughters of the Republic of Texas, the Elks, the Muslims or the Water Buffalo Club." The Daughters retaliated with righteous indignation. Pauline Wilson, president of the Alamo Mission Chapter, announced that DRT "sweat has mixed with the blood of their ancestors shed there." A writer for the *Dallas Morning News* agreed. "This shrine of freedom is wonderfully and sensitively maintained. Far from taking the Alamo away from the Daughters, I would give to the Daughters control of the Parks and Wildlife Department. I bet we'd see some improvements." When San Antonio mayor Henry Cisneros, one of the state's most influential Hispanics, sided with the Daughters, the jurisdictional fight vanished.[21]

★

The third battle subsided, at least locally and temporarily. But the broader cultural divide only deepened. In 1991, the New Western History engulfed the Alamo with the publication of Jeff Long's *Duel of Eagles*. For Long, the Alamo defenders were neither heroes nor martyrs, just good-for-nothing, white-trash no-accounts gone to the huge Texas land grab. It was as if Long plumbed the depths of Santa Anna's ego in search of pejorative adjectives. He wielded the term "mercenary" with enthusiasm, painting in broad brush strokes new stereotypes no less ideological than the old ones. The men who died at the Alamo were "pirates," "freebooters," "fanatics," "heretics," "adventurers," "smugglers," and "hairy, wild-eyed rebels" without redeeming qualities, whose vision for "an independent Texas became viciously racist, devouring every Hispanic to the Rio Grande." They were "Manifest Destiny killers . . . with dirt under their fingernails, lice in their hair . . . and the stink of ignorant, trigger-pulling white trash."[22]

Long took calculated aim at Texas heroes, hoping to bring them down a notch. Sam Houston "was a kamikaze in search of fame and glory," a man "conspicuous for his debauchery," an alcoholic and cocaine addict, a vain, would-be transvestite of sorts who occasionally donned girdles and corsets, an unconvicted felon who made land fraud his raison d'être. Along with the other Ango Texans, Houston "dreamed their dream of theft and he spoke their language of glory. He knitted his path with theirs and together they called their conspiracies destiny."[23]

Bowie was even worse. "Spawned in shadow, wary of the light," Long wrote, he "was . . . by nature crafty and acquisitive . . . a man who saw the world as his bastard slave." A "frontier shadow creature" whose marriage to Ursula de Veramendi "was less romantic than fiscal," since her father was willing to finance "the restless treasure hunter." Bowie spent his days searching for and never finding the rumored lost gold and silver mines of northern Mexico. According to Long, Bowie amounted to nothing more than a thug, a vicious knife fighter who filled a "lifetime [with] fraud and hoaxes" and was unmoved when his wife died suddenly.[24]

Equally lacking in moral fiber was Davy Crockett, whom Long described as a legend in his own mind, a man who "witnessed the extraordinary flowering of his alter ego [and] saw the crowds and heard the applause, and he forgot what he really was . . . an aging, semiliterate squatter of average talent." Crockett's life meant nothing; at the time of his death he was just "an arrogant mercenary with gunsmoke staining his creased face . . . a slave trader and a smuggler . . . [a] pirate . . . [a] heretic," and in the end, a coward. Long harbored no doubts about Crockett's death. "The Go Ahead man quit. He did more than quit. He lied. He dodged. He denied his role in the fighting."[25]

William Travis was a buffoon whom Long derisively nicknamed "Great

Heart," a venereal-disease-ridden "womanizer, a gambler . . . and a martyr-rebel." Long depicted him as a "petulant Southern gentleman . . . certifiably a lover . . . [but] certifiably not a fighter." Instead of being the patriot and hero Texans had long considered him to be, Travis "was young, vain, ambitious, and stuffed full of heroic nonsense." And he was certainly no leader. "He had never learned the difference between bravado and courage, nor the meaning of diplomacy. He had long aspired to military leadership, but he lacked any real connection with his men." Without any convictions, Travis was morally bankrupt, a crusader without a cause, a man "who faced defeat like a mystic facing a mountain." While Santa Anna tightened the noose, "Travis turned his back on reality. He . . . retreated to the only religion he knew: propaganda. He propagandized the colonies, the States, the world. He even propagandized his own men." What Texans had long considered the most noble of words—"VICTORY or DEATH"—Long held to be the ranting of an egomaniac.[26]

Finally, Long reduced early Texas history to a series of epithets. "In order to rationalize, if not sanction, the Anglo-American seizure of Texas," he sermonized, "the Anglo-Americans needed to be bewitched. They needed an artificial history that would present piracy as heroism, wrong as right, aggression as defense. . . . By plucking heroes and martyrs from the still-smoking ash of its battlefields, by copying the colors of Old Glory, the Lone Star bastard declared itself worthy." Adding irony to insult, in his preface Long thanked the Daughters of the Republic of Texas for assisting his research effort.[27]

Reactions to the book were predictable. Academics hailed *Duel of Eagles* as revisionary history at its best. "Legendary figures like James Bowie, Davy Crockett, and William Travis," according to *Choice,* "are shown to be much less the heroes that folklore has made them. . . . One of Long's major contributions is to show . . . the racism of the Anglo-Saxons against the Hispanics in Texas, both before and after 1836." Another reviewer credited Long with "adroitly extract[ing] fact from a deep pit of fiction. The result is the best history of the Alamo fight yet produced." Many Texans reacted differently. The review in the Texas State Historical Association's *Southwestern Historical Quarterly* was decidedly critical, classifying Long as one of the "New Western Historians . . . whose hallmark is a dark sense of negativism. . . . [They] condemn what they interpret as the celebrationist tone of previous western historians and seek to set the record straight on the many sins of our ancestors. . . . The rhetorical overkill employed by Jeff Long . . . actually undercuts his ability to provide any sense of balance to the historical record. His book . . . will not stand the test of time."[28]

After the publication of *Duel of Eagles* the third battle resumed, as seizing control of the Alamo from the DRT again became a cause célèbre in liberal circles. Carlos Guerra, a writer for the *San Antonio Express-News,* accused the DRT of mismanagement, claiming that the Alamo "was deteriorating rapidly. Age isn't the greatest culprit. DRT-installed air-conditioning and vehicular traffic is." By keeping the Alamo too cool, Guerra claimed, water vapor formed on the exterior limestone walls, which absorbed the moisture. Exhaust fumes from internal combustion engines mixed with the moisture, which damaged the walls. "We need professionals there." In 1993 Ronald Wilson resurrected his bill to shift jurisdiction over the Alamo from the DRT to the Parks and Wildlife Department, claiming that "Daffy Duck could run the Alamo. It's a no-brainer." State senator Gregory Luna filed legislation to place the Alamo under the control of the Texas Historical Commission.[29]

In 1994 San Antonio boosters suggested a major architectural renovation of the Alamo compound—demolishing several neighboring buildings and fast food joints and converting the grounds into a major historical park. Supporters argued that the change would attract more visitors to the city, and Native American and Hispanic activists promoted the idea. On March 21, 1994, Gary Gabehart, head of the Inter-Tribal Council of American Indians, staged a protest at the Alamo, proudly displaying an arrow and saying, "This is the arrow of truth, justice and historical fact." With his arms outstretched, Gabehart surveyed the Alamo and proclaimed, "This is *campo santo,*" or sacred earth, a burial site for Native Americans. By expanding the Alamo, the site could be recognized for what it was—holy ground.

Restoring the eighteenth-century mission would de-emphasize, in the words of historian Cynthia Orozco, "the Alamo [as] part of Anglo-American creation myth." A Hispanic journalist insisted, "Here's a mission that existed for 120 years and the only people you hear about had been in Texas for two months." The site would be rebuilt as an eighteenth-century Spanish mission, with a first-class museum and strategically placed interpretive exhibits explaining day-to-day mission activities. In the process, the events of March 6, 1836, would move backstage and the chapel would become part of a much larger complex. It was just what Clara Driscoll had opposed. The DRT responded by accusing proponents of wanting to create an "Alamoland" theme park that would destroy the shrine. DRT head Gail Loving Barnes remarked, "We have been content all these years to work to preserve the Alamo, the shrine of Texas liberty. . . . We will never give up, just to put it bluntly." DRT tenacity was nearly as well known around Texas as the Lone Star flag, prompting one longtime San Antonian to joke, "If the Daughters had been *at* the battle of the Alamo, Santa Anna would have been driven back to Mexico."[30]

The Daughters had learned the rules of late-twentieth-century politics, taking a cue from feminists and suggesting that the minority activists had a subtext of their own. What was really at the heart of the dispute, argued Ana Hartman, head of the DRT's Alamo Committee, was gender. "There's something macho about it," she insisted. "Some of the men who are attacking us just resent what has been a successful female venture since 1905." In truth, criticism of the Daughters had often reeked of gender bias. The nastiest voices accused the Daughters of transforming "redneck culture" into history and history into political power. One critic demeaningly insisted, "You can't always expect good management from a private organization whose leadership changes every two years. Sooner or later, you get some mudhead from out of town with a lot of weird ideas, just because it's good old Madge's or good old Nellie's turn." Professor Holly Beachly Brear, author of *Inherit the Alamo: Myth and Ritual at an American Shrine* (1994), told a San Antonio reporter, "For years, the Alamo was seen as not economically significant. Men were content to let women have it. Women were allowed to *preserve* history, but men are supposed to create it. Now the Daughters are being opposed because of the way they *present* history."[31]

Part of the new strength of the critics stemmed from the rising political power of Mexican Americans as an interest group. For sociologist Alvarado Valdez, "Mexican Americans do not view the Alamo as something that symbolizes some kind of symbol of freedom. . . . I still believe they see it as a symbol of racism." Chicano historian Rodolfo Acuña proclaimed the Alamo "the single most important source of racism toward Mexicans in this country." In 1992, while attending the convention of the National Association for Chicano Studies, he led a protest march on the Alamo, debated Alamo history with a DRT guide, pointed to children at the site, and told his students, "When you know the truth about the Alamo, I want you to get more than angry. Internalize that anger in a positive way. Learn the truth and one day come with children like those and tell them the truth."[32] As just one measure of new Mexican American political strength, the Mexican American Legal Defense and Education Fund (MALDEF), founded in San Antonio in 1968, had by the eighties become a grant recipient of major national foundations and had successfully waged a number of court battles.

Still, proposals to snatch the Alamo from the DRT left Texas's real power brokers unmoved. Governor George W. Bush cast his lot with tradition. In 1994 and again in 1995, he promised to veto any legislation to alter DRT custodianship of the Alamo. "I'd veto it. I believe the Daughters ought to run it. I don't believe it ought to become part of a state agency, and I think it's the best way to preserve the historic significance not only for Texas but for San Antonio."[33]

But the Daughters were also savvy enough to realize that unless they played the political game with more sophistication, self-defense would become a full-time job. "We have an image problem, and I'm trying to change that," admitted Bernice Everitt, president of the DRT Alamo Mission Chapter. Although the Daughters would not compromise on their conviction that the Alamo was a monument to heroic virtues, they did broaden their horizons. John Wayne, for example, loomed large in the culture wars, even though he had died in 1979. Many liberals considered Wayne and the DRT to be fellow travelers in marketing mythology. Back in 1959, during the filming of *The Alamo,* Wayne's publicity crew commissioned an oil painting showing him as Davy Crockett atop an Alamo wall battling Mexican soldiers. The painting was used to fashion promotional posters, and when the film premiered in October 1960, Wayne gave it to the DRT. The DRT proudly displayed it in the gift shop.

It remained there until 1987, when the Daughters quietly moved the painting out of public sight to the foyer of their offices. Critics charged that the painting had for years hung in the shrine itself, an accusation the Daughters bitterly denied. In 1994, when the authors of *John Wayne's "The Alamo"* scheduled a book signing at the Alamo, the Daughters debated whether or not to put the painting back on display. Several DRT leaders worried that bringing it back would trigger a hostile reaction. In the end, they decided to make it part of an exhibit in the gift shop entitled "The Alamo Through the Eyes of Hollywood."[34]

Other changes were afoot as well. In 1994–95, the DRT erected markers to Adina De Zavala and recognized her, along with Clara Driscoll, as an early-twentieth-century savior of the Alamo. A similar marker identified the Alamo grounds as a burial site for eighteenth-century Native Americans. In 1994, the DRT began sponsoring "Bravo at the Alamo," a series of folk dances and displays representing the contributions of Native Americans, Canary Islanders, and Mexican Americans to Alamo history. An Alamo History Seminar at the compound allowed scholars to freely discuss the past and to suggest that dozens of defenders remain unrecognized. And by the late 1990s, the annual March 6 anniversary of the fall of the Alamo had all but become a multicultural event. With historical reenactors from the San Antonio Living History Association gathered in period costumes as Mexican soldiers and Alamo defenders, the official activities began with prayers offered in English and Spanish, and an official script acknowledging that on March 6, 1836, the representatives of "two great peoples" sacrificed their lives in a heroic struggle that rendered the Alamo "sacred ground."[35]

Cultural conflict over the Alamo soon spread from Austin and San Antonio to other Texas communities. Adina De Zavala had spent a lifetime getting public schools named after the defenders, and the same groups who wanted to wrest control of the Alamo from the DRT also wanted to end Texas's obsession with them. In 1988, when the school board in Austin, Texas, opened hearings on whether to name a new high school after Jim Bowie, the local chapter of the National Association for the Advancement of Colored People picketed the meeting, insisting that black children "should not have to attend a school named after a man who smuggled slaves." One year later, the school board in Bryan, Texas, considered naming a new elementary school after William Barret Travis. Walter Buenger, a professor at nearby Texas A&M University, reminded board members that Travis had abandoned his pregnant wife before coming to Texas, that he had owned and trafficked in slaves, and that he had been a notorious womanizer, hardly a role model for children. Others appearing before the school board, of course, defended Travis as a hero, but in the end the board bypassed the name of William Travis because "his character was too flawed." A similar dispute erupted in Dallas, Texas, in 1999 when the NAACP demanded that Bowie Elementary School be renamed.[36]

*

If the left had gained power, so had the far right. During the 1990s, the siege of March 6, 1836, became a symbolic beacon for right-wing extremists involved in the militia movement. In August 1992, when FBI agents tried to serve a summons to Randy Weaver, a conservative Christian survivalist in Ruby Ridge, Idaho, who had sold two illegally sawed-off shotguns, leading to a siege of his remote cabin for eleven days, many Texans drew the obvious comparison. Weaver defied the federal agents, and a gunfight erupted, leaving a government agent and Weaver's son dead. FBI sharpshooters then proceeded to kill Weaver's wife and wound him. In a subsequent trial, Weaver was acquitted of murder charges, and the radical right had a poster boy.[37]

In the spring of 1993, when federal agents raided the Branch Davidian compound outside Waco, Texas, the participants themselves made the connection. David Koresh, a charismatic religious cult leader, had gathered eighty-four of his followers into a compound, where he preached an apocalyptic, end-of-the-world Christianity. On a tip that Koresh bought and sold illegal guns, federal agents approached the compound with a search warrant. Koresh denied them entry, and in the ensuing gun battle, six Branch Davidians and four federal agents were killed. Government agents then laid siege to the compound. Throughout Texas, conservatives raised the specter of the Alamo, and so did Texas native David Koresh, who saw himself not only as divine but also as a modern-day reincarnation of Davy Crockett or Jim Bowie or William Travis, under siege by a vastly superior army of federal agents. "This is just like the Alamo," he told one of his followers. "I will never surrender." In this case, Koresh was prophetic. The Branch Davidians held out for fifty-one days until federal agents and troops, equipped with tanks, armored personnel carriers, and incendiary bombs, launched an assault that took the lives of seventy-five people, including several dozen children. Few Texans sympathized with Koresh's unusual religious views, but many were convinced that a dangerous federal government had surpassed its authority once again.[38]

Texas produced its own militias. In the spring of 1997, newspapers and talk shows crackled with descriptions of the so-called Republic of Texas, a secessionist group convinced that Texas had been illegally annexed in 1845 by the United States. Like other militia groups, the Republic of Texas nurtured political opinions that would have made Governor George Wallace of Alabama look liberal. They hated the federal government, gun control laws, large corporations, banks, stock exchanges, checking accounts, credit cards, and every other political and economic reflection of modern society, and they claimed to be free of state and local laws.

Early in May 1997, Republic of Texas leader Richard L. McLaren announced that he would stage a "second Alamo" to resist arrest warrants issued on him. But instead of mission walls and a limestone chapel, his Alamo was a ramshackle house trailer in the high desert foothills of the Davis Mountains of west Texas. The trailer was stocked with guns, junk food, and such videos as *The Alamo, Thelma and Louise,* and *The Wild Bunch.* McLaren first became intoxicated with Alamo rhetoric as a third-grader in Illinois, when he wrote an essay about the siege. The Republic of Texas movement counted far more guns than members, but McLaren's followers identified viscerally with Travis, Crockett, and Bowie. "This is his Alamo, and he believes he's Davy Crockett," said the brother of Mike Matson, one of McLaren's most devoted disciples. They did not hold out as long as Koresh. McLaren ran short of Twinkies and beer after just a week, and with the grudging cooperation of Texas state troopers, he surrendered in a mock military ceremony.[39]

★

By now, the Alamo was everyone's favorite symbol. Presidents embraced it, from Ronald Reagan's reference in his second inaugural address to the "men of the Alamo [who] call out encouragement to each other" to George Bush's notation in his diary in response to Iraq's invasion of Kuwait: "I think we can draw a line in the sand—draw it in the sand of American belief." Candidates embraced it, from Pat Robertson broadcasting an episode of *The 700 Club* from there in 1986 to George W. Bush reading Travis's "VICTORY or DEATH" letter to America's Ryder Cup golf team in 1999. Iconoclastic intellectual Michael Lind even wrote an epic poem about it, which was dismissed by reviewer Garry Wills in the *New York Times* as a thing "not worth doing."[40]

In 1998, when the family of the late John Peace, an Austin rare books dealer, decided to sell the de la Peña diary, a firestorm erupted. Many major newspapers and newsmagazines in the United States, Great Britain, Mexico, Italy, Spain, and Germany, as well as television news and radio talk shows, debated how Davy had died, how the Alamo should be remembered, and whether the diary was authentic. Rumors circulated that a right-wing cabal of Davy Crockett cultists had raised a fortune to buy the manuscript and then burn it. Professor James Crisp, a North Carolina State University professor whose meticulous research had long since concluded that the de la Peña manuscript was authentic, worried that "some right-wing nut case will put down a bunch of money and then throw it in the fireplace." To keep the diary in the state, the University of Texas decided to participate in the auction. When the bidding started, the price rocketed up in $25,000 increments, quickly pushing UT out of the bidding. Eventually, however, two wealthy alums put in the top bid of $387,500 and subsequently donated the manuscript to the university. Two years later, in the spring of 2000, the University of Texas announced the results of an exhaustive investigation of the document, concluding that the ink and the paper on which it had been written had been manufactured in Portugal in the early 1800s and had been commonly used in Mexican army correspondence, and that the paper had not been treated by modern chemicals, a common tactic of forgers. But even that evidence could not convince true believers. The controversy was not about to die, remarked historian Edward Linenthal, because "what people have invested in this debate is . . . a genuine passion for how the story of Texas is written and how it affects real life."[41]

The extraordinary interest and controversy surrounding the diary stunned the directors of Butterfield & Butterfield, the Los Angeles auction that had handled the sale. "It's the weirdest thing I've ever seen," remarked a spokesman. "We're sitting out here in California scratching our heads, going what the heck? . . . We didn't anticipate this. We didn't have the faintest idea what we were in for." James Crisp could have anticipated the obsession. "What you're looking at is an icon inside an icon. It's the icon of Crockett inside the icon of the Alamo. The Alamo is a significant part of the American mythic narrative of how we became a nation, and Davy

Crockett is the most famous person at the Alamo. It's a pretty emotional subject for most people."[42]

★

The mystery of Davy's death will live on, no matter the fate of the diary. The stakes held in all competing versions are simply too high. Never mind that a surrender and execution is hardly less honorable or less tragic or less inspiring than fighting to the death. In John Sayles's 1996 film *Lone Star,* the filmmaker tried to suggest a resolution. Set in the south Texas of the 1990s, a time when school boards are debating who were the heroes of the Alamo and the Hispanic majority is asserting its political power, Sheriff Sam Deeds discovers the murdered body of Sheriff Charlie Wade, the very symbol of the ruthless Anglo conqueror, a man whose Colt .45 Peacemaker was singularly misnamed. Sam suspects his own father, Sheriff Buddy Deeds, of the crime, and he is forced to confront the meaning of his father's life. Though Buddy Deeds was more politically sophisticated and less violent than Charlie Wade, was he any less corrupt or racist? What Sam uncovers is as ambiguous as it is complex. Buddy was a racist who loved his Hispanic mistress, a pawn of the Anglo elite who aided his town's African Americans and Mexican Americans. By the end of the film, the heroine concludes that the past is a burden to the future. "Start from scratch," she tells Sam. "Forget the Alamo."

Forget the Alamo. In an age of multiculturalism and shifting political alliances, the past is a handicap. What happened at the Alamo, the absolute clarity of the choices and the issues, simply seemed, for many, out of touch with the end of the century. But others believed that Americans could forget the Alamo only at their peril. At an anniversary celebration of the battle of the Alamo, historian T. R. Fehrenbach warned that any "age that does not exalt courage will be confounded by the Alamo, and baffled by the men who stayed in it. Any age that fears war more than servitude, or death more than honor, must denigrate the Alamo. Ages that do not honor the concept of liberty or death will fight no Alamos. Ages that do not cling to the great values of love, honor, courage, and sacrifice, the soldier values, will not only fail to remember the Alamo, they may not long endure."[43]

Forget the Alamo? That'll be the day.

EPILOGUE

———— ✯ ————

Around 4:30 A.M., like ghosts emerging from the dark in twos and threes, they solemnly began to gather, clustering in small knots near the benches and oak trees in front of the Alamo. Unlike the original defenders, who had been doing anything they could on March 6, 1836, to keep warm and get some sleep, the modern-day pilgrims approached the shrine carrying sweaters and coats but not wearing them. The wind was blowing from the southeast, not the north. Nobody had to bundle up, breathe into clutched fists, or keep moving to stay warm.

The ghosts came on March 6, 1999, for the last anniversary of the twentieth century. They were true believers, men and women who loved history, who had cast their lot with a state and embraced its identity. As on every March 6, several had come from great distances—Los Angeles, London, San Francisco, Cleveland, and Seattle—proving the old adage that life might pull people out of Texas but could never get Texas out of them. Many got their directions from the Alamo's recorded telephone message, which, after explaining how to exit the nearby interstates, reminded listeners that since 1905 the Daughters of the Republic of Texas have been entrusted by the Texas state legislature to maintain the Alamo "as a sacred memorial to those heroes who immolated themselves upon that hallowed ground."

Prominent in the crowd were public school teachers, spiritual descendants of Adina De Zavala, each accompanied by a few favorite students.
A young mother appeared with three little boys in tow, each dressed in
T-shirt and jeans, with the cuffs folded up several inches. Coonskin caps
covered their heads and buckskin vests draped their chests. Strapped to
their left shoulders were toy replicas of Davy Crockett's "Pretty Betsey"
long rifle; on their right shoulders were plastic powder horns. Except for
the Payless boots, they looked like they had just marched out of Frontierland in the 1950s. The one person truly out of place was a wino startled
from his mumbling slumber by the unusual noise. He stumbled over to
the oak trees, hungover but not wanting to miss an opportunity to pan-
handle a few coins, enough at least for a sausage biscuit at the nearby
McDonald's or an early bottle of Boone's Farm. His clothes—darkened
by grime that must have bonded molecularly with the fabric—probably
had not been washed, or even changed, in months. San Antonio summers had
blistered his head and neck into a deep reddish brown. No sooner had he
hit on his first mark than a San Antonio cop hustled him away.

In hushed voices, the pilgrims speculated on what it must have been
like 163 years ago. The bugles had blown just before first light creased the
eastern horizon, and for half an hour or so, the cacophony of battle—artillery booming, sabers rattling, muskets firing, and men screaming and
groaning—had sounded a symphony of death. By first light it was over,
except for Mexican soldiers converting a battle into a massacre by shooting and bayoneting the last few breathing defenders. The modern visitors
tried to recapture those moments. They knew more history than most,
and their fingers pointed to likely spots—where Mexican soldiers had
breached the north wall, where the palisade had protected the chapel,
where Davy might have died, where Travis might have drawn his line,
where Bowie was killed, where the funeral pyre consumed the corpses.

A little after 5 A.M., some thirty reenactors from the San Antonio Living History Association—some in the bright colors of Mexican military
dress uniforms and others in Anglo-Texan buckskins—mustered into separate lines. The last of the actors to appear was Santa Anna's body double, a young, handsome Hispanic man whose dignity and charisma would
have pleased *el presidente*. One visitor, no doubt a first-timer, wondered
if the morning's activities would include a reenactment; the query raised
a smirk or two. There would be, of course, no reenactment. Downtown

San Antonio had crowded in on the Alamo, and little remained of the original compound except the chapel. There was no room left to stage the battle. And a realistic re-creation of the events of March 6, 1836, would have required a cast of thousands. Anything less would look silly. Only John Wayne in 1960 had ever really tried to do the battle justice. Besides, for the DRT, a noisy, touristy anniversary reenactment would have been sacrilege anyway. The ground here is sacred. A passion play is one thing, a reenactment of crucifixion quite another.

Around 5:25 A.M., the doors to the Alamo chapel opened and an honor guard of the Daughters of the Republic of Texas solemnly paraded out. The crowd quieted immediately; the very presence of Daughters evoked reverence. Just before first light, exactly 163 years after the bugles had sounded, the ceremony began. Invocations in Spanish and English, delivered by a Protestant pastor and a Catholic priest, requested the approbation of heaven and acknowledged the blessings of the past. Honor guards, with dignity and respect, smartly presented the Mexican, American, and Republic of Texas colors. Wreaths were laid at the base of the cenotaph. The main speaker reminded all present that 163 years ago, the "soldiers of two great peoples did battle here, and we gather to honor their sacrifice." The ceremony reflected a clarity and simplicity the Daughters had long nurtured. By 6 A.M. it was all over, just like the battle they had remembered that morning.

The crowd dispersed, back to hotels for naps or off to local greasy spoons for breakfast. During the course of the next three hours, a new generation of heavily armed defenders assumed their posts. San Antonio police showed up in powder blue uniforms, as did state troopers in DPS gray. To bolster their own beige-uniformed Alamo police, the Daughters had hired a platoon of private security. The new defenders were overwhelmingly Hispanic, their plastic ID badges bearing such names as García, Gómez, Mendez, Guajardo, Martínez, and López. By 1999, San Antonio had become more than 60 percent Hispanic, a number destined for geometric increase. Without firing a shot, Tejanos had won back the Alamo.

By 9 A.M., the first of what would eventually become more than fifteen thousand visitors that day strolled back and forth between the Alamo chapel, the DRT Library, and the rest rooms at the back of the complex. Orange school buses from around the state soon disgorged an army of junior high schoolers, most of them deeply absorbed in the sounds emanating from portable CD players. In an age of sophisticated electronic games, theme and water parks, and music videos, there is little at the Alamo to keep the attention of a thirteen-year-old. Most immediately recognized the Alamo chapel and stopped short, momentarily stunned in their tracks, to examine it. They quit talking for a few seconds, then pointed and chattered and moved toward the chapel doors. "Hey, that's where Davy bought it," exclaimed one boy to his friend. "I saw it in the movie with that old cowboy."

All day long, schoolteachers fought the good fight, trying to hold pop culture at bay. It seemed a losing battle. Teaching history to most children is like trying to explain what it's like to have cancer. Until it's happened to you, you cannot really understand. A handful tuned in, listening intently to the guides and not needing to be shushed by their teachers when entering the Alamo chapel, but most found the gift shop the best stop on the tour. One long-suffering teacher explained to an exhausted, discouraged colleague, who had spent the day telling kids far more than they ever wanted to know about the Alamo, "Don't lose hope! All we can expect is that when they go home tonight, they'll remember that once upon a time, real men died for a worthy cause."

Missionaries of another stripe fought their battles on the Alamo grounds that Saturday, rejecting the prevailing consensus and hoping for converts to their version of the truth. A pudgy middle-aged man with long gray hair, braided Indian style, worked the crowd on behalf of Native Americans. He was, no doubt, self-appointed, claiming to be Comanche and insisting that the bones of his ancestors were buried at the Alamo. He looked like an Anglo. The fact that the Comanches had arrived relatively late on the central plains of Texas did not preoccupy him, nor did the fact that they most decidedly had not been part of the mission Indians in Spanish days. His passion was inversely related to his blood quantum. He vilified Spaniards, Mexicans, and whites, blaming all three for plundering and wiping out Texas's indigenous people. "The Spaniards and Mexicans," he preached to anyone who would listen, "were just as bad as the whites. They laid waste to my people. The United States only did to Mexico what Spain and Mexico did to us." Waxing apocalyptic, he then warned, "Perhaps in the not so distant future, Americans will get theirs. Somebody bigger and better and stronger is going to come along and take all this from them." A security guard escorted the "Comanche" from the premises.

After lunch, an Anglo graduate student from the University of Texas, filled with passionate intensity, showed up at Alamo Plaza on a personal crusade to convert laymen to the New Western History. Plain, metal-rimmed glasses rested down on his nose, and his goatee was trimmed à la Leon Trotsky. He was a bit too portly for Trotsky; radical chic had not worked its way to his physique. He considered the annual Alamo com-memoration a travesty. He compared the Alamo to the Holocaust, with the defenders standing in for the Nazis. "Celebrating Davy Crockett and Jim Bowie," he lectured, "is like holding a birthday party for Adolf Hitler. Texas should be ashamed of itself." Holding out a copy of Jeff Long's *Duel of Eagles,* he repeated again and again, "Here is the truth, not the white-washed tripe the DRT is dishing out. They won't even sell this book in the gift shop." Despite his grandiose vocabulary—"racism," "imperialism," "colonialism," "Holocaust," and "genocide"—nobody listened, and he grew increasingly disheartened. He then took a break from his missionary endeavors and headed across Crockett Street to the Häagen-Dazs shop.

After lunch a bright red Lincoln Navigator pulled up to Crockett Street and out jumped a Hispanic mother with three girls, ranging in age from eight to twelve. Her husband parked the car in a nearby lot and returned bearing a video camera. The three daughters, dressed in matching white pullovers and Gap skirts, were striking. Their father, a CPA with a Whar-ton degree, posed his family in front of the limestone walls of the chapel and triggered the camera. They waved on cue but smiled spontaneously, obviously delighted to be where they were. He then told them briefly about the Alamo, delivering the Daughters' version of the battle, and he let his girls know that it stood for courage and integrity, virtues they needed to cultivate in their own lives.

At that point, the Anglo graduate student arrived at the chapel door. He asked, "Why are you even here today? Don't you know what this place stands for? It represents the rape and destruction of your people." Looking just the least bit annoyed, the Hispanic man politely replied, "We're not so bad off, you know." The Anglo student was persistent. "You don't understand, you just don't understand," he continued. "You shouldn't be teaching your kids this stuff." The CPA stopped short. "*Es-cúcheme, bolillo* [Listen to me, white bread]," he said sharply. "If Santa

Anna would have won the war, this whole city would be a shithole just like Reynosa. *Soy tejano* [I'm a Texan]. Mind your own goddamned business. It's my Alamo too."

Two other men stood out in sharp relief on March 6, 1999. Wearing loose-fitting, flower-printed cotton shirts and plaid Bermuda shorts, with cheap sneakers and black socks stretching up to their knees, they looked like they had just come from a shuffleboard tournament in Atlantic City. One of them appeared mentally off. He was too young for the shell shock of World War I, too old for Vietnam's post-traumatic stress disorder. Perhaps he suffered from World War II's battle fatigue. But on closer examination, his troubles appeared to be of more recent vintage. An expressionless face and rheumy eyes revealed a terminal case of bewilderment, and his feet danced the Alzheimer's shuffle. Locked arm in arm and marching to a very slow cadence, the two former comrades moved about carefully, one doing all the talking, the other all the listening. They were devoted to each other.

Both men wore olive green baseball caps bearing the logo "Semper Fi." Fifty-six years before, they had fought in the Marine Corps's bloodiest battle, storming the coconut logs of Tarawa in the Pacific. Just teenagers, they were in the first wave to hit the beach, and Japanese defenders exacted a terrible toll, killing and wounding 90 percent of the men in those unlucky rifle companies. Their caps stood as monuments of their own, simple statements of fact that when their country drew a line in the sand, the boys crossed over, knowing full well that they might not survive. Death was not the worst of alternatives. Both men, even the wounded one, radiated a special glow in front of the Alamo. Old soldiers understand sacred ground.

"They stayed and fought here," the talker told his muted brother. "They could have made a run for it but didn't."

"Yeh," the other replied.

"They knew they didn't have a prayer, but they fought on anyway."

"Yeh."

"They all died."

"Yeh."

"God, what men they must have been."

"Yeh."

NOTES

PROLOGUE

1. Thomas Ricks Lindley, "James Butler Bonham: October 17, 1835–March 6, 1836," *Alamo Journal*, August 1988.
2. Fox Butterfield, *All God's Children: The Bosket Family and the American Tradition of Violence* (1995), 7.
3. James Butler Bonham to Sam Houston, December 1, 1835, in John H. Jenkins, ed., *The Papers of the Texas Revolution 1835–1836* (1973), III:61.
4. Lon Tinkle, *The Alamo* (1958), 110–11. There remains some dispute among historians about Bonham's presence in the Alamo, but historian Stephen L. Hardin, the premier scholar of the military history of the Texas Revolution, makes a good case for Bonham's departure from the Alamo on February 16, 1836, and his return on March 3. See Stephen L. Hardin, "Where Was Bonham?" http://home.flash.net/~alamo3/archives/articles/bonham/bonham.htm.

CHAPTER 1. IN THE FOOTSTEPS OF HISTORY

1. Jeff Long, *Duel of Eagles: The Mexican and U.S. Fight for the Alamo* (1990), 91.
2. Ruth R. Olivera and Liliane Crété, *Life in Mexico Under Santa Anna, 1822–1855* (1991), 113–17.
3. Quoted in Enrique Krauze, *Mexico. Biography of Power: A History of Modern Mexico, 1810–1996*, trans. Hank Heifetz (1997), 141.
4. José C. Valadés, *México, Santa Anna y la guerra de Texas* (1982), 97; Antonio López de Santa Anna, *The Eagle*, ed. Ann Fears Crawford (1967), 245. Santa Anna quoted in Krauze, *Mexico*, vii.
5. Quoted in Olivera and Crété, *Life in Mexico Under Santa Anna*, 112.
6. Robert A. Potash, "Testamentos de Santa Anna," *Historia Mexicana* 13 (1964): 428–40.

7. Fanny Calderón de la Barca, *Life in Mexico During a Residence of Two Years in That Country* (1843), 31–33.

8. Quoted in Wilfrid Hardy Callcott, *Santa Anna: The Story of an Enigma Who Once Was Mexico* (1936), 7–8.

9. José Fuentes Mares, *Santa Anna, el hombre* (1984), 24–25; Lorenzo De Zavala, "El Historiador y el representante popular: Ensayo crítico de las revoluciones de México desde 1808 hasta 1830," *Obras históricas* (1969), 113.

10. Quoted in Fernando Díaz Díaz, *Caudillos y caciques* (1972), 86. Also see Harold Dana Sims, *The Expulsion of Mexico's Spaniards 1821–1836* (1990), 152–59; Romeo Flores Caballero, *La contrarevolución en la independencia: Los españoles en la vida política, social, y económica de México (1804–1838)* (1969), 160–65; Calderón de la Barca, *Life in Mexico*, 439–41.

11. Callcott, *Santa Anna*, 7–8; Basil Hedrick, J. Charles Kelley, and Carroll L. Riley, eds., *The North Mexican Frontier: Readings in Archaeology, Ethnohistory, and Ethnography* (1971), 50–72; Ross Hassig, *War and Society in Ancient Mesoamerica* (1978), 119–20; Lorenzo De Zavala, "El Historiador," 56.

12. Quoted in Krauze, *Mexico*, 28.

13. Quoted in S. Jeffrey Wilkerson, "Following Cortés: Path to Conquest," *National Geographic* 166 (October 1984): 445–46.

14. Ibid., 448.

15. *Diario del Gobierno*, August 5, 1837; Calderón de la Barca, *Life in Mexico*, 460–62; John Lynch, *Caudillos in Spanish America 1800–1850* (1992), 320.

16. Michael P. Costeloe, *The Central Republic in Mexico, 1835–1846* (1993), 31–50; Sims, *The Expulsion of Mexico's Spaniards*, 3–31.

17. *Fénix de la Libertad*, June 4, 1834.

18. M. Dublán and J. M. Lozano, eds., *Legislación mexicana* (1876), III:3, 38; Basilio José Arrillaga, *Recopilacíon de leyes, directos, bandos, reglamentos, circulares, y providencias de los supremos poderes y otras autoridades de la república mexicana* (1844), 186–97; *El Sol*, February 26 and 28, 1835; *El Mosquito Mexicano*, April 3, 1835.

19. Quoted in A. A. Greene, trans. and ed., "The Battle of Zacatecas," *Texana* 7 (1969): 192.

20. José Antonio Serrano Ortega, *El contingente de sangre: Los gobiernos estatales y departamentos y los métodos de reclutamiento del ejército permanente mexicano, 1824–1844* (1933), 60–61; José María Bocanegra, *Memorias para la historia de México independiente* (1986), II:603; Eliseo Rangel Gaspar, *Francisco García Salinas: "Tata Pachito"* (1984), 241–42; *El Sol* (Zacatecas), February 24, 1835, and April 10, 1835; *El Telégrafo*, June 22, 1834.

21. Greene, "The Battle of Zacatecas," 196.

22. John H. Jenkins, ed., *The Papers of the Texas Revolution 1835–1836* (1973), I:194–97.

23. Elizabeth Andros Foster, ed., *Motolinia's History of the Indians of New Spain* (1950), 25–26; Philip Wayne Powell, *Soldiers, Indians, and Silver: The Northward Advance of New Spain, 1550–1600* (1952), 10–12, 227–30. Also see Peter John Bakewell, *Silver Mining and Society in Colonial Mexico: Zacatecas, 1546–1700* (1971); E. L. Blichfeldt, *A Mexican Journey* (1919), 228–29.

24. For a brilliant account of Spanish imperial expansion in North America, see David J. Weber, *The Spanish Frontier in North America* (1992).

25. Charles E. Cobb, "Mexico's Bajío–The Heartland," *National Geographic* 178 (December 1990): 122–43.

26. Hugh M. Hamill Jr., *The Hidalgo Revolt* (1966), 209–11; John Collis and David M. Jones, *Mexico* (1997), 529; Juan E. Hernández y Dávalos, *Colleción de documentos para la historia de la guerra de independencia*, 6 vols. (1877–1882), 1:119–30; 2:402–410; Krauze, *Mexico*, 97.

NOTES

27. José M. de la Fuente, *Hidalgo íntimo* (1910), 528–30; Hamill, *The Hidalgo Revolt,* 216; Krauze, *Mexico,* 97–102.
28. José María Luis Mora, *Méjico y sus revoluciones* (1836), IV:264–66, 445–49.
29. Quoted in Krauze, *Mexico,* 121–23.
30. Valadés, *México, Santa Anna y la guerra de Texas,* 119; Elías Amador, *Bosquejo histórico de Zacatecas* (1943), II:415.
31. Terry Pindell, *Yesterday's Train: A Rail Odyssey Through Mexican History* (1997), 158–59; Donald Fithian Stevens, *Origins of Instability in Early Republican Mexico* (1991), 40, 76–77.
32. For the battle of Zacatecas, see Amador, *Bosquejo histórico,* II:403–30; Rangel Gaspar, *Francisco García Salinas,* 241–61; Emilio Rodríguez Flores, *Compendio histórico de Zacatecas* (1977), 70–75, 214–15; Jesús Flores Olague, Mercedes D. Vega, Sandra Kuntz Ficker, and Laura del Alizal, *Breve historia de Zacatecas* (1991), 110–11; Arnoldo Grácia, *Zacatecas* (1910), 22–45.
33. Pindell, *Yesterday's Train,* 195–96.
34. For brilliant discussions of tactics and weapons in the Army of Operations, see Stephen L. Hardin, *Texian Iliad: A Military History of the Texas Revolution* (1994).
35. For the equipment and arms of the Army of Operations, see Angelina Nieto, Joseph Hefter, and Mrs. John Nicholas Brown, *El soldado mexicano, 1837–1847: Organización, vestuario, equipo* (1958); Greene, "The Battle of Zacatecas," 196–97.
36. Amador, *Bosquejo histórico,* II:403–18; Rangel Gaspar, *Francisco García Salinas,* 247–49.
37. Rodríguez Flores, *Compendio histórico de Zacatecas,* 70–75, 214–15; Salvador Vidal, *La Imprenta y el periodismo en Zacatecas* (1949), 5; Flores Olague et al., *Breve historia de Zacatecas,* 110–11; Fayette Robinson, *Mexico and Her Military Chieftains from the Revolution of Hidalgo to the Present Time* (1847), 174; Carlos Macías, "La minería en Fresnillo durante el gobierno de Francisco García Salinas," *Relaciones: Estudios de historia y sociedad* 19 (Spring 1988): 31–54; Amador, *Bosquejo histórico,* II:418–25.
38. Josefina Zoraida Vázquez, *Don Antonio López de Santa Anna: Mito y enigmo* (1987), 22–23; Rafael F. Muñoz, *Antonio López de Santa Anna* (1937), 104; Amador, *Bosquejo histórico,* II:419.
39. Amador, *Bosquejo histórico,* II:422; Valadés, *México, Santa Anna y la guerra de Texas,* 120.

CHAPTER 2. "THE FREE BORN SONS OF AMERICA"

1. William C. Davis, *Three Roads to the Alamo: The Lives and Fortunes of David Crockett, James Bowie, and William Barret Travis* (1998), 190–202.
2. John Spencer Bassett, ed., *Correspondence of Andrew Jackson,* 3 vols. (1926–33), I:220.
3. Alexis de Tocqueville, *Democracy in America,* ed. J. P. Mayer and Max Lerner (1966), 215.
4. Alexis de Tocqueville, *Democracy in America,* ed. Richard D. Heffner (1956), 139, 142; *Democracy in America,* ed. Mayer and Lerner, 375.
5. W. W. Newcomb Jr., *The Indians of Texas* (1961), 335; Armando C. Alonzo, *Tejano Legacy: Rancheros and Settlers in South Texas, 1734–1900* (1998), 53–55. For additional accounts of the the Spanish conquest of south Texas, see Hodding Carter, *Doomed Road of Empire: The Spanish Trail of Conquest* (1963); Sandra Myers, *The Ranch in Spanish Texas* (1969); Oakah L. Jones, *Los Paisanos: Span-

ish Settlers on the Northern Frontier of New Spain (1979); David J. Weber, *The Spanish Frontier in North America* (1992).

6. Nettie Lee Benson, "Texas As Viewed from Mexico, 1820–1834," *Southwestern Historical Quarterly* 90 (January 1987): 220.

7. Mary Virginia Henderson, "Minor Empresario Contracts for Colonization, 1825–1834," *Southwestern Historical Quarterly* 31 (April 1928): 295–324; 32 (July 1928): 1–28; Gregg Cantrell, *Stephen F. Austin: Empresario of Texas* (1999), 174–75, 198–99, 223–24.

8. C. E. Castañeda, trans., "Statistical Report on Texas by Juan N. Almonte," *Southwestern Historical Quarterly* 27 (January 1925): 179.

9. Maurine T. Wilson and Jack Jackson, *Philip Nolan and Texas: Expeditions into the Unknown Land, 1791–1801* (1987).

10. James R. Jacobs, *Tarnished Warrior: Major-General James Wilkinson* (1938).

11. Henry P. Walker, ed., "William McLane's Narrative of the Magee-Gutiérrez Expedition, 1812–1813," *Southwestern Historical Quarterly* 66 (January 1963): 457–79; 66 (October 1962): 234–51; Felix D. Almaraz, *Tragic Cavalier: Governor Manuel Salcedo of Texas, 1808–1813* (1971); Harry McCorry Henderson, "The Magee-Gutiérrez Expedition," *Southwestern Historical Quarterly* 55 (July 1951): 43–61.

12. Harris Gaylord Warren, "The Origin of General Mina's Invasion of Mexico," *Southwestern Historical Quarterly* 42 (July 1938): 1–20, and "Xavier Mina's Invasion of Mexico," *Hispanic American Historical Review* 23 (February 1943): 52–76.

13. John Henry Brown, *Long's Expedition* (1930); Harris Gaylord Warren, *The Sword Was Their Passport: A History of American Filibustering in the Mexican Revolution* (1943); Frank L. Owsley Jr. and Gene A. Smith, *Filibusters and Expansionists: Jeffersonian Manifest Destiny, 1800–1821* (1997).

14. Zozaya quoted in Benson, "Texas As Viewed from Mexico," 235; Robert V. Remini, *Andrew Jackson and the Course of American Democracy, 1833–1845* (1984), 151–52; Samuel Flagg Bemis, *John Quincy Adams and the Foundations of American Foreign Policy* (1949), 563–64; James C. Curtis, *Andrew Jackson and the Search for Vindication* (1976), 173.

15. Jordan Holt, "The Edwards Empresarial Grant and the Fredonia Rebellion" (M.A. thesis, Stephen F. Austin State University, 1977).

16. Cantrell, *Stephen F. Austin*, 190–93, 200, 203–4. For the best analysis of the centrality of slavery in early Texas history, see Randolph B. Campbell, *An Empire for Slavery: The Peculiar Institution in Texas, 1821–1865* (1989).

17. Jack Jackson, ed., and John Wheat, trans., *Texas by Terán: The Diary Kept by General Manuel de Mier y Terán on His 1828 Inspection of Texas* (2000), 33–36.

18. Ibid., 178–79. For a discussion of the fundamental issues dividing Texans and Mexico City, see Paul D. Lack, *The Texas Revolutionary Experience: A Political and Social History, 1835–1836* (1992), 3–16.

19. Quoted in Cantrell, *Stephen F. Austin*, 219–21, 270–75.

20. Ibid., 291.

21. Margaret S. Henson, *Anahuac in 1832: The Cradle of the Texas Revolution* (1982), and *Juan Davis Bradburn: A Reappraisal of the Mexican Commander of Anahuac* (1982); Davis, *Three Roads to the Alamo*, 262–74.

22. Davis, *Three Roads to the Alamo*, 274; Cantrell, *Stephen F. Austin*, 256–60.

23. Ibid., 278.

24. Cantrell, *Stephen F. Austin*, 261–65.

25. Ibid., 271.

26. Davis, *Three Roads to the Alamo*, 369–76.

27. Davis, *Three Roads to the Alamo*, 450–58; John H. Jenkins, ed., *The Papers of*

the Texas Revolution 1835–1836 (1973), I:90–93, 232–33, 247, 294–98, 381–82.

28. Quoted in Davis, *Three Roads to the Alamo*, 456–57.
29. Cantrell, *Stephen F. Austin*, 286–314; Jenkins, *Papers*, I:359–62, 423–27, 465–66.
30. Cos quoted in Craig H. Roell, *Remember Goliad!* (1994), 36; Cantrell, *Stephen F. Austin*, 286–314; Jenkins, *Papers*, I:359–62, 423–27, 465–66; José Ramón Malo, *Diario de sucesos notables, 1832–1853* (1948), I:104.
31. Henderson Yoakum, *History of Texas from Its First Settlement in 1685 to Its Annexation to the United States in 1846* (1855), 334–35; Jenkins, *Papers*, I:197–98; Dudley G. Wooten, ed., *A Comprehensive History of Texas, 1685 to 1897* (1989), I:173–76.
32. Cantrell, *Stephen F. Austin*, 315; Davis, *Three Roads to the Alamo*, 461.
33. Quoted in Stephen L. Hardin, *Texian Iliad: A Military History of the Texas Revolution* (1994), 15.
34. Malo, *Diario de sucesos notables*, I:104; James W. Pohl and Stephen L. Hardin, "The Military History of the Texas Revolution: An Overview," *Southwestern Historical Quarterly* 89 (January 1986): 287–88.
35. Quoted in Alwyn Barr, *Texans in Revolt: The Battle for San Antonio, 1835* (1990), 6.
36. Noah Smithwick, *The Evolution of a State; or, Recollections of Old Texas Days* (1900), 72, 75. Smithwick's recollections, dictated to his daughter when he was almost ninety years old, are colorful (and useful) but not always reliable.
37. Ibid., 77; Davis, *Three Roads to the Alamo*, 440–43.
38. *A Visit to Texas, Being the Journal of a Traveler Through Those Parts Most Interesting to American Settlers, with Descriptions of Scenery, Habits, Etc.* (1836), 173–74; William T. Austin, "Account of the Campaign of 1835 by William T. Austin, Aid to Gen. Stephen F. Austin & Gen. Ed Burleson," *Texana* 4 (Winter 1966): 287. For the best accounts of the battle of Concepción, see Stephen L. Hardin, *Texian Iliad*, 25–35; Cantrell, *Stephen F. Austin*, 321–22; and Barr, *Texans in Revolt*, 23–26.
39. Jenkins, *Papers*, II:287–88.
40. Davis, *Three Roads to the Alamo*, 470.
41. Cantrell, *Stephen F. Austin*, 323–27.
42. Jeff Long, *Duel of Eagles: The Mexican and U.S. Fight for the Alamo* (1990), 42, 58, 84, 323, 334; Rodolfo Acuña, *Occupied America: A History of Chicanos* (2000), 46; Josefina Zoraida Vásquez, *De la rebelión de Tejas a la guerra del 47: Interpretaciones de la historia de México* (1994).
43. Quoted in Arnoldo De León, *They Call Them Greasers: Anglo Attitudes Toward Mexicans in Texas, 1821–1900* (1983), 7, 9, 11–13.
44. Cantrell, *Stephen F. Austin*, 114–15, 275–76; De León, *They Call Them Greasers*, 2–3.
45. Grady McWhiney, *Cracker Culture: Celtic Ways in the Old South* (1988), xiv–xv, xxi, 268–71; Thomas C. Cochran, *Business in American Life: A History* (1972), 10–14.
46. Launcelot Smither to Stephen F. Austin, November 4, 1835, in Jenkins, *Papers*, II:318; Stephen F. Austin, "General Austin's Order Book for the Campaign of 1835," *Quarterly of the Texas State Historical Association* 11 (July 1907): 39; Stephen F. Austin to the President of Consultation, in Jenkins, *Papers*, II:320–22; Noah Smithwick, *The Evolution of a State*, 71, 76; "Uncle Frank Sparks' Story," *San Antonio Express*, December 8, 1935.
47. Elliott J. Gorn, "Gouge and Bite, Pull Hair and Scratch: The Social Significance of Fighting in the Southern Backcountry," *American Historical Review* 90 (February 1985): 18–43.

48. De Tocqueville, *Democracy in America*, ed. Heffner, 139; Amelia Williams, "A Critical Study of the Siege of the Alamo and of the Personnel of Its Defenders" (Ph.D. dissertation, University of Texas, 1931), 110; quoted in Bill Groneman, *Alamo Defenders. A Genealogy: The People and Their Words* (1990), 132.
49. Joel Poinsett, *Notes on Mexico Made in the Autumn of 1822 Accompanied by an Historical Sketch of the Revolution, and Translations of Official Reports on the Present State of that Country . . . by a Citizen of the United States* (1824), 119; Ruth R. Olivera and Liliane Crété, *Life in Mexico Under Santa Anna 1822–1855* (1991), 19–43.
50. Olivera and Crété, *Life in Mexico Under Santa Anna*, 101–2; Nettie Lee Benson, "Texas As Viewed from Mexico," 228.
51. Robert Ryal Miller, *Mexico: A History* (1885), 203; Michael P. Costeloe, *The Central Republic in Mexico, 1835–1846: Hombres de Bien in the Age of Santa Anna* (1993), 136–39, 158–60, 230.
52. Hardin, *Texian Iliad*, 14–15, 16, 29, 41–42, 83.
53. Bolívar quoted in Enrique Krauze, *Mexico. Biography of Power: A History of Modern Mexico, 1810–1996* (1997), 130–31; Jenkins, *Papers*, I:53–54, 313–14, 327–28; IV:88; Cantrell, *Stephen F. Austin*, 230–31; Davis, *Three Roads to the Alamo*, 449.
54. Jenkins, *Papers*, I:327–28, 343–44; Davis, *Three Roads to the Alamo*, 373.
55. Costeloe, *The Central Republic in Mexico*, 99–101; Fanny Calderón de la Barca, *Life in Mexico*, 438–42.
56. Groneman, *Alamo Defenders*, 4–5, 7–8, 12–13, 17–18, 26–29, 32, 36–37, 48, 60–61, 69–70, 82–83, 88–89, 107–8.
57. Jenkins, *Papers*, I:62–63, 194–97.
58. Forrest T. Ward, "Pre-Revolutionary Activity in Brazoria County," *Southwestern Historical Quarterly* 64 (October 1960): 212–31; Jenkins, *Papers*, II:475–76; Amos Pollard to Henry Smith, January 27, 1836, in Jenkins, *Papers*, IV:160; Hardin, *Texian Iliad*, 9.
59. Jenkins, *Papers*, III:130–31.
60. Cantrell, *Stephen F. Austin*, 327–28; Kenneth Kesselus, *Edward Burleson: Texas Frontier Leader* (1990).
61. Lois A. Garver, "Benjamin Rush Milam," *Southwestern Historical Quarterly* 38 (October 1934): 79–121; 38 (January 1935): 173–202.
62. Milam quoted in Long, *Duel of Eagles*, 77.
63. Herman Ehrenberg, *With Milam and Fannin in Texas: Adventures of a German Boy in Texas' Revolution* (1935), 71.
64. Barr, *Texans in Revolt*, 45–57.
65. Benson, "Texas As Viewed from Mexico," 291; Hobart Huson, *Captain Phillip Dimmitt's Commandancy of Goliad, 1835–1836: An Episode of the Mexican Federalist War in Texas Usually Referred to As the Texas Revolution* (1974), 194; Frank W. Johnson, *A History of Texas and Texans* (1914), I:359–60; Hardin, *Texian Iliad*, 81–91; Micajah Autry to Martha Autry, January 13, 1836, in *Quarterly of the Texas State Historical Association* 14 (April 1911): 319–20; Barr, *Texans in Revolt*, 56–57. For a description of Béxar as it appeared in 1828, see Jackson and Wheat, *Texas by Terán*, 3–5, 9–10, 16–27, 209–10.

CHAPTER 3. "THE BONES OF WARRIORS"

1. Richard G. Santos, *Santa Anna's Campaign Against Texas, 1835–1836* (1968), 54.

2. Jean-Louis Berlandier, *Journey to Mexico During the Years 1826 to 1834* (1980), 283–84.

3. Richard W. Gronet, "United States and the Invasion of Texas, 1810–1814," *The Americas* 25 (January 1969): 281–306.

4. "Diary of José Bernardo Gutiérrez de Lara," *American Historical Review* 34 (October 1928): 59; Gronet, "United States and the Invasion of Texas," 281–306; Julia Kathryn Garrett, *Green Flag over Texas: The Last Years of Spain in Texas* (1939); Harry McCorry Henderson, "The Magee-Gutiérrez Expedition," *Southwestern Historical Quarterly* 55 (July 1951); 43–61; Félix D. Almaráz Jr., *Tragic Cavalier: Governor Manuel Salcedo of Texas, 1808–1813* (1971), 170–71.

5. "Joaquín de Arredondo's Report of the Battle of the Medina, August 18, 1813," *Quarterly of the Texas Historical Association* 11 (1907–8): 220–36; Berlandier, *Journey to Mexico,* 283–84.

6. Garrett, *Green Flag over Texas;* Stephen F. Austin, "Descriptions of Texas, 1828," *Southwestern Historical Quarterly* (October 1924): 101; Vicente Ribes Iborra, *Ambiciones estadounidenses sobre la provincia novohispana de Texas* (1982), 194; Almaráz, *Tragic Cavalier,* 174–82.

7. José Enrique de la Peña, *With Santa Anna in Texas: A Personal Narrative of the Revolution,* ed. Carmen Perry (1975), 19.

8. Brantz Mayer, *Mexico As It Was and As It Is* (1844), 71; *El Sol,* June 19, 1835; *Diario del Gobierno,* November 7, 1835; Michael P. Costeloe, *The Central Republic in Mexico, 1835–1846* (1993), 48–58; Fanny Calderón de la Barca, *Life in Mexico During a Residency of Two Years in That Country* (1843), 203–5, 376–82; Wilfrid Hardy Callcott, *Santa Anna: The Story of an Engima Who Once Was Mexico* (1936), 35–37; John Anthony Caruso, *The Liberators of Mexico* (1967), 267; Jeff Long, *Duel of Eagles: The Mexican and U.S. Fight for the Alamo* (1990), 91–92, 146–47; De la Peña, *With Santa Anna,* 19.

9. José Urrea, *Diary of the Military Operations of the Division Which Under the Command of General José Urrea Campaigned in Texas,* in Carlos E. Castañeda, ed., *The Mexican Side of the Texas Revolution* (1928), 211; Santos, *Santa Anna's Campaign,* 34–35.

10. Michael Robert Green, "El Soldado Mexicano, 1835–1836," *Military History of Texas and the Southwest* 13 (1995): 9.

11. Quoted in Stephen L. Hardin, *Texian Iliad: A Military History of the Texas Revolution, 1835–1836* (1994), 102; de la Peña, *With Santa Anna,* 12, 16, 79.

12. Green, "El Soldado Mexicano," 8.

13. De la Peña, *With Santa Anna,* 19.

14. Santos, *Santa Anna's Campaign,* 1, 11; José Ramón Malo, *Diario de Sucesos Notables, 1832–1833* (1948), 104; Miguel A. Sánchez Lamego, *Sitio y toma del Alamo, 1836* (1966), 11–12; William A. DePalo Jr., *The Mexican National Army, 1822–1852* (1997), 48–49; Antonio López de Santa Anna to José María Tornel, October 26, 1835, in John H. Jenkins, ed., *The Papers of the Texas Revolution* (1973), II: 226–29.

15. Callcott, *Santa Anna,* 119; Ramón Martínez Caro, *A True Account of the First Texas Campaign and the Events Subsequent to the Battle of San Jacinto,* in Castañada, *The Mexican Side of the Texan Revolution,* 97; Berlandier, *Journey to Mexico,* 122, 147.

16. De la Peña, *With Santa Anna,* 18; Callcott, *Santa Anna,* 125–26; Santos, *Santa Anna's Campaign,* 11–12.

17. Robert V. Remini, *Andrew Jackson and the Course of American Democracy, 1833–1845* (1984), 151–52; de la Peña, *With Santa Anna,* 12.

18. Antonio López de Santa Anna, *Manifesto Relative to His Operations in the Texas*

Campaign and His Capture, in Castañeda, *The Mexican Side of the Texan Revolution,* 12.

19. Eugene C. Barker, "The Tampico Expedition," *Quarterly of the Texas State Historical Association* 6 (January 1903): 169–86.

20. D. Anthony Butler to John Forsythe, January 26, 1836, in Jenkins, *Papers,* IV:147–50.

21. Vicente Filisola, *Memorias para la historia de la guerra de Texas* (1849), 2:577; Callcott, *Santa Anna,* 162–63; Barker, "The Tampico Expedition," 169–86.

22. DePalo, *The Mexican National Army,* 49.

23. Lucas Alamán, *Historia de México: Desde los primeros movimientos que preparan su independencia en el año de 1808 hasta la época presente* (1985), 5:55; Manuel Muro, *Historia de San Luis Potosí* (1910), 1:365–66; Filisola, *Memorias,* 2:242.

24. Filisola, *Memorias,* 2:334–38, 351; Amelia Williams, "A Critical Study of the Siege of the Alamo and of the Personnel of Its Defenders," *Southwestern Historical Quarterly* 37 (July 1933): 4–5; De Palo, *The Mexican National Army,* 50.

25. Green, "El Soldado Mexicano," 5–10.

26. De la Peña, *With Santa Anna,* 6–7.

27. Miguel A. Sánchez Lamego, *El Soldado Mexicano, 1837–1848* (1958), 60; Waddy Thompson, *Recollections of Mexico* (1846), 172–73; De la Peña, *With Santa Anna,* 6–9.

28. Martínez Caro, *A True Account of the First Texas Campaign,* 97–99; De la Peña, *With Santa Anna,* 7.

29. Martínez Caro, *A True Account of the First Texas Campaign,* 99; De la Peña, *With Santa Anna,* 12, 18–19; Filisola, *Memorias,* 2:296–97; Santos, *Santa Anna's Campaign,* 9; De la Peña, *With Santa Anna,* 22.

30. Martínez Caro, *A True Account of the First Texas Campaign,* 90; De la Peña, *With Santa Anna,* 11–12, 15; DePalo, *The Mexican National Army,* 52–53; Antonio López de Santa Anna to José Urrea, December 20, 1835, in Jenkins, *Papers,* III:273–74.

31. Berlandier, *Journey to Mexico,* 230–32.

32. De la Peña, *With Santa Anna,* 29–31; Filisola, *Memorias,* 2:260–68; López de Santa Anna, *Manifesto,* 11.

33. Urrea, *Diary* of the Military Operations, 212; De la Peña, *With Santa Anna,* 19–20, 67.

34. Martínez Caro, *A True Account of the First Texas Campaign,* 90; Berlandier, *Journey to Mexico,* 122, 147; Santos, *Santa Anna's Campaign,* 35.

35. John Collis and David M. Jones, *Mexico* (1997), 529.

36. Frederick C. Chabot, ed., *Texas in 1811: The Las Casas and Sambrano Revolutions* (1941), 35–105; J. Villasana Haggard, "The Counter-Revolution of Bexar, 1811," *Southwestern Historical Quarterly* 43 (October 1938): 222–35.

37. Carlos Sánchez Navarro, ed., *La guerra de Tejas: Memorias de un soldado* (1960), 78–79; also see Helen Hunnicutt, trans., "A Mexican View of the Teas War: Memoirs of a Veteran of the Two Battles of the Alamo," *Library Chronicle of the University of Texas* IV (summer 1951): 62.

38. Martínez Caro, *A True Account of the First Texas Campaign,* 100; Hunnicutt, "A Mexican View," 61.

39. Caro, *A True Account,* 101; De la Peña, *With Santa Anna,* 22.

40. Sánchez Navarro, *La guerra de Tejas,* 137; Hardin, *Texian Iliad,* 103–4.

41. Carlos E. Castañeda, ed. and trans., "Statistical Report on Texas by Juan N. Almonte," *Southwestern Historical Quarterly* 28 (January 1925): 195.

42. James Presley, "Santa Anna in Texas: A Mexican Viewpoint," *Southwestern His-*

torical Quarterly 62 (April 1959): 499; Sánchez Navarro, *La guerra de Tejas,* 127; De la Peña, *With Santa Anna,* 24–25, 30, 34.

43. Hardin, *Texian Iliad,* 104; Filisola, *Memorias,* 2:114–23, 260.
44. Berlandier, *Journey to Mexico,* 263; Juan Nepomuceno Almonte, "The Private Journal of Juan Nepomuceno Almonte, February 1–April 16, 1836," *Southwestern Historical Quarterly* 48 (1944): 14; De la Peña, *With Santa Anna,* 36–40; Filisola, *Memorias,* 2:353.
45. Urrea, *Diary of the Military Operations,* 212–15, 360; Martínez Caro, *A True Account of the First Texas Campaign,* 100; De la Peña, *With Santa Anna,* 26–28; Filisola, *Memorias,* 2:155–59.
46. Filisola, *Memorias,* 2:158–65; De la Peña, *With Santa Anna,* 27–28.
47. De la Peña, *With Santa Anna,* 37–38; Berlandier, *Journey to Mexico,* 283–84.
48. Castañeda, "Statistical Report on Texas by Juan N. Almonte," 211; Sánchez Navarro, *La guerra de Texas,* 76–78; Hardin, *Texian Iliad,* 90.
49. Quoted in Callcott, *Santa Anna,* 125–26.

CHAPTER 4. "THOSE PROUD TOW'RS"

1. For Crockett's background see especially William C. Davis, *Three Roads to the Alamo: The Lives and Fortunes of David Crockett, James Bowie, and William Barret Travis* (1998), and James Atkins Shackford, *David Crockett: The Man and the Legend,* ed. John B. Shackford (1956); David Crockett, *A Narrative of the Life of David Crockett,* ed. Paul Andrew Hutton (1987), 68.
2. Shackford, *David Crockett,* 253–64.
3. Davis, *Three Roads to the Alamo,* 319; Daniel J. Boorstin, *The Image: A Guide to Pseudo-Events in America* (1961), 57–58.
4. Alexis de Tocqueville, *Democracy in America* (1945), II:66–67.
5. Quoted in Davis, *Three Roads to the Alamo,* 407.
6. Quoted in Shackford, *David Crockett,* 210; quoted in Davis, *Three Roads to the Alamo,* 411.
7. David Crockett to Wiley and Margaret Flowers, January 9, 1836, in John H. Jenkins, ed., *The Papers of the Texas Revolution 1835–1836* (1973), III:453–54.
8. *Arkansas Gazette,* May 10, 1836.
9. Quoted in William St. Clair, *That Greece Might Still Be Free: The Philhellenes in the War of Independence* (1972), 54.
10. Quoted in C. M. Woodhouse, *The Philhellenes* (1969), 102.
11. Quoted in David M. Robinson, *America in Greece: A Traditional Policy* (1948), 41; *Annals of Congress,* 18th Congress, 1st Session, I, 1823–24, 1160–63.
12. *Jackson Mississippian,* May 6, 1836; Thurston quoted in Bill Groneman, *Alamo Defenders. A Genealogy: The People and Their Words* (1990), 130–31; Goodrich quoted in Groneman, *Alamo Defenders,* 129.
13. Parker quoted in Jenkins, *Papers,* II:475–76.
14. Herman Ehrenberg, *With Milam and Fannin in Texas: Adventures of a German Boy in Texas' Revolution* (1935), 1–5; Gary Brown, *The New Orleans Greys* (1999).
15. Ehrenberg, *With Milam and Fannin in Texas,* 7–15.
16. Johnson quoted in Jenkins, *Papers,* III:467–68.
17. Henry Smith to the Legislative Council of Texas, November 16, 1835, ibid., II:439; Henry Smith to the Council, December 18, 1835, ibid., III:248.
18. Paul Lack, *The Texas Revolutionary Experience: A Political and Social History 1835–1836* (1992), 53–74; Sam Houston to the Soldiers, January 15, 1836, in Jenkins, *Papers,* IV:29–30.

19. Stephen F. Austin to F. W. Johnson, December 22, 1835, in Jenkins, *Papers,* III:284–86; Lack, *The Texas Revolutionary Experience,* 57–58.
20. R.R. Royall to Sam Houston, February 8, 1836, in Jenkins, *Papers,* IV:292.
21. Dimmitt quoted in Jenkins, *Papers,* II:262–63; III:77–78.
22. James W. Robinson Proclamation, February 12, 1836, ibid., IV:307–8; Henry Smith to Asa Hoxey, January 15, 1836, ibid., IV:36.
23. W. Roy Smith, "The Quarrel between Governor Smith and the Council of the Provisional Government of the Republic," *Quarterly of the Texas State Historical Society* 5 (April 1902): 269–346.
24. Frank Johnson to James W. Robinson, December 25, 1835, in Jenkins, *Papers,* III:325–27.
25. Sam Houston to Henry Smith, January 30, 1836, ibid., IV:191.
26. Ibid., IV:187–96; Hobart Huson, *Captain Philip Dimmitt's Commandancy of Goliad, 1835–1836* (1974).
27. Crockett to Wiley and Margaret Flowers, January 9, 1836, in Jenkins, *Papers,* III:453–54; James Gaines to Lieutenant Governor J. W. Robinson, January 9, 1836, ibid., III:454–55.
28. Quoted in Davis, *Three Roads to the Alamo,* 416; Crockett to the Flowerses, January 9, 1836, in Jenkins, *Papers,* III:454.
29. Micajah Autry to Martha Autry, December 7, 1835, *Quarterly of the Texas State Historical Association* 14 (April 1911): 317–18; Micajah Autry to Martha Autry, December 13, 1835, ibid., 318–19.
30. Micajah Autry to Martha Autry, January 13, 1836, ibid., 319–20.
31. Cloud quoted in Groneman, *Alamo Defenders,* 132; *Jackson Mississippian,* May 5, 1836, in Daniel W. Cloud File, Daughters of the Republic of Texas Library.
32. Quoted in Stephen L. Hardin, "James Clinton Neill," in Ron Tyler, ed., *The New Handbook of Texas* (1996), 4:973; also see Stephen L. Hardin, "J. C. Neill: The Forgotten Alamo Commander," http://home.flash.net/~alamo3/archives/feature/net
33. Frederick Charles Chabot, *The Alamo: Mission, Fortress and Shrine* (1935); George Nelson, *The Alamo: An Illustrated History* (1998), 31–39.
34. Green Jameson to Sam Houston, January 18, 1836, in Jenkins, *Papers,* IV:58–61.
35. Alan C. Huffines, *Blood of Noble Men: The Alamo Siege and Battle* (1999), 122–27; Stephen L. Hardin, *Texian Iliad: A Military History of the Texas Revolution* (1994), 112–16; George Nelson, *The Alamo,* 12–13.
36. Green Jameson to Sam Houston, January 18, 1836, in Jenkins, *Papers,* IV:58–61; Green Jameson to Henry Smith, February 16, 1836, ibid., IV:352.
37. J. C. Neill to Sam Houston, January 14, 1836, ibid., IV:14; J.C. to Governor and Council, January 14, 1836, ibid., IV:15.
38. Quoted in De Zavala, *The Alamo,* 18–20; Green Jameson to Sam Houston, January 18, 1836, in Jenkins, *Papers,* IV:58–59.
39. Robinson Proclamation, January 19, 1836, in Jenkins, *Papers,* IV:75–76.
40. Sam Houston to Henry Smith, January 17, 1836, ibid., IV:46; Marquis James, *The Raven: A Biography of Sam Houston* (1929), 221.
41. The ensuing material on Jim Bowie can be found in Davis, *Three Roads to the Alamo,* 94, 100–101, 355; James L. Batson, *James Bowie and the Sandbar Fight* (1992); Raymond W. Thorp, *Bowie Knife* (1948).
42. Davis, *Three Roads to the Alamo,* 100–101, 355; Thorp, *Bowie Knife;* Smithwick, *The Evolution of a State,* 112–15.
43. James Bowie to Henry Smith, February 2, 1836, in Jenkins, *Papers,* IV:236–38; Green Jameson to Sam Houston, January 18, 1836, ibid., IV:58–61; J. C. Neill to the Governor and Council, January 23, 1836, ibid., IV:127. The exact nature of Houston's orders to Bowie remain a mystery, but historian William Davis argues

that Houston asked Bowie to demolish any fortifications still standing in Béxar and, if the Army of Operations appeared, to withdraw to the Alamo compound. In the meantime, Houston would try to secure permission from Governor Smith to blow up the Alamo and pull Neill's forces and their supplies and artillery back to Gonzales and Copano.

44. J. C. Neill to Governor and Council, January 23, 1836, ibid., IV:127; J. C. Neill to the Council, January 27, 1836, ibid., IV:159; Sam Houston to Henry Smith, January 30, 1836, ibid., IV:195; William Travis to Henry Smith, January 28, 1836, ibid., IV:176–77.

45. J. C. Neill to the Government, January 28, 1836, ibid., IV:174; James Bowie to Henry Smith, February 2, 1836, ibid., IV:237

46. Quoted in Davis, *Three Roads to the Alamo,* 511–12.

47. Ibid., 512–13, 717–18; John M. Swisher, *The Swisher Memoirs* (1932), 18–19.

48. J. C. Neill to the Council, January 27, 1836, in Jenkins, *Papers,* IV:159.

49. Green Jameson to Henry Smith, February 11, 1836, ibid., IV:303.

50. J. J. Baugh to Henry Smith, February 13, 1836, ibid., IV:320.

51. J. C. Neill to Sam Houston, January 14, 1836, ibid., IV:14; William Travis and James Bowie to Henry Smith, February 14, 1836, ibid., IV:339; William Travis to Henry Smith, February 13, 1836, ibid., IV:327.

52. J. J. Bauch to Henry Smith, February 13, 1836, ibid., IV:320–21; Davis, *Three Roads to the Alamo,* 521.

53. Hardin, *Texian Iliad,* 120; Davis, *Three Roads to the Alamo,* 521–24.

54. Milledge L. Bonham, "James Butler Bonham: A Consistent Rebel," *Southwestern Historical Quarterly* 35 (October 1931).

55. William Travis to Sam Houston, January 17, 1836, in Jenkins, *Papers,* IV:51; William Travis to Henry Smith, February 12, 1836, ibid., IV:318.

56. José María Rodríguez, *Memoirs of Early Texas* (1900), 8–9.

57. Quoted in Davis, *Three Roads to the Alamo,* 528.

58. Ruth R. Olivera and Liliane Crété, *Life in Mexico Under Santa Anna, 1822–1835* (1991), 37–38.

59. Rodríguez, *Memoirs of Early Texas,* 8–9; Davis, *Three Roads to the Alamo,* 528–29.

CHAPTER 5. "VICTORY OR DEATH"

1. John Sutherland, *The Fall of the Alamo* (1936), 15–17.

2. José María Rodríguez, *Rodríguez Memoirs of Early Texas, 1913,* in Timothy Matovina, ed., *The Alamo Remembered: Tejano Accounts and Perspectives* (1995), 113–15.

3. Sutherland, *The Fall of the Alamo,* 18–19.

4. Antonio López de Santa Anna, *Manifesto,* in Carlos E. Castañeda, ed., *The Mexican Side of the Texas Revolution* (1928), 13.

5. Juan Seguín to William Winston Fontaine, June 7, 1890, Chronological File, Daughters of the Republic of Texas Library at the Alamo.

6. Juan Seguín to William Winston Fontaine, June 7, 1890, in John H. Jenkins, ed., *The Papers of the Texas Revolution 1835–1836* (1973), IV:420; William B. Travis and James Bowie to James Fannin, February 23, 1836, ibid., IV:419.

7. *San Antonio Light,* September 1, 1907; Samuel E. Asbury, ed., "The Private Journal of Juan Nepomuceno Almonte," *Southwestern Historical Quarterly* 48 (July 1944): 16–17.

8. José Enrique de la Peña, *With Santa Anna in Texas: A Personal Narrative of the Revolution,* trans. and ed. by Carmen Perry (1975), 38.

9. James Bowie to Santa Anna, February 23, 1836, in Jenkins, *Papers,* IV:414; Walter Lord, *A Time to Stand: The Epic of the Alamo* (1961), 102.

10. José Batres to James Bowie, February 23, 1836, in Jenkins, *Papers,* IV:415.

11. *San Antonio Express,* June 23, 1878; Asbury, "Private Journal," 17.

12. Reuben Potter, "The Fall of the Alamo," *Magazine of American History* 2 (January 1878): 6.

13. William Barret Travis to the People of Texas and All Americans, February 24, 1836, in Jenkins, *Papers,* IV:423.

14. Stephen L. Hardin, *Texian Iliad: A Military History of the Texas Revolution* (1994), 128–31.

15. Quoted ibid., 129.

16. Travis to the People of Texas and All Americans, in Jenkins, *Papers,* IV:423; Asbury, "Private Journal," 17; James T. DeShields, *Tall Men with Long Rifles: The Glamorous Story of the Texas Revolution As Told by Captain Creed Taylor* (1935), 163.

17. For a good discussion of Bowie's illness, see William C. Davis, *Three Roads to the Alamo: The Lives and Fortunes of David Crockett, James Bowie, and William Barret Travis* (1998), 540; also Lord, *A Time to Stand,* 106; Alan C. Huffines, ed., *Blood of Noble Men* (1999), 42.

18. Asbury, "Private Journal," 17.

19. For a description of the skirmish, see ibid., 17–18; Ramón Martínez Caro, *A True Account of the First Texas Campaign* (1837), in Castañeda, *The Mexican Side of the Texas Revolution,* 101–2; William Barret Travis to Sam Houston, February 24, 1836, in Jenkins, *Papers,* IV:433–34.

20. William Barret Travis to Sam Houston, February 24, 1836, in Jenkins, *Papers,* IV:433–34; Asbury, "Private Journal," 18.

21. Jesus F. de la Teja, ed., *A Revolution Remembered: The Memoirs and Selected Correspondence of Juan Seguín* (1991), 107. Seguín said he left on February 28, but given the other events he describes, it had to have been the night of February 25–26.

22. Travis and Bowie to Fannin, February 23, 1836, in Jenkins, *Papers,* IV:419; Richard G. Santos, *Santa Anna's Campaign Against Texas, 1835–1836: Featuring the Field Commands Issued to Major General Vicente Filisola* (1968), 65.

23. Ruby C. Smith, "James W. Fannin, Jr., in the Texas Revolution," *Southwestern Historical Quarterly* 23 (October 1919, January and April 1920).

24. James W. Fannin to James W. Robinson, February 22, 1836, in Jenkins, *Papers,* IV:398.

25. Quoted in William A. DePalo Jr., *The Mexican National Army, 1822–1852* (1997), 60.

26. James W. Fannin to James W. Robinson, February 16, 1836, in Jenkins, *Papers,* IV:350–51; James W. Fannin to James W. Robinson, February 17, 1836, ibid., IV:371.

27. James W. Fannin to James W. Robinson, February 16, 1836, ibid., IV:350–51; James W. Fannin to James W. Robinson, February 22, 1836, ibid., IV:398–401.

28. Quoted in Clinton P. Hartman, "James Walker Fannin, Jr.," in Ron Tyler, ed., *The New Handbook of Texas,* 6 vols. (1996), II:945.

29. James W. Fannin to James W. Robinson, February 25, 1836, in Jenkins, *Papers,* IV:429–30; James W. Fannin to James W. Robinson, February 26, 1836, ibid., IV:443–44.

30. James W. Fannin to Joseph Mims, February 28, 1836, ibid., IV:454; Hobart Huson, ed., *Dr. J. H. Barnard's Journal, Dec. 1835–June 1836* (1950), 14.

31. James W. Fannin to James W. Robinson, February 28, 1836, in Jenkins, *Papers,* IV:455–56.

32. De la Teja, *A Revolution Remembered,* 26, 107.
33. William F. Gray, *From Virginia to Texas, 1835: Diary of Col. Wm. F. Gray* (1901), 119; Asbury, "Private Journal," 18.
34. Martínez Caro, *A True Account of the First Texas Campaign,* 102.
35. Quoted in Huffines, *Blood of Noble Men,* 76.
36. Asbury, "Private Journal," 19.
37. Henry Smith to the People of Texas, February 27, 1836, in Jenkins, *Papers,* IV:450; Henry Smith to Fellow Citizens of Texas, February 1836, in Wallace O. Chariton, ed., *100 Days in Texas: The Alamo Letters* (1990), 287.
38. Huffines, *Blood of Noble Men,* 86–90, makes a persuasive case for the armistice; López de Santa Anna, *Manifesto,* 14.
39. Matovina, *The Alamo Remembered,* 81–82; Davis, *Three Roads to the Alamo,* 546.
40. De la Peña, *With Santa Anna,* 36; Gray, *From Virginia to Texas,* 121.
41. William B. Travis to Jesse Grimes, March 3, 1836, in Jenkins, *Papers,* IV:504–5; Lord, *A Time to Stand,* 128.
42. Hardin, *Texian Iliad,* 133.
43. Lord, *A Time to Stand,* 124–27.
44. Ibid., 127–28.
45. Quoted in Huffines, *Blood of Noble Men,* 96.
46. Paul Lack, *The Texas Revolutionary Experience: A Political and Social History, 1835–1836* (1992), 82–86.
47. Quoted ibid., 75.
48. Ibid., 78, 87; David G. Burnet to Henry Clay, March 30, 1836, in Jenkins, *Papers,* V:238–39.
49. Sam Houston to the Soldiers, January 15, 1836, in Jenkins, *Papers,* IV:30; James W. Fannin to James W. Robinson, February 21, 1836, ibid., IV:392.
50. William Travis to Henry Smith, February 12, 1836, ibid., IV:317; James W. Fannin to James W. Robinson, February 17, 1836, ibid., IV:371.
51. James W. Fannin to James W. Robinson, February 7, 1836, ibid., IV:280; John W. Hall to the "People," February 1836, ibid., IV:470.
52. James K. Greer, "The Committee on the Texas Declaration of Independence," *Southwestern Historical Quarterly* 30 (April 1927): 239–51.
53. Texas Declaration of Independence, March 2, 1836, in Jenkins, *Papers,* IV:493–97.
54. Reuben R. Brown, "Expedition Under Johnson and Grant," in James M. Day, ed., *Texas Almanac, 1857–1873: A Compendium of Texas History* (1967), 218–24; General José Urrea, *Diary of the Military Operations of the Division Which Under the Command of General José Urrea Campaigned in Texas,* in Castañeda, *The Mexican Side of the Texas Revolution,* 216; *Southwestern Historical Quarterly* 9: 192–95.
55. Davis, *Three Roads to the Alamo,* 547–48.
56. James W. Fannin to Convention, March 3, 1836, in Jenkins *Papers,* IV: 502–4; DePalo, *The Mexican National Army;* De la Peña, *With Santa Anna,* 36–37; William B. Travis to Convention, March 3, 1836, in Jenkins, *Papers,* V:503.
57. Juan N. Seguín to William Winston Fontaine, June 7, 1890, in Matovina, *The Alamo Remembered,* 50–51; Huffines, *Blood of Noble Men,* 102.
58. Robert L. Williamson to James B. Fannin, March 1, 1836, in Huffines, *Blood of Noble Men,* 103.
59. William B. Travis to Convention, March 3, 1836, in Jenkins, *Papers,* IV:502–4.
60. William B. Travis to Jesse Grimes, March 3, 1836, ibid., IV:504–5; William B. Travis to David Ayres, March 3, 1836, ibid., 501.

61. De la Peña, *With Santa Anna*, 43–44; DePalo, *The Mexican National Army*, 57; López de Santa Anna, *Manifesto*, 13–14; Asbury, "Private Journal" 20–21.
62. De la Peña, *With Santa Anna*, 43–44.
63. López de Santa Anna, *Manifesto*, 13.
64. De la Peña, *With Santa Anna*, 43–44.
65. Ibid., 43–45; Santos, *Santa Anna's Campaign Against Texas*, 72–73; Alsbury, "Private Journal," 19–20.
66. Huffines, *Blood of Noble Men*, 114.

INTERLUDE

1. Timothy M. Matovina, *The Alamo Remembered: Tejano Accounts and Perspectives* (1995), 52–53, 58–62.
2. William P. Zuber, *My Eighty Years in Texas*, ed. Janis Boyle Mayfield (1971), 248–52.
3. Wallace O. Chariton, *Exploring the Alamo Legends* (1992), 175–206; Jeff Long, *Duel of Eagles: The Mexican and U.S. Fight for the Alamo* (1990), 77.
4. José Enrique de la Peña, *With Santa Anna in Texas* (1975), 43–45; Richard G. Santos, *Santa Anna's Campaign Against Texas, 1835–1836* (1968), 72–73.
5. Captain Fernando Urizza, "Urizza's Account of the Alamo Massacre," in James Day, comp. and ed., *The Texas Almanac, 1857–1873* (1967), 173.
6. Santa Anna Order, March 5, 1836, in John H. Jenkins, ed., *The Papers of the Texas Revolution 1835–1836* (1973), IV:518–19; Stephen Hardin, *Texian Iliad* (1994), 140–45; Reuben M. Potter, *The Fall of the Alamo: A Reminiscence of the Revolution of Texas* (1977), 56–57.
7. Santos, *Santa Anna's Campaign Against Texas*, 73–74.
8. De la Peña, *With Santa Anna*, 45–46; Sánchez quoted in Walter Lord, *A Time to Stand* (1961), 150.
9. Vicente Filisola, *The History of the War in Texas* (1985–87), II:176; Urizza, "Urizza's Account of the Alamo Massacre," 173. The Santa Anna and Almonte conversation quoted in Lord, *A Time to Stand*, 151.
10. De la Peña, *With Santa Anna*, 47.
11. William Fairfax Gray, *From Virginia to Texas, 1835* (1837), 137–138; *Memphis Enquirer*, April 14, 1836; *Frankfort Commonwealth*, May 25, 1836.
12. De la Peña, *With Santa Anna*, 46–47.
13. Ibid., 46–50; Alan C. Huffines, *Blood of Noble Men. The Alamo: Siege and Battle* (1999), 143.
14. De la Peña, *With Santa Anna*, 47–51. Filisola quoted in Long, *Duel of Eagles*, 246.
15. De la Peña, *With Santa Anna*, 47–51.
16. Ibid.; Juan José Sánchez Navarro, "A Mexican View of the Texas War: Memoirs of a Veteran of the Two Battles of the Alamo," trans. Helen Hunnicutt, *Library Chronicle* 4 (summer 1951): 62–64.
17. Enrique Esparza, "The Alamo's Only Survivor," *San Antonio Express*, May 12, 1907; Huffines, *Blood of Noble Men*, 145.
18. De la Peña, *With Santa Anna*, 51.
19. J. M. Morphis, *History of Texas* (1875), 176; *San Antonio Express*, April 27, 1881; "Susanna Dickinson," *Alamo de Parras*, http://home-flash.net/~alamo3/bios/dickenson/susannah.htm
20. De la Peña, *With Santa Anna*, 50–51.
21. Ibid.
22. Ibid., 52; John Sutherland, *The Fall of the Alamo* (1936), 40.

23. Vicente Filisola, *The History of the War in Texas,* II:179.

CHAPTER 6. IN SEARCH OF DAVY'S GRAVE

1. E. N. Gray to (no name), March 11, 1836; Sam Houston to James W. Fannin, March 11, 1836; Sam Houston to James Collinsworth, March 13, 1836; in John H. Jenkins, ed., *The Papers of the Texas Revolution 1835–1836* (1973), V:48, 52–53, 69–71.
2. Sam Houston to Henry Raguet, March 13, 1836, ibid., V:71–72.
3. Benjamin Goodrich to Edmund Goodrich, March 15, 1836, ibid., V:80–82.
4. E. Bowker to Daniel Bowker, March 29, 1836, ibid., V:223–25.
5. Thomas J. Chambers Broadsheet, March 1836, ibid., V:260–67.
6. Susan Prendergast Schoelwer, ed., *Alamo Images: Changing Perceptions of a Texas Experience* (1986), 5.
7. Ibid., 6.
8. Walter Lord, *A Time to Stand: The Epic of the Alamo* (1961), 175–82; Jeff Long, *Duel of Eagles: The Mexican and U.S. Fight for the Alamo* (1990), 264–65.
9. Antonio López de Santa Anna to the Inhabitants of Texas, March 7, 1836, in Jenkins, *Papers,* V:20–21.
10. Sam Houston to James Collinsworth, March 15, 1836, ibid., V:82–84; William F. Gray, *From Virginia to Texas, 1836* (1909), 129–36.
11. Gray, *From Virginia to Texas, 1836,* 136–42.
12. *Columbia Observer,* April 14, 1836; *Frankfort Commonwealth,* May 25, 1836; William C. Davis, "How Davy Probably Didn't Die" (manuscript, William C. Davis Papers), 11–12. Davis's insightful essay is published in the *Journal of the Alamo Battlefield Association* 2 (fall 1997): 3–35.
13. Davis, "How Davy Probably Didn't Die," 11–13.
14. José Urrea, "Diary of the Military Operations on the Division Which Under the Command of General José Urrea Campaigned in Texas," in Carlos E. Casteñeda, ed., *The Mexican Side of the Texas Revolution* (1928), 213–19.
15. Sam Houston to James W. Fannin, March 11, 1836, in Jenkins, *Papers,* V:51–52.
16. Quoted in Craig H. Roell, *Remember Goliad!* (1994), 59.
17. For Fannin's retreat, see Stephen L. Hardin, *Texian Iliad: A Military History of the Texas Revolution, 1835–1836* (1994), 166–71.
18. Urrea, "Diary," 228–31.
19. José Enrique de la Peña, *With Santa Anna in Texas: A Personal Narrative of the Revolution* (1975), 83–84; William Corner, "John Crittendan Duval: The Last Survivor of the Goliad Massacre," *Quarterly of the Texas State Historical Association* 1 (July 1897): 47–67; Roell, *Remember Goliad!,* 69; Urrea, "Diary," 228–35.
20. De la Peña, *With Santa Anna,* 92; Roell, *Remember Goliad!,* 69–70; Urrea, "Diary," 242.
21. De la Peña, *With Santa Anna,* 92; Roell, *Remember Goliad!,* 68–73; Hardin, *Texian Iliad,* 173–74.
22. De la Peña, *With Santa Anna,* 92; Roell, *Remember Goliad!,* 71.
23. Quoted in Lord, *A Time to Stand,* 169; Philip Hay Hornthwaite, *The Alamo and the War of Texan Independence 1835–36* (1986), 16.
24. Reprinted in the *Lafayette Free Press and Commercial Advertiser,* May 20, 1836.
25. Reprinted in the *Ohio State Journal,* April 30, 1836; *Richmond Enquirer,* May 6, 1836.
26. *Kentucky Gazette,* April 16, 1836; reprinted in the *Ohio State Journal,* April 30, 1836; *Richmond Enquirer,* May 17, 1836.

27. *United States Gazette,* April 11, 1836; *Niles Register,* April 16, 1836; *Ohio State Journal,* April 16, 1836; *Richmond Enquirer,* May 17, 1836.

28. Lord, *A Time to Stand,* 167.

29. William A. DePalo Jr., *The Mexican National Army, 1822–1852* (1997), 58–59.

30. Sam Houston to James Collinsworth, March 17, 1836, in Jenkins, *Papers,* V:122–24; Richard G. Santos, *Santa Anna's Campaign Against Texas, 1835–1836, Featuring the Field Commands Issued to Major General Vicente Filisola* (1968), 92; Hardin, *Texian Iliad,* 180.

31. Sam Houston to Thomas J. Rusk, March 23, 1836, in Jenkins, *Papers,* V:168–70; Frank X. Tolbert, *The Day of San Jacinto* (1959), 50–51; [Robert M. Coleman], *Houston Displayed; or, Who Won the Battle of San Jacinto? By a Farmer in the Army, Reproduced from the Original* (1837), 4; Hardin, *Texian Iliad,* 187.

32. Sam Houston to Thomas J. Rusk, March 29, 1836, in Jenkins, *Papers,* V:234–35; Hardin, *Texian Iliad,* 184–87.

33. Quoted in Hardin, *Texian Iliad,* 189.

34. Quoted in Michael Fluent, "San Jacinto," *American History Illustrated* 21 (May 1986): 27; Hardin, *Texian Iliad,* 200.

35. Sam Houston to Henry Raguet, April 19, 1836, in Jenkins, *Papers,* V:504.

36. James W. Pohl, *The Battle of San Jacinto* (1989), 28–31.

37. Hardin, *Texian Iliad,* 205–17.

38. For the battle of San Jacinto, see ibid., 107–115; Pedro Delgado, *Mexican Account of the Battle of San Jacinto* (1919), 10; Pohl, *The Battle of San Jacinto,* 41–43.

39. DePalo, *The Mexican National Army,* 61–65.

40. Ramón Martínez Caro, "A True Account of the First Texas Campaign and the Events Subsequent to the Battle of San Jacinto," in Casteñeda, *The Mexican Side of the Texas Revolution,* 104.

41. Thomas Lawrence Connelly, ed., "Did Davy Crockett Surrender at the Alamo? A Contemporary Letter," *The Journal of Southern History* 26 (August 1960): 368–76.

42. Samuel E. Asbury, ed., "The Private Journal of Juan Nepomuceno Almonte, February 1–April 16, 1836," *Southwestern Historical Quarterly* 48 (June 1944): 23; Francisco Antonio Ruíz Deposition, in Timothy M. Matovina, ed., *The Alamo Remembered: Tejano Accounts and Perspectives* (1995), 37. Though beyond the range of this book, there exists a quite lively literature on the Dolson letter. See especially Thomas Ricks Lindley, "Killing Crockett: It's All in the Execution," *Alamo Journal* 96 (May 1995); Lindley, "Killing Crockett: Theory Paraded as Fact," *Alamo Journal* 98 (July 1995); Lindley, "Killing Crockett: Lindley's Opinion," *Alamo Journal* 98 (October 1995); James E. Crisp, "Davy in Freeze-Frame: Methodology or Madness," *Alamo Journal* 98 (October 1995); Crisp, "Back to Basics: Conspiracies, Common Sense, and Occam's Razor," http://home.flash.net/~alamo3/archives/confused/crisp.htm.; Crisp, "Trashing Dolson: The Perils of Tendentious Interpretation," http://home.flash.net/~alamo3/archives/confused/dolson.htm.

43. Davis, "How Davy Probably Didn't Die," 18; Michael P. Costeloe, "The Mexican Press of 1836 and the Battle of the Alamo," *Southwestern Historical Quarterly* 91 (April 1988): 540.

44. Oakah L. Jones, *Santa Anna* (1968), 70–75.

45. Quoted ibid., 75.

46. Martínez Caro, "A True Account of the First Texas Campaign," 103–4.

47. James M. Day, ed., *The Texas Almanac, 1857–1873: A Compendium of Texas History* (1967), 173–74.

48. See discussion in Davis. "How Davy Probably Didn't Die," 39–40.

CHAPTER 7. RETRIEVING THE BONES OF HISTORY

1. For a brief survey of her life, see "Adina De Zavala: Preservationist Extraordinaire," *The Medallion*, March 1991, 1–8; L. Robert Ables, "Adina Emilia De Zavala," in Ron Tyler, *The New Handbook of Texas* (1996), VI:1146–47; and Frank W. Jennings with Rosemary Williams, "Adina De Zavala, Alamo Crusader," *Alamo de Parras*, http://home.flash.net/~alamo3/bios/zavala/zavala.htm.

2. *Advance Guard* (Goliad, Texas), March 10, 1955; *San Antonio Light,* February 11, 1908; Frank Jennings, "Adina De Zavala: Alamo Crusader," *Texas Highways,* March 1995, 19–20; *Houston Chronicle,* February 14, 1908; Charles Heuermann statement, August 4, 1937, Chronological File, 1900–1909, Daughters of the Republic of Texas Library; *San Augustine Tribune,* March 12, 1936; *Dallas Morning News,* March 30, 1955; *Des Moines Daily News,* February 19, 1908.

3. *Telegraph and Texas Register,* March 24, 1836; *Beaumont Enterprise,* May 31, 1836.

4. *New York Sun,* April 12, 1836; Don Graham, "Remembering the Alamo: The Story of the Texas Revolution in Popular Culture," *Southwestern Historical Quarterly* 89 (1985–86): 35–66.

5. *San Antonio Express,* July 1, 1906; Tom W. Glaser, "Victory or Death," in Susan Prendergast Schoelwer, ed., *Alamo Images* (1985), 97–98; "Story of Felix Nuñez at the Alamo," *San Antonio Express,* July 1, 1906.

6. *Telegraph* (Columbia, Texas), March 28, 1837; R. M. Potter, "The Fall of the Alamo," *Magazine of American History* 1 (January 1878): 19–20; Marilyn McAdams Sibley, "The Burial Place of the Alamo Heroes," *Southwestern Historical Quarterly* 70 (1966–67): 272–80. Bernice Strong, "José Francisco Ruiz (1783–1840)," *Alamo de Parras,* http://home.Flash.net/~alamo3/mexican/tenoxtitlan/ruiz.htm.

7. Adina De Zavala, *History and Legends of the Alamo* (1917), 55–56.

8. J. H. Barnard, *Dr. J. H. Barnard's Journal* (1949).

9. Charles I. Sellon to Marilla, September 6, 1846, Chronological File, 1840–49, DRTL, San Antonio; John Frost, *Incidents and Narratives of Travel in Europe, Asia, Africa and America* (1855), 59–60; *San Antonio Express,* April 9, 1905.

10. Quoted in Edward Tabor Linenthal, *Sacred Ground: Americans and Their Battlefields* (1991), 65; Jack C. Butterfield, "Women Restored the Alamo," *Inn Dixie* 27 (May 1960): 5–6, 28; George Nelson, *The Alamo: An Illustrated History* (1998), 62–72; Stephen Gould, *The Alamo City Guide* (1882), 16; Kevin R. Young, "Major Babbitt and the Alamo 'Hump,'" *Military Images* 6 (July–August 1984): 16–17; Schoelwer, *Alamo Images,* 40; "The Journal of Edward Everett," manuscript in the Cushing Library, Texas A&M University, 21–22.

11. "E. I. Coyle and Trouble at the Alamo," *Our Heritage* 34 (winter 1992–93): 18–21.

12. William Corner, *San Antonio de Bexar* (1890); Irwin Sexton, *Samuel A. Maverick* (1964).

13. Quoted in John F. Sears, *Sacred Places: American Tourist Attractions in the Nineteenth Century* (1989), 39, 122–23.

14. Quoted in Linenthal, *Sacred Ground,* 90–91.

15. Quoted in Sears, *Sacred Places,* 30, and David Glassberg, *American Historical Pageantry: The Uses of Tradition in the Early Twentieth Century* (1990), 44.

16. Glassberg, *American Historical Pageantry,* 41.

17. See Linenthal, *Sacred Ground,* 28–37, 104–11, 143–55.

18. *San Antonio Daily Express,* March 6, 1886.

19. Adele B. Looscan, "The Work of the Daughters of the Republic of Texas in Behalf of the Alamo," *Texas Historical Association Quarterly* 8 (1904): 81–82; Daughters of the Republic of Texas, *Ninety Years of Achievement: History of the Daughters of the Republic of Texas* (1981).

20. Pompeo Coppini, *From Dawn to Sunset: Autobiography* (1949), 106–7; Jennings, "Adina De Zavala: Alamo Crusader," 16–19.

21. *San Antonio Express,* April 29, 1900; March 7, 1903.

22. Martha Anne Turner, *Clara Driscoll: An American Tradition* (1979), 1–16; Karen Tipton, "Clara Driscoll, Savior of the Alamo," *Alamo de Parras,* http://home.flash.net/~alamo3/bios/driscoll/clara.htm.

23. Transcript of 1939 interview of Clara Driscoll by Charles White, Chronological File, 1900–1939, DRT Library.

24. Peter Molyneaux, "How the Alamo Was Saved," *Bunker's Monthly* (1928): 1–14, copy in Chronological File, 1900–1909, DRT Library; *Plain Talk* (Newport, Tennessee), March 29, 1906; *San Antonio Light,* March 5, 1904; January 21 and 29, 1905; February 5, 1905; *San Antonio Daily Express,* April 16, 1903; *San Antonio Light,* April 17, 1955; Jack C. Butterfield, *Women of the Alamo* (1960), 1–7; *San Antonio Express,* March 2, 1955; David McLemore, "Remembering the Alamo," *Dallas Morning News,* March 2, 1994.

25. *San Antonio Light,* September 13, 1906.

26. Ibid.

27. *San Antonio Daily Express,* March 21, 1907; *San Antonio Light,* March 21 and April 21, 1907; *Houston Chronicle,* February 20, 1907; *San Antonio Daily Express,* April 21, 1909.

28. *San Antonio Light,* September 12–14, 1906; July 8, 1907; February 12, 1908.

29. *Houston Daily Post,* May 31, 1908; *San Antonio Light,* September 12–14, 1906; July 8, 1907; February 12, 1908; *Houston Chronicle,* February 12–13, 1908; Coppini, *From Dawn to Sunset,* 181–82; "The Modern Story of the Alamo," *Texas Field and National Guardsman,* Historic Sites, Alamo Clippings, DRTL.

30. *San Antonio Daily Express,* June 16–17, 1908.

31. *San Antonio Express,* March 12, 1909; DRT *Report* (1909), 11.

32. *San Antonio Light,* February 11 and 20, 1909; *San Antonio Express,* March 12, 1909.

33. George P. Uckaby, "Oscar Branch Colquitt: A Political Biography" (Ph.D. dissertation, University of Texas, 1946), 169; *San Antonio Express,* July 1, 1913; *Dallas Morning News,* December 31, 1911; Clara Driscoll, "To All Texans," April 22, 1912, pamphlet in Chronological File, 1900–1909, DRTL.

34. Quoted in *San Antonio Express,* April 30, 1913. For a well-researched, pro–De Zavala account of the entire controversy, see L. Robert Ables, "The Second Battle for the Alamo," *Southwestern Historical Quarterly* 70 (January 1967): 372–413.

35. Holly Beachley Brear, *Inherit the Alamo: Myth and Ritual at an American Shrine* (1995), 94; Richard R. Flores, "Private Visions, Public Culture: The Making of the Alamo," *Cultural Anthropology* 10 (February 1995): 112; Schoelwer, *Alamo Images,* 52–53.

36. "The Journal of Edward Everett," 27–28, 33–34; John S. D. Eisenhower, *So Far from God: The U.S. War with Mexico 1846–1848* (1989), 103.

37. Walter Prescott Webb, *The Texas Rangers: A Century of Frontier Defense* (1965), 477–78.

38. U.S. Congress, House of Representatives, House Executive Document No. 52, *Difficulties on the Southwestern Frontier,* 36th Congress, 1st Session, 1861, 81; Richard J. Mertz, "No One Can Arrest Me: The Story of Gregorio Cortez," *Journal of South Texas* (1974); Charles W. Goldfinch and José T. Canales, *Juan N. Cortina: Two Views* (1974).

39. Gilbert M. Cuthbertson, "Catarino E. Garza and the Garza War," *Texana* 13 (1975).

40. Mertz, "No One Can Arrest Me"; Américo Paredes, *With His Pistol in His Hand: A Border Ballad and Its Hero* (1958).

41. Madison Grant, *The Passing of the Great Race* (1916).

42. Don Graham, "Remembering the Alamo: The Story of the Texas Revolution in Popular Culture," *Southwestern Historical Quarterly* 89 (1985–86): 39–48; Patrick McInroy, "The Star Film Ranch: Gastón Méliès in San Antonio, 1910–1911," unpublished manuscript, Chronological File, 1910–19, DRTL; Frank Thompson, *Alamo Movies* (1991), 17–30.

43. Molyneaux, "How the Alamo Was Saved," 5; Mary Lasswell, "Clara Driscoll Sevier As I Knew Her," in Jack Butterfield, *Clara Driscoll Rescued the Alamo* (1961), 1–2.

44. Jennings, "Adina De Zavala: Alamo Crusader," 15–21; "The Modern Story of the Alamo," *Texas Field and National Guardsman,* Historic Sites, Alamo Clippings, DRTL; Coppini, *From Dawn to Sunset,* 181.

45. Newspaper article, Rites and Ceremonies File, March 6, 1917, DRT Library.

46. *San Antonio Express,* April 22, 1920.

47. *San Antonio Light,* October 18, 1931; *San Antonio Express,* January 29, 1932.

48. *San Antonio Light,* March 17, 1935; February 15, 1933; April 17, 1955.

49. *San Antonio Evening News,* March 17, 1935.

50. *San Antonio Express,* March 6–8, 1936.

51. Shelby Hearon, "The Guardian," *Texas Monthly,* January 1986, 166; *San Antonio Evening News,* March 5–7, 1936.

52. *San Antonio Light,* March 7, 1935; *San Antonio Express,* March 6, 1936; *San Antonio Evening News,* March 5–7, 1936.

53. *San Antonio Light,* June 12–14, 1936.

54. Quoted in the *Crockett Courier,* June 22, 1936.

55. Butterfield, *Women of the Alamo,* 6–7.

56. *San Antonio Evening News,* March 7, 1934; *San Antonio Light,* June 12, 1936; Charles White interview with Clara Driscoll, manuscript in Chronological File, 1930–39, DRTL.

57. Edwin Muller, "Remember the Alamo," *Reader's Digest,* October 1940, 10–14.

58. Quoted in Linenthal, *Sacred Ground,* 79–80.

59. Evelyn M. Carrington, "Memorial Service and Service Flag Dedication," March 6, 1943, Historic Sites, Rites and Ceremonies File, DRTL; *San Antonio Evening News,* March 7, 1944; Charles Jeffries, "The Lights of the Alamo," *Southwestern Historical Quarterly* 46 (July 1942); *San Antonio Evening News,* April 13, 1945.

60. *Austin-American Statesman,* July 21–22, 1945; *San Antonio Express,* July 21, 1945; *Corpus Christi Caller-Times,* July 18–22, 1945; *Houston Post,* July 20–22, 1945; *Dallas Morning News,* May 29, 1961; *San Antonio Evening News,* July 19, 1945; *Time,* July 30, 1945, 23; *San Antonio Evening News,* July 19, 1945.

61. *Fort Worth Star-Telegram,* March 2 and 6, 1955; *San Antonio Light,* March 2–6, 1955; *Houston Post,* March 2, 1955; *San Antonio Express,* March 2–6, 1955.

CHAPTER 8. KING OF THE WILD FRONTIER

1. *New York Times,* June 29, 1941.

2. For a good discussion of Disney's labor problems see Steven Watts, *The Magic Kingdom: Walt Disney and the American Way of Life* (1997), 203–27.

3. *New York Times,* May 1 and 28, 1941.

4. Watts, *The Magic Kingdom,* 209; *New York Times,* June 14, 1941.

5. Watts, *The Magic Kingdom*, 209–11.
6. Ibid., 214–20; *New York Times*, June 29, 1941.
7. For Disney's speech, see Watts, *The Magic Kingdom*, 221–23.
8. Ibid., 225–26.
9. Ibid., 251–59.
10. Larry Ceplair and Steven Englund, *The Inquisition in Hollywood: Politics in the Film Community, 1930–1960* (1980), 84.
11. For the emergence of the Motion Picture Alliance for the Preservation of American Ideals, see *Variety*, February 9, 1944; "The Battle in Hollywood," *Time*, February 4, 1944; Matthew Bernstein, *Walter Wanger: Hollywood Independent* (1994), 193; R. B. Wood to J. Edgar Hoover (February 9, 1944), Motion Picture Alliance for the Preservation of American Ideals file, FBI; Ronald Brownstein, *The Power and the Glitter: The Hollywood-Washington Connection* (1992), 88–92.
12. Ceplair and Englund, *The Inquisition in Hollywood*, 209–12.
13. Watts, *The Magic Kingdom*, 241.
14. Quoted ibid., 265.
15. Richard Schickel, *The Disney Version: The Life, Times, Art, and Commerce of Walt Disney*, 3rd ed. (1997), 316–37.
16. Quoted in Watts, *The Magic Kingdom*, 393.
17. Ibid., 287.
18. *Chicago Tribune*, May 9, 1948.
19. Schickel, *The Disney Version*, 312; for the Disney-ABC deal, see 312–14 and Watts, *The Magic Kingdom*, 384–86.
20. Arthur M. Schlesinger Jr., *The Age of Jackson* (1945), 216, 278–79.
21. Margaret Jane King, "The Davy Crockett Craze: A Case Study in Popular Culture" (Ph.D. dissertation, University of Hawaii, 1976), 111–13.
22. "The Ballad of Davy Crockett," in Charles K. Wolfe, "Davy Crockett Songs: Minstrels to Disney," in Michael A. Lofaro, ed., *Davy Crockett: The Man, the Legend, and the Legacy, 1786–1986* (1985), 181.
23. Paul F. Anderson, *The Davy Crockett Craze: A Look at the 1950s Phenomenon and the Davy Crockett Collectibles* (1996), 49; King, "The Davy Crockett Craze," 8.
24. King, "The Davy Crockett Craze," 8.
25. For the merchandise, see ibid., 17; Anderson, *The Davy Crockett Craze*, 87–160. On the economic impact see the *New York Times*, June 1, 1955.
26. *Life*, April 25, 1955, 27–33.
27. Peter H. White, "Ex-King of the Wild Frontier," *New York Times Magazine*, December 11, 1955, 27; King, "The Davy Crockett Craze," 16.
28. Anderson, *The Davy Crockett Craze*, 69–73.
29. Ibid., 49–55.
30. *New York Times*, June 1, 1955.
31. J. Fred Macdonald, *One Nation Under Television: The Rise and Decline of Network TV* (1990), 149; Eric Barnouw, *Tube of Plenty: The Evolution of American Television* (1990), 99; King, "The Davy Crockett Craze," 130–31.
32. David Karp, "Television Shows Are Not *Supposed* to Be Good," *New York Times Magazine*, January 23, 1966, 9.
33. Neal Gabler, *Life the Movie: How Entertainment Conquered Reality* (1999), 3–95.
34. Ibid., 53–58. See Daniel J. Boorstin, *The Image: A Guide to Pseudo-Events in America* (1961), 12–17, for a discussion of the "graphic revolution."
35. Kenneth S. Davis, "Coonskin Superman," *New York Times Magazine*, April 24, 1955, 20.
36. E. J. Kahn Jr., "Be Sure You're Right, Then Go Ahead," *New Yorker*, September

3, 1955, 71–74, 77; John Haverstick, "The Two Davy Crocketts," *Saturday Review,* July 9, 1955, 19, 30.

37. Bernard Kalb, "Dan'l, Dan'l Boone," *New York Times Magazine,* October 9, 1955, 42.
38. Boorstin, *The Image,* 45–49.
39. John Fischer, "The Embarassing Truth About Davy Crockett, the Alamo, Yoknapatawpha County, and Other Dear Myths," *Harper's Magazine,* July 1955, 16–18.
40. Letters to the Editor, *Saturday Review,* July 13, 1955, 23; August 6, 1955, 23; Letters, *Harper's Magazine,* September 1955, 5–6; *Newsweek,* July 18, 1955, 60–61.
41. *Newsweek,* July 4, 1955, 56; July 18, 1955, 60–61.
42. *New York Times,* May 22, 1955; King, "The Davy Crockett Craze," 33–34; White, "Ex–King of the Wild Frontier," 27.
43. Richard Hofstadter, *Anti-Intellectualism in American Life* (1964), 161–66.

CHAPTER 9. ONLY HEROES, ONLY MEN

1. For the Catholic question, see Thomas C. Reeves, *A Question of Character: A Life of John F. Kennedy* (1991), 162–63, 190–92.
2. Mary St. John interview. Congressman Maury Maverick insisted that he had made the comment about "no back door" to Kennedy. See *San Antonio Express-News,* April 22, 1979.
3. *Life,* July 4, 1960.
4. For Wayne in World War II, see Randy Roberts and James S. Olson, *John Wayne: American* (1995), 203–63. For a different view, see Garry Wills, *John Wayne's America: The Politics of Celebrity* (1997), 102–13.
5. *Playboy,* May 1971, 82.
6. John Wayne interview, John Ford Papers, Indiana University; *Los Angeles Examiner,* March 24, 1949.
7. John Wayne interview, Maurice Zolotow Papers, University of Texas at Austin.
8. Mary St. John interview.
9. John Wayne to Famous Artists (Feldman's agency), October 21, 1948, Charles K. Feldman Papers, American Film Institute.
10. Donald Clark and Christopher Anderson, *John Wayne's "The Alamo": The Making of the Epic Film* (1994), 7.
11. Wills, *John Wayne's America,* 200; Clark and Anderson, *John Wayne's "The Alamo,"* 9.
12. Mary St. John interview.
13. Ibid.
14. Frank T. Thompson, *Alamo Movies* (1991), 59–66.
15. James T. "Happy" Shahan interview; *San Antonio Light,* July 18, 1958; *Los Angeles Times,* November 1, 1959; *Hollywood Reporter,* July 29, 1959; *New York Times,* October 4, 1959; *Variety,* October 24, 1960; Clark and Anderson, *John Wayne's "The Alamo,"* 20.
16. Mary St. John interview. Other friends of Wayne have told the same story. Widmark denied the episode in an interview with Garry Wills. See Wills, *John Wayne's America,* 222.
17. Clark and Anderson, *John Wayne's "The Alamo,"* 6.
18. Mary St. John interview.
19. James T. "Happy" Shahan interview; Clark and Anderson, *John Wayne's "The Alamo"*; Wills, *John Wayne's America,* 222.

20. Ken Curtis interview in *John Wayne's "The Alamo,"* United Artists video; Harry Carey Jr. interview; James T. "Happy" Shahan interview.
21. Aissa Wayne with Steve Delsohn, *John Wayne: My Father* (1991), 46.
22. Quoted in Clark and Anderson, *John Wayne's "The Alamo,"* 103–4.
23. Ibid., 105. Clark and Anderson have a fine discussion of Birdwell's campaign.
24. *Life,* July 4, 1960.
25. John Wayne to Russell Birdwell, November 23, 1960, Alamo File, Daughters of the Republic of Texas Library.
26. Tino Balio, *United Artists: The Company That Changed the Film Industry* (1987), 127–28, 208–10.
27. *Southern California Promoter,* October 1960, 26; *New Yorker,* November 5, 1960; *Time,* September 7, 1960; *Newsweek,* October 31, 1960.
28. *Variety,* October 26, 1960; Brian Huberman interview.
29. *Hollywood Reporter,* January 11, 1960.
30. *Variety,* March 21, 1961; *Los Angeles Mirror,* March 1, 7, and 15, 1961.

CHAPTER 10. DE LA PEÑA'S REVENGE

1. Robert A. Caro, *The Years of Lyndon Johnson: The Path to Power* (1982), 44; *New York Times,* June 3–4, 1965; Eric Goldman, *The Tragedy of Lyndon Johnson* (1969), 426–30.
2. *San Antonio Light,* August 19, 1982; *San Antonio Express,* April 9, 1966.
3. Hugh Sidey, "The Presidency," *Life,* October 10, 1969, 4; Ronnie Dugger, *The Politician: The Life and Times of Lyndon Johnson. The Drive for Power—From the Frontier to the Master of the Senate* (1982), 28–35.
4. Julie Leininger Pycior, *LBJ and Mexican Americans* (1992), 5; Dugger, *The Politician,* 34.
5. Susan Prendergast Schoelwer, *Alamo Images: Changing Perceptions of a Texas Experience* (1985), 166, 168.
6. *San Antonio Light,* November 7, 1965, and May 21, 1967; *San Antonio Express,* November 7, 1965.
7. Schoelwer, *Alamo Images,* 171.
8. Ibid., 168.
9. *New York Times,* March 3, 1968.
10. *San Diego Union-Tribune,* November 24, 1998
11. *San Antonio Express,* January 13, 1964.
12. Ibid., December 31, 1963, and January 3, 1964.
13. Ibid., January 3, 9, 13, and 15, 1964.
14. Ibid., June 12, 1975; *New York Times,* January 23, 1970.
15. José Enrique de la Peña, *With Santa Anna in Texas: A Personal Narrative of the Revolution* (1997).
16. Ibid., 52–53.
17. Ibid., 53. Also see James E. Crisp, "The Little Book That Wasn't There: The Myth and Mystery of the de la Peña Diary," *Southwestern Historical Quarterly* 98 (1994–95): 288–89, for a slightly different translation.
18. For an insightful discussion of the de la Peña controversy, see Crisp, "The Little Book That Wasn't There," 261–96.
19. Dan Kilgore, *How Did Davy Die?* (1978), 17–22.
20. De la Peña, *With Santa Anna,* 50; Michael Lind, "The Death of David Crockett," *Wilson Quarterly* (winter 1998): 53.
21. Crisp, "The Little Book That Wasn't There," 274–75; Lind, "The Death of David

Crockett," 52–53; also see James E. Crisp's response to Lind, http://home.flash.net/~alamo3/archives/lind-crisp/crisp.htm.

22. Schoelwer, *Alamo Images,* 14–15; Barbara Paulsen, "Say It Ain't So, Davy," *Texas Monthly* 14 (November 1876): 129.

23. Schoelwer, *Alamo Images,* 15–16.

24. Bill Groneman, *Defense of a Legend: Crockett and the de la Peña Diary* (1994), xiii.

25. Kilgore, *How Did Davy Die?,* 9–48.

26. Paulsen, "Say It Ain't So, Davy," 129; Paul Andrew Hutton, "Introduction," in Schoelwer, *Alamo Images,* 16–17.

27. Gregory Curtis, "Forgery Texas Style," *Texas Monthly,* March 1989, 108.

28. Ibid., 104–9, 187–95.

29. Larry McMurtry, introduction to W. Thomas Taylor, ed., *Texfake: An Account of the Theft and Forgery of Early Texas Documents* (1991), xvi.

30. Curtis, "Forgery Texas Style," 109, 185.

CHAPTER 11. THE THIRD BATTLE OF THE ALAMO

1. *Houston Post,* March 3, 1984.

2. *San Antonio Express,* September 6, 1979; *Houston Post,* September 7, 1979.

3. *San Antonio Express,* September 9 and 15, 1979; *Houston Post,* September 7, 1979; *San Antonio Light,* September 13, 1979.

4. *San Antonio Light,* September 9, 1979; *San Antonio Express,* September 9, 1979.

5. *San Antonio Light,* October 3, 1985; June 16, 1988; May 2, 1988; January 23, 1989; *San Antonio Express-News,* November 8, 1985; May 2, 1987; *International Herald-Tribune,* May 3–4, 1986; *Dallas Morning News,* April 15, 1989.

6. *San Antonio Light,* June 25, 1975; *Newsweek,* June 23, 1975.

7. *San Antonio Light,* February 13, 1982; *San Antonio Express,* February 23, 1982.

8. Rodolfo Acuña, *Occupied America: The Chicano's Struggle Toward Liberation* (1972), 7–8; Matt S. Meier and Feliciano Rivera, *The Chicanos: A History of Mexican Americans* (1972), 56, 72.

9. William Cronon, George Miles, and Jay Gitlin, eds., *Under an Open Sky: Rethinking America's Western Past* (1992), ix–xii; Patricia Limerick, "Beyond the Agrarian Myth," in Patricia Limerick, Clyde A. Milner II, and Charles E. Rankin, eds., *Trails: Toward a New Western History* (1991), 15–16.

10. Quoted in Forrest G. Robinson, *The New Western History* (1997), 5–6; Miriam Horn, "How the West Was Really Won," *U.S. News and World Report,* May 21, 1990, 55–65.

11. Limerick et al., *Trails,* 59–61.

12. Larry McMurtry, "How the West Was Won or Lost," *New Republic,* October 22, 1990, 32–38; John Mark Faragher, "The Frontier Trail: Rethinking Turner and Reimagining the American West," *American Historical Review* 98 (1993): 111–12; Alan Brinkley, "The Western Historians: Don't Fence Them In," *New York Times Book Review,* September 20, 1992, 25.

13. Gerald D. Nash, "Point of View: One Hundred Years of Western History," *Journal of the West,* January 1993, 3–4.

14. *San Antonio Express,* March 29, 1992; *Austin-American Statesman,* June 4, 1994.

15. "LULAC, Imax Latest Controversies," Alamo Chronological Files, 1980s, DRT Library; Julie Catalano, "The Second Battle of the Alamo," *Vista,* August 6, 1989, 12–13.

16. *Waco Herald-Tribune,* March 21, 1980; *San Antonio Express-News,* March 15, 1988.

17. Catalano, "The Second Battle of the Alamo," 12.

18. *Houston Chronicle,* March 15, 1989; *El Paso Herald-Post,* April 23, 1988; *Houston Post,* April 20, 1988.

19. *San Antonio Express-News,* October 4 and 9, November 16, December 4, 1988; *Houston Post,* December 14, 1988; *San Antonio Light,* November 12, 1988.

20. *San Antonio Express-News,* October 9, 1988; *Houston Post,* December 14, 1988; *San Antonio Light,* October 27, December 29, 1988; Catalano, "The Second Battle of the Alamo," 12.

21. *San Antonio Light,* March 8 and 22, 1989; *San Antonio Express-News,* March 8, 1989; *Dallas Morning News,* April 15, 1989.

22. Jeff Long, *Duel of Eagles: The Mexican and U.S. Fight for the Alamo* (1991), 22, 57, 107, 317, 331, 334.

23. Ibid., 23–27.

24. Ibid., 27–28, 31–32.

25. Ibid., 105, 258.

26. Ibid., 34–35, 187–90, 248.

27. Ibid., 323.

28. *Choice* 28 (December 1990): 693; *Southwestern Historical Quarterly* 96 (July 1992): 135; *New York Times,* March 29, 1995.

29. *Houston Post,* March 3, 1993; *San Antonio Express-News,* December 12 1994; February 14–16, 1995; May 5, 1995.

30. *San Antonio Express-News,* March 18, 1993; *Washington Post,* May 29, 1994; "The New Battle of the Alamo," *Newsweek,* March 28, 1994, 27; *New York Times,* March 29, 1994; "The Alamo Debate," *The Medallion* 6, Chronological File, 1990–1999, DRT Library.

31. *San Antonio Express-News,* January 17, February 5 and 14, 1995; Paula Allen, "Under Siege," *San Antonio Express-News Magazine,* May 16, 1993, 3.

32. *Houston Chronicle,* March 6, 1993; *Austin American-Statesman,* April 13, 1994; *San Antonio Light,* March 28, 1992.

33. *Houston Post,* January 23, 1995; *San Antonio Express-News,* January 17, 1995; November 9, 1996.

34. Paula Allen, "Under Siege," 5; *San Antonio Express-News,* May 25, 1991; September 2, 1994.

35. *San Antonio Express-News,* October 18, 1994; *Dallas Morning News,* March 12, 1995.

36. J. R. Edmondson, *The Alamo Story: From Early History to Current Conflicts* (2000), 420.

37. Richard White, "The Current Weirdness in the West," *Western Historical Quarterly* XXVII (spring 1997): 7–8; *Dallas Morning News,* August 16–31, 1992.

38. *Houston Chronicle,* March 10–17 and April 17–26, 1993.

39. *New York Times,* May 4, 1997.

40. George Bush and Brent Scowcroft, *A World Transformed* (1998), 381–83; *Cold War,* CNN broadcast, December 12, 1999.

41. *New York Times,* November 18, 1998; *Houston Chronicle,* November 18 and 23, 1998; Don Carleton, "Post-Mortem of a Hero," *Texas,* June 25, 2000, 8–12.

42. *Boston Globe,* November 19, 1998; *Houston Chronicle,* November 23 1998.

43. John Knaggs, "San Antonio: Alamo Encore," *Texas Republic,* May/June 1994, 40.

BIBLIOGRAPHIC ESSAY

———— ✯ ————

THE SLAUGHTER AND SACRIFICE of March 6, 1836, continue to simmer deep inside the Texas psyche, and like a case of post-traumatic stress syndrome, flashbacks erupt frequently into the public consciousness and assume political lives of their own. A recent feature article in the *Houston Chronicle* posed the questions: "Did Davy Crockett go down fighting, or was he executed at the Alamo? After all this time, why does it matter, anyway?" But it does matter, and coming to terms with the Alamo is a prerequisite to understanding Texas. History is to Texans what food is to other species, and no event is more central to Texas history and the Texan identity than the battle of the Alamo. Depending upon one's politics, the Alamo is either the creation story, or the creation myth, of the Lone Star state.

For those interested in primary sources relevant to the Texas Revolution, the key collections are housed in the Texas State Library in Austin, Texas; the Benson Latin American Collection and the Barker Center for American History at the University of Texas at Austin; the Daughters of the Republic of Texas Library in San Antonio, Texas; and the Texana collection at Yale University in New Haven, Connecticut. Much of the key material from the Mexican Military Archives in Mexico City is also available on microfilm at the library in Palo Alto, Texas. Most readers, of course, will have no need to peruse such documents, and for them the

345

most accessible collection of primary sources is John H. Jenkins's monu-mental, eight-volume *The Papers of the Texas Revolution 1835–1836* (1973). For other eyewitness Anglo-American accounts of the events of the Texas Revolution, see Noah Smithwick, *The Evolution of a State; or, Recollections of Old Texas Days* (1900); Andrew Forest Muir, ed., *Texas in 1837: An Anonymous, Contemporary Narrative* (1958); William Fairfax Gray, *From Virginia to Texas, 1835* (1965); Hobart Huson, ed., *Dr. H. Barnard's Journal* (1949); and Herman Ehrenberg, *With Milam and Fannin in Texas: Adventures of a German Boy in Texas' Revolution* (1935).

Mexican and Tejano participants, of course, often had a different take on the revolution. For the Tejano point of view, see Timothy M. Matovina, *The Alamo Remembered: Tejano Accounts and Perspectives* (1995), and Juan N. Seguín, *Personal Memoirs* (1858). The best accounts by Mexican participants in the battle of the Alamo are Samuel E. Asbury, ed., "The Private Journal of Juan Nepomuceno Almonte, February 1–April 16, 1836," *Southwestern Historical Quarterly* 48 (July 1944): 10–32; Carlos E. Castañeda, ed. and trans., *The Mexican Side of the Texan Revolution* (1928); José Enrique de la Peña, *With Santa Anna in Texas,* trans. Carmen Perry (1975); General Vicente Filisola, *Memoirs for the History of the War in Texas,* trans. Wallace Woolsey, 2 vols. (1987); Richard G. Santos, *Santa Anna's Campaign Against Texas, 1835–1836* (1968); and Ann Fears Crawford, *The Eagle: The Autobiography of Santa Anna* (1988).

Enrique Krauze's *Mexico. Biography of Power: A History of Modern Mexico, 1810–1996* is indispensable for beginning an inquiry into Mexican history. For social life in Mexico during the era of the Texas Revolution, see Ruth R. Olivera and Liliane Crété, *Life in Mexico Under Santa Anna 1822–1855* (1991). The best account of Mexican politics at the time is Michael Costeloe's *The Central Republic in Mexico, 1835–1846: Hombres de Bien in the Age of Santa Anna* (1993). For Mexican military history during the era of the Texas Revolution, see William A. DePalo Jr., *The Mexican National Army, 1822–1852* (1997).

The Texas Revolution has a rich historiography, and the best place to begin is Paul D. Lack's *The Texas Revolutionary Experience: A Political and Social History, 1835–1836* (1992). Alwyn Barr's *Texans in Revolt: The Battle for San Antonio, 1835* (1990) is excellent. Stephen L. Hardin's *Texian Iliad: A Military History of the Texas Revolution 1835–1836*

(1994) has become the last word on the subject. Also see Joseph G. Dawson III, ed. *The Texas Military Experience: From the Texas Revolution Through World War II* (1995). Several recent biographies are especially revealing. Marshall De Bruhl's *Sword of San Jacinto: A Life of Sam Houston* (1993) raised the ire of many Houston apologists, but it remains the best recent work on his life. Gregg Cantrell's brilliant *Stephen F. Austin: Empresario of Texas* (1999) sets a new standard in Texas historiography. For the lives of the three most prominent Americans at the Alamo, see William C. Davis, *Three Roads to the Alamo: The Lives and Fortunes of David Crockett, James Bowie, and William Barret Travis* (1998). The best English-language biographies of Santa Anna are the dated Wilfrid Hardy Callcott, *Santa Anna: The Story of an Enigma Who Once Was Mexico* (1936), and Oakah L. Jones, *Santa Anna* (1968).

For years Anglo-American historians all but ignored the history of Tejanos, but the seminal work of several prominent scholars has recently begun to fill the gap. For the Spanish period of early Texas history, see David J. Weber, *The Spanish Frontier in North America* (1992). Arnoldo De León's *The Tejano Community, 1836–1900* (1982) reversed four generations of Anglo-American bias in treating the Tejano historical experience. Also see Armando C. Alonzo, *Tejano Legacy: Rancheros and Settlers in South Texas, 1734–1900* (1998), and David Montejano, *Anglos and Mexicans in the Making of Texas, 1836–1986* (1987).

The siege and battle for the Alamo has enjoyed a rich and controversial literature. Lon Tinkle's *13 Days to Glory; The Siege of the Alamo* (1958) and Walter Lord's *A Time to Stand* (1961) were written from a Cold War perspective and left readers with few doubts about the moral stakes of the battle. Jeff Long's *Duel of Eagles: The Mexican and U.S. Fight for the Alamo* (1990), on the other hand, turned conventional historiography upside down and interpreted the Alamo through the lens of the New Western History. William C. Davis's recent *Three Roads to the Alamo: The Lives and Fortunes of David Crockett, James Bowie, and William Barret Travis* (1998) achieves an appropriate balance, as does Stephen Harrigan's fine novel *The Gates of the Alamo* (2000). Also see Alan C. Huffines, *Blood of Noble Men: The Alamo Siege and Battle* (1999).

A number of excellent works deal with the Alamo as an American icon. Holly Beachley Brear's *Inherit the Alamo: Myth and Ritual at an*

American Shrine (1995) looks at the Alamo from an anthropologist's perspective. Even better is Susan Prendergast Schoelwer's (with Tom W. Gläser) *Alamo Images: Changing Perceptions of a Texas Experience* (1986). For the Alamo on film, see Frank Thompson, *Alamo Movies* (1991). Steven Watts's *The Magic Kingdom: Walt Disney and the American Way of Life* (1997) explains the Davy Crockett craze of the mid-1950s. For John Wayne's role in popularizing the Alamo, see Randy Roberts and James S. Olson, *John Wayne: American* (1995), and Donald Clark and Christopher Anderson, *John Wayne's "The Alamo": The Making of the Epic Film* (1994).

Of course, the last word on the Alamo has not been nor ever will be written, and for historians, its grounds remain as treacherous as they are sacred. A shrine to some and symbol of racism to others, the Alamo's history has become a cultural battleground in its own right, a place where fact, fable, and political ideology blend and the boundaries between history and mythology blur. Perhaps José Enrique de la Peña said it best: "It is important to avoid partiality if one wants to be believed. Be very careful because it is very difficult to be a historian."

INDEX

—————— ✦ ——————

Abamillo, Juan, 4, 302
Acuña, Rodolfo, 47, 298, 308
Adams, John Quincy, 34, 86
Adams-Onís Treaty (1819), 34
Alamo, The (film), 256, 257, 261–76, 281, 309
Alamo Acquisition Board, 221
Alamo Purchase Bill, 277, 280
Alamo . . . The Price of Freedom (film), 301
Aldama, Juan de, 18, 19, 77
Allen, Gen. Henry T., 220
Allen, James, 53
Allende, Ignacio de, 18, 19, 77
Allred, James, 223–24
Almonte, Col. Juan Nepomuceno, 84, 125, 138, 139, 151, 152, 161, 173, 193, 196
Alsbury, Horace, 129
Alsbury, Juana Navarro de, 129
Alvarez de Toledo, José, 63
Amat, Col. Agustín, 151, 164
American Federation of Labor (AFL), 231, 232
American Revolution, 16, 54–56, 240
Ampudia, Gen. Pedro de, 75
Amrendáriz, Pedro, 19
Andrade, Gen. Juan José, 24, 72, 75, 82, 200
Apaches, 80, 105, 134
Army of Operations, 17, 20–22, 25, 41, 66–68, 71–72, 76–77, 79–84, 97, 99, 104, 112–14, 116–17, 142–43, 149, 153, 161, 184, 191
Army of the People, 44, 56, 99, 102, 115, 118, 134

Arredondo, Gen. José Joaquín de, 8, 19, 20, 33, 63–65, 84, 153
Arruza, Carlos, 265
Austin, Moses, 32
Austin, Stephen F., 32, 35–40, 42–44, 48, 49, 56, 57, 65, 98–99
Austin, William T., 46
Autry, Micajah, 55, 59, 103–4
Avalon, Frankie, 265, 267
Aztecs, 10–12, 20

Babbitt, Art, 233
Babbitt, Bruce, 295–96
Babbitt, Maj. E. B., 201
Badillo, Juan Antonio, 4, 302
Baker, William C. M., 123
Ballentine, Richard, 56
Banks, Thomas, 96
Baptists, Southern, 297
Barcana, Andrés, 169–70, 182, 195
Barnard, J. H., 177
Barnes, Maj. Charles, 220
Barnes, Gail Loving, 308
Batres, Col. José, 125
Baugh, John J., 115, 161–62
Baylor, John, 54
Beauchamp, Jerry, 304
Becerra, Francisco, 196
Begara, Anselmo, 169–70, 182, 195

Berlandier, Jean-Louis, 61
Béxar, battle of, 56–59, 111, 142
Billington, Ray Allen, 299
Birdwell, Russell, 271–73, 276
Birth of a Nation, The (film), 218, 263, 265
Blackburn, Tom, 240
Blazeby, William, 123
Bolívar, Simón, 53
Bonaparte, Napoleon, 66–68, 74, 85, 159, 171
Bond, Ward, 258
Bonham, Col. James Butler, 1–4, 116–17, 149, 228, 265, 302
Bonilla, Ruben, 296
Boone, Daniel, 92, 240, 241, 244, 249–50, 283
Boone, Richard, 265
Boone and Crockett Club, 283
Boorstin, Daniel, 248, 250
Bowie, Jim, 4, 45, 109–13, 115–20, 123, 125–28, 156, 182, 219, 296, 302; background of, 54; death of, 154, 155, 168, 170, 171, 173, 175, 194, 196, 316; film depictions of, 262–64, 269, 275, 276, 301; identification of militia movement with, 311, 312; illnesses of, 2, 111, 119, 129; in Indian wars, 55; naming of schools after, 310, 311; pleas sent to Fannin for reinforcements by, 132, 133, 135; portrait in Alamo chapel of, 228; revisionist historians on, 305, 319; in Sandbar Fight, 110–11; Tejanos and, 139–40; WPA murals of, 283
Bowles, Samuel, 203
Branch Davidians, 311
Brear, Holly Beachly, 308
Brown, Reuben, 148
Brown, Robert, 131
Bryan, Guy M., 205
Buckley, William F., 252
Bullock, Bob, 304
Bunton, John Wheeler, 279
Burgin, Abner, 91
Burleson, Edward, 56–57
Burnet, David G., 48, 143, 186–87, 191
Burr, Aaron, 33
Bush, George, 295, 312
Bush, George W., 309, 312
Bustamante, Anastasio, 10, 36, 53
Butterfield & Butterfield, 313
Byron, George Gordon, Lord, 94, 95, 171, 172

Cabanne, William Christy, 218
Calderón de la Barca, Franes, 8, 9
Campbell, Thomas, 211
Candelaria, Madam (Castañón Villanueva, Andrea), 154–55

Carey, Harry, Jr., 268
Carey, William, 59
Carner, John Nance, 228
Carrington, Evelyn, 227
Castañón Villanueva, Andrea (Madam Candelaria), 154–55
Catholicism, 12–14, 48, 50–51, 173, 201, 202, 217–19, 222–23, 254–55
Chambers, Thomas J., 172
Cherokees, 3, 108
Chichimecas, 8, 16, 17
Childress, George, 144, 175
Cisneros, Henry, 304
Civil War, 203–5
Clarke, Matthew St. Clair, 87–88
Clay, Henry, 86, 143
Clayton, Bill, 296
Clements, Bill, 295, 296, 304
Clothier, William, 270
Cloud, Daniel, 50, 95, 104
Cody, William F. "Buffalo Bill," 283
Cohn, Harry, 234
Cold War, 230, 237, 242, 253, 259, 271, 297
Coleman, Robert, 186
Coleridge, Samuel Taylor, 171
Colquitt, Oscar, 213–14, 217
Comanches, 80, 105, 318–19
Communists, 235–36, 259
Concepción, battle of, 45–47, 101, 111, 133, 142
Conference of Studio Unions (CSU), 231–32
Connally, John, 282
Connally, Thomas, 228
Conroy, T. L., 212
Cooper, Gary, 236, 258
Cooper, James Fenimore, 241
Coppini, Pompeo, 206, 219
Cortés, Hernán, 10–12, 17, 20
Cortez, Gregorio, 217
Cortina, Juan, 216, 217
Cos, Gen. Martín Perfecto de, 41–47, 52, 68, 71, 76, 78, 97, 188, 189, 196; in assault on Alamo, 151, 158, 159, 163–66; during siege of December, 1835, 56–59, 85, 107, 112, 124; surrender of, 59, 75, 98, 100, 102–5, 108, 125, 126, 139
Coyle, E. I., 202
Crisp, James, 313
Cristal, Linda, 265
Crockett, Davy, 4, 50, 86–93, 109, 114, 123, 131, 201, 202, 219, 285, 293, 296, 297, 302, 316; arrival in Texas of, 102–4; during assault on Alamo, 165, 167; autobiography of,

87–89; Candelaria's claims about, 154–55; in Congress, 86, 89–91; death of, 168, 171, 173, 175–76, 182–84, 191–96, 287–91; film depictions of, 229, 238–53, 263, 269–71, 274–77, 289, 301, 309, 318; iconic status of, 313–14; identification of militia movement with, 311, 312; in Indian wars, 55; journey to Texas of, 91–93, 97; portrait in Alamo chapel of, 228; revisionist historians on, 290–91, 305, 319; at Washington's Birthday celebration in Béxar, 119, 120; WPA murals of, 283

Cummings, David, 109
Curtis, Ken, 265, 268
Custer, Gen. George Armstrong, 204–5

Daniels, Price, 263, 273
Daughters of the Republic of Texas (DRT), 198, 206, 208–9, 211–14, 220–22, 226–28, 255–56, 277, 286, 290–91, 297, 301–4, 306–10, 315, 317
David, C. Dorman, 292–93
Davis, John, 55
Davis, Kenneth S., 248
Declaration of Independence, 53, 55, 145
Dellet, James, 28
de Man, Paul, 300
Democratic Party, 90, 205, 221, 224, 225, 256, 258, 296, 303, 304
Despallier, Charles, 131
DeWitt, Green, 36
De Zavala, Adina, 197–98, 206–15, 219, 220, 222, 224–25, 229, 270, 310, 316
Díaz, Juan, 124
Díaz del Castillo, Bernal, 11–12
Dickinson, Almaron, 55, 166–67, 169, 171
Dickinson, Susanna, 166–67, 173–76, 182, 185
Dies, Martin, 252
Dimmitt, Philip, 99–100
Disney, Walt, 230–38, 277, 279, 282, 294; depiction of Crockett by, 229, 238–53, 263, 274, 276, 289, 290
Disneyland, 237–39, 243, 247
Dobie, J. Frank, 261
Dolson, George M., 192–95, 291
Driscoll, Clara, 207–15, 212, 219–29, 277, 279, 280, 308, 310
Dromundo, Col. Ricardo, 74, 79
Drossaerts, Arthur J., 222–23
Duque, Col. Francisco, 151, 158, 159, 162, 164
Duval, John C., 177–78

Ebsen, Buddy, 241, 245

Edgren, Charles, 303
Edwards, Haden, 34–35
Ehrenberg, Herman, 96
Eisenhower, Dwight D., 271
Elizondo, Col. Ignacio, 64
Espalier, Carlos, 302
Esparza, Enrique, 141, 149, 166
Esparza, José Gregorio, 4, 140, 302
Ethridge, LeJean, 268
Evans, Samuel, 54
Everett, Edward, 201, 215
Everitt, Bernice, 309

Fannin, Col. James W., 2, 45, 46, 100–102, 116, 118, 124, 132–38, 141–43, 148, 150–52, 157, 170, 176–81, 185
Farley, James A., 228
Federal Bureau of Investigation (FBI), 311
Fehrenbach, T. R., 314
Feldman, Charles, 260
Fellows, Robert, 262
Ferdinand XII, King of Spain, 33
Ferguson, J. F., 135
Fernández Castrillón, Gen. Manuel, 85, 151, 153, 161, 192, 195, 287
Filisola, Gen. Vicente, 67, 71–72, 75, 76, 81, 127–28, 161, 164, 168, 188, 191, 195, 287
Fischer, John, 250–52
Fisher, Rachel, 212
Fonda, Henry, 257
Ford, John (antiquarian), 196
Ford, John (film director), 257, 258, 261, 275
Ford, Pat, 261
Franciscans, 104–5
Franklin, Benjamin, 88, 244, 247
Fredonian Rebellion (1826), 34–35
Fuqua, Galba, 166–67

Gabehart, Gary, 307
Gable, Clark, 257, 258, 264, 265
Gabler, Neal, 247
Ganilh, Anthony, 199
Gaona, Gen. Antonio, 72, 75, 148, 184, 185
García, Francisco, 15–16, 21–22, 25
García, Orlando, 303, 304
García de Lara, José, 302, 303
García Ugarte, Col. Ramón, 51
Garza, Catarino, 216–17
General Federation of Women's Clubs, 206
George III, King of England, 53, 56
Gish, Lillian, 265
Godkin, E. L., 248
Goldman, Eric, 246

Gómez Farías, Valentín, 14, 40, 53
Gómez Pedraza, Manuel, 9, 53
Gone With the Wind (film), 235, 247, 263, 265, 271–72, 274
Gonzales, battle of, 43, 47, 49, 55, 101, 133, 142
Gonzales Ranging Company of Mounted Volunteers, 2, 141
González, José María, 161
Goodrich, John Camp, 95, 171
Grant, James, 101, 102, 104, 116, 118, 133, 147–48
Grant, Jimmy, 261, 262, 268, 269
Grant, Madison, 217–18
Gray, E. N., 170
Gray, William Fairfax, 137, 140, 174
Great Depression, 228, 230, 283
Greek war for independence, 94
Grenet, Honoré, 201
Griffith, D. W., 218
Groce, Jared, 174–76, 186
Groneman, Bill, 290, 293
Guadalupe Hidalgo, Treaty of (1848), 215
Guerra, Carlos, 307
Guerrero, Vicente, 9, 35
Gutiérrez, José Bernardo, 62–63
Gutiérrez de Lara, José Bernardo, 33
Guzmán, Gordiano, 51

Hackett, James, 87
Hall, Mrs. Charles, 290
Harbord, Gen. James A., 221
Hardin, Stephen L., 127
Harper's Magazine, 250
Harrison, Benjamin, 228
Hart, L. J., 212
Hartman, Ana, 308
Harvard University Press, 291
Harvey, Laurence, 264, 265
Haverstick, John, 249, 251
Hayden, Sterling, 262
Henry, Patrick, 171
Hersey, John, 278, 284
Heston, Charlton, 264, 278
Hidalgo, Miguel, 17–20, 62, 77
Highsmith, Ben, 54
Hitler, Adolf, 225, 226, 235, 271, 300, 319
Hofstadter, Richard, 253
Holden, William, 264
Hollywood Ten, 258
Hopper, Hedda, 238
House Committee on Un-American Activities (HUAC), 258
Houston, Sam, 4, 47, 91, 99, 105, 113, 118,

143, 151, 155, 176, 196, 279; Bowie ordered to Alamo by, 109, 111–12, 117; in Congress, 95; defeat of Santa Anna by, 187–91; fall of Alamo reported to, 169, 170, 174, 195; film depiction of, 265; Jackson and, 70; Neill's appeals for help to, 108, 115; removed by Council as commander in chief, 100–102, 133; retreat from Gonzales of, 184–87; revisionist historians on, 305; Tejanos and, 98, 137, 215; Travis's letters to, 116, 130, 131, 148
Hudson, Rock, 264, 265
Hugo & Schmeltzer Company, 198, 202, 207–13
Hull, Cordell, 228
Huntsman, Adam "Blackhawk," 90
Hutton, Paul Andrew, 173

Iguala, Plan of, 51
Immortal Alamo, The (film), 218
Indian wars, 55, 93, 240, 241
Inter-Tribal Council of American Indians, 307
International Alliance of Theatrical Stage Employees (IATSE), 231–32
Iturbide, Agustín de, 9, 18, 19, 51, 66, 72

Jackson, Andrew, 4, 29, 34, 54, 70, 86, 89–91, 108, 171, 241, 283
Jagger, Mick, 297
Jameson, Green B., 105–9, 112, 114, 125
Jefferson, Thomas, 4, 33, 56, 95, 145
Jeffries, Charles, 226–27
Jenkins, John, 288, 292–93
Jews, 51, 217, 223
Jiménez, Mariano, 18, 19, 77
Jiménez Battalion, 130
John Birch Society, 284
Johnson, Frank, 96–97, 100, 101, 104, 116, 118, 133
Johnson, Lyndon B., 225, 228, 277–86, 294, 395
Johnson, Samuel Ealy, Jr., 209, 277, 279
Jones, Jesse, 221

Kahn, E. J., Jr., 249
Kalb, Bernard, 249
Karp, David, 246–47
Kefauver, Estes, 252
Kellogg, Johnnie, 141
Kempton, Murray, 252
Kennedy, Jacqueline, 278, 284
Kennedy, John Fitzgerald, 254–56, 273, 278, 280, 281, 284–85
Kerr, Joseph, 54

Khrushchev, Nikita, 271, 273
Kilgore, Dan, 290–91
King, William P., 141
Korean War, 243, 280
Koresh, David, 311, 312
Ku Klux Klan, 296, 303

Labadie, Nicholas, 195–96
Laffite, Jean, 110
Lamar, Howard Robert, 298
Lancaster, Burt, 264
Lanham, Samuel W. T., 209
Las Casas, Juan Bautista, de, 77–78
Last Command, The (film), 262
Last Patrol, 297
Law of April 6, 1830, 55, 93
League of United Latin American Citizens (LU-LAC), 296, 301–3
Leigh, Vivien, 265
Lemus, Pedro, 76
Leonidas, 172
Lewis, Nathaniel, 121
Lewis, Rogert, 272
Liggett & Meyers Tobacco Company, 282
Limerick, Patricia, 298–99
Lind, Michael, 288–89, 312–13
Linenthal, Edward, 313
Locke, John, 145, 146
Lone Star (film), 314
Long, Huey, 259
Long, James, 34
Long, Jeff, 47, 57, 304–7, 319
Long, Walter, 218, 277, 288
Losoya, Torbio, 302
Lowell, Robert, 278, 284
Luce, Henry, 273
Luna, Gregory, 307
Lyon, G. F., 51

MacArthur, Gen. Douglas, 243
Macdonald, Dwight, 278, 284
Maddox, Thomas, 110
Magee, Augustus, 33
Manifest Destiny, 11, 17, 298, 305
Maoist Revolutionary Party, 282–83
Marion, Francis "the Swamp Fox," 54, 237, 238
Martin, Capt. Albert, 125–26, 141
Martínez, Antonio, 34
Martinez, Walter, 301
Martínez Caro, Ramón, 74, 78–79, 83, 192, 194, 195
Martyrs of the Alamo, The (film), 218

Matson, Mike, 312
Mattox, Jim, 304
Maverick, Maury, Jr., 252
Maverick, Samuel, 203
Mayans, 14, 73, 77
Mayer, Louis B., 234
Mayes, William Harding, 214
McAlister, Hill, 223–24
McAllister, Walter W., 282
McCall, Mary, 235
McCullough brothers, 263–64
McKinley, William, 228
McKnight, Roxanne, 296–97
McLaren, Richard L., 312
McLean, Angus W., 204
McMurtry, Larry, 292, 299–300
Metro-Goldwyn-Mayer (MGM), 231, 235
Mexía, José Antonio, 70, 71
Mexican American Legal Defense and Education Fund (MALDEF), 309
Mexican American Unity Council, 296
Mexican-American War, 201, 215, 303
Mexican Congress, 10, 13–16, 27, 36, 37, 39–40, 51, 54, 66, 68–69, 74, 153, 191, 194
Mexican Constitution of 1824, 7, 14, 22, 32, 35, 39–40, 42, 44, 52–53, 57, 59, 76, 93, 98–99, 101
Mexican Revolution, 62, 72, 77, 134
Mier y Terán, Manuel de, 35–36, 53
Milam, Ben, 57, 58, 100, 156, 279, 280
Miller, Thomas R., 141
Mills, Evelyn, 246
Millsaps, Isaac, 141, 293
Mina, Francisco Xavier, 33
Mitchell, Margaret, 272
Mobile Grays, 96, 117
Moctezuma, 12
Mora, Gen. Ventura, 128, 175
Morales, Col. Juan, 158–59, 165, 166, 176
Morelos y Pavón, José María, 18
Morgan, Col. James, 192
Morris, W. T. "Brack," 217
Motion Picture Alliance for the Preservation of American Ideals, 235, 238, 258–59
Movimiento Estudianil Chicanos de Aztlán, 290
Murat, Joachim, 67
Murchison, Clint W., 263–64
Muslims, 51
Músquiz, Ramón, 38–40
Musselman, Robert, 55
Mussolini, Benito, 225

Nash, Gerald, 300

National Association for Chicano Studies, 301, 309
National Association for the Advancement of
    Colored People (NAACP), 310, 311
National Council on Family Relations, 246
National Endowment for the Humanities,
    299
National Labor Relations Board, 234
National Youth Administration (NYA), 225
Nava, Andrés, 302
Neill, Capt. James C., 58, 104–9, 112–15
New Deal, 258, 283
New Orleans Greys, 96
New Western History, 298–300, 304–7, 319
Nichols, Dudley, 258
Nixon, Richard, 290
Nolan, Philip, 33

Olarte, Marione, 51
Olivares, Antonio de, 104–5
Orozco, Cynthia, 307
Osbourne, Ozzy, 297
Oswald, Lee Harvey, 285
Ottoman Empire, 94

Padilla, Ruben, 270
Parker, Charles, 55, 95
Parker, Christopher, 54
Parker, Fess, 240, 243, 245, 289
Parker, Louis Napoleon, 204
Parrington, Vernon L., 249
Patton, William, 91
Paulding, James Kirke, 87, 88
Peace, John, 313
Peace Party, 40, 46–47, 99
Peale, Norman Vincent, 255
Pearl Harbor, Japanese attack on, 226
Pegler, Westbrook, 234
Peña, Col. José Enrique de la, 66–69, 73, 74, 79,
    84, 140, 151–53, 158, 160, 161, 163–67,
    178–80; publication of diary of, 286–91, 293
Perry, Carmen, 287, 288, 290
Pinocchio (film), 230, 233, 234
Poinsett, Joel, 50
Pollard, Amos, 56
Ponton, Andrew, 123, 175
Populists, 205
Portilla, Col. José Nicolás de la, 179, 180
Postman, Neil, 248
Potter, R. M., 200
Pound, Ezra, 292
Prieto, Guillermo, 4
Protestantism, 51, 173, 217, 223, 254
Publicity League of San Antonio, 212

Pyle, Denver, 265

Quetzalcóatle, 12
Quinn, C. K., 222

Rafferty, Max, 248
Ramírez y Sesma, Gen. Joaquín, 26, 67–68,
    71–72, 74–75, 78, 81, 84, 108, 117, 122,
    142, 151–52, 159–60, 168, 184–88, 196, 287
Rayburn, Sam, 228
Reagan, Ronald, 257, 312
Reconstruction, 205
Red Scare, 220–21
Republic studios, 260–63
Republican Army of the North, 62–63
Republican Party, 256, 295
Revenue Act (1944), 258
Revolutionary War, *see* American Revolution
Rife, Tom, 202
Robertson, Pat, 312
Robertson, Sterling, 144
Robinson, James W., 100, 102, 109, 116, 118,
    133–36, 143, 144
Rodríguez, José María, 121–22
Rodriquez, Chatto, 264
Roe v. Wade, 296
Rogers, Peter, 266
Rolling Stones, 297
Romero, Col. José María, 158, 159, 163, 164, 167
Romero, Col. Manuel, 151
Roosevelt, Eleanor, 224, 225
Roosevelt, Franklin D., 223–25, 227, 228, 258
Roosevelt, Theodore, 283
Rose, Moses (Louis), 155–56, 251
Rossen, Robert, 259–60
Rosten, Leo, 246
Royall, R. R., 143
Ruíz, Francisco Antonio, 193–94, 199
Rusk, Thomas, 185–86
Russell, Jane, 271, 272

St. John, Mary, 262
Salcedo, Manuel de, 63
San Antonio Living History Association, 310, 316
Sánchez, Don Melchor, 76
Sánchez Garza, Jesús, 289
Sánchez Navarro, Col. José Juan, 59, 78, 85,
    160, 165
Santa Anna, Gen. Antonio López de, 1, 3, 5–12,
    18–19, 27, 41, 55, 61, 92, 97–99, 103, 112,
    134, 144, 148, 170, 172–74, 182, 184, 185,
    219, 277, 302; advance north led by, 77–78,
    83–84, 108–9, 114–17; arrest of Texas busi-

nessmen in Monclova ordered by, 111; assault on Alamo by, 146, 150–53, 158–64; Cos's relationship with, 42; defeated by Houston, 187–91; in defeat of Texas rebellion of 1812–13, 62–64; execution of prisoners ordered, 168, 175, 179–81, 192–96, 287–89; film depictions of, 218, 242, 271; Indians and, 80; Napoleonic fantasies of, 66–68, 85; in New Western History, 305, 306; numerical superiority of, 107; parley on surrender terms with, 124–26; Peña's account of, 286–91; planning of invasion of Texas by, 55, 59–60, 65–66, 68–70; poem about, 281; political power of, 6, 9, 10, 14–15, 53, 57; preparations for invasion of Texas by, 71–76; reenactor of, 316; refuses to bury Alamo dead, 199, 200; rumors of sightings in Béxar of, 119, 122; siege of Alamo by, 4, 127–30, 134, 138, 140, 142, 145, 151, 157; surprise attack planned by, 122–23; Tampico expedition against, 70–71; Tejanos and, 52, 118, 139, 143, 152, 214; Urrea deployed to Matamoros by, 176; Zacatecan rebellion crushed by, 15–17, 20–26, 68, 122

Santos, Richard, 303
Saxton, Brendan, 252
Sayles, John, 314
Schickle, Richard, 238
Schlesinger, Arthur M., Jr., 239
Scott, Sir Walter, 28, 171
Screen Cartoonists Guild (SCG), 231, 233
Seguín, Erasmo, 116
Seguín, Juan, 52, 111, 116–18, 123, 126, 132, 137, 139, 199, 215, 219, 302
Seminole war, 181
Shahan, James T. "Happy," 264, 267
Shelley, Percy Bysshe, 94, 172
Sherman, Sidney, 188
Shiga, Shigetaka, 226
Sidey, Hugh, 280–81
Simpson, William, 292–93
Smith, Charles Harvey, 268
Smith, Deaf, 174
Smith, Henry, 47, 98–100, 109, 112–18, 133, 139, 144
Smith, John W., 122–23, 140, 141, 175
Smith, W. P., 55
Smither, Launcelot, 49
Smithwick, Noah, 44–46, 190
Snow White and the Seven Dwarfs (film), 230, 233, 234
Sons of the Republic of Texas, 290
Sorensen, Theodore, 256

Sorrell, Herb, 231–32
Spanish-American War, 220
Stagecoach (film), 258
Stalin, Joseph, 225
Sterling, Ross, 221
Stewart, Jimmy, 257
Streeter, Thomas, 291, 292
Sutherland, John, 54, 122–123, 140
Swartz, Morey, 245
Swisher, John, 114

Taft, William Howard, 228
Taylor, Bayard, 203
Taylor, Creed, 47
Taylor, Gen. Zachary, 215
Tejeda, Frank, 304
Tennessee Mounted Volunteers, 96, 103
Tenorio, Capt. Antonio, 41
Terry, Samuel, 227
Texas, University of, 291, 313, 319
Texas A&M University Press, 286, 290
Texas Congress, 147, 279
Texas Declaration of Independence, 144–46, 292, 293
Texas Declaration of Rights, 147
Texas Department of Parks and Wildlife, 304, 307
Texas Federation of Women's Clubs, 228
Texas Historical Commission, 307
Texas Independence Day, 294
Texas Landmarks Association, 220
Texas Legislature, 214, 277
Texas Rangers, 216
Texas State Historical Association, 290, 306–7
Texas Veterans Association, 205
Thermopylae, battle of, 172
Thurston, John M., 95
Tinkle, Lindsay, 91
Tiomkin, Dimitri, 270
Tlaxcalans, 11–12
Tocqueville, Alexis de, 30, 50, 88–89
Tolosa, Juan, 16
Tolsa, Gen. Eugenio, 72, 75, 186
Tornel, José María, 68, 72, 85, 151, 195
Tower, John, 294–95
Tracy, Spencer, 236
Travis, Col. William Barret, 2–4, 28–29, 121–27, 144, 148–51, 153, 182, 202, 219, 285, 296, 302, 316; arrest of, 37–38; arrival in Texas of, 30–31; during assault on Alamo, 161–62; bounty on, 41–42; Candelaria's claims about, 154, 155; at Concepción, 46; death of, 170, 171, 175, 194, 196, 288; film depictions of,

263, 264, 269, 270, 275, 276, 301; identification of militia movement with, 311, 312; Johnson's evocation of, 280–81; joint command of Bowie and, 115–16, 123, 125; law practice of, 27, 39; March 5 speech to troops of, 155–57; Mexican government denounced by, 53, 54; naming of schools after, 310–11; ordered to Béxar, 113–14; pleas for reinforcements of, 117, 123–24, 132–33, 135, 138–39, 157; portrait in Alamo chapel of, 228; reenactment at centennial observances of, 222; revisionist historians on, 305–6; during siege of Alamo, 128–31, 157; Tejanos and, 117–18, 121; VICTORY OR DEATH letter of, 126–27, 129, 292, 294–95, 312; and War Party, 40, 41; at Washington's Birthday celebration in Béxar, 119, 120

Truman Doctrine, 242

Turner, Frederick Jackson, 298, 299

Ugartechea, Col. Domingo, 38, 41, 43, 58

United Artists, 263, 272–74

United Veterans' Council, 282

U.S. Army, 201

U.S. Congress, 86, 88–90, 92, 93, 95, 240–42, 248, 252, 258

U.S. Constitution, 29, 53, 147; First Amendment, 297

U.S. Military Academy (West Point), 132–35

U.S. Navy, 70

U.S. Senate, 214, 295; Armed Services Committee, 296

Urizza, Capt. Fernando, 184, 195–96

Urrea, Gen. José, 51, 72, 75–76, 83, 97, 108, 117, 133–34, 136–37, 142, 145, 147–48, 152, 177–80, 184–86, 188, 195

Ustinov, Peter, 286

Valdez, Alvarado, 308

Van Buren, Martin, 90

Vanguard Brigade, 122, 124

Vásquez, Josefina, 47

Vásquez y Sánchez, Ramón, 302

Velasco, Treaty of (1836), 191

Veramendi, Ursula de, 45, 111, 305

Vidor, King, 236

Vietnam War, 278, 280–82, 285, 290, 297, 298, 300

Viva Max (film), 286

Wagner Act (1935), 231, 232

Walker, Jacob, 167

Walsh, Bill, 240, 243

War of 1812, 54, 55, 56, 93, 103, 110

War Party, 40, 41, 46–48, 97, 99, 112

Warner Bros., 262, 263

Warner, Harry, 234

Warren, Robert Penn, 259

Washington, George, 4, 54, 118

Watts, H. Bascom, 225

Watts, Steven, 237

Wayne, Aissa, 265, 271, 275

Wayne, John, 256–72, 274–77, 279, 281, 282, 289–91, 293, 294, 309, 317

Wayne, Patrick, 265

Weaver, Randy, 311

Webb, Walter Prescott, 216, 299

Webster, Daniel, 86

Wellington, Duke of, 67, 171

Wells, Samuel, 110

Wertham, Frederic, 248

Wharton, William H., 40, 48

Whig Party, 89, 239, 241

White, Mark, 296

White, Richard, 299

White House Festival of the Arts, 277–78

Widmark, Richard, 264–65, 267

Wilkinson, Gen. James, 33

Williamson, R. M., 43, 149–50

Williamson, "Three Legged Willie," 2, 3

Wills, Chill, 265

Wills, Garry, 261, 313

Wilson, Ronald, 304, 307

Wood, Sam, 235

Worden, Hank, 265

Works Progress Administration (WPA), 225, 283

World War I, 220, 279

World War II, 225–28, 234–35, 243, 257, 259, 280, 300, 320

Worster, Donald, 299

Wright, Norris, 110

Ximénes, Damacio, 302

Ximénes, Doña Santos, 122

Yale Foundation, 264

Yale University, 291, 298–300

Yates, Herbert, 261–63

Ybarra, Alfred, 264

Yngloria, Ignacio, 78

Ypsilantis, Alexandros, 94

Zavala, Lorenzo de, 197, 219

Zolotow, Maurice, 259

Zozaya, José, 34

Zuber, William P., 155, 156